The WAY of CHINESE CHARACTERS

漢字之道

The ORIGINS of 670 ESSENTIAL WORDS

SECOND EDITION

JIANHSIN WU

ILLUSTRATED BY CHEN ZHENG AND CHEN TIAN

CHENG & TSUI

BOSTON

Second Edition

27 26 25 24 23   4 5 6 7 8

Published by
Cheng & Tsui Company, Inc.
25 West Street
Boston, MA 02111-1213 USA
Fax (617) 426-3669
www.cheng-tsui.com
"Bringing Asia to the World"™

ISBN 978-1-62291-046-5

Illustrated by Chen Zheng and Chen Tian

The Library of Congress has cataloged the first edition as follows:

Wu, Jian-hsin.
    The Way of Chinese characters : the origins of 400 essential words = [Han zi zhi dao] / by Jianhsin Wu ; illustrations by Chen Zheng and Chen Tian.
    p. cm.
    Parallel title in Chinese characters.
    ISBN 978-0-88727-527-2
  1. Chinese characters. 2. Chinese language--Writing. I. Title. II. Title: Han zi zhi dao.

PL1171.W74 2007
808'.04951--dc22

                                            2007062006

Printed in the United States of America

Photo Credits
front cover ©Fotohunter/ShutterStock

CONTENTS

ABOUT *the* AUTHOR

JIANHSIN WU received her Ph.D from the Department of East Asian Languages and Literatures at University of Wisconsin, Madison. A professor of Chinese at Pomona College since 1990, she concentrates her research on etymology, the pedagogy of teaching Chinese to heritage students, classical Chinese novels, and modern Chinese poetry.

PREFACE

Mastering characters is often the most challenging task for learners of Chinese. Unlike an alphabetical language with a writing system composed of a limited number of letters, the Chinese writing system is built upon about 200 radicals, which are the most basic components of Chinese characters. (Radicals, along with stroke counts, also provide the organizing principle for Chinese dictionaries.) Although there are over 50,000 Chinese characters, 2,500 characters are required for basic literacy. Furthermore, the pronunciation of a particular character does not necessarily relate to its meaning. The sheer number of Chinese characters, in addition to the frequent lack of visual pronunciation guides, makes character memorization a significant challenge for many.

Paradoxically, this complexity is precisely what draws many people to learn Chinese. The presence of pictographic elements in Chinese characters is one of the unique and fascinating aspects of the language. Most radicals, for example, are pictographs, or visual representations of objects or concepts. Given a pictograph, learners can turn the character into a vivid picture, or associate the character with a shape, color, sound, smell, feeling, emotion, movement, or action. When using this method of employing pictographs as memory aids, students will find that learning Chinese characters can be enjoyable, and can provide valuable insight into Chinese culture.

We believe that each and every Chinese character is a crystallization of the wisdom and creativity of our ancient Chinese ancestors. When given the logical and historical origins of each character, as described in this book, learners can also remember characters in an efficient and intelligent manner, rather than mechanically reproducing strokes that may seem meaningless to them. Students can also acquire knowledge of Chinese history and culture while learning the origins and evolution of characters, as their pictographic features often reflect vivid aspects of ancient life, such as agricultural and domestic life, war, trade materials, crafts, rituals, etc.

After studying *The Way of Chinese Characters*, learners will understand pictographic forms, interpret the logic behind the meanings of characters, and know something about the ancient forms of the most commonly occurring characters.

WHAT'S NEW IN THE SECOND EDITION?

The second edition of *The Way of Chinese Characters* includes over 220 more characters than the first edition. It now covers all the characters in both Part 1 and Part 2 of *Integrated Chinese Level 1*. The book has also been redesigned to be easier to read and carry, and reordered alphabetically by *pinyin* to make it easier to find characters. New example words and phrases have been added to each entry to help students learn how each character is used.

SELECTION AND PRESENTATION OF CHARACTERS

The 670 characters included in this book are frequently used in modern Chinese, and cover all the characters in the glossary of *Integrated Chinese, Level 1, Part 1* and *Level 1, Part 2* (by Yuehua Liu, Tao-chung Yao, et. al.), the Chinese textbook most widely used at schools across the United States.

Explanations are given in both English and Chinese. The English entries are meant for beginning and intermediate students, while the Chinese entries may serve as references for teachers and advanced learners.

For each entry, we display the character in its various ancient scripts (see Types of Script below), and we include each character's classification, which indicates how the character was constructed (see Types of Characters below). Most characters have illustrations that help readers instantly connect the characters' pictographic elements to their meanings, both ancient and modern. Some characters are not accompanied by illustrations. Many of these are pictophonetic characters that have developed meanings largely unrelated to their visual aspects.

Also included are four indexes, organized alphabetically by *pinyin*, by *Integrated Chinese* lesson, and by stroke count (of both traditional and simplified characters), respectively. We hope all readers will find these indexes convenient and practical.

TYPES OF SCRIPT

KEY TO SCRIPT TYPES

SYMBOL	SCRIPT	EXAMPLES (報)	SYMBOL	SCRIPT	EXAMPLES (報)
甲	Oracle-Bone Inscriptions	𢀖	篆	Seal Script	報
金	Bronze Inscriptions	報	草	Cursive Script	報

The characters in *The Way of Chinese Characters* are written in "Regular Script" (or traditional characters) and simplified characters. Regular Script can be traced to the late Han Dynasty (207 B.C.–220 A.D.) and is still used in Taiwan, Hong Kong, and many overseas Chinese communities. Simplified characters were introduced and promoted by the government of the People's Republic of China in the 1950s, and have since remained the standard in mainland China.

In this book we focus on Regular Script, or traditional form, because we have found that it is often difficult for beginning learners to appreciate the visual flavor of simplified Chinese characters. We present the ancient forms of the characters and provide illustrations, so that students can identify characters' original pictographic traits. We hope that with such imagery in mind, students will have a much easier time remembering Chinese characters.

This book also introduces other forms of Chinese script including "Oracle-Bone Inscriptions 甲骨文," "Bronze Inscriptions 金文," "Seal Script 篆文," and "Cursive Script 草書." "Oracle-Bone Inscriptions" come from carvings on ox bones or tortoise shells, which were used during the Shang Dynasty (ca.1600–ca.1100 B.C.) to record events and devise predictions. "Bronze Inscriptions" are found on bronze vessels of the Shang and Zhou Dynasties (Zhou Dynasty: ca. 1100–ca. 221 B.C.). "Seal Script" includes both "Big Seal Script" and "Small Seal Script." The former was used in the Qin State during the Eastern Zhou Dynasty (ca. 770–ca. 221 B.C.) and the latter became official in the Qin Dynasty (221–207 B.C.). As an abbreviated form of traditional Chinese characters, "Cursive Script" originates from the Han Dynasty (207 B.C.–220 A.D.). These characters are written swiftly such that the strokes flow together, and were thus considered an artistic form of Chinese calligraphy. Many of the simplified characters used in mainland China today were born out of this cursive style.

In the book, we display each character in its various forms: Oracle-Bone Inscriptions, Bronze Inscriptions, and Seal Script, alongside Regular Script and simplified forms. You will notice that some characters are without ancient forms, however, such as 她 (tā, she), 您 (nín, polite form of the pronoun you), and 啤(pí, beer), as these were created in later periods. Cursive Script is also shown for those simplified characters which were derived from the cursive style.

TYPES OF CHARACTERS

Chinese characters are constructed differently from alphabetic languages. According to the Han dynasty scholar Xu Shen, in his *Analysis and Explanation of Characters*, they can be divided into six basic categories: pictographs (象形), explicit characters (指事), associative compounds (會意), pictophonetic characters (形聲), mutually explanatory characters (轉注), and phonetic loan characters (假借).

Pictographs delineate the shape of certain objects or their parts. Examples include: 木 (mù, wood; tree), 刀 (dāo, knife), 女 (nǚ, woman), and 馬 (mǎ, horse). Although such characters are relatively easy to identify, the limitation of this particular category is that pictographs cannot convey more abstract meanings.

Explicit characters are simple diagrammatic indications of abstract ideas, such as 上 (shàng, above), or 下 (xià, below). Others are formed with the addition of a symbol to an existing pictograph, such as 本 (běn, root; basic), or 刃 (rèn, edge). Explicit characters constructed via this method comprise only a small proportion of all Chinese characters.

The meanings of associative compound characters are derived from their components, which may combine two or more ideographs. Examples include 明 (míng, bright, the combination of 日 rì, sun and 月 yuè, moon), and 森 (sēn, forest, the combination of three trees 木 mù).

The majority of Chinese characters are pictophonetic, which combine semantic and phonetic components. For instance, the character 媽 (mā, mother) consists of 女 (nǚ, female) and 馬 (mǎ, horse). 女 suggests the general meaning of the character while 馬 signals its pronunciation.

According to Xu Shen, mutually explanatory (or synonymous) characters refer to those that are of the same or similar meanings, and thus can be used to define one another, e.g., 老 (lǎo, old; aged) and

考 (kǎo, aged; long life; test). However, the exact meaning of this category is ambiguous. Some contemporary scholars consider that the characters in this category actually refer to those later invented characters for recovering their original meanings. A common way to make this type of character is to add radicals or other components to the original characters. The character 蛇 (shé, snake) is an example from this category. The character 它 (tā) was a pictograph of a cobra-like snake and originally meant "snake". Later 它 was borrowed to mean "other," "it," etc., and these meanings overwhelmed its original meaning. Therefore, a worm radical 虫 was added to the left of 它 to make a new character 蛇.

Phonetic loan characters refer to those that originally had no written form, and so borrowed existing characters of the same or similar pronunciation. For example, the character 我 resembles a weapon with a saw-toothed blade and long shaft, and originally referred to a kind of ancient weapon. Because the pronunciation of this character is similar to that of the pronoun "I," 我 was borrowed to mean "I" or "me."

USING THIS BOOK AS A TEACHING TOOL

This book is the result of a serious, meticulous, and extensive study of the origins of Chinese characters. Many of the books currently on the market on this topic offer learners imaginative, yet inaccurate pictorial representations of characters. While imagination can help learners remember Chinese characters, such historically groundless explanations may misinform them. This book's academic, accurate, and straightforward explanations allow learners to study Chinese characters thoughtfully, but without the risk of becoming overwhelmed by overly detailed information on origin and evolution.

It is our belief that this book will provide teachers with a new, efficient, interesting, and scholarly way to teach Chinese characters to learners of Chinese, as well as learners of Japanese and Korean, whose writing systems employ Chinese characters.

The characters in this edition have been organized by *pinyin* for easy and universal reference, with separate sections for some Basic Radicals and numerals. New students of Chinese should first familiarize themselves with these radicals and numerals, as they will make learning more complex characters easier. Multiple indexes have been provided to help students and teachers look up specific characters.

USING THIS BOOK WITH *INTEGRATED CHINESE*

The Way of Chinese Characters contains all the characters taught in *Integrated Chinese Level 1 Part 1* and *Level 1 Part 2*. Students of *Integrated Chinese* should use the "Character Index by *Integrated Chinese* Lesson" to easily find each character grouped by lesson as they proceed through the course.

It is our expectation that this book will benefit all learners of Chinese characters, especially those who have difficulty memorizing numerous characters. In short, we hope that reading *The Way of Chinese Characters* helps learners overcome the obstacles to memorizing Chinese characters in an academically sound and creatively engaging way.

Jianhsin Wu

BIBLIOGRAPHY

Gu, Yankui 谷衍奎, ed. *Hanzi yuanliu zidian* 《漢字源流字典》. Beijing: Huaxia chubanshe, 2003.

Hanyu dazidian bianji weiyuanhui 漢語大字典編輯委員會, ed. *Hanyu dacidian* 《漢語大字典》. Chengdu: Sichuan cishu chubanshe & Hubei cishu chubanshe, 1993.

Jiang, Lansheng 江藍生 and Zunwu Lu 陸尊梧, eds. *Jianhuazi fantizi duizhao zidian* 《簡化字繁體字對照字典》. Shanghai: Hanyu dacidian chubanshe, 2004.

Jiang, Shanguo 蔣善國. *Hanzixue* 《漢字學》. Shanghai: Shanghai jiaoyu chubanshe, 1987.

Liu, Yuehua 劉月華 and Yao, Tao-chung 姚道中, et. al. *Integrated Chinese* 《中文聽説讀寫》, *Level 1, Part 1 Textbook*. 3rd ed. Boston: Cheng & Tsui Company, 2009.

Liu, Yuehua 劉月華 and Yao, Tao-chung 姚道中, et. al. *Integrated Chinese* 《中文聽説讀寫》, *Level 1, Part 2 Textbook*. 3rd ed. Boston: Cheng & Tsui Company, 2009.

Rong, Geng 容庚, ed. *Jinwen bian* 《金文編》. Beijing: Zhonghua shuju, 1985.

Shi, Dingguo 史定國, et al., eds. *Jianhuazi yanjiu* 《簡化字研究》. Beijing: Shangwu yinshuguan, 2004.

Wan, Zhiwen 宛志文, et al., eds. *Gujin hanyu changyong zidian* 《古今漢語常用字典》. Wuhan: Hubei renmin chubanshe, 2002.

Weng, Zhifei 翁志飛, et al., eds. *Xinbian caoshu zidian* 《新編草書字典》. Hangzhou: Zhejiang guji chubanshe, 2005.

Xie, Guanghui 謝光輝, et al., eds. *Hanyu ziyuan zidian* 《漢語字源字典》. Beijing: Beijing daxue chubanshe, 2002.

Xu, Shen [漢] 許慎. *Shuowen jiezi* 《說文解字》. Beijing: Zhonghua shuju, 1978.

Xu, Shen. Preface to *Analysis and Explanation of Characters* in Zang, Kehe 臧克和 and Ping Wang 王平, ed. *Shuowen jiezi xinding* 《說文解字新訂》. Beijing: Zhonghua shuju, 2002.

Xu, Zhongshu 徐中舒, et al., eds. *Hanyu guwenzi zixingbiao* 《漢語古文字字形表》. Chengdu: Sichuan renmin chubanshe, 1981.

Xu, Zhongshu 徐中舒, et al., eds. *Jiaguwen zidian* 《甲骨文字典》. Chengdu: Sichuan cishu chubanshe, 1998.

Zhang, Shuyan 張書岩, et al., eds. *Jianhuazi suyuan* 《簡化字溯源》. Beijing: Yuwen chubanshe, 2005.

BASIC RADICALS

RADICALS are components of Chinese characters which often indicate the character's meaning. They are useful to know not only because they can provide clues to the meanings of characters, but also because many Chinese dictionaries are organized by radicals. Most radicals are common characters (often pictographs) and can be used on their own in addition to being components in more complicated characters like associative compounds and pictophonetic characters. When used as components, radicals may appear in variant forms. For example, 心 (heart) may appear as 心 or 忄 in compound characters.

See the "Types of Script" section on page vi of the Preface for more information about the different scripts.

rén
man; person

PICTOGRAPH In the Oracle-Bone and Bronze Inscriptions, the character 人 presents the profile of a person with a head, an arched back, arms and legs, possibly indicating a figure from an early stage of human evolution. In Regular Script, 人 looks like someone with two rather long legs. As a radical, 人 often appears as 亻, and is often used in characters related to human beings and their activities, e.g., 你 (nǐ, you), 他 (tā, he; him), 住 (zhù, to live), and 休 (xiū, to rest).

人　象形。甲骨文、金文像人側立之形。

人民 rénmín the people
客人 kèrén visitor; guest; customer

人們 rénmen people; the public
病人 bìngrén sick person; patient

dāo
knife

PICTOGRAPH In ancient writing systems, the character 刀 resembles a knife, with the upper part as the handle and the lower part as the edge. In Regular Script, the handle is shortened so that it becomes almost unnoticeable. Characters with the knife radical 刂 usually have something to do with knives or cutting, such as 別 (bié, to separate), 刺 (cì, to stab), and 利 (lì, sharp).

刀　象形。像刀形。上像刀柄，下像刀刃及刀背。

刀子 dāozi knife
剪刀 jiǎndāo scissors

刀刃 dāorèn knife blade
開刀 kāidāo to perform or have an operation

力

lì
power; strength

PICTOGRAPH In both the Oracle-Bone and Bronze Inscriptions, the character 力 resembles an ancient plow, with the upper part as the handle and the lower part as the plowshare. Since plowing requires great physical strength, 力 means "strength." In Regular Script, 力 is similar in form to 刀 (dāo, knife) except that its top sticks out.

力　象形。甲骨文、金文均像耕田用具。因耕田要有力，引申為力氣。

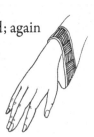

甲 力 金 力 篆 力

力氣 lìqi strength
精力 jīnglì energy

能力 nénglì capability; ability
有力 yǒulì strong; powerful; vigorous

又

yòu
right hand; again

PICTOGRAPH In its ancient form, the character 又 was shaped like a right hand, meaning "right hand." Today 又 is used to mean "again," "also," "in addition," "both... and...," etc.

又　象形。甲骨文像右手形。

甲 又 金 又 篆 又

又及 yòují P.S.; postscript
又… 又… yòu... yòu... both... and...

又名 yòumíng a.k.a.; alternative name

口

kǒu
mouth; entrance

PICTOGRAPH The character 口 looks like an open mouth. Characters with the mouth radical are often associated with the movement of the mouth, e.g., 吃 (chī, to eat), 喝 (hē, to drink), 唱 (chàng, to sing), and 叫 (jiào, to shout).

口　象形。像人口形狀。

甲 口 金 口 篆 口

口紅 kǒuhóng lipstick
門口 ménkǒu doorway

口語 kǒuyǔ spoken language; vernacular language
人口 rénkǒu population

口

wéi
enclose

PICTOGRAPH 口 represents the periphery or border of an area. Characters relating to boundaries often include the radical 口, such as 國/国 (gúo, country; state), 園/园 (yuán, garden; park), 圖/图 (tú, map). Note that 口 is larger than the radical 口 (kǒu, mouth), indicating a large area that can contain many objects.

口 象形。像環圍形。從口的字多有外圍或邊界。

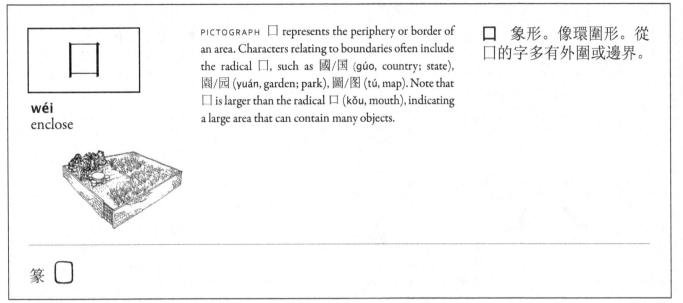

篆

土

tǔ
earth; soil

PICTOGRAPH In the Oracle-Bone Inscriptions, the upper part of 土 represents a small hill or mound of soil, while the bottom line stands for the ground. In Regular Script, a cross replaces the mound.

土 象形。像一土塊狀，下方 "一" 字意指大地。

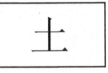

甲  金 土 篆 土

土地 tǔdì land; soil
土氣 tǔqì rustic; unsophisticated

國土 guótǔ country's territory; national land
土豆 tǔdòu potato

夕

xī
sunset; evening

PICTOGRAPH In its ancient forms, the character 夕 resembles a half moon, meaning "sunset," "dusk," "evening," or "night." Sometimes the moon can be seen rising from the east at dusk.

夕 象形。像半個月亮，傍晚或夜晚之意。

甲 𝒟 金 𝐃 篆 𝓅

夕陽 xīyáng sunset; the setting sun
除夕 chúxī lunar New Year's Eve

前夕 qiánxī eve; the day before
朝夕 zhāoxī morning and night; all the time

dà
big; great

PICTOGRAPH In the ancient writing systems, the character 大 portrays a figure standing with arms stretching out and legs spread apart. This posture seems to suggest that humans are the greatest creatures on earth. The primary meanings of 大 are "big," "large," "great," "age," and "older."

大　象形。像正面人形。天地萬物中以人為大為貴，故用人形來表示大。

甲 大　金 大　篆 大

大人 dàren adult; grown-up
大家 dàjiā all; everyone

大學 dàxué college; university
長大 zhǎngdà grow up

女

nǚ
female;
woman

PICTOGRAPH In the Oracle-Bone Inscriptions, the character 女 depicts a woman kneeling with her arms lowered and hands clasped on her lap, reflecting the lower social status of women in ancient times. In later forms, the kneeling component is transformed as women are recognized as having a status more equal to men. The Regular Script forms of 女 and 大 are similar, but 女 emphasizes the female bosom.

女　象形。甲骨文像女子俯首，雙臂交叉下跪形。

甲 女　金 女　金 女

女人 nǚrén woman
女生 nǚshēng female student; girl

女兒 nǚ'ér daughter
女士 nǚshì lady; madam

子

zǐ
baby; child

PICTOGRAPH In its ancient form, the character 子 shows a baby swaddled in cloth, with its head sticking up and arms stretching out. In Regular Script, the head of the baby is represented by a horizontal hook instead of a round shape. 子 is used as suffix after some nouns, such as 桌子, 椅子 etc.

子　象形。像頭部突出、手臂在外、裹在襁褓中的嬰兒。

甲 子　金 子　篆 子

孩子 háizi child
房子 fángzi house; building

兒子 érzi son
餃子 jiǎozi dumpling; pot-sticker

寸

cùn
inch

EXPLICIT CHARACTER In Seal Script, 寸 combines 又 with 一. 又 means "right hand" while 一 indicates the section of the forearm one inch from the wrist, where a traditional Chinese doctor would feel a patient's pulse and diagnose ailments.

寸 指事。從又，從一。"又"為右手，"一"指手後一寸之處。中醫所言寸口。

篆

尺寸 chǐcùn size; dimension; measurement　寸口 cùnkǒu a person's pulse on the wrist
寸步難行 cùnbù nánxíng unable to move a single step (idiom)

小

xiǎo
small

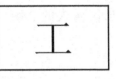

ASSOCIATIVE COMPOUND In the Oracle-Bone and Bronze Inscriptions, the character 小 consists of three dots, like three tiny grains of sand. In its later forms, 小 resembles a knife (represented by the vertical hook in the middle) cutting something into two smaller pieces.

小 會意。甲骨文及金文作三點，像細小的沙粒形，表示微小的意思。

甲 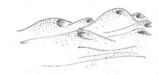 金 篆

小孩兒 xiǎoháir child; kid; kiddy　小學 xiǎoxué elementary/primary school
小時候 xiǎo shíhou in one's childhood　小姐 xiǎojie Miss; young lady

工

gōng
tool; work; labor

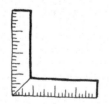

PICTOGRAPH In the ancient writing systems, the character 工 looks like a carpenter's square or ruler. The original meaning of 工 was "tool," from which derived the meanings "work," "labor," "skill," "craftsmanship," and "construction project."

工 象形。像工匠用的曲尺。

甲 金 工 篆 工

工具 gōngjù tool　工人 gōngrén worker
工作 gōngzuò to work; job　工程 gōngchéng engineering; engineering project

幺

yāo
tiny; small

PICTOGRAPH   In the Oracle-Bone and Bronze Inscriptions, the character 幺 represents a wisp of silk. Since a wisp is a small quantity, 幺 extends to mean "small," "tiny," or "youngest."

幺　象形。像一小把細丝。甲骨文幺、糸（mì）、絲为同源字。糸、絲都像絲束形，不同的是糸为一束絲，絲为两束絲。系(xì) 字在甲骨文中為一隻手握兩束絲。

甲 〰 金 〰 篆 〰　　幺 yāo one (spoken form when spelling out numbers, esp. on telephone)
老幺 lǎoyāo youngest

弓

gōng
bow

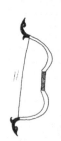

PICTOGRAPH   In the Oracle-Bone Inscriptions, the character 弓 resembles an entire bow. In the Bronze Inscription form, 弓 depicts a bow without its string, which is how a bow should be stored. Just like human beings, bows need time for relaxation!

弓　象形。甲骨文像有弓弦弓背的完整弓形。金文簡化。

甲 〰 金 〰 篆 弓　　弓箭 gōngjiàn bow and arrow　　彈弓 dàn'gōng catapult; slingshot

---

心

xīn
heart

PICTOGRAPH   In its ancient forms, the character 心 represents a heart. There are two forms of the heart radical, 心 and 忄. 心 is usually positioned at the bottom of a character as in 想 (xiǎng, to think) and 愁 (chóu, to worry), while 忄 is on the left, as in 忙 (máng, busy) and 怕 (pà, fear). Characters with heart radicals are often associated with feelings or other mental activities.

心　象形。像人的心臟。

甲 〰 金 〰 篆 〰
心理 xīnlǐ psychology; mentality　　關心 guānxīn care for; be concerned with
擔心 dānxīn worry; to be anxious　　心情 xīnqíng mood; state of mind

gē
dagger-axe

PICTOGRAPH The dagger-axe 戈 is a weapon from the Shang (ca.1600–C.1100 B.C.) and Zhou Dynasties (ca.1100–221 B.C.). In the Oracle-Bone and Bronze Inscriptions, the character 戈 delineates such a weapon with a long shaft and a blade at the end. 戈 is used as a component of many characters, such as 我 (wǒ, I), 國/国 (guó, nation), and 錢/钱 (qián, money).

戈　象形。戈是古代常用的一種長柄橫刃的兵器。

甲 金 篆

干戈 gān'gē weapons of war; arms
大動干戈 dàdòng gān'gē to go to war; to make a big fuss over something

倒戈 dǎogē to change sides in a war; turncoat

---

niú
cow; ox

PICTOGRAPH In its ancient forms, 牛 is the front view of an ox head. Its primary meaning is "ox," "cow," or "bull," but due to the way the Chinese think of an ox, it has been extended to mean "stubborn," "headstrong," "capable," "arrogant," and "to boast."

牛　象形。甲骨文像正面有腳的牛頭形狀。本義為牛，引申義有固執、倔強、高傲、有本領、吹牛、説大話等這些在人看來與牛的特性有關聯的詞語。

甲 金 篆

牛肉 niúròu beef
放牛 fàngniú grazing cattle

牛奶 niúnǎi milk
吹牛 chuīniú to brag

---

shǒu
hand

PICTOGRAPH The ancient form of the character 手 looks like an outspread hand, with five fingers comprising the upper part, and the forearm below. Characters with the hand radical 扌 are often related to acts performed with the hands, e.g., 打 (dǎ, to beat), 推 (tuī, to push), and 擦 (cā, to wipe).

手　象形。像五指伸開的手掌。

金 篆

握手 wòshǒu shake hands
手錶 shǒubiǎo watch

分手 fēnshǒu to split up; to break up
手套 shǒutào glove

rì
sun; day

PICTOGRAPH   In the Oracle-Bone and Bronze Inscriptions, 日 represents the sun. Since the sun rises daily, 日 extended to mean "day." Regular Script is also called "Square Script" and usually there are no round components, so the character 日 in Regular Script is drawn as a rectangle with a horizontal line through its middle, which indicates that the sun is not just a circle but a solid thing, and distinguishes 日 from the character 口.

日　象形。甲骨文、金文像太陽的輪廓。日字寫成方形則出於楷书書寫的習慣。

甲 ⊖　金 ⊟　篆 日

生日 shēngrì birthday
日期 rìqī date

節日 jiérì holiday; festival
日本 rìběn Japan

---

yuè
moon; month

PICTOGRAPH   In the Oracle-Bone and Bronze Inscriptions, the character 月 depicts a crescent moon, which may be compared to a large eye, following and watching people quietly at night. The dot or lines in the character 月 represent the darker areas of the moon's surface. Given that the moon's orbit takes approximately thirty days, the extended meaning of 月 is "month." When used as a radical, 月 can mean "moon" or "flesh." For example, the characters 腿 (tuǐ, leg), 臉/脸 (liǎn, face), 腦/脑 (nǎo, brain), and 腳/脚 (jiǎo, foot) all contain the flesh radical 月 (derived from 肉, ròu).

月　象形。甲骨文、金文中像彎月形。作為部首，也稱為肉月旁。

甲 ☽　金 ☾　篆 ♫

月亮 yuèliang the moon
月餅 yuèbǐng mooncake

月光 yuèguāng moonlight
月份 yuèfèn month

---

mù
tree; wood

PICTOGRAPH   In its ancient forms, the character 木 depicts a tree with branches on top and roots at the bottom. "Tree" is the original meaning of 木, while extended meanings today are "wood" or "lumber."

木　象形。像一棵樹。上像樹枝，中像樹幹，下像樹根。

甲 朩　金 朩　篆 朩

樹木 shùmù trees
木頭 mùtou log; timber; blockhead

木刻 mùkè woodcut
木匠 mùjiàng carpenter

水 shuǐ
water

PICTOGRAPH In its ancient form, the character 水 looks like a flowing body of water. The line in the middle represents the main stream and the dots on the sides look like the spray or waves of the water. In Regular Script, the dots extend into lines, resembling the tributaries of a river. The original meaning of 水 was "river," but later it came to mean "water."

水 象形。甲骨文中間像流水，旁似浪花或水的支流。

甲 〔水〕 金 〔水〕 篆 〔水〕

汽水 qìshuǐ soda
水平 shuǐpíng level; standard

水果 shuǐguǒ fruit
開水 kāishuǐ boiled water; boiling water

方 fāng
square; side; method

PICTOGRAPH In the Oracle-Bone Inscriptions, 方 looks like a shovel or spade. Its original meaning was "shovel," but today it means "to dig a hole," "cubic meter," "square," "upright," "place," "region," "side," "direction," etc.

方 象形。像剷土的工具。甲骨文上短橫像手握的橫柄，中間一長橫是腳踩的地方，下為分叉的鍤。本義為土鍤，引申義包括正方形、方面、方向、地域、正、才等。

甲 〔方〕 金 〔方〕 篆 〔方〕

長方形 chángfāngxíng rectangle
地方 dìfang place; space

方便 fāngbiàn convenient
方向 fāngxiàng direction

火 huǒ
fire

PICTOGRAPH In the Oracle-Bone Inscriptions, the character 火 represents flames. In Regular Script, 火 resembles flames on firewood. There are two forms of the fire radical: 火 and 灬, as in 燙/烫 (tàng, scalding), 燒/烧 (shāo, burn), and 熱/热 (rè, hot).

火 象形。像火焰形。

甲 〔火〕 篆 〔火〕

火紅 huǒhóng fiery; blazing
火車 huǒchē train

火山 huǒshān volcano
火藥 huǒyào gunpowder

王

wáng
king; (surname)

PICTOGRAPH   In the Oracle-Bone and Bronze Inscriptions, the character 王 looks like an ax-type tool, with the handle on the top and the blade at the bottom. This 王 symbol of an ax suggests power and authority, therefore meaning "king." In Regular Script, one can hardly find the ax in the character 王, as it evolved into a simple 三 with a vertical stroke running down the middle. When used as a radical, 王 usually refers to jade, because it is similar to 玉 (yù, jade).

王　象形。甲骨文、金文中像斧形，上像其柄，下像其圓弧形的鋒刃。王是一種斧狀的的兵器，後來成為執法的刑具，是權威的象徵。引申義指以武力征服天下者為王。

甲 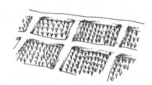 金 篆

國王 guówáng king
王子 wángzǐ prince; son of a king

女王 nǚwáng queen
王室 wángshì royal family

田

tián
field; (surname)

PICTOGRAPH   The character 田 depicts plots of land, divided by vertical and horizontal lines, as if seen from above. Today it is also a common surname.

田　象形。像阡陌縱橫的田地。

甲  金 田 篆 田

田地 tiándì field; farmland; cropland
油田 yóutián oil field

種田 zhòngtián to farm; farming
稻田 dàotián paddy field

目

mù
eye

PICTOGRAPH   In the Oracle-Bone and Bronze Inscriptions, the character 目 represents an eye. In Seal Script, this eye becomes vertical and the curves in the character are straightened. 目 is often used as a radical in characters related to eyes, e.g., 看 (kàn, see), 瞎 (xiā, blind), and 睡 (shuì, sleep). The extended meanings of 目 are "item," "catalogue," "goal," "title," etc.

目　象形。甲骨文、金文像人眼形。為書寫方便，小篆將橫目改為豎目。

甲 金 篆 目

目光 mùguāng sight; vision; gaze
目的 mùdì purpose; aim; goal

目前 mùqián at present; currently
題目 tímù title; topic

示

shì
to show

PICTOGRAPH In the Oracle-Bone Inscriptions, the character 示 looks like a T-shaped stone table upon which sacrificial offerings to gods or ancestors were placed. In Seal Script, more lines are added beneath, as if to make the altar more stable. In combinations, 示 usually means "to show" but its radical form 礻 often appears in characters related to religious ritual, such as 禮/礼 (lǐ, rite), and 祝 (zhù, pray).

示 象形。甲骨文中像用石塊搭起的簡單祭臺。

甲 示 篆 示

表示 biǎoshì to express; to indiciate
出示 chūshì to show for inspection

示好 shìhǎo to express goodwill
示威 shìwēi demonstrate; a demonstration

糸

mì
silk

PICTOGRAPH In the Oracle-Bone and Bronze Inscriptions, 糸 depicts a silk string. Characters with the silk radical 糸/纟 often relate to the process of making cloth, including dyeing, such as 織/织 (zhī, weave), 線/线 (xiàn, thread), 紅/红 (hóng, red), and 綠/绿 (lǜ, green). In Regular Script, the character 糸 combines 幺 (yāo, tiny) and 小 (xiǎo, small).

糸 象形。甲骨文、金文中像丝束形。

甲 金 篆 糸

耳

ěr
ear

PICTOGRAPH In the Oracle-Bone and Bronze Inscriptions, the character 耳 delineates the contour of an ear. In Regular Script, 耳 still somewhat resembles the shape of an ear, with the two lines in the middle representing the helix, earlobe, and internal structure.

耳 象形。甲骨文、金文中像耳朵的形狀。

甲 金 篆 耳

耳朵 ěrduo ear
打耳光 dǎ ěrguāng slap someone's face

耳環 ěrhuán earring
木耳 mù'ěr edible tree fungus

衣

yī
clothing

PICTOGRAPH In its ancient forms, the character 衣 outlines a garment with a collar and sleeves in the upper part, and the hemline in the lower part. In Regular Script, 衣 resembles a garment on a clothes hanger. There are two forms of the clothing radical, 衣 and 衤. 衣 is usually positioned at the bottom of a character as in 袋 (dài, bag; sack) and 表 (biǎo, surface; outside), while 衤 is on the left, as in 襯衫 (chènshān, shirt) and 褲 (kù, pants).

衣　象形。像衣領、衣袖、衣襟形。

甲 𧘇　金 𧘇　篆 𧚎

衣服 yīfu clothes
雨衣 yǔyī raincoat

大衣 dàyī overcoat; topcoat
毛衣 máoyī (wool) sweater

米

mǐ
uncooked rice

PICTOGRAPH In the Oracle-Bone Inscriptions, 米 resembles grains scattered around a rack, meaning "hulled or husked uncooked rice." Its extended meanings include "rice-shaped things," and "meter."

米　象形。甲骨文像一段有米粒的穀穗，或散落在稻稭下的穀粒。本義為去皮的稻穀，引申泛指稻穀、像米粒的食物以及長度單位。一米是 100 釐米，合 3 市尺。

甲 ⁂　金 朮　篆 米

米飯 mǐfàn (cooked) rice
玉米 yùmǐ corn

花生米 huāshēng mǐ peanut
米老鼠 mǐlǎoshǔ Mickey Mouse

車/车

chē
vehicle; car

PICTOGRAPH In the Oracle-Bone and Bronze Inscriptions, the character 車 depicts a chariot, complete with frame, axle, wheels, and yokes. In Seal Script, 車 is simplified to one wheel on its axle. The simplified character 车 developed from the cursive style of 車.

車　象形。篆文像簡化了的車形，只有車架、一個輪子與軸。簡體字车是繁體字車的草書楷化字。

甲 車　金 車　篆 車　草 车

汽車 qìchē car; automobile
自行車 zìxíngchē bicycle; bike

火車 huǒchē train
車站 chēzhàn rail station; bus stop

The Way of Chinese Characters

言 yán
word; speech

ASSOCIATIVE COMPOUND   In the Oracle-Bone and Bronze Inscriptions, the character 言 looks like a tongue (the upper part) sticking out from a mouth (the bottom part), referring to the act of speaking with excitement and energy. In Regular Script, the mouth 口 comprises the lower part of 言, but the upper part resembles a sound wave more than a tongue.

言　會意。甲骨文、金文字形下像嘴，上像伸出的舌頭。意指言乃從舌上發出的聲音。

甲 〔oracle〕　金 〔bronze〕　篆 〔seal〕

語言 yǔyán language
寓言 yùyán fable

發言 fāyán to speak; to make a statement/ speech
預言 yùyán to predict; prophecy

貝/贝 bèi
cowry shell

PICTOGRAPH   In the Oracle-Bone and Bronze Inscriptions, the character 貝 resembles a cowry shell. Since cowry shells were used as currency in ancient times, characters with 貝 as a component often relate to money, trade, or wealth, e.g., 買/买 (mǎi, buy), 賣/卖 (mài, sell), 貴/贵 (guì, expensive), and 財 (cái, fortune). The simplified character 贝 derives from the cursive style of the traditional character 貝.

貝　象形。甲骨文、金文中像貝殼形。簡體字贝是由繁體字貝的草書楷化而來。

甲 〔oracle〕　金 〔bronze〕　篆 貝　草 〔cursive〕

貝殼 bèiké cowry shell

寶貝 bǎobèi treasure; darling

見/见 jiàn
to see

ASSOCIATIVE COMPOUND   In the Oracle-Bone and Bronze Inscriptions, the character 見 looks like a person with one large eye in place of a head, meaning "to see" or "meet." In Regular Script, 見 looks like a stylized rendition of a figure with a big eye above two thin legs. The simplified character 见 derives from the cursive style of the traditional form 見.

見　會意。從目從儿。儿指人，表示人看東西時要睜大眼睛。簡體字见是繁體字見的草書楷化字。

甲 〔oracle〕　金 〔bronze〕　篆 見　草 〔cursive〕

見面 jiànmiàn to meet
看見 kànjiàn to see

再見 zàijiàn goodbye; see you again later
聽見 tīngjiàn to hear

走

zǒu
to walk

ASSOCIATIVE COMPOUND In the Bronze Inscriptions, the upper part of 走 looks like a person walking rapidly with arms swinging, while the lower part depicts a human foot. In Regular Script, the lower part resembles a person striding forward with one arm swinging high, and the upper part becomes 土 (tǔ, earth), the surface upon which we walk.

走　會意。金文上像人擺動雙臂，下從止（腳），表示人用腳快步前行。

金 𦓐 篆 𧺆

走路 zǒulù to walk; to go on foot
走狗 zǒugǒu running dog; lackey

走走 zǒuzǒu take a walk
走私 zǒusī to smuggle

足

zú
foot; enough

PICTOGRAPH In the Oracle-Bone Inscriptions, the upper part of 足 represents the calf of a leg, while the lower part presents an image of a foot, which is the same as the lower part of 走. In Regular Script, the calf part is replaced by 口. Characters with the foot radical ⻊ are often associated with acts that involve using one's feet, such as 跟 (gēn, follow), 踢 (tī, kick), and 跳 (tiào, jump). The extended meanings of 足 are "enough," "ample," etc.

足　象形。從口、從止。口像小腿；止是腳。合起來表示人足。

甲 𤴚 金 𧾷 篆 𧾷

足跡 zújì footprint; track
不足 bùzú not enough; insufficient; deficiency

足球 zúqiú soccer; football
滿足 mǎnzú satisfied; content

金

jīn
gold; metal; money

PICTOGRAPH AND ASSOCIATIVE COMPOUND In the Bronze Inscriptions, the character 金 consists of three parts: 人 (arrowhead), 王 (axe), and two dots (representing bronze ingots), suggesting that both arrowheads and axes are made of bronze. The primary meaning of 金 is "metal," with the extended meanings "gold" and "money."

金　象形兼會意。金文左邊像兩塊青銅塊，右邊上是箭頭下是斧，指可用來製作箭、斧等器具的金屬。本義為金屬，引申為黃金、金錢等。

金 𨥀 篆 𨥉

金屬 jīnshǔ metal
金魚 jīnyú goldfish

現金 xiànjīn cash
獎學金 jiǎngxuéjīn scholarship

門/门
mén
door; gate

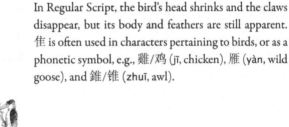

PICTOGRAPH The character 門 depicts a door with two panels. Characters with the 門 radical include: 開/开 (kāi, open), 關/关 (guān, close), 問/问 (wèn, ask), etc. The simplified character 门 derives from the cursive style of 門.

門 象形。像兩扇門之形。门是門字的草書楷化字。

甲 𪩘 金 𨳇 篆 門 草 门

出門 chūmén to go out; to go on a journey
大門 dàmén entrance door; gate
門票 ménpiào admission ticket
對門 duìmén the house or room opposite

隹
zhuī
short-tailed bird

PICTOGRAPH In the Oracle-Bone and Bronze Inscriptions, the character 隹 depicts a short-tailed bird. In Regular Script, the bird's head shrinks and the claws disappear, but its body and feathers are still apparent. 隹 is often used in characters pertaining to birds, or as a phonetic symbol, e.g., 雞/鸡 (jī, chicken), 雁 (yàn, wild goose), and 錐/锥 (zhuī, awl).

隹 象形。意指短尾巴鳥。

甲 𠁥 金 𨾴 篆 隹

雨
yǔ
rain

PICTOGRAPH The character 雨 could indicate heavy rain, as one can see four large rain drops. Characters with the rain radical often relate to natural phenomena or weather, e.g., 雪 (xuě, snow), 雷 (léi, thunder), 霧/雾 (wù, fog), and 雲/云 (yún, cloud).

雨 象形。像雨滴從天上落下形。

甲 𡈼 金 雨 篆 雨

下雨 xiàyǔ to rain; rainy
雨傘 yǔsǎn umbrella
雨衣 yǔyī raincoat
雨季 yǔjì rainy season

食

shí
to eat

ASSOCIATIVE COMPOUND   In the Oracle-Bone Inscriptions, the lower part of 食 resembles a high-legged container full of food, while the upper part represents an open mouth, referring to the act of eating. In Regular Script, the lower part of 食 looks like legs in movement, which could suggest that one derives energy from eating. The food radical 飠/饣 always appears on the left side of a character, e.g., 飯/饭 (fàn, food; cooked rice), 餓/饿 (è, hungry), and 餅/饼 (bǐng, pancake).

食　會意。甲骨文中
"食"字上邊像是向下
張開的嘴，下邊像是盛
滿了食物的容器，表示
張口向下吃容器中的食
物。一説下像裝滿食物
的容器，上則為蓋子。

甲 🥢 金 🥢 篆 食

食物 shíwù food
食堂 shítáng dining hall; canteen

飲食 yǐnshí food and drink; diet
食言 shíyán to break a promise (literally: to eat one's words)

馬/马

mǎ
horse

PICTOGRAPH   In the Oracle-Bone Inscriptions, the character 馬 delineates a horse. In its later forms, the character becomes more simple and abstract. Yet the shape of a horse, complete with body, mane, and legs, can still be seen in the Regular Script form. The simplified character 马 derives from the cursive style of the traditional character 馬.

馬　象形。上像馬頭與鬃
毛，下像身、腿、尾。
簡體的马字保留了繁體
馬字的大體輪廓，十分
接近馬字的草書。

甲 🐎 金 🐎 篆 馬 草 🐎

馬上 mǎshàng at once; right away
馬虎 mǎhu careless

出馬 chūmǎ go into action; take up a matter
馬路 mǎlù street; road

魚/鱼

yú
fish

PICTOGRAPH   In its ancient forms, 魚 is the drawing of a complete fish with its head, body, fin, scales, and tail. In Regular Script, 魚 still resembles a fish with its head on the top, body and scales in the middle, and tail at the bottom. In the simplified form 鱼, the fish tail is replaced by a horizontal line.

魚　象形。像魚的素描，
上是頭，中是身，下是
尾。意指水生脊椎动物。
簡化字鱼將魚字下面四點
改成一橫，清代已見。

甲 🐟 金 🐟 篆 魚

打魚 dǎyú to fish (with a net)
金魚 jīnyú goldfish

海魚 hǎiyú sea fish
魚網 yúwǎng fish net

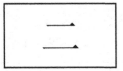

yī
one

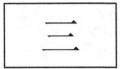

èr
two

sān
three

EXPLICIT CHARACTERS In Chinese writing systems, one horizontal stroke represents the number one, two horizontal strokes stand for the number two, and three strokes for the number three. 一, 二, 三 are probably the easiest Chinese characters to remember. From ancient times until now, these three characters have not changed much.

There is a Chinese joke about a silly boy who began to learn numerals. After the boy learned 一, 二, 三 from his teacher, he told his father he was able to write any number. His father was very proud. One day he asked his son to write the number "ten thousand" to show his guests. The boy remained worked for half a day, but was still unable to finish the task. When the guests saw what he wrote, they all laughed. On the paper were thousands of horizontal strokes! In fact, numbers larger than three are expressed in a different pattern.

一二三 指事。以一至三画表示數字一到三，是原始的計數符號。

甲 一 金 一 篆 一

甲 二 金 二 篆 二

甲 三 金 三 篆 三

一直 yìzhí straight forward; continuously; always
一點兒 yìdiǎr a little; a bit
二胡 èrhú two-stringed Chinese instrument
二百五 èrbǎi wǔ idiot; stupid person
三角 sānjiǎo triangle
三明治 sānmíngzhì sandwich

四

sì
four

PHONETIC LOAN CHARACTER In the Bronze Inscriptions, the character 四 resembles a big nose, or nostrils on a face. Therefore it originally meant "gasp" or "pant." Later 四 came to mean the numeral "four." In the Oracle-Bone inscriptions, "four" was represented by four horizontal lines, but this character was replaced by 四.

四 假借。在甲骨文中是四橫。金文"四"像臉部的口鼻。本義為喘息，是呬的本字，因讀音相近而借用為四字。

甲 三 金 四 篆 四

四方 sìfāng the four directions; all sides   四季 sìjì four seasons
四面八方 sìmiàn bāfāng in all directions; all around; far and near

五

wǔ
five

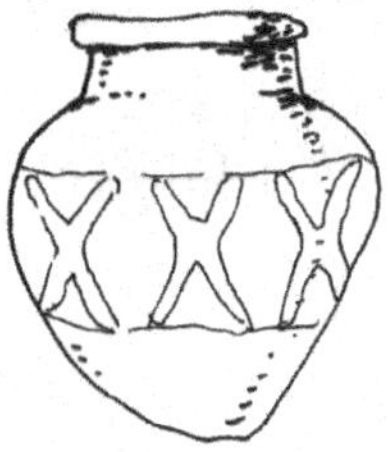

EXPLICIT CHARACTER In the Neolithic signs around 4,000 B.C., the symbol "X" was used to indicate "five." In the Oracle-Bone and Bronze Inscriptions, a line was added above and below the X. In Regular Script, the middle part of 五 resembles a cross that corners at its right end.

五 指事。在西安半坡仰韶文化遺址出土的陶器上，X即五。 甲骨文、金文在X上下各加一橫。

甲  金  篆 

五官 wǔguān five sense organs (nose, eyes, lips, tongue, ears 鼻目口舌耳); facial features
五行 wǔxíng five elements of Chinese philosophy (wood, fire, earth, metal, water 木火土金水)

六

liù
six

PHONETIC LOAN CHARACTER In the Oracle-Bone and Bronze Inscriptions, the character 六 outlines a hut or shed, possibly some sort of prehistoric dwelling. Later, 六 came to indicate the number six. In Regular Script, 六 still resembles a simple house, with the roof on top and two pillars beneath.

六 假借。在甲骨文、金文中為茅棚狀，本義為廬。由於讀音相近的關係，借用為六字。

甲  金  篆 

六百 liùbǎi six hundred
六千 liùqiān 6,000
六萬 liùwàn 60,000
六億 liùyì 600,000,000

七

qī
seven

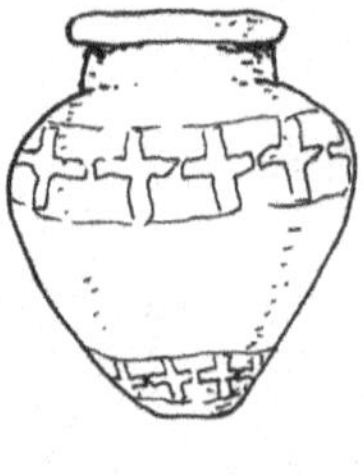

EXPLICIT CHARACTER In the Neolithic, Oracle-Bone, and Bronze Inscriptions, 十 represented the number seven. However, in Seal Script, 十 was used to mean "ten" and the vertical line of 十 was bent to mean "seven." In Regular Script, you may still see similarities between 十 (shí, ten) and 七 (qī, seven), as 七 looks like 十 with a tail.

七 指事。在半坡陶器上以及甲骨文、金文中，十的意思皆是七。小篆將十的意思改為十，而將十的一竪彎曲，另造七字，以區別于十。

甲  金  篆 

十七 shíqī seventeen
七十 qīshí seventy
七嘴八舌 qīzuǐ bāshé "With seven mouths and eight tongues;" lively discussion with many talking at once

八

bā
eight

PHONETIC LOAN CHARACTER The character 八 suggests is the act of dividing something into parts. Originally the character did mean "to divide" or "to separate." Later 八 came to mean the numeral eight.

八 假借。甲骨文中用兩劃來表示將一物分開，是分字的初文，後借用為數字。

甲 金 篆 

十八 shíbā eighteen
八十 bāshí eighty
第八 dìbā eighth
八百 bābǎi eight hundred

九

jiǔ
nine

PHONETIC LOAN CHARACTER In the Oracle-Bone and Bronze Inscriptions, the character 九 looks like the posterior of an animal with a long tail, possibly a monkey. Hence, the original meaning of 九 was "behind" or "buttocks." Later 九 came to mean the number nine.

九 假借。甲骨文像是獸類臀部上長出的尾巴，是尻（kāo 屁股）的初文。後借為數目字。

甲 金 篆 

第九 dìjiǔ ninth
十九 shíjiǔ nineteen
九十 jiǔshí ninety
九月 jiǔyuè September

十

shí
ten

EXPLICIT CHARACTER In the Neolithic signs, as well as in the Oracle-Bone Inscriptions, one vertical line stood for ten, two lines for twenty and three for thirty. In the Bronze Inscriptions, a circular dot was added in the middle of the vertical line. Later, in Seal Script, this dot became a horizontal line, making the character for "ten" look like a cross.

十 指事。在半坡陶器上，十字為一豎畫，甲骨文同。金文中間加一點，篆文又由一點延長為一橫。一說在一根繩上打一個結表示一个十。

甲 金 篆 

十分 shífēn very; extremely
十全十美 shíquán shíměi perfect in every way
十字架 shízì jià cross; crucifix
十字路口 shízì lùkǒu crossroads; intersection

bǎi
hundred

ASSOCIATIVE COMPOUND In the Oracle-Bone Inscriptions, the upper part of 百 may represent a ruler and the lower part a grain of white rice 白, suggesting a long line of rice grains. Meanings of 百 are "hundred," "numerous," and "all kinds of."

百　會意。一說甲骨文字
形上像一把尺子，下像白
米粒，表示擺下一尺長
的米粒，引申為一百。
白，象形。像一粒白米

甲 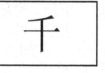 金 　 篆 百

幾百　jǐbǎi　several hundred; how many hundred
百貨公司　bǎihuò gōngsī　department store

百姓　bǎixìng　ordinary people
二百　èrbǎi　two hundred

---

qiān
thousand

ASSOCIATIVE COMPOUND In its ancient forms, the top part of 千 is a person 人 and the bottom part a ten 十, implying that the maximal life span of ten persons is 1000 years. The primary meaning of 千 is "thousand" and its extended meanings are "many," "numerous," etc.

千　會意。甲骨文從十，
從人。人壽以一百歲為
限，十人壽限加起便是
千。本義為千，引申義
為很多、無數。

甲 　 金 千 篆 　

千萬　qiānwàn　ten million; millions and millions; to be sure
成千上萬　chéngqiān shàngwàn　thousands upon thousands

Heavenly Stems and Earthly Branches

In addition to these numerals, the Chinese also traditionally used two sets of numbers to count up to sixty: ten heavenly stems and twelve earthly branches. Together, they were used to count years, months, days, and hours. Today, the heavenly stems still often appear as ordinal numbers, choices in multiple choice questions, or as abbreviations of parties in legal documents (Party A, Party B, etc.). Many also commonly appear as components in more complex characters.

TEN HEAVENLY STEMS

甲	乙	丙	丁	戊	己	庚	辛	壬	癸
jiǎ	yǐ	bǐng	dīng	wù	jǐ	gēng	xīn	rén	guǐ

TWELVE EARTHLY BRANCHES

子	丑	寅	卯	辰	巳	午	未	申	酉	戌	亥
zǐ	chǒu	yín	mǎo	chén	sì	wǔ	wèi	shēn	yǒu	xū	hài

CHARACTERS *by* PINYIN
(A–Z)

KEY TO SCRIPT TYPES

SYMBOL	SCRIPT	EXAMPLES (報)	SYMBOL	SCRIPT	EXAMPLES (報)
甲	Oracle–Bone Inscriptions		篆	Seal Script	
金	Bronze Inscriptions		草	Cursive Script	

See the "Types of Script" section on page vi of the Preface for more information.

阿

ā
(a prefix)
ē
big mound

PICTOPHONETIC CHARACTER The character 阿 (pronounced ē) is made up of the mound radical ß and the phonetic element 可 (kě), originally referring to "a big mound." Its extended meanings are "riverbank," "the corner or edge," "be bent," "to pander to," "to play up to," "graceful," etc. When 阿 is pronounced ā, it functions as a prefix to a monosyllabic name or a kinship term of address to indicate familiarity. In the Oracle-Bone Inscriptions, 可 resembles a mouth exhaling and means "to approve," "okay," "may," "can," and "but."

阿　形聲。從阜（左阝），可聲。本義為大土山，音讀作 ē。引申義有山水的彎曲之處、角落、屈從迎合、阿諛奉承等。作為人名與親屬稱謂的前綴時讀作 ā，如阿毛，阿爸、阿姨。可，從口，從丂(kǎo)。丂，气欲舒出狀。以口中舒气以示認可、同意等。

 金　篆

阿姨 āyí aunt; nursemaid

阿拉伯 ālābó Arab; Arabic

啊

a
(exclamation particle)

PICTOPHONETIC CHARACTER The character 啊 is used as an exclamation, and consists of the mouth radical 口 and the phonetic component 阿 (ā/ē). 阿 contains the mound radical ß and the phonetic 可 (kě), meaning "large mound."

啊　形聲。從口，阿聲。用作嘆詞。阿，形聲。金文從阜（脬坑；土山），可聲，本義為山的彎曲處。

啊呀 āyā interjection of surprise

啊喲 āyo interjection of surprise or pain

āi
(exclamatory particle)

PICTOPHONETIC CHARACTER   The character 哎 combines the mouth radical 口 and the phonetic indicator 艾 (ài) and functions as an interjection to express surprise, dissatisfaction, regret, greeting, or to draw attention. 艾 is Chinese mugwort or wormwood. The dried leaves of mugwort can be made into moxa cones (a cylinder of cotton wool or other combustible material) and used in moxibustion (a traditional treatment of Chinese medicine in which moxa cones are placed on the skin and ignited in order to treat disease or produce analgesia).

哎　形聲。從口，艾聲，是後起字。用做嘆詞，表示傷感、嘆息或提醒、打招呼、呼應等。哎呀用來表示驚訝，哎喲表示驚訝、痛苦。艾，形聲。從艹，乂 (yì) 聲，本義指艾草，曬乾后可制成艾絨用作灸療。

哎呀 āiyā ah!; Oh, my!　　　　哎喲 āiyō ouch; whoops

ài
love; to love

ASSOCIATIVE AND PICTOPHONETIC COMPOUND   In the Seal Script, the top part of 愛 is both the phonetic and signifying component (pronounced ài, meaning "love") and the bottom part is the signifying element (夊 suī, walk back and forth; hover). It seems a man is falling deeply in love with a woman, hovering around her house and being reluctant to leave. The simplified character 爱 derives from the cursive style of the traditional form 愛.

愛　會意兼形聲。篆文上部標聲兼表意 (ài, love)，下部從夊 (suī 腳)，表示心有所愛而腳下徘徊不忍離去，有慈愛、情愛、喜愛等意。爱是愛字的草書楷化字，去掉愛字中間的心字而將夊字改為友。

篆　　　草

愛人 àirén spouse (PRC); lover (non-PRC)　　愛好 àihào hobby
可愛 kě'ài cute; lovely　　　　　　　　　　親愛的 qīn'àide dear; beloved; darling

---

ān
calm; safe

ASSOCIATIVE COMPOUND   The character 安 consists of the roof radical 宀 on top and the woman 女 underneath, suggesting when there is no war or natural calamity, women can stay home peacefully and life is safe and tranquil. Hence, 安 means "tranquil," "peaceful," "quiet," "calm," "stable," "safe," "secure," "at ease," "content," "satisfied," "to pacify," "to stabilize," "to settle down," and "to install."

安　會意。從女，從宀，表示一女在房中。本義為安靜、安寧，引申義有安定、安全、舒適、感到滿足、使安定、安置、安裝等。

甲　　金　　篆

安靜 ānjìng quiet　　　　　　平安 píngān safe and sound
安心 ānxīn to feel at ease　　晚安 wǎn'ān Good night!

22

bǎ
(MW for objects
with handles)

PICTOPHONETIC CHARACTER The character 把 is made up of the hand radical 扌 and the phonetic element 巴, meaning "to grasp," "to hold," "to take hold of," "a handle," or "handful." 把 can be used as a measure word for objects that can be held or handled with one hand. It also functions as a particle before a direct object, followed by a transitive verb. In Seal Script 巴 looks like a snake with a large mouth. The original meaning of 巴 was "snake." Later it came to mean "to cling to" or "to stick to," for when a snake moves, its body always clings to something.

把　形聲。從扌，巴聲。本義為以手握持。引申義有把守控制、東西的柄，也用於能以一手所握的東西（一把米），以及能以一隻手握持的一些東西的量詞（一把刀）。另外，把也作為介詞引出動作受事的對象，使賓語前置。巴，象形。篆文像一條張著大嘴的蛇。

篆 𤔲 巴 篆 𢍏

把手 bǎshǒu knob
一把刀 yìbǎ dāo a knife

火把 huǒbǎ torch
一把椅子 yìbǎ yǐzi a chair

---

bà
father; dad

PICTOPHONETIC CHARACTER The character 爸 is made up of the radical 父 (fù, father) and the phonetic 巴 (bā, cling to). In its ancient form, 父 delineates a hand holding a stone ax—an important tool and weapon in primitive society. In Seal Script 巴 looks like a snake with a large mouth.

爸　形聲。從父、巴聲。父，象形。甲骨文、金文字形像手持石斧工作狀。巴，象形。篆文中像一條張著大嘴的蛇。本義為蛇，引申為依附、靠近、巴結等。

父 甲 𠂇 金 𠂇 篆 𠃋 巴 篆 𢀩

爸爸 bàba (informal) father
親爸 qīnbà biological father

爸媽 bàmā dad and mom
阿爸 ābà (dialect) father

---

ba
(sentence-
ending particle)

PICTOPHONETIC CHARACTER 吧 has the mouth radical 口 and the phonetic element 巴 (bā). 吧 can be used as a question indicator, onomatopoeic word, or particle for making a suggestion. In Seal Script, 巴 resembles a snake with a large, open mouth. Today's meanings of 巴 are still related to the characteristics of a snake, such as "cling to," "stick to," and "wait anxiously" (as a snake waiting for prey).

吧　象聲詞、語氣詞。巴，象形。篆文像嘴大能吞象的蛇形。本義為蛇，引申為依附、靠近、巴結等。

巴 篆 𢀩

好吧 hǎoba alright; fine
酒吧 jiǔbā bar; pub

走吧 zǒuba let's go
網吧 wǎngbā Internet café

bái
white; (surname)

PICTOGRAPH In its ancient form, 白 resembles bright rays spreading out from the sun, or as some scholars say, a grain of white rice. The original meaning of 白 is "white." Extended meanings include "pure," "clear," and "in vain."

白　象形。像太陽初升、光芒四射狀。一說像一粒白米。

甲 ◌ ◌ 金 ◌ 篆 ◌

白天 báitiān daytime; day
白人 báirén white people; caucasian
白色 báisè white color
白菜 báicài Chinese cabbage; bok choi

bān
class

ASSOCIATIVE COMPOUND In its ancient forms, the character 班 looks like two pieces of jade with a knife in between. The original meaning of 班 was "to divide a jade stone into two," from which the meanings "to distribute," "class," "group," "work shift," and "schedule (of flights, bus, etc.)" have derived.

班　會意。金文中間是刀，左右為兩塊玉（珏），指以刀將玉一分為二。本義為分割玉石，引申為分工作或學習的班組，按時間分成的工作時段，定時開行的班車、航班等。

金 珏 篆 班

三班 sānbān Class Three
上班 shàngbān to go to work
中文班 zhōngwén bān Chinese class
班機 bānjī a scheduled flight

bān
to move

PICTOPHONETIC CHARACTER The character 搬 consists of the hand radical 扌 and the phonetic element 般 (bān), meaning "to move," "to take away," or "to copy mechanically." 般 is made up of 舟 (zhōu, boat) and 殳 (shū, a type of ancient weapon made of bamboo), suggesting the act of using a boat-pole to change the direction a boat is taking. Originally 般 meant "to rotate," and has been borrowed to mean "sort," "type," or "the same as." In its ancient forms, 舟 is the pictograph of a boat and 殳 a hand holding a weapon.

搬　形聲。從扌，般聲。意指搬動、搬運，引申義有套用等。般，會意。從舟，從殳，本義為用篙使舟旋轉，後借指樣、種、相同。舟，象形，古文字中像船形。殳（shū），會意。古文字中像手持一兵器，本義為古代一種竹製的兵器。如今不單用，只作為偏旁。

篆 般 舟 甲 ◌ 金 ◌ 篆 ◌

搬家 bān jiā to resettle, to move (house)
搬運 bānyùn to transport; to carry
搬桌子 bān zhuōzi to move a table
搬運工 bānyùngōng porter

The Way of Chinese Characters

bàn
half

ASSOCIATIVE COMPOUND In its ancient form, the character 半 consists of 八 (bā, divide; eight) and 牛 (niú, ox), indicating cutting an ox in half. In the Oracle-Bone Inscriptions, the character 牛 depicts the front view of an ox's head. In the character 半 in Regular Script, 八 is upside down and 牛 loses one stroke on the left.

半　會意。上從八（分開），下從牛。表示將牛從中切為兩半，意為事物的二分之一。

金 𠦂 篆 半

半天 bàntiān half a day
半個月 bàngeyuè half a month

半年 bànnián half a year
一半 yíbàn half

拌

bàn
to mix

PICTOPHONETIC CHARACTER The character 拌 consists of the hand radical 扌 and the phonetic element 半 (bàn), indicating the act of mixing things with hands. Literally 拌嘴 (bànzuǐ) is "to mix mouths" and therefore means "to wrangle" or "to quarrel." In its ancient forms, 半 (bàn, half) contains 八 (bā, divide; eight) on top and 牛 (niú, ox) underneath, indicating cutting an ox into halves. In the character 半 in Regular Script, 八 is upside down and 牛 loses one stroke on the left.

拌　形聲。從手，半聲。是後起字。本義為攪拌、攪和，引申義有爭吵等。半，會意。金文、篆文上從八（分開），下從牛。表示將牛從中切為兩半，意為事物的二分之一。

涼拌面 liángbàn miàn cold noodles with sauce
拌嘴 bànzuǐ to quarrel

涼拌菜 liángbàn cài salad
搅拌 jiǎobàn to stir; to agitate

辦／办

bàn
to manage

PICTOPHONETIC CHARACTER The character 辦 consists of the signifying element 力 (lì, power) and the phonetic element 辡 (biàn, to debate), meaning "handle," "manage," "do," or "punish." You can memorize this character by imagining a person "managing" to split something in two using all their strength. 辡 is made up of two 辛 (xīn). In the Oracle-Bone and Bronze Inscriptions, 辛 is a pictograph of a chiseled instrument used to tattoo the faces of prisoners. Extended meanings of 辛 are "pungent," "laborious," "suffering," and "hot (in flavor)." The simplified character 办 uses two short strokes to replace the two 辛 of the traditional form 辦.

辦　形聲。從力，辡（biàn 剖分、爭辯）聲。辛，象形。甲骨文、金文像在犯人臉上刺字的刑具。簡體字办用一撇一點代替兩個辛字，舊時已見。

篆 辦 辛甲 ▽ 金 ♈ 篆 辛

辦公 bàngōng to work (esp. in an office)
辦法 bànfǎ means; method

辦公室 bàngōngshì office
怎麼辦 zěnmebàn what's to be done?

幫/帮

bāng
to help

PICTOPHONETIC CHARACTER The character 幫 consists of the signifying element 帛 (bó, silk) and the phonetic 封 (fēng, seal). The original meaning of 幫 was "the upper part of a shoe" while extended meanings include "side" (of a boat, cart, etc.), "assist," and "help." The character 帛 combines 白 (bái, white) and 巾 (jīn, pictograph of a scarf), referring to un-dyed silk. In Regular Script, 封 is comprised of two 土 (tǔ, soil) and one 寸 (cùn, inch). 幚 is a variant of 幫, and the middle part 白 was deleted from 幫 to form the simplified 帮.

幫 形聲。從帛，封聲。本義為鞋幫，引申為輔助等意。封，會意。甲骨文像在土堆上植樹，以此來劃定邊界。帛，從巾，從白；本義指素白絲織物，引申為絲織品的總稱。巾，象形。像垂下的佩巾。繁體字幫的另一寫法是幚。簡體字帮去掉了幫字中間的白字。

幫助 bāngzhù to help; aid
幫手 bāngshǒu helper
幫忙 bāngmáng to help; to do a favor
幫派 bāngpài faction

棒

bàng
fantastic; stick

PICTOPHONETIC CHARACTER The character 棒 is comprised of the wood radical 木 and the phonetic 奉 (fèng), originally meaning "a stick" or "a club." The extended meanings of 棒 are "to hit with a stick," "strong," "capable," and "excellent." In the Oracle-Bone Inscriptions, 奉 looks like two hands holding a plant. Its original meaning is "to hold in both hands respectfully," from which it has derived the meanings "to offer with respect," "to esteem," "to serve," "to believe in," etc.

棒 形聲。從木，奉聲。本義為棍子，引申義有健壯、能力強、水平高等。奉，會意。甲骨文像雙手恭敬地捧著一物。本義為捧，是捧的本字。引申義有奉上、尊崇、信仰、侍侯等。

篆  **奉** 甲  金  篆 

棒子 bàngzi stick; club
冰棒 bīngbàng popsicle
棒球 bàngqiú baseball
真棒 zhēnbàng excellent (interjection)

包

bāo
bag; sack; bundle; package

PICTOGRAPH In its ancient forms, 包 looks like a fetus in its mother's womb. Originally 包 referred to "afterbirth," from which it has derived the meanings "to wrap," "to surround," "to contain," "to contract," "to charter," "to guarantee," "package," "bundle," "bag," "lump," etc. 包 also serves as a measure word for things in the shape of a bale, a box, a bundle, a package, a packet, or a sack, as in "一包衣服 (a bundle of clothes)," and "兩包米 (two sacks of rice)."

包 象形。甲骨文像腹中有孕狀，本義為胎衣，引申為把東西包起、包圍、包含、全部承擔、擔保、袋子、包裹、像包的東西、包裹起來的東西、腫起的疙瘩，也可以作為量詞（一包衣服|兩包米）。

甲  篆 

包餃子 bāo jiǎozi to make dumplings
錢包 qiánbāo wallet; purse
麵包 miànbāo bread
書包 shūbāo schoolbag; satchel

保

bǎo
to protect;
insurance

ASSOCIATIVE COMPOUND In the Oracle-Bone Inscriptions, the character 保 depicts a person carrying a child on his/her back. Its original meaning was "to carry somebody/something on one's back," from which the Chinese have derived the meanings "to bring up," "to safeguard," "to protect," "to defend," "to maintain," "to guarantee," "to insure," etc. In Seal Script, 保 becomes the combination of the person radical 亻 and 呆 (dāi, dull; slow-witted; wooden), possibly because a dull-witted child needs more protection.

保 會意。甲骨文從人，
從子，像人負子於背。
本義為背在背上，引申
義有養育、保護、保持、
保證等。

甲 金 篆

保姆 bǎomǔ nanny	保險 bǎoxiǎn insurance
保安 bǎoān to ensure safety; security guard	保重 bǎozhòng to take care of oneself

---

抱

bào
to hold or carry
in one's arms

ASSOCIATIVE AND PICTOPHONETIC COMPOUND The character 抱 consists of the hand radical 扌 and the phonetic and signifying component 包 (bāo, wrap), signifying the act of holding or carrying something in one's arms. Its extended meanings include "to hug," "to embrace," "to surround," "to harbor," "to adopt," etc. 包 is also used in the character 跑.

抱 會意兼形聲。從扌，
從包，包亦聲。本義為
以手抱持，引申義有擁
抱、圍繞、胸中懷有等。
跑字也以包為聲旁。

篆

抱孩子 bào háizi to hold a baby in one's arms	擁抱 yōngbào to hug
抱歉 bàoqiàn to feel apologetic	抱著 bàozhe keep holding

報／报

bào
to report;
newspaper

ASSOCIATIVE COMPOUND In the Oracle-Bone and Bronze Inscriptions, the character 報 depicts a hand pressing the head of a handcuffed person, forcing him or her onto his or her knees, signifying that the prisoner will be executed. The original meaning of 報 was "to pass a sentence on someone who is guilty of a crime." Since a judge needs to report the conviction to the appropriate authorities and make it public, 報 extended to mean "to report," "to announce," and "newspaper." The simplified character 报 is developed from the cursive style of 報, with the hand radical 扌 replacing 幸.

報 會意。甲骨文、金文
中像一隻手從後按住一個
像帶手銬跪著的人，表
示行將處決犯人。報的
本義是判決犯人。因這
類事情要通報，引申為
報告、報刊、回報等。
簡體字报是繁體字報的
草書楷化字，左邊以扌
替換幸字。

甲 金 篆 草

報告 bàogào report; paper	報紙 bàozhǐ newspaper
日報 rìbào daily newspaper	海報 hǎibào poster

杯

bēi
cup; glass

PICTOPHONETIC CHARACTER 杯 consists of the wood radical 木 and the phonetic element 不 (bù), which may have referred to a wooden cup.

杯　形聲。從木，不聲，意為裝飲料的器皿或指木做的杯子。

篆 𣏻

杯子 bēizi cup; glass
一杯茶 yìbēichá a cup of tea

茶杯 chábēi teacup
乾杯 gānbēi bottoms up; to drink a toast; cheers

北

běi
north

ASSOCIATIVE COMPOUND In the Oracle-Bone Inscriptions, the character 北 depicts two people standing back-to-back, meaning "contrary," "deviate from," or "back." Since traditional Chinese houses usually face south (with their backs toward the north), 北 means "north."

北　會意。甲骨文中像二人背對背站着，本義為違背，引申為脊背。後來加肉月旁作"背"，表示脊背之義，而"北"則借用為方位名詞。

甲 𨅥 金 北 篆 𨸏

北京 Běijīng Beijing
東北 dōngběi northeast

北邊 běibiān north side; northern part
西北 xīběi northwest

被

bèi
by; quilt

PICTOPHONETIC CHARACTER The character 被 consists of the clothes radical 衤 and the phonetic element 皮 (pí). The original meaning of 被 is "quilt", and has been extended to mean "to cover," "to suffer from," and "by (an indicator of passive voice)." In Bronze Inscriptions, 皮 looks like a hand stripping the skin off an animal, meaning "skin," "fur," "leather," "surface," etc.

被　形聲。從衤，皮聲。本義為被子，引申義有覆蓋、遭受、表示被動等。皮，會意。金文下像手，上像獸形，表示以手剝去獸皮。本義為剝皮，引申為獸皮、皮膚、皮制的（皮包、皮鞋、皮帶）、表面的等。

篆 𧟌 皮 甲 𠂷 金 𤿎 篆 𤿤

被子 bèizi quilt
被動 bèidòng passive

被單 bèidān bed sheet
被告 bèigào defendant

備 / 备

bèi
to prepare

ASSOCIATIVE COMPOUND In the Oracle-Bone and Bronze Inscriptions, the character 備 looks like an arrow in the quiver, signaling ready for a battle. Hence, the meanings of 備 are "cautious," "prepare," or "ready." 俻 is a variant form of 備, and the simplified character 备 remains only the right part of 俻.

備 會意。甲骨文、金文皆像箭在箭匣中，意指準備、防備、預備、裝備等。俻是備字的異體字，簡體字备去掉了俻字的部首亻。

甲 ▨ 金 ▨ 篆 ▨

準備 zhǔnbèi preparation; to prepare
設備 shèbèi equipment; facilities

預備 yùbèi to prepare; to make ready
具備 jùbèi posess; to have

本

běn
(MW for books);
foundation

EXPLICIT CHARACTER The character 本 represents a tree 木 with a horizontal line added at the bottom. Its original meaning is "the root of a tree," from which its present meanings "foundation," "basis," "based on," "source," "origin," "original," "capital (in business)," and "oneself" have been derived. 本 also functions as a measure word for books, periodicals, etc.

本 指事。木字下面加一橫，本義是樹根。引申為基礎、根源、原來的、自身的、本錢、書本雜誌的量詞等。

金 ▨ 篆 ▨

本人 běnrén oneself
本來 běnlái originally

本地 běndì local
課本 kèběn textbook

鼻

bí
nose

ASSOCIATIVE AND PICTOPHONETIC COMPOUND The character 鼻 is made up of the signifying part 自 and the phonetic element 畀 (bì), indicating the "nose" that breathes air. In the Oracle-Bone Inscriptions, 自 shows the shape of a nose, referring to "nose" in the first place, and later is borrowed to mean "self," "one's own," "from," or "since." Now 自 does not mean "nose" anymore since the character 鼻 is used instead. In its ancient forms 畀 looks like someone holding a container with both hands and means "to give" or "to confer upon."

鼻 會意兼形聲。篆文從自（鼻子），畀（bì，給與）聲，表示用鼻子吸氣。自，象形。甲骨文像鼻形。自的本義是鼻子，因後來引申用作為自己，而用鼻字來表示鼻子的意思。

篆 ▨ 自甲 ▨ 金 ▨ 篆 ▨

鼻子 bízi nose
鼻音 bíyīn nasal sound/tone

鼻孔 bíkǒng nostril
鼻頭 bítóu the tip of the nose

比

bǐ
to compare

ASSOCIATIVE COMPOUND The ancient form of 比 depicts two people standing side by side, meaning "to juxtapose." The extended meanings of 比 include "close together," "next to," "to cling to," "to compare," "to compete," "to model after," "than," etc. Can you tell what the differences are between the left and right part of 比?

比 會意。古文的比字像靠在一起的兩個人。本義為並列，引申為靠近、比較、對比、模仿等。

甲  金  篆 

比較 bǐjiào to compare; relatively
比賽 bǐsài competition; match
比如 bǐrú for example; proportion
三比二 sān bǐ èr three to two

筆/笔

bǐ
pen;
writing brush

ASSOCIATIVE COMPOUND In the Oracle-Bone and Bronze Inscriptions, 聿 (yù) shows a hand holding a brush. You can see 聿 in the character 書 (shū, book); 畫 (huà, to paint; painting) and 律 (lǜ, law). The character 筆 combines the bamboo radical ⺮ and 聿, signifying a writing brush or writing instrument. The simplified character 笔 combines the bamboo radical and the character 毛 (máo, hair; fur) since the nib of a Chinese brush is made of animal fur and bamboo shafts.

筆 會意。從聿（手持筆形），從竹，指手握竹子做的筆杆寫字。簡體笔字保留上邊竹字頭，因毛筆筆端用獸毛之故，下邊改用毛字。屬新創的會意字。

篆 

毛筆 máobǐ writing brush
筆試 bǐshì written examination
圓珠筆 yuánzhūbǐ ballpoint pen
筆畫 bǐhuà strokes of a Chinese character

幣/币

bì
currency; coin

PICTOPHONETIC CHARACTER The character 幣 consists of the scarf radical 巾 (jīn) and the phonetic indicator 敝 (bì), originally referring to "silk fabric used as a present." 幣 has extended to mean "a present," "money," "coin," and "currency." In the Oracle-Bone Inscriptions, the left part of 敝 depicts a piece of broken cloth with four big holes and the right part the tap/rap radical 攴, meaning "shabby," "tattered," and "worn out." 巾 looks like a piece of hanging cloth , meaning "scarf," "towel," or "napkin." In the simplified 币, a left falling stroke replaces 敝 in 幣.

幣 形聲。從巾，敝聲。本義指作為禮物的絲織品，引申為禮物、財物、錢幣。敝，會意。左邊像衣物有洞，右邊手持棍拍打，本義為衣服破爛，引申為破舊、衰敗等。巾，象形。像佩巾下垂形。簡化字币用一撇代替繁體字幣上部的敝字。

篆 

貨幣 huòbì money; currency
人民幣 rénmínbì PRC Currency (RMB)
外幣 wàibì foreign currency
紙幣 zhǐbì paper currency

邊/边

biān
side

ASSOCIATIVE AND PICTOPHONETIC COMPOUND 邊 is comprised of the walk radical 辶 and the signifying and phonetic element 臱 (biān, side), meaning "side," "edge," "border," or "next." In the Bronze Inscriptions, 臱 combines 自 (zì, nose; oneself) with 旁 (páng, side), referring to the sides of a nose. In Regular Script, 臱 is the combination of 自, 穴 (xuè, cave), and 方 (fāng, square). In the simplified character 边, 力 replaces 臱.

邊 會意兼形聲。從辶，臱(biān)聲。臱，會意。從自，從旁，金文像鼻的兩翼。自，象形。像鼻形，本義為鼻子，後引申為自己。簡體字边用力替代臱，屬符號替代字。元明時已有边字。

金 𦥑 篆 𩵋

上邊 shàngbian above; on top of
前邊 qiánbian in front

下邊 xiàbian below; under
後邊 hòubian behind

便

biàn
convenient

pián
inexpensive

ASSOCIATIVE COMPOUND The character 便 combines the person radical 亻 with the character 更 (gēng, change), referring to the ways in which people create shortcuts to make things easier. Meanings of 便 include: "suitable," "beneficial," "convenient," "informal" (biàn), and "inexpensive" (pián). In the Oracle-Bone Inscriptions, 更 resembles a hand holding a spatula to turn a pancake on a griddle. Hence its meanings: "change" or "alternate."

便 會意。篆文從人、從更。人有不便時，更改方能使之安妥方便。更，會意兼形聲。甲骨文字形像手持鏟翻餅狀，引申為更改。

金 𠊱 篆 𠊱 更 甲 𠬝 金 𠬝

方便 fāngbiàn convienient
便利店 biànlìdiàn convenience store

隨便 suíbiàn as one pleases; casual
便宜 piányi inexpensive; cheap

遍

biàn
(MW for actions)

PICTOPHONETIC CHARACTER The character 遍 is composed of the walk radical 辶 and the phonetic indicator 扁 (biǎn, flat), signifying "to walk all over." Its extended meanings include "everywhere," "all over," "throughout," and "one time." In the Seal Script, 扁 is the combination of 戶 (hù, household) and 冊 (cè, volume; copy) and originally meant a horizontal board bearing an inscription hanging over the door. Nowadays 扁 is used to mean "flat". In the Oracle-Bone Inscriptions, 戶 is the pictograph of a single leaf door. In ancient writing systems, 冊 depicts a scroll of bamboo slips bound together.

遍 形聲。從辵（辶），扁聲。意為普遍、到處；也用作表示次數的量詞。扁，會意。從戶，從冊，本義為題字的匾，引申義指物體平而薄等。

篆 𧹝

一遍 yíbiàn one time
普遍 pǔbiàn common; universal

遍地 biàndì everywhere; all over the place
千遍萬遍 qiānbiàn wànbiàn thousands of times

表

biǎo
surface;
matrilineal
relatives

ASSOCIATIVE COMPOUND In its ancient form, the character 表 looks like a fur coat with the fur facing out, signifying "a fur coat." Later 表 came to mean "outside," "surface," "appearance," "to show," "example," "chart," or "form." In addition, 表 refers to the children of paternal aunts or maternal uncles or aunts, while 堂 (táng, [main] hall) is used for the children of paternal uncles. The original meanings of 堂 and 表 indicate that traditionally, children of paternal uncles were considered closer to the inner family and more important. In Chinese, 表親 (maternal relatives) are also called 外親 (literally "outside relatives").

表　會意。篆文從衣，從毛。古代以獸皮為衣，毛皆在外，故表字本義為外衣，引申為外面、外表、表格、表率、表達、外親（表親）等。

甲 𧘇　篆 𧘇

表面 biǎomiàn surface
表姐 biǎojiě older female cousin via female line

外表 wàibiǎo appearance
表現 biǎoxiàn behavior; performance

別／别

bié
other; do not

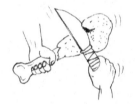

ASSOCIATIVE COMPOUND In the Oracle-Bone Inscriptions, the left part of 別 represents a knife and the right part resembles bone fragments, signifying the action of separating bones from flesh. The primary meaning of 別 is "to separate" or "part." Its extended meanings include "distinguish," "other," "another," and "do not." In the simplified character 别, the right part is the knife radical 刂, just as in the traditional version, but the left bottom part is 力, which differs slightly from the traditional character 別.

別　會意。甲骨文從刀，從冎（guǎ），本義指以刀剔下骨頭上肉。另，象形，与冎本為一字，甲骨文中像剔乾淨用來占卜的牛骨。簡體字别的左下方寫作力，與繁體字別稍有不同。

甲 𠛠　篆 𠛮

別的 biéde else; other
特別 tèbié special; especially

別人 biérén other people; others
別字 biézì mispronounced or wrongly written character

冰

bīng
ice

ASSOCIATIVE COMPOUND The character 冰 is the combination of the ice radical 冫 and water 水, signifying that ice is frozen water. 冰 can be used as a verb meaning "to cool things with ice," "to make cold," and as an adjective meaning "iced," "ice-cold," etc. In some word combinations like 冰糖 (bīngtáng, crystal sugar), 冰 stands for an ice-like substance.

冰　会意。從冫（冫的意思是冰），從水，意指水結成冰。另外可用作動詞，指使人感到寒冷或用冰使東西變涼。也可用做形容詞，指像冰一樣。

金 𣲺　篆 𣲺

冰箱 bīngxiāng fridge
滑冰 huábīng to skate; skating

冰水 bīngshuǐ iced water
冰激淩 bīngjīlíng ice cream

bìng
illness; to become ill

PICTOPHONETIC CHARACTER The character 病 is made up of the sick radical 疒 (nè) and the phonetic component 丙 (bǐng, third), meaning "illness," "ailment," "sickness," "disease," "to fall ill," "defect," or "fault." In Seal Script, 疒 looks like a bed for the sick. The characters with the sick radical are often associated with illnesses or unhealthy conditions, such as 癌 (ái, cancer), 痛 (tòng, ache), 瘦 (shòu, skinny), 癢 (yǎng, itchy), 瘋 (fēng, mad; crazy), etc. In ancient forms, 丙 depicts a fish tail and later was borrowed to mean "third," or "third heavenly stem" (see page 20).

病 形聲。從疒，丙聲。篆文疒像是一張病床。病古代為重病，引申為疾病的統稱、缺點、毛病等。有疒字旁的字多與身體的疾病或不適有關，譬如瘡、瘋癲、瘟疫、疼痛、痰、瘦、癌、癢。丙，象形。意指魚尾，後被借用為天干的第三位，也表示順序中的第三。

篆

生病 shēngbìng to fall sick
病人 bìngrén patient

看病 kànbìng to go to a doctor
毛病 máobìng shortcoming; defect

不

bù
not; no

PHONETIC LOAN CHARACTER In the Oracle-Bone Inscriptions, the horizontal stroke of the character 不 represents the ground, and the three strokes underneath signify a germinating seed. The original meaning of 不 was "seed of a plant," but later was borrowed to mean "no" or "not."

不 假借。像種子萌芽即將破土而出時的形狀，是胚的本字。後多借為否定詞，本義遂不用。

甲  金 不 篆 不

不錯 búcuò not bad; pretty good
不久 bùjiǔ before long; near future

不同 bùtóng different; not the same
不用 búyòng need not

步

bù
step; pace

ASSOCIATIVE COMPOUND In the Oracle-Bone and Bronze Inscriptions, the character 步 represents two footprints, one in front of the other. Its original meaning is "to go on foot" or "to walk," from which it has derived the meanings "step," "pace," "stage," "degree," and "situation." In Regular Script, 步 still bears a resemblance to two footprints, one on the top and the other underneath.

步 會意。甲骨文、金文、篆文像左右腳一前一後行走狀。本義為用腳行走，引申為腳步、階段、地步等。

甲 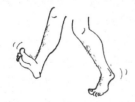 金 步 篆 步

跑步 pǎobù to run
散步 sànbù take a walk

進步 jìnbù progress; to progress
同步 tóngbù to synchronize; synchronization

A - F

cái
not until; only then

EXPLICIT CHARACTER The character 才 looks like a seedling just breaking through the ground. The horizontal stroke represents the ground and the part underneath is the root of the seedling. The meanings of 才 include "just," "only," "not until," "ability," "talent," etc.

才 指事。甲骨文中一橫畫象徵土地，表示種子已生根發芽、破土而出。本義為草木初生，引申為剛剛。

甲 ╪ 金 ╪ 篆 才

剛才 gāngcái just now; a moment ago
口才 kǒucái eloquence

才能 cáinéng talent; ability
天才 tiāncái genius; talented

cài
dish; cuisine; vegetable

ASSOCIATIVE AND PICTOPHONETIC COMPOUND The character 菜 is composed of the grass/plant radical 艹 and phonetic and signifying component 采 (cǎi), meaning "vegetable." In the Oracle-Bone Inscriptions, the character 采 looks like a hand picking fruits from a tree, and means "pick," "pluck," or "gather." When vegetables are ripe, people will gather them.

菜 會意兼形聲。本義為蔬菜。從艸，采聲。采亦有採摘之意。采，會意。像以手採樹上果實。

篆 菜 采 甲 ╪ 金 采 篆 采

青菜 qīngcài green vegetable
點菜 diǎncài to order dishes

做菜 zuòcài to cook
菜單 càidān menu

---

cān
meal

PICTOPHONETIC CHARACTER The character 餐 consists of the radical 食 (shí, eat) and phonetic element 飧 (cán), meaning "to eat," "food," or "meal." In the Oracle-Bone Inscriptions, the lower part of 食 resembles a high-legged container full of food, while the upper part represents an open mouth, referring to the act of eating. In the Oracle-Bone Inscriptions, the character 飧 depicts a hand next to a skeleton or bones, meaning "remnant," "ferocious," etc.

餐 形聲。從食，飧聲，意為吞嚥、吃飯。甲骨文中 "食" 字上邊像是向下張開的嘴，下邊像是盛滿了食物的容器，表示張口向下吃容器中的食物。

篆 餐

餐廳 cāntīng dining hall
中餐 zhōngcān Chinese food

餐館 cānguǎn restaurant
西餐 xīcān Western-style food

廁/厕

cè
toilet

PICTOPHONETIC CHARACTER The character 廁 contains the radical 广 (yǎn, shed; roof; shelter) and the phonetic element 則 (zé, rule; regulation), meaning "lavatory" or "toilet." In the Bronze Inscriptions, 則 is the combination of 鼎 (dǐng) and a knife. 鼎 is a large, three-legged bronze caldron. In ancient times, laws and regulations were often carved on 鼎. Hence, 則 means "law," "rule," or "regulation." In Seal Script, 鼎 is replaced by 貝 in the character 則, but the knife part 刂 remains. 厠 is a variant of 廁, from which the simplified character 厕 has derived. 贝 is the simplified form of 貝.

廁 形聲。從广（敞屋），則聲，意為廁所。則，會意。金文從鼎，從刂，因古代的法律條文曾經刻鑄在鼎上，讓人遵守，本義為規則，也用作副詞，表示轉折。因鼎、貝二字在古文中形近，篆文將則的左邊由鼎改為貝。厠是廁的俗體字，簡化字厕來源於厠。

篆 廁　則 金 則　鼎 甲 鼎　篆 鼎

廁所 cèsuǒ bathroom; toilet
男廁 náncè men's room

公廁 gōngcè public toilet
女廁 nǚcè women's room

查

chá
to check; to look up

PICTOPHONETIC CHARACTER The character 查 consists of the wood radical 木 and the phonetic component 旦 (dàn), originally referring to a wooden raft. 查 has been extended to mean "to check," "to examine," "to investigate," "to look into," or "to consult (a reference book, dictionary, etc)," probably because one has to check a raft carefully before setting off on it. 旦 is composed of 日 and a horizontal stroke underneath, symbolizing the sun rising above the horizon. 旦 therefore means "daybreak" or "dawn."

查 形聲。篆文從木，且聲。楷書從木，且聲。本義一說是木筏，一說為砍剩的木樁。引申義有檢查、調查、翻檢（查字典，查資料等）。且，指事。一代表地平綫，表示太陽剛從地平綫上升起，本義為日出天亮時。

篆 查

檢查 jiǎnchá to check; to inspect
調查 diàochá to investigate

查問 cháwèn to interrogate
查字典 chá zìdiǎn to consult a dictionary

茶

chá
tea

PICTOPHONETIC CHARACTER In Seal Script, the character 茶 consists of 艸 (the grass or herb radical), and the phonetic element 余 (yú), meaning tea. In Rgular Script, 茶 contains ⁺⁺ (grass radical), 人 (rén, man; person), and 木 (mù, wood; tree), resembling a person harvesting tea leaves.

茶 形聲。茶与荼本為一字，從艸，余聲，本義為一種苦菜。唐代時將"荼"減去一筆而成為"茶"。

篆 茶

茶葉 cháyè tea; tea-leaves
茶館 cháguǎn tea house

茶杯 chábēi teacup
紅茶 hóngchá black tea

A - F

差

chà/chā
to fall short of

ASSOCIATIVE COMPOUND In the Bronze Inscriptions, the character 差 consists of 麥 (mài, wheat) on top and a hand and 工 (gōng, to work) underneath, suggesting the act of rubbing off wheat husks with one's hands. Its extended meanings include "to differ from," "to fall short of," "lacking," "wrong," "poor," "not up to standard," and "inferior." In Regular Script, the top part of 差 is similar to 羊 (yáng, sheep) and the bottom part is 工.

差 會意。金文上從小麥，下是一隻手與工，表示以手搓麥粒，當是搓的本字。引申為相差（差不多、差一點）、欠缺、缺少（差五分九點，差兩毛錢），不好、不夠標準（成績差、質量差）等。

金  篆

差不多 chàbùduō almost; about the same
差別 chābié difference

差一點 chàyìdiǎn almost; missed by just a little bit
差距 chājù gap; disparity

長/长

cháng
long

zhǎng
to grow;
leader

PICTOGRAPH In its ancient form, the character 長 looks like an old man with long hair and a walking stick. The original meaning of 長 is "long hair," and the extended meanings include "long," "length," "strong point," "be good at," etc. When 長 means "head," "leader," or is used as the verb "to grow," it is pronounced as zhǎng.

長 象形。古字像一長髮拄杖之老人。本義為髮長，引申義有長度、長久、長處、擅長等。長作為動詞時，意為生長。

甲 金 篆 草 長

長城 chángchéng the Great Wall
生長 shēngzhǎng grow; grow up

長期 chángqī long term
校長 xiàozhǎng (school) president; headmaster

常

cháng
often;
ordinary

PICTOPHONETIC CHARACTER In Seal Script, 常 consists of the radical 巾 (jīn, scarf) and the phonetic indicator 尚 (shàng, uphold; esteem). The original meaning of 常 was "skirt" or "clothes," but later came to mean "often," "constant," and "ordinary." In its ancient form, 巾 is a pictograph of a scarf, whereas 尚 resembles smoke drifting from a window.

常 形聲。篆文從巾，尚聲。本義指裙子，與裳本為一字，後分開，常意為經常、常規、日常等。

篆 常

常常 chángcháng often; frequently
常識 chángshí common sense; general knowledge

非常 fēicháng unusual; extraordinary
正常 zhèngcháng regular; normal

The Way of Chinese Characters

場/场
chǎng
field

PICTOPHONETIC CHARACTER The character 場 is comprised of the earth radical 土 and the phonetic element 易 (yáng), meaning "field," "stage," or "a large place used for a specific purpose." In the Oracle-Bone Inscriptions, the upper part of 易 is 日 (rì, sun), while the lower part resembles sunlight piercing through the clouds. 易 means "sun" or "sunshine." When comparing 易 with 易 (yì, easy), note that 易 has a horizontal line under the sun part. The simplified character 场 derives from the cursive style of the traditional character 場.

場 形聲。從土，易聲。古代祭神用的平地，引申為場地、處所等。易，會意。從日，從勿（像陽光穿過雲層射出狀），意指日出。簡體字场是由繁體字場的草書楷化而來。

篆 場 草 场 易 甲 旦 金 弓

商場 shāngchǎng mall; department store
球場 qiúchǎng ball field; sports ground

機場 jīchǎng airport
廣場 guǎngchǎng public square

唱
chàng
to sing

PICTOPHONETIC CHARACTER The character 唱 contains the mouth radical 口 and the phonetic component 昌 (chāng, flourishing), meaning "to sing." 昌 consists of 日 (rì, sun) on top and 曰 (yuē, speak; say) at the bottom. Its original meaning was "to speak openly" or literally "speak under the sun" and symbolizes being truthful and frank. 昌 can also mean "prosperous" or "flourishing."

唱 形聲。從口，昌聲。昌，會意。從日，從曰（説話）。本義指光明磊落的言詞，引申為美好、昌盛等。

篆 唱 昌 篆 昌

唱歌 chànggē to sing a song
演唱 yǎnchàng sing (in a performance)

合唱 héchàng chorus; to chorus
唱片 chàngpiàn gramophone record

超
chāo
to exceed; to surpass

PICTOPHONETIC CHARACTER The character 超 is comprised of 走 (zǒu, walk) and the phonetic component 召 (zhào). Its original meaning is "to jump over," from which it has derived the meanings "to surpass," "to exceed," "to overtake," "to excel," "to go beyond," "to transcend," "superb," "detached," "super-," "ultra-," etc. In the Bronze Inscriptions, the upper part of 走 looks like a person walking rapidly with arms swinging, while the lower part represents a human foot. 召 is made up of 口 (kǒu, mouth) and the phonetic indicator 刀 (dāo, knife), meaning "to call," "to convene," or "to summon."

超 形聲。從走，召聲。本義為跳躍，引申義有超過、不同尋常的、在某個範圍之外等。召，形聲。從口，刀聲。意為呼喚、召集。

篆 超 走 金 夵 篆 夵

超級市場 chāojí shìchǎng supermarket
超重 chāozhòng overweight

超人 chāorén superman
超速 chāosù to go over the speed limit

吵

chǎo
to quarrel;
noisy

PICTOPHONETIC CHARACTER The character 吵 consists of the mouth radical 口 and the phonetic element 少 (shǎo), meaning "noisy," "to quarrel," "to wrangle," or "to disturb." In the Oracle-Bone Inscriptions, 少 depicts four grains of sand, suggesting "few," "little," "less," "to be short of," and "missing." In Regular Script, the bottom grain becomes a downward left stroke.

吵 形聲。篆文從言，少聲。楷書改為從口。本義為喧嚷，引申為爭吵、吵架、擾亂等。少，象形。在甲骨文像是四粒細小的沙子。意指數量不多、時間短、短缺、丟失等。

篆  少 甲  金  篆 

吵架 chǎojià to quarrel

吵鬧 chǎonào noisy

襯/衬

chèn
lining

PICTOPHONETIC CHARACTER The character 襯 consists of the clothing radical 衤 and the phonetic component 親 (qīn), meaning "lining." 襯 also extends to mean "place something underneath," "provide a background for," or "set off." In the Bronze Inscriptions, 親 contains the radical 見 and the phonetic component 辛 (xīn), meaning "close" or "intimate." In the simplified character 衬, 寸 replaces 親, since the pronunciation of 寸 (cùn) is similar to that of 襯 (chèn).

襯 形聲。從衣/衤，親聲。意指内衣、襯裹。親，形聲。從見，亲聲。本義為常見，引申為親近。簡體字衬右邊以寸代替親，因寸與襯聲音相近。

襯衫 chènshān shirt; blouse

襯托 chèntuō set off; serve as a foil to

襯褲 chènkù underpants

反襯 fǎnchèn set off by contrast

成

chéng
to become;
to succeed

ASSOCIATIVE COMPOUND In the Oracle-Bone and Bronze Inscriptions, the character 成 depicts the act of splitting something with a battle-axe 戊 (wù). Its original meaning is "cease-fire" or "to complete a task," from which the meanings "to finish," "to accomplish," "to succeed," "achievement," "to become," "to turn into," "capable," "all right," "established," and "one-tenth" have derived. In the Oracle-Bone Inscriptions, 戊 is the pictograph of a battle-axe. Later 戊 was borrowed to mean "the fifth heavenly stem" (see page 20) and "the fifth (in order)."

成 會意。甲骨文、金文字形像以戊（斧型兵器）劈一物，本義為休兵言和結盟或完成任務。引申義有完成、成功、成就、變成、成為、成全、成就等。戊（wù），象形。甲骨文、金文像一種刃寬柄長的斧型古代兵器，屬斧鉞類。後假借為天干的第五位。

甲  金  篆 

完成 wánchéng to complete

成人 chéngrén adult

成功 chénggōng success; to succeed

成為 chéngwéi to become

城

chéng
city; town

PICTOPHONETIC CHARACTER The character 城 is comprised of the soil/earth radical 土 and the phonetic element 成 (chéng, succeed), originally meaning "wall." Since all cities had walls in ancient times, 城 extended to mean "city."

城 形聲。從土，成聲。本義指城牆。古代城市皆有墻，因而引申為城市。

金 𩫏 篆 城

城市 chéngshì city
古城 gǔchéng anceint city

長城 chángchéng the Great Wall
城堡 chéngbǎo castle; tower

程

chéng
journey; schedule

PICTOPHONETIC CHARACTER The character 程 consists of the growing grain radical 禾 and the phonetic element 呈, signaling the act of weighing or measuring grain. Originally 程 was a general name of measurements of all kinds, and later came to mean "to measure," "to assess," "rule," "regulation," "order," "procedure," "formula," "schedule," "journey," or "distance." 呈 is formed with 口 (kǒu, mouth) and 壬 (tǐng, a person standing on the ground), representing a man standing on the ground and speaking. It's used to mean "to appear," "to show," "to submit," and "petition."

程 形聲。從禾，呈聲，意指稱量穀物。本義為度量衡的總稱，引申為稱量、規矩、程序、路程、里程等。呈，形聲。從口，從壬。像一人站在地上發言。意為顯露、呈現、呈送、呈子等。

篆

日程 rìchéng daily schedule; agenda
里程 lǐchéng mileage

單程 dānchéng single trip; one-way
計程車 jìchéngchē taxi; cab

吃

chī
to eat

PICTOPHONETIC CHARACTER The character 吃 combines the mouth radical 口 and the phonetic 乞 (qǐ), meaning "to eat." The character 乞 is derived from the character 气 (qì, air) meaning "to supplicate" or "beg for alms," etc. In the Oracle-Bone and Bronze Inscriptions, 气 looks like three thin clouds in the sky, meaning "air" or "breath." Be sure to note the difference between 气 and 乞.

吃 形聲。從口，乞聲，意為進食。乞，本為气，甲骨文、金文中像天上的雲氣浮動狀。后省去一筆為乞。乞由气字分化而來，意為請求、乞討。

篆

吃飯 chīfàn to have a meal; to eat
小吃 xiǎochī snack; refreshments

好吃 hǎochī tasty; delicious
吃醋 chīcù to feel jealous

寵 / 宠

chǒng
to dote on

ASSOCIATIVE AND PICTOPHONETIC COMPOUND The character 寵 combines the roof radical 宀 with the semantic and phonetic element 龍 (lóng, dragon), originally meaning "to worship," "respectable," or "glory." Extended meanings of 寵 are "favor (especially of the emperor)," "to favor," or "to pamper." In the Oracle-Bone and Bronze Inscriptions, 龍 is the sketch of a dragon. In Chinese tradition, the dragon is considered an auspicious totem that can bring rain to the fields, and is also the symbol of the emperor. 尨 is a variant form of 龍, from which the simplified character 龙 derives. In the character 宠, the "dragon" part is simplified.

寵 形聲兼會意。從宀，龍聲，龍亦兼表神聖之意。本義為地位尊崇、榮耀，引申為上給下恩惠使之榮耀、偏愛、驕縱等。龍，象形。像傳說中神異動物龍的形狀。古時已有將龍字寫成尨，簡化字龙是在尨字的基礎上進一步簡化。宠屬於偏旁類推簡化。

金 𡩠 篆 𡩊 龍 甲 𤜼 金 𤜺

寵物 chǒngwù pet	寵愛 chǒng'ài to dote on; to love dearly
寵兒 chǒngér favorite	寵壞 chǒnghuài spoiled

出

chū
to go out

ASSOCIATIVE COMPOUND In the Oracle-Bone and Bronze Inscriptions, the character 出 resembles a foot on top of a cave dwelling, meaning "to go or come out." Extended meanings of 出 include "to appear," "happen," "issue," "produce," etc. In Regular Script, 出 looks quite different from its earlier forms.

出 會意。甲骨文、金文中本字上部從止，下部像洞穴，表示人從穴居走出。

甲 𡴆 金 𡴆 篆 𡴆

出來 chūlai come out	出去 chūqu go out
出口 chūkǒu exit; export	出現 chūxiàn to appear; to emerge

初

chū
beginning;
elementary

ASSOCIATIVE COMPOUND The character 初 is made up of the clothes radical 衤 (衣) and 刀 (dāo, knife), suggesting that "cutting cloth is the beginning of making a dress." Its extended meanings are "beginning," "start," "first," "original," "elementary," "basic," "junior," and "early." Note the differences between the clothes radical 衤 (衣) and the show/altar radical 礻 (示).

初 會意。甲骨文從衤/衣，從刀，本義為裁衣是制衣之始。引申為開始、第一次（初版，初戀，初賽）、原來的（初衷）、最低的（初級、初中）、每月開始的頭十天等。

甲 𥘉 金 𥘉 篆 𥘉

初期 chūqī initial stage	初次 chūcì first time
初中 chūzhōng junior middle school	初學者 chūxuézhě beginner

除

chú
except

ASSOCIATIVE AND PICTOPHONETIC COMPOUND The character 除 is comprised of the mound radical 阝 and the signifying and phonetic element 余 (yú, hut). Its original meaning was "doorstep," and later came to mean "leave," "remove," "get rid of," "except," etc. The character 余 combines 亼 (jí, gather together) and 木 (mù, wood), signifying "hut." In classical Chinese 余 means "I."

除 會意兼形聲。篆文從阜（土山），從余；余亦聲。本義為階梯，引申為除去等。余，形聲。甲骨文、金文上像屋頂，下像支撐的木頭。本義為茅屋，引申為剩下、多出來等。

篆 餘

除了… 以外 chúle… yǐwài besides; except for
清除 qīngchú to eliminate; to get rid of

除非 chúfēi only if; unless
開除 kāichú to expel; to fire

廚 / 厨

chú
kitchen

PICTOPHONETIC CHARACTER The character 廚 consists of 广 (yǎn, shelter; shed) and the phonetic 尌 (shù), meaning "kitchen." 尌 combines 壴 (zhù, drum) with 寸 (cùn, inch), suggesting the act of setting up a drum with hands (寸 refers to the hand in the character 尌). Hence, 尌 means "to set up," "to stand (something) up." 厨 is the variant form of 廚 and is now used as its simplified form. Note that in 厨 the dot on the top of 廚 is removed and 壴 replaced with 豆.

廚 形聲。從广，尌（shù）聲。本義為廚房。尌，會意。從壴（zhù），從寸。本義為樹立，是古樹字。后加木字旁為樹。現在尌不單用。簡化字厨原是廚的俗體字，去掉廚上面一點，把下面的壴改為豆。

篆 廚

廚房 chúfáng kitchen
幫廚 bāngchú to help in the kitchen

廚師 chúshī cook
廚具 chújù kitchen ware

楚

chǔ
clear; neat

PICTOPHONETIC CHARACTER In its ancient forms, the character 楚 combined the signifying part 林 (lín, grove; forest) and the phonetic element 足 (zú, foot), originally referring to a type of tree known in the West as the "Judas tree." Since the branches of this tree were used to beat criminals, 楚 has been extended to mean "pain" or "suffering." 楚 can also mean "neat" and "clear." In Regular Script, 疋 (shū, foot) replaces the 足 part of 楚. 足 and 疋 were the same character in their ancient forms.

楚 形聲。從林，疋（shū）聲。甲骨文、金文從足，從林。本義為一種落葉灌木，也叫牡荊，因用荊木作刑杖，引申為杖刑，痛苦，清晰，整齊等。楚也是春秋時國名，也特指現今湖北省。

甲 金 篆

痛楚 tòngchǔ pain; suffering
一清二楚 yìqīng èrchǔ to be perfectly clear about something

清楚 qīngchǔ clear

---

chuān
to wear; to pass through

ASSOCIATIVE COMPOUND The character 穿 consists of the radical 穴 (xué, cave; hole) and the character 牙 (yá, tooth), referring to animals creating holes with their sharp teeth. The primary meaning of 穿 is "pierce through," and extended meanings include "pass though," "cross," "string together," and "wear." The cave radical is also used in the character 空 (kòng, free time) and 牙 in 呀 (ya, a grammatical particle).

穿 會意。從穴，從牙，表示用牙咬穿或掘洞。本義為穿透，引申為穿戴。

 篆 𡧛

穿上 chuānshang to put on (clothes etc.)
吃穿 chīchuān food and clothing

穿越 chuānyuè to pass through; to cross
穿著 chuānzhuó dress; apparel

---

chuāng
window

ASSOCIATIVE COMPOUND In its ancient form, the character 窗 is the pictograph of a skylight. In Seal Script, a cave radical 穴 (xué) is added to the top of 囪 (cōng, the original form of skylight; chimney; funnel). 窗 originally referred to "skylight" and has been extended to mean "window." 囪 is the old form of 窗, but means only "chimney" today. 穴 is a pictograph of a cave dwelling in Seal Script.

窗 會意。此字最初只有下面的囪，本義指屋頂上的天窗，篆文後在囪上加穴（洞穴）以突出窗洞之意。而囪字後專用來表示煙囪。窗則表示開在屋頂、墙上、船上等用來採光、通風的洞。穴，象形。像古人居住的半地下的土窖。引申泛指洞穴。

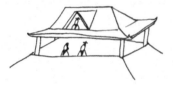
囪 古 篆 篆

窗戶 chuānghù window
天窗 tiānchuāng skylight

窗簾 chuānglián window curtains
櫥窗 chúchuāng display window

---

chuáng
bed

ASSOCIATIVE COMPOUND In the Oracle-Bone Inscriptions, the character 牀 depicts the outline of a bed (爿 pán). In Seal Script, the character wood (木) is added to the right side of 爿, indicating that the bed is made of wood. 床 is a variant form of 牀, combining 广 (yǎn, shed; shelter) and 木, suggesting a bed is a wooden article used inside of a house. The simplified character for bed is also 床.

牀/床 會意。牀，從木，從爿 (pán)，泛指臥具。爿，象形。像床形。牀亦寫作床。床，從广，從木。牀與床是異體字，兩者通用，但舊時多用牀。簡體字為床。

甲 爿 篆 牀

起床 qǐchuáng to get up
床單 chuángdān bed sheet

單 (雙)人床 dān(shuāng)rénchuáng single (double) bed
床墊 chuángdiàn mattress

春

chūn
spring

ASSOCIATIVE AND PICTOPHONETIC COMPOUND In the Bronze Inscriptions, the character 春 consists of grass 艸 (cǎo), bud 屯 (tún), and the sun 日 (rì), representing a vigorous "spring." Its extended meanings are "youthful," "love," "lust," etc. In Regular Script, the upper part of 春 resembles grass or plants growing from the soil while 日 in the lower part remains unchanged.

春 會意兼形聲。金文從日，從艸，從屯(tún植物發芽)；屯亦聲。春字是春天陽光普照，草木萌發，生機勃勃的寫照。本義為春季，引申義有生機勃勃、男女情欲等。

金 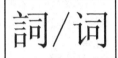 篆

春天 chūntiān spring
青春 qīngchūn youth

春假 chūnjià spring break
春節 chūnjié Spring Festival (Chinese New Year)

詞 / 词

cí
word

ASSOCIATIVE COMPOUND The character 詞 consists of the word radical 言 and the character 司 (sī, to manage), meaning "word," "term," or "statement." In the Oracle-Bone Inscriptions, 司 resembles a hand over a mouth, symbolizing a person issuing orders. Therefore, the meanings of 司 are "to take charge of," "manage," etc. The speech radical is simplified to form the character 词.

詞 會意。從司，從言。司有主管義，表示人對語言的駕馭掌握。司，會意。甲骨文、金文像把手遮在嘴上發號施令。簡體字词為部首簡化。

司 甲 金

生詞 shēngcí new word
名詞 míngcí noun

詞彙 cíhuì vocabulary; list of words
動詞 dòngcí verb

次

cì
(MW for occurrences)

ASSOCIATIVE COMPOUND In the Oracle-Bone Inscriptions, the character 次 combines 二 (èr, two) and 欠 (qiàn, yawn), referring to a person yawning again and again. The meanings of 次 include: "next," "second," "time," "order," "second-rate," "inferior," and "the measure word for occurrences." In Regular Script, the ice radical 冫 replaces the 二 part of 次, even though ice has nothing to do with the original meaning of 次. In the Oracle-Bone Inscriptions, 欠 looks like a man in the act of breathing or yawning, originally meaning "to yawn." Extended meanings of 欠 include "not enough," "to owe," etc.

次 會意。從二，從欠（張口出氣），像人連連打哈欠狀。意思有動作的次數、順序、等級、次等的。欠，象形。像人打哈欠狀。本義為打哈欠，引申義有欠缺、虧欠等。

甲 金 篆

上次 shàngcì last time
每次 měicì every time

下次 xiàcì next time
名次 míngcì ranking

聰 / 聪

cōng
able to hear well; smart

ASSOCIATIVE AND PICTOPHONETIC COMPOUND The character 聰 combines the radical 耳 (ěr, ear) and the phonetic element 悤 (cōng). Originally 聰 referred to "hearing" or "hearing well" and has been extended to mean "quick intelligence," "acute," "clever," and "intelligent." 悤 is made up of heart 心 (xīn) and the phonetic 囱 (cōng), meaning "agitated" or "hurried." 囱 is the pictograph of a skylight and has been extended to mean "chimney."

聰 會意兼形聲。從耳，悤 (cōng) 聲。本義為通過聽來明辨是非。引申為聽力、聽覺靈敏、智力高等。悤，形聲。從心，囱聲，古與聰同義，後作為匆的異體字。囱，象形。像天窗形。是窗的本字，後引申為煙囱。簡體字用聪代替聰，屬同音替代。清代已有此字。

篆 聰

聰明 cōngming smart
耳聰目明 ěrcōng mùmíng can hear and see well; quick-eared and sharp-eyed

失聰 shīcōng deafness; loss of hearing

從 / 从

cóng
from

ASSOCIATIVE COMPOUND In the Oracle-Bone Inscription, 從 contains two persons "从" with one following the other, meaning "to follow." Its extended meanings are "follower," "to comply with," "subordinate," "to attend," "from," "whence," "since," and "through." In Regular Script, the radical 彳 (walk slowly; left step) and 止 (zhǐ, foot; stop) are added to the two persons (从) to form the character 從. In fact the simplified character 从 restores its original form.

從 會意。甲骨文像二人相隨之形。楷書寫做從。從字本義為相隨、跟隨，引申義有跟隨者（隨從）、聽從、從屬的、參與（從政，從軍）、以及作為表示起點的介詞。從字簡化為从，實際上是恢復了古本字。元代已見。

甲 从 金 从 篆 从

從不 cóngbù never
自從 zìcóng ever since

從前 cóngqián before; once upon a time
服從 fúcóng to obey

醋

cù
vinegar

PICTOPHONETIC CHARACTER The character 醋 combines the wine jar radical 酉 (yǒu) with the phonetic 昔 (xī), suggesting something in a jar and meaning "vinegar." 醋 has been extended to mean "jealous" or "envy," since the Chinese think such feelings are rather sour—like vinegar. In the Oracle-Bone and Bronze Inscriptions, the upper part of 昔 looks like a flood and the lower part like the sun 日, referring to severe floods which overwhelmed the sun in prehistoric times. Hence 昔 means "the past" or "former times."

醋 形聲。從酉，昔聲。本義為調味用的酸味液體，引申為嫉妒，如"吃醋"。昔，會意。甲骨文、金文下是日，上像洪水泛濫、遮天蔽日狀，指古代大洪水時期。

篆 醋 昔 甲 昔 金 昔 篆 昔

糖醋魚 tángcùyú sweet and sour fish
醋味 cùwèi smell of vinegar; feeling of jealousy

陳醋 chéncù aged vinegar
吃醋 chīcù to be jealous

錯 / 错

cuò
wrong; error

PICTOPHONETIC CHARACTER The character 錯 consists of the radical 金 (jīn, gold; metal) and the phonetic element 昔 (xī, the past). The original meaning of 錯 was "gold inlay." Later it came to mean "interlocked," "jagged," "grind," "alternate," or "wrong," In the Oracle-Bone and Bronze Inscriptions, the upper part of 昔 looks like a flood and the lower part resembles the sun 日, referring to prehistoric times when there was an extraordinarily big flood. Hence 昔 means "the past" or "former times." The gold/metal radical is simplified in the character 错.

錯 形聲。從金，昔聲，本義為用金塗飾。昔，會意。甲骨文、金文下是日，上像洪水泛濫、遮天蔽日狀，指古代大洪水時期。簡體字错的部首由金 簡化為钅。

篆 錯 昔 甲 日 金 日 篆 日

錯誤 cuòwù error; mistake
錯字 cuòzì incorrect character

出錯 chūcuò to make a mistake
不錯 búcuò not bad; pretty good

打

dǎ
to hit

ASSOCIATIVE COMPOUND The character 丁 (dīng) depicts a nail, and originally meant "nail." Later, the radical 金 (metal) was added to the left of 丁 (釘). The character 打 combines the hand radical 扌 with the nail 丁, conveying the act of striking a nail with a hammer. Hence 打 means "to strike," "hit," or "beat," and its extended meanings include "to calculate," "to make," "to play (a game)," etc.

打 會意。從手，從丁。丁本義為釘，用手釘釘子來表示敲打。

篆 打

打算 dǎsuàn to plan; plan
打針 dǎzhēn to give or have an injection

打球 dǎqiú to play ball
打電話 dǎ diànhuà to make a telephone call

帶 / 带

dài
to bring;
to take;
to carry

PICTOGRAPH In Seal Script, the character 帶 looks like a cloth belt tied into a bow (top part) at the waist (middle part) with the belt ends hanging down (bottom part). The original meaning of 帶 is "waistband" or "girdle," from which derived the meanings "belt," "band," "ribbon," "string," "tire," "area," "zone," "region," "to carry," "to take along," "to bring," and "to look after." The simplified character 带 derives from the cursive style of 帶. Note that only the top part of 帶 is simplified.

帶 象形。篆文像腰間繫的帶子。上部像束在腰間的一根帶子和用帶打成的結，中間是腰，下為帶子垂下的部分。本義為繫在腰間的帶子，引申為各類帶子、攜帶、帶領、地區、連接、養育等。簡化字带是繁體字帶的草書楷化字，僅上部簡化。

篆 帶 草 带

皮帶 pídài leather belt
帶頭 dàitóu to take the lead

鞋帶 xiédài shoelaces
熱帶 rèdài tropical zone

The Way of Chinese Characters

單／单

dān
single

PICTOGRAPH   In the Oracle-Bone and Bronze Inscriptions, the character 單 resembles a Y-shaped stick with stones fastened to the top, referring to a kind of ancient weapon. Its extended meanings are "simple," "single," "sole," "odd number," "unlined (clothing)," "sheet," "bill," and "list." The simplified character 单 derives from the cursive style of 單.

單 象形。甲骨文、金文像帶叉的木棍上捆著石頭。原指古代一種武器，用於狩獵與戰鬥，引申為不複雜、單獨、奇數、薄的衣服、記載事物用的紙片等。

甲 單　金 單　篆 單

簡單 jiǎndān simple
菜單 càidān menu

單號 dānhào odd number
名單 míngdān name list; roster

擔／担

dān
to be burdened with

PICTOPHONETIC CHARACTER   The character 擔 is made up of the hand radical 扌 and the phonetic component 詹 (zhān). Its original meaning is "to carry with a shoulder pole," from which the meanings "to shoulder," "to be burdened with," "to undertake," "to endure" have derived. 擔 means "shoulder pole," and "a unit of weight (=50 kilograms)" when it is pronounced as dàn. 詹 is the combination of 厃 (yán, tall; look upward), 八 (bā, eight), and 言 (yán, words), meaning "to talk too much." Today 詹 by itself is only used as a surname. In the simplified 担, 旦 (dàn, dawn; morning) replaces 詹 as the phonetic element.

擔 形聲。從扌，詹聲。是儋的異體字。本義為肩挑，引申為擔負、承擔等。當擔發音為dàn時，意為扁擔、重量單位（一擔等於一百斤）。詹，會意。從厃(yán，人立於崖上)，從八，從言。本義為話多，現只用作姓。擔的簡化字担右邊以旦代替詹，屬同音替代。

篆 擔

負擔 fùdān burden
擔保 dānbǎo to guarantee; to warrant

擔心 dānxīn to worry
擔任 dānrèn hold the post of; to serve as

但

dàn
but; however

PICTOPHONETIC CHARACTER   但 consists of the person radical 亻 and the phonetic component 旦 (dàn). Its original meaning was "to be stripped to the waist." It later came to mean "but," "yet," and "nevertheless." A new character 袒 was created to convey the original meaning of 但. 旦 is comprised of 日 with a horizontal stroke underneath, symbolizing the sun rising above the horizon. 旦, therefore, means "daybreak" or "dawn."

但 形聲。從人，旦聲。本義為袒露，是袒的古字，今用為副詞或連詞。旦，指事。一代表地平綫，表示太陽剛從地平綫上升起。

但是 dànshì but; however
不但…而且… búdàn... érqiě...   not only ... but also...

但願 dànyuàn if only; I wish

The Way of Chinese Characters

蛋

dàn
egg

ASSOCIATIVE AND PICTOPHONETIC COMPOUND The character 蛋 is the combination of 疋 (shū, foot) and 虫 (chóng, worm; insect), referring to eggs of various animals including birds, reptiles, etc., or egg-shaped things. Sometimes 蛋 is used as a term of abuse. In its ancient forms, the top part of 疋 looks like a human calf and the bottom part of a foot. In the Oracle-Bone Inscriptions, 虫 resembles the shape of a snake, originally representing a kind of poisonous snake and extended to refer to all insects or worms.

蛋 會意兼形聲。從疋 (shū，足)，從虫。本義 指禽鳥龜蛇所產的卵。引 申為形狀似蛋的東西、罵 人的話等。虫，象形。 像長蛇之形。本義為一 種毒蛇，後泛指蟲類。

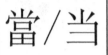

雞蛋 jīdàn chicken egg
完蛋 wándàn to be ruined

蛋糕 dàngāo cake
壞蛋 huàidàn bad egg; bastard

當/当

dāng
to serve as; to be

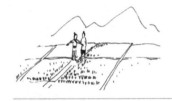

PICTOPHONETIC CHARACTER The character 當 consists of the signifying part 田 (tián, field) and the phonetic element 尚 (shàng), originally meaning "the prices of two pieces of farmland are equal." The extended meanings of 當 include "equal," "well-matched," "to face," "to work as," "to serve as," "to be in charge of," "just at (a time or a place)," "ought," "should," etc. In its ancient forms, 尚 looks like a drinking vessel. Since people toast to show respect, 尚 means "to uphold" or "to esteem." The simplified character 当 derives from the cursive style of 當.

當 形聲。篆文從田，尚 聲。本義表示兩塊田价 相等，引申為相等、對 著、擔任（當官）、主 持、以往的某時或某地 （當時|當地）、應該 等。尚，會意。一說像酒 器，一說像煙氣由窗口向 外散出。意思有推崇、崇 尚、高尚等。簡化字当 由當的草書演化而來。

篆 當 草 当

當然 dāngrán of course
門當戶對 méndāng hùduì (of a marriage) be well-matched in social and economic status

當時 dāngshí at the time

導/导

dǎo
to lead; to guide

ASSOCIATIVE AND PICTOPHONETIC COMPOUND The character 導 combines a hand 寸 (cùn, inch, but symbolizing a hand in the character 導) and the semantic and phonetic element 道 (dào, way; road), signaling the act of guiding others with the hand pointing the way to go. The meanings of 導 include "to guide," "to lead," "to direct," "to instruct," "to inspire," and "to conduct." The simplified character 导 derives from the cursive style of 導.

導，會意兼形聲。從 寸（手），從道，道亦 聲。表示手在道路上引 領前行。本義為引領， 引申義有引導、指導、 啟發、開導、傳導等。 簡化字导由導的草書演 化而來。

金 導 篆 導 草 导

導遊 dǎoyóu tour guide
教導 jiàodǎo to instruct; to educate

導師 dǎoshī advisor; supervisor
導演 dǎoyǎn director (of a film, play, etc.)

到

dào
to arrive

PICTOPHONETIC CHARACTER The character 到 has the signifying element 至 (zhì, arrive) on the left, and the knife radical and phonetic symbol 刂 (dāo) on the right, meaning "arrive," "reach," "go to," or "leave for." In its ancient form, 至 depicts an arrow reaching its target, and means "arrive," "reach," "extremely," and "most."

到 形聲。篆文從至，刀聲。至，象形，像箭頭射中地面或箭靶狀。

金 𝍎 篆 𝍎

看到 kàndào to see
得到 dédào to get; to obtain

找到 zhǎodào to find
遲到 chídào to arrive late

道/道

dào
road; way

ASSOCIATIVE COMPOUND The character 道 consists of the walk radical 辶 and 首 (shǒu, head), suggesting that a person is walking on the road. Thus, 道 means "road," "way," "the (natural) way (of things)," "method," "doctrine," and "Taoism." In the Oracle-Bone Inscriptions, 首 looks like a head with hair on top. The primary meaning of 首 is "head," and extended meanings include "leader," "chief," and "first."

道 會意。從辶，從首，表示一人在路上向前行走，意為道路、事理、道教等。首，象形。甲骨文、金文像有髮的人頭。

金 𝍎 篆 𝍎

道路 dàolù road; path; way
道家 dàojiā Taoism

道理 dàolǐ principle; truth; reason
知道 zhīdào to know

得

dé
to obtain; to get

děi
must;
have to

de
(particle)

ASSOCIATIVE COMPOUND In the Oracle-Bone Inscriptions, the character 得 resembles a hand holding a cowry shell, suggesting obtaining money or something valuable. In the Bronze Inscriptions, the radical 彳 (left step; walk slowly) was added, implying that one acquires valuable things while traveling. In Regular Script the 彳 part of the character 得 remains the same; 寸 depicts the hand, but 貝 (bèi, shell) becomes 日 with 一 underneath.

得 會意。甲骨文從又（右手）持貝（錢幣），意指有所得。金文又加彳（街道），以示行有所獲。

甲 𝍎 金 𝍎 篆 𝍎

得到 dédào to get; to obtain
得意 déyì proud of oneself

得失 déshī gain and loss; success and failure
覺得 juéde to feel; to think

The Way of Chinese Characters

的

de
(possessive particle)

PICTOPHONETIC CHARACTER The character 的 consists of 白 (bái, white) and the phonetic component 勺 (sháo, ladle; spoon). Its original meaning was "bright-colored" or "distinctive." Now 的 is used to connect an attributive to a noun. Both 白 and 勺 are pictographs. In its ancient form, 白 may resemble the bright rays spreading from the sun or a grain of white rice—scholars differ on the explanation. 勺 is the outline of a ladle containing something.

的 形聲。篆文從日，勺聲，楷書寫作"的"。白，象形。像日出光芒射出狀。一説像白米粒。勺，象形。像用勺舀物。

篆 䀅 勺 金 𠣀 篆 𠂔

我的 wǒde my; mine
別的 biéde other; else

大的 dàde big one(s)
有的 yǒude some

登

dēng
to climb; to ascend

ASSOCIATIVE COMPOUND In the Oracle-Bone and Bronze Inscriptions, the character 登 is made up of a pair of hands (bottom part) carrying a high-legged vessel 豆 (middle part) and a pair of feet 癶 (top part), suggesting the act of ascending to a high platform and offering newly harvested grains to God or the king. In Seal Script, the hands at the bottom are removed. The meanings of 登 include "to ascend," "to mount," "to climb," "to enter," "to record," "to publish," "to register," "grain harvest," "ripe," etc.

登 會意。甲骨文、金文中其字形下是雙手捧豆（器皿），上是雙足向上（癶 bō），表示升階進獻新穀。引申義為登高、記載、刊登、登記、穀物成熟等。篆文簡化而去掉下面的雙手，僅保留豆與癶兩部分。

甲 𤼁 金 𤼷 篆 登

登山 dēngshān to climb a mountain; hiking
登機 dēngjī to board a plane

登高 dēnggāo to ascend a height
登記 dēngjì to register

燈/灯

dēng
light; lamp

PICTOPHONETIC CHARACTER The character 燈 consists of the fire radical 火 and the phonetic indicator 登 (dēng), meaning "lamp," "light," or "lantern." In the simplified character 灯, 丁 (dīng) replaces 登 as the phonetic indicator since their pronunciations are similar.

燈 形聲。從火，登聲，指照明器具。簡化字灯把燈字左邊換成丁，屬於同音替代。其實灯是燈的俗字，元代已見。

篆 䥗 燈 登 甲 𤼁 金 𤼷

電燈 diàndēng electric light
紅綠燈 hónglùdēng traffic light

路燈 lùdēng street light
臺燈 táidēng desk lamp

等

děng
to wait; rank

ASSOCIATIVE COMPOUND The character 等 consists of the bamboo radical ⺮ and the character 寺 (sì, to manage; temple), meaning "to tidy bamboo pieces." Extended meanings of 等 include "sort," "equal," and "rank." After the Tang Dynasty, 等 came to mean "wait." In the Bronze Inscriptions, 寺 consists of stop (止) and a hand (又), meaning "hold," "handle," or "manage." Later 寺 came to mean "temple" or "monastery."

等 會意。從竹，從寺。有等級、類別、相等、等候、等等之意。寺，會意兼形聲。金文從又（手），從止。手之所止為持，本義為持有、操持，是持的本字。後借用為寺廟的寺。

篆

等級 děngjí grade; rank; status
平等 píngděng equal; equality

上等 shàngděng highest quality; top-notch
等等 děngděng etc.; and so on

地

dì
earth

de
(particle)

PICTOPHONETIC CHARACTER The character 地 consists of the earth radical 土 and the phonetic component 也 (yě, also), meaning "earth," "land," "soil," "ground," "floor," etc. 地 (pronounced de) can also be used to link an adverb to a verb.

地 形聲。從土，也聲。本義指土地，引申為地區、領域等。

篆

土地 tǔdì land; soil
地方 dìfang place; area; space

地球 dìqiú the earth
地位 dìwèi position; status

弟

dì
younger brother

ASSOCIATIVE COMPOUND In its ancient form, the character 弟 looks like a man with a bow on his shoulder. Some scholars believe the character 弟 refers to a cord wound around something. The original meaning of 弟 was "order" and it came to mean "younger brother." In Regular Script, we can still see the bow 弓 (gōng) in the character 弟. Other than the bow, the top part of 弟 looks like a child's hair twisted in two knots and the lower part the two legs.

弟 會意。像人身上背弓箭形，古時年輕人挂弓箭祭奠死去的長者。一説上像總角，下像腿形。另一説弟本義指纏繞的次序。

甲 金 篆

弟弟 dìdi younger brother
表弟 biǎodì younger male cousin

兄弟 xiōngdì brothers
弟子 dìzǐ disciple; follower

第

dì
(ordinal prefix)

PICTOPHONETIC CHARACTER The character 第 consists of the bamboo radical ⺮ and the phonetic element 弟 (dì, younger brother). The original meaning of 第 was "the arrangement of bamboo" and its extended meaning is "order" or "sequence." 第 is also placed before a number to form ordinal numbers. Please note the differences between 第 and 弟.

第 形聲。從竹，從弟；弟也兼表聲。本義為竹的層次，引申為次第、順序。

第一 dìyī first; number one
次第 cìdì order; sequence

第一課 dìyīkè Lesson 1
門第 méndì family status

點／点

diǎn
dot; o'clock

PICTOPHONETIC CHARACTER The character 點 combines the radical 黑 (hēi, black) and the phonetic symbol 占 (zhàn, divination), meaning "speck" or "spot." Extended meanings include "drop," "point," "a little," "o'clock," "to choose," etc. In the Bronze Inscriptions, the character 黑 looks like a sweaty person whose face is blackened from the smoke of fire. 灬 is a radical form of the character 火 (huǒ, fire). The character 占 consists of 卜 (bǔ, a crack on an oracle bone) and 口 (kǒu, mouth), suggesting the interpretation of cracks on oracle bones. The simplified 点 retains the fire radical 灬 under 占.

點 形聲。從黑，占聲。黑，會意。甲骨文、金文中像一個被煙熏火烤、大汗淋漓、滿面污垢的人。占，會意。從卜（龜殼燒裂後出現的兆紋），從口，意指觀察兆紋解釋凶吉。簡體字点去掉黑字的上半部，把灬移到占字下。明清已有此字。

篆 點 占 甲 占 篆 占

點鐘 diǎnzhōng o'clock
點心 diǎnxin dessert; dim sum

點菜 diǎncài to order dishes (in a restaurant)
重點 zhòngdiǎn important point; main point

店

diàn
store; shop

PICTOPHONETIC CHARACTER In Seal Script, the character 店 consists of the soil/earth radical 土 and the phonetic element 占 (zhàn), originally referring to a clay stand designed for storing things in the main room of a house. Later it extended to mean "store," "shop," "inn," etc. In Regular Script, the shed/shelter radical 广 is used to replace the soil/earth radical 土. It shows the progress of selling things inside a shed instead of on a stage made of soil.

店 形聲。篆文從土，占聲。本義為置放物品的土臺子。後改土字旁為广（敞屋），有商店、旅店等意。店字展示了由在土臺上售貨到在大房內售貨的演變過程。

篆 坫

商店 shāngdiàn store; shop
酒店 jiǔdiàn wine shop; pub; restaurant

書店 shūdiàn bookstore
飯店 fàndiàn restaurant; hotel

電/电

diàn
electricity

ASSOCIATIVE COMPOUND In the Bronze Inscriptions, the character 電 has 雨 (yǔ, rain) in the upper part and 申 (shēn, lightning) in the lower part, symbolizing lightning in a rainstorm. The extended meanings of 電 are "swift," "electricity," and "electric shock." The character 申 resembles lightning streaking across a field, with extended meanings such as "stretch," "express," and "state." The simplified character 电 does not include the rain radical 雨.

電 會意。金文從雨，從申，像雷雨時閃電劃過長空狀。簡體字去掉上部的雨字。

金 霝 篆 電

電視 diànshì television; TV
電話 diànhuà telephone; phone call
電影 diànyǐng movie; film
電燈 diàndēng electric light

碟

dié
disc; saucer

PICTOPHONETIC CHARACTER The character 碟 is comprised of the radical 石 (shí, stone) and the phonetic element 枼 (yè), meaning "plate" or "small dish." Certain objects similar to the shape of a plate are also called 碟, such as 飛碟 (fēi dié, UFO) and 光碟 (guāng dié, compact disc). In its ancient forms, 石 resembles a rock (bottom part) underneath a cliff (upper left). 枼 is the ancient form of 葉 (yè, leaf), which looks like leaves (top part) on a tree (木) in the Bronze Inscriptions.

碟 形声。從石，枼 (yè) 聲。本義為盛食物的小盤子，引申為類似碟子的東西。石，象形，古文寫法像山崖下的一石塊。枼是葉的古體字。

石甲 石 金 石 枼 金 枼

碟子 diézi small plate
影碟 yǐngdié DVD
光碟 guāngdié optical disc; compact disc; CD; CD-ROM
飛碟 fēidié flying saucer

定

dìng
settled; decided

ASSOCIATIVE COMPOUND In its ancient forms, the character 定 is comprised of the roof radical 宀 and the signifying part 正 (zhèng, straight; right; proper; correct), meaning settling down in the right place. Its extended meanings include "settled," "stable," "to agree on," "to decide," "to fix," and "to be sure." In the Oracle-Bone Inscriptions, 正 is the combination of 囗 (wéi, enclosure, here standing for a city) and a foot 止, suggesting people marching toward enemy territory, from which have derived the meanings "righteous," "correct," "upright," "precisely," "just now," etc. Note that in Regular Script, the bottom part of 定 is no longer 正.

定 會意。甲骨文從宀（房屋），從正（止［足］，指到達一處，是前往之意）。本義指到房中為止，即安居，引申為安定、約定、決定、規定的、確定等。

甲 定 金 定 篆 定

安定 āndìng stable
定做 dìngzuò custom-tailored; to customize
決定 juédìng to decide
一定 yídìng surely

訂 / 订

dìng
to reserve; to book

PICTOPHONETIC CHARACTER The character 訂 consists of the word/speech radical 言 and the phonetic 丁 (dīng), originally meaning "to appraise through discussion." Its extended meanings include "to agree on," "to arrange," "to make corrections," "to reserve," "to order (merchandise, etc.)," "to book (a ticket, a hotel room, etc.)," "to subscribe to (magazine, newspaper, etc.)," or "to bind." 丁 (dīng) originally meant "nail." Later, the metal radical 金 was added to the left of 丁 (釘) to mean "nail," whereas 丁 is used to mean "male adult," "robust," "population," "the fourth heavenly stem," and "fourth." In 订, 讠 is in its simplified form.

訂 形聲。從言，丁聲。本義為評議。引申義有經商議後而確定、修改、糾正、預定、裝訂。丁，象形。像平放的釘子。後借用來表示成年男子、強壯、人口、天干的第四位、第四等。簡化字订的部首言屬偏旁類推簡化。

篆

訂報 dìngbào to subscribe to a newspaper
預定 yùdìng to book in advance

訂貨 dìnghuò to order (goods)
訂書機 dìngshūjī stapler

冬

dōng
winter

ASSOCIATIVE COMPOUND The character 冬 consists of "end" (zhōng) on top and "ice" (bīng) at the bottom, referring to winter: the cold period at the end of a year. In its ancient form, the word ice 仌 (bīng) looks like "frost." 仌 is written as 冫 when it functions as a radical. Make sure to distinguish between the ice radical 冫 and the water radical 氵.

冬 會意。上部為古文終字，下部兩點水代表冰，意指冬天是年終天寒地凍到處結冰的日子。

甲  金 篆

冬天 dōngtiān winter
寒冬 hándōng cold winter

冬季 dōngjì winter season
冬泳 dōngyǒng winter swimming

東 / 东

dōng
east

ASSOCIATIVE COMPOUND The character 東 consists of 日 (rì, sun) and 木 (mù, tree; wood), representing the sun rising behind a tree. Given that this scene may be observed in the east at dawn, the meaning of 東 is "east." The simplified character 东 derives from the cursive style of 東.

東 會意。從木，從日，以示太陽剛從東方升起，以此來表示東邊。簡體字东是繁體字東的草書楷化字。

甲  金 東 篆 東 草 东

東方 dōngfāng the East; the Orient
東北 dōngběi northeast; Northeast China

東部 dōngbù the east; eastern part
東西 dōngxi thing; stuff

懂
dǒng
to understand

PICTOPHONETIC CHARACTER 懂 consists of the vertical heart radical ↑ and the phonetic symbol 董 (dǒng, to supervise), meaning "understand" or "know." 董 combines the grass radical ⺍ and the phonetic component 童 (tóng). In the Bronze Inscriptions, 童 depicts a figure with implements of punishment, carrying a heavy sack on his back, referring to "criminal slave." Its extended meanings include "boy servant," "child," etc.

懂 形聲。從忄，董聲。董，形聲。篆文從艸，童聲。童，金文像身背重物、頭上有刑具的人，指男子有罪受刑罰的奴隸，引申為童僕、兒童等。

懂事 dǒngshì sensible; thoughtful 　看懂 kàndǒng to understand by reading or watching
半懂不懂 bàndǒng bùdǒng to not completely understand

動/动
dòng
to move

ASSOCIATIVE AND PICTOPHONETIC COMPOUND The character 動 combines 力 (lì, physical strength; power) with the semantic and phonetic component 重 (zhòng, heavy), suggesting the action of carrying heavy things with one's strength. 動 means "get to move," "to change," "to act," "to use," "to start," or "to touch (one's heart)." In the ancient forms, 力 resembles an ancient plow and 重 is the sketch of a man carrying a heavy sack on his back. The simplified character 动 derives from the cursive style of 動 and replaces 重 with 云.

動 會意兼形聲。從力，重聲。本義為用力背起重物，引申義為位置或狀態的改變、使用、開始、感動等。簡體字动源於動字的草書，將其中的重改為了云。

金 𤩪 篆 𫝀 草 动

活動 huódòng activity
動詞 dòngcí verb

動物 dòngwù animal
動畫 dònghuà cartoon

都
dōu
all; both

dū
capital

PICTOPHONETIC CHARACTER When the radical 阝 appears on the right side of a character, it means "town" or "city" as 阝 is derived from 邑 (yì, town; city; county). In the Bronze Inscriptions and Seal Script, 都 consists of the phonetic symbol 者 (zhě) and 邑 as the signifying component, meaning "big city" or "capital" (pronounced dū). 都 is also used as an adverb, meaning "all" (pronounced dōu). In Regular Script, the upper part of 者 is the same as that of 老, but the bottom part is 曰.

都 形聲。金文從邑，者聲。本義為都市，引申義為全部（副詞）。者，會意。甲骨文、金文中像將食物投到鍋中煮。者是煮的本字。

金 𨝵 篆 𩫏

首都 shǒudū capital (city)
誰都 shéidōu anybody; everyone

全都 quándōu all; without exception
都市 dūshì city; metropolis

豆

dòu
bean

PICTOGRAPH The character 豆 looks like a high-legged food container. It originally meant "food container" and was also used as a measurement in ancient times. Later 豆 was borrowed to mean "beans," "peas," or "bean-shaped," and no longer carries its original meaning of a food container.

豆 象形。像古代高腳的盛食品容器。本義為古代食器，也曾作為古代的容量單位。（左傳・昭公三年：“齊舊四量：豆、區、釜、鐘。四升為豆。”）後借用指豆類植物。

甲 豆 金 豆 篆 豆

綠豆 lǜdòu green bean
土豆 tǔdòu potato

黃豆 huángdòu soy bean
豆腐 dòufu tofu

肚

dù
belly;
abdomen

PICTOPHONETIC CHARACTER The character 肚 consists of the flesh radical 月 and the phonetic component 土 (tǔ), referring to "belly," "stomach," or "abdomen." 肚 also refers to the mind or brain in certain word combinations, such as 牽腸挂肚 (qiān cháng guà dù) "to be very worried about," "to be deeply concerned." When 肚 is pronounced as dǔ, it means tripe—the stomach of a pig, cow, or ox when it is cooked and served. In the Oracle-Bone Inscriptions, 土 looks like a mound of soil and means "earth" or "soil."

肚 形聲。從月（肉月），土聲。本義為人與動物肚子的部分，引申為內心、物體突出的部分；又指牛、羊等動物的胃囊，讀作dǔ，在中國，這是一種不錯的菜。

肚子 dùzi stomach
牛肚 niúdǔ cow tripe

腿肚子 tuǐdùzi calf (leg muscle)
羊肚 yángdǔ goat tripe

短

duǎn
short

PICTOPHONETIC CHARACTER The character 短 is comprised of the arrow radical 矢 and the phonetic element 豆 (dòu, bean), meaning "short." In the Oracle-Bone and Bronze Inscriptions, 矢 is the pictograph of an arrow. In ancient times people could use an arrow to measure the length of other things, therefore the character 短 has the arrow radical.

短 形聲。從矢，豆聲。意為不長。矢即是箭，古人可用矢量長度，故短從矢部。

篆

短信 duǎnxìn text message
長短 chángduǎn length; right and wrong

短期 duǎnqī short-term
短處 duǎnchù shortcoming; weak point

對/对

duì
correct; toward

ASSOCIATIVE COMPOUND   In its ancient form, the character 對 delineates a hand (寸) holding a tablet, meaning "to answer" or "respond." In the past, an official often referred to his notes on a small narrow tablet made of jade, ivory, or bamboo, which he held in his hands when discussing state affairs with his sovereign or answering questions. The extended meaning of 對 is "right" or "correct." In the simplified character 对, 又 replaces the left part of the traditional character 對.

對 會意。篆文左邊一半是板子，右邊從寸（手），本義為手持笏板回答，引申為對答、正確、面對等。簡體对字左邊以又替代。明代已有此字。

甲 金 篆

對不起 duìbuqǐ I'm sorry; excuse me
反對 fǎnduì to fight against; to oppose

對話 duìhuà dialogue
針對 zhēnduì to be directed against; to be aimed at

多

duō
many; much

ASSOCIATIVE COMPOUND   In its ancient form, the character 多 looks like two pieces of meat, meaning "extra," "large amount," or "many." In Regular Script, 多 became one 夕 (xī, sunset; evening) on the top of another 夕.

多 會意。多字像兩塊肉形。古時祭祀用肉，用兩塊以表示多。

甲 金 篆

很多 hěnduō many; a lot of; much
多少 duōshǎo how much; how many

多半 duōbàn most; mostly; most likely
多少錢 duōshǎoqián how much money?

餓/饿

è
hungry

PICTOPHONETIC CHARACTER   The character 餓 is comprised of the food radical 食 and the phonetic element 我 (wǒ, I), meaning "hungry," "hunger," and "covetous." Though 我 serves as the phonetic in 餓, it may help you to remember the character if you imagine that it means that "I" am hungry and need to eat food. The food radical 食 is simplified to 饣 to form the simplified character 饿.

餓 形聲。從食，我聲。意為飢餓。雖然我在餓字中是聲符，但可想成餓是我需要吃東西。簡化字饿屬於偏旁類推簡化。

篆

飢餓 jī'è hunger; starvation; famine
挨餓 ái'è suffer from hunger or starvation

餓鬼 èguǐ, hungry ghost
餓死 èsǐ starve to death; extremely hungry

The Way of Chinese Characters

而

ér
(conjunction)

PICTOGRAPH In the Oracle-Bone Inscriptions, 而 resembles a long beard on someone's chin, originally meaning "beard." 而 is now often used as a conjunction, meaning "and," "but," "moreover," "so that," etc.

而 象形。甲骨文像幾縷鬍鬚從下巴上垂下，本義為鬍鬚。引申義有但是、並且、和、到、及等。

甲 𣎳　金 而　篆 而

而且 érqiě (not only ...) but also; moreover
反而 fǎn'ér on the contrary; instead

然而 rán'ér however; but
時而 shí'ér occasionally

兒/儿

ér
son; child

PICTOGRAPH In its ancient form, 兒 looks like a baby whose skull has not finished forming. 兒 means "small child" and "son." In Regular Script, 兒 resembles a baby with a big head and two thin legs. The simplified form of the character (儿) uses only the bottom part of the traditional form (兒).

兒 象形。像頭囟未合的嬰儿。簡體字儿僅保存兒字的下半部。

甲 𠤎　金 𠤎　篆 兒

兒子 érzi son
兒女 érnǚ sons and daughters; children

女兒 nǚ'ér daughter
哪兒 nǎr where

發/发

fā
to emit; to issue

PICTOPHONETIC CHARACTER The character 發 consists of the radical 弓 (gōng, bow) and the phonetic element 癹 (bá), meaning "to shoot an arrow." The extended meanings of 發 include "to shoot," "issue," "emit," "send out," "utter," "express," etc. The character 發 combines 癶 (bō, two feet) with 殳 (shū, throw a weapon), meaning "to trample" or "tread on." The simplified character 发 is derived from the cursive style of the traditional character 發.

發 形聲。從弓，從癶（bō 兩隻腳相並），從殳（投擲），本義為射箭。簡體字发是繁體字發的草書楷化字。

金 𤼲　篆 發　草

發言 fāyán speak; to make a statement
沙發 shāfā sofa

發燒 fāshāo to have a fever
發財 fācái get rich; make a fortune

法
fǎ
method; way; law

ASSOCIATIVE COMPOUND The character 法 consists of the water radical 氵 and the character 去 (qù, to go). The original meaning of 法 was "to live on a river," and extended meanings include "standard," "law," "method," and "way." Many ancient cities were built on rivers, such that this practice became almost "standard" or "law."

法 會意。金文從人，從口，從水，從鷹（zhì 公牛）。指人趕著牛羊，逐水草而居。逐水草而居是遊牧民族的規矩，世界上不少古老的城市也都沿河而建，因此引申為規律、法律等。篆文簡化，從水，從去。

金 𣲺 篆 𣿳

法律 fǎlù law
辦法 bànfǎ method; means; way

語法 yǔfǎ grammar
法國 fǎguó France

煩/烦
fán
to bother;
to trouble

ASSOCIATIVE COMPOUND The character 煩 consists of 火 (huǒ, fire) and 頁 (yè, originally meaning "head," now meaning "page"), implying that one has fire in one's head. Meanings of 煩 therefore, are "to be vexed," "irritated," "tired of," "trouble," "bother," etc. You can also see 頁 in 題/题 (tí, topic), 預/预 (yù, prepare), and 顏/颜 (yán, face; color). The right part 頁 is simplified to form the simplified character 烦.

煩 會意。從頁（人頭），從火，表示腦袋發熱，煩躁不安。簡體字烦右邊的页由頁簡化而來。

篆 煩

煩人 fánrén to annoy; annoying
煩惱 fánnǎo to be worried; worries

麻煩 máfan troublesome; trouble; to trouble or bother sb.
不耐煩 bú nàifán impatient

返
fǎn
to return

ASSOCIATIVE AND PICTOPHONETIC COMPOUND The character 返 consists of the walk radical 辶 and the semantic and phonetic element 反 (fǎn, reverse; return), meaning "to return," In its ancient forms, 反 depicts a hand next to a cliff, suggesting a person climbing the cliff on hands and knees. Its original meaning is "to turn over," and extended meanings include "contrary," "opposite," "reverse," "return," "oppose," "rebel," etc.

返 會意兼形聲。篆文從辵（辶），從反，反亦聲。意為回、歸。反，會意。甲骨文從厂（hǎn 山崖），從又（右手），表示人以手攀崖。本義為手翻轉。引申義有相反的、顛倒的、回、反對、反抗等。

篆 𫝑 反 甲 𠬝 金 𠬝 篆 𠬝

返回 fǎnhuí to return
返老還童 fǎnlǎo huántóng to rejuvenate

往返 wǎngfǎn to go back and forth; round trip

飯/饭

fàn
meal;
(cooked) rice

篆 餖 草 饭

PICTOPHONETIC CHARACTER The character 飯 consists of the food radical 食 and the phonetic element 反 (fǎn), meaning "cooked rice," "meal," or "food." In its ancient form, 反 depicts a hand next to a cliff, suggesting a person climbing. Its original meaning was "to climb," and extended meanings included "against," "opposite" and "turn over." Note the difference between the food radical 食 and the character for food 食 (shí). The food radical 饣 developed from the cursive of 食 and is always written as 饣 in simplified characters.

飯 形聲。從食，反聲。反，會意。從厂（hǎn 山崖），從又（右手），表示以手攀崖。簡體字中，作為部首的食 一律簡化為饣。饣 由食 的草書楷化而來。

吃飯 chīfàn to have a meal; to eat
午飯 wǔfàn lunch

米飯 mǐfàn (cooked) rice
法國飯 fǎguó fàn French food

房

fáng
house

篆 房

PICTOPHONETIC CHARACTER The character 房 is formed with the radical 戶 (hù, door) and the phonetic indicator 方 (fāng). Originally 房 meant "side room" and later has been extended to mean "room," "house," "building," "a house-like structure," and "a branch of a family (in the past)". In its ancient forms, 戶 represents a single-paneled door, meaning "door" or "household."

房 形聲。從戶，方聲。本義指正室兩邊的房屋。引申為房子、房間、類似房子形狀的東西、家族的一支等。戶，本義指單扇的門。一扇為戶，兩扇為門。戶引申為住戶、人家、門第等。

房子 fángzi house
廚房 chúfáng kitchen

房間 fángjiān room
房租 fángzū rent

放

fàng
to put; to place

金 放 篆 放

PICTOPHONETIC CHARACTER 放 is the combination of the phonetic element 方 (fāng) and the tap/rap radical 攵. Originally 放 means "to expel" or "to exile," from which derive the meanings: "to release," "to set free," "to place," "to put," "to put out to pasture," "to stop," "to light up," "to enlarge," etc. In its ancient forms, 攵 depicts a hand holding a stick. You can see it in the character 教 (jiāo, to teach), and as a component 攵 suggests the physical punishment a teacher would give a student in the past.

放 形聲。金文、篆文從攴 pū（攴指手持棍狀，作為部首，攴通常寫做攵，被稱作反文旁 "tap/rap radical"），方聲。本義為驅逐、流放，引申義有不約束、使自由、放置、放養、結束等。

放假 fàngjià to have a holiday/vacation
放心 fàngxīn be at ease; feel relieved

放羊 fàngyáng to herd sheep
開放 kāifàng to open; to open up (to the outside)

fēi
not; non-

PICTOGRAPH In its ancient forms, 非 resembles the two wings of a flying bird. Since these two wings are opposite to each other, 非 originally meant "to run against," and later came to mean "to not conform with," "wrong," "non-," "not to be," "to blame," etc.

非 象形。甲骨文、金文像鳥展開雙翅飛翔狀。由於兩翅相背，本義為違背，引申為不是、不對、不正確、責備等。

甲 飛 篆 非

非常 fēicháng extraordinary
是非 shìfēi right and wrong; quarrel

非法 fēifǎ illegal
非洲 fēizhōu Africa

啡

fēi
coffee

PICTOPHONETIC CHARACTER The character 啡 was created to transliterate some English words, such as coffee (咖啡) and morphine (嗎啡). 啡 consists of the mouth radical 口 and the phonetic component 非 (fēi). In its ancient form, 非 resembles the two wings of a flying bird. Since these two wings are opposite each other, 非 originally meant "run counter to," and came to mean "not conform with," "wrong," "non-," etc.

啡 譯音用字。非，象形。甲骨文、金文像鳥展開雙翅飛翔狀。由於兩翅相背，本義為違背，引申為不正確等。

咖啡 kāfēi coffee
咖啡館 kāfēiguǎn coffee shop; café

咖啡因 kāfēiyīn caffeine
嗎啡 mǎfēi morphine

飛/飞

fēi
to fly

PICTOGRAPH In Seal Script, 飛 resembles a flying bird flapping its wings, meaning "to fly," "flit," "hover," or when used as an adjective, "swiftly." In Regular Script, the character 飛 combines 升 (shēng, ascend; go up) and two 飞, which look like the two wings of a bird. In the simplified character 飞, only the top part of 飛 remains, still resembling a flying bird.

飛 象形。篆文中上像鳥頭，下像鳥身與展開的雙翅，意為飛翔。簡體字飞僅沿用了飛字的一部分，但仍像一隻飛鳥的輪廓。

篆 飛

飛機 fēijī airplane
飛快 fēikuài very fast; extremely sharp

起飛 qǐfēi (of an aircraft) to take off
飛盤 fēipán flying saucer; Frisbee

費/费

fèi
to spend;
to take
(effort)

ASSOCIATIVE AND PICTOPHONETIC COMPOUND The character 費 combines the cowry shell radical 貝 (bèi) with the semantic and phonetic element 弗 (fú, not), meaning "to spend money." Its extended meanings are "to spend," "to use," "to consume," "to waste," "wasteful," and "fee." Cowry shells were used as currency in ancient times. Therefore characters with 貝 are often related to money. In its ancient forms 弗 depicts the act of straightening arrows by wrapping a string around them, suggesting "to straighten out" or "to rectify." 弗 was borrowed to mean "not" in classical Chinese. The shell radical 貝 is simplified in 费.

費 會意兼形聲。從貝，弗（fú）聲。本義為花去錢財、消費，引申為消耗、費用等。貝，象形。像貝殼形。弗，會意。像捆箭桿而使之變直狀。本義為矯正。在古文中常用來表示否定，類似現代漢語中的"不"。簡化字费屬於偏旁簡化（部首貝簡化）。

金 𧶚 篆 𧶜

小費 xiǎofèi tips
費時 fèishí time-consuming

學費 xuéfèi tuition
費力 fèilì to take great effort

分

fēn
penny; minute

ASSOCIATIVE COMPOUND 分 consists of 八 (bā, divide; eight) and 刀 (dāo, knife), conveying the act of cutting something in half. The primary meanings of 分 are "separate," "divide," "part," while extended meanings include "share," "distribute," "distinguish," "branch," "minute," "fen" (the smallest unit of Chinese currency), etc.

分 會意。上從八，下從刀，指用刀將一物體切為兩半。八的本義是分，後加刀以強化此意。分的意思包括分開、分配、辨別、分支、以及錢幣、時間、成績等單位名。

甲 𢁢 金 分 篆 𠔿

分開 fēnkāi to separate; to part
一分錢 yìfēn qián one cent

分別 fēnbié to leave each other; to distinguish
兩分鐘 liǎng fēnzhōng two minutes

份

fèn
(MW for meal
order, job)

ASSOCIATIVE AND PICTOPHONETIC COMPOUND The character 份 is composed of the person radical 亻 and the semantic and phonetic component 分 (fēn, to divide), referring to "a portion or part (of a whole)." Other meanings of 份 include "unit," "limits," and "one's duty." It is also used as a measure word for meal orders, jobs, gifts, newspapers, reports, contracts, etc.

份 會意兼形聲。從人，從分，分亦聲。是"彬"的異體字，本義為文質兼備。後借用來指整體的一部分、劃分的單位、自身的責任、一些事物（報紙、文件、合同、工作、菜等）的量詞。

篆 𠤵

年份 niánfèn year
月份 yuèfèn month

身份 shēnfèn identity; status
一份報紙 yífèn bàozhǐ a copy of a newspaper

封

fēng
(MW for letters)

ASSOCIATIVE COMPOUND In the Oracle-Bone and Bronze Inscriptions, the right part of the character 封 is a hand (cùn, 寸) and left part depicts a tree on the ground, suggesting the act of planting trees to define a boundary. Extended meanings of 封 are "boundary," "limit," "seal," and "envelope," and it is also used as a measure word for letters (as in mail). In Regular Script, the tree part of 封 is replaced with two 土. You can also see 封 in the character 幫 (bāng, to help).

封 會意。甲骨文、金文中像用手在土地上植樹，用種樹木來劃定疆界。引申為封閉，書信的量詞等。

甲 ⿰ 金 封 篆 封

信封 xìnfēng envelope
封鎖 fēngsuǒ to blockade; to block

封閉 fēngbì to seal; to close
封建 fēngjiàn feudal; feudalistic

服

fú
clothing; to serve

ASSOCIATIVE COMPOUND In the Oracle-Bone Inscriptions, the right part of 服 consists of a person on his or her knees, and a hand, with a plate comprising the left part, signifying a person with a serving plate. The original meaning of 服 is "to serve" or "wait upon," and the extended meanings include "to take," "to wear," "clothing," etc. In Regular Script, the flesh radical 月 replaces the left part of 服, while the right part is the same as the right part of the character 報.

服 會意。甲骨文從凡（盤），從跪人，從手，表示人跪着端盤服侍。衣服為其引申義。

甲 ⿰ 金 ⿰ 篆 朋

服務 fúwù to serve; service
衣服 yīfu clothes

服務員 fúwùyuán waiter; waitress; attendant
舒服 shūfu comfortable; feeling well

腐

fǔ
rotten; to turn bad

PICTOPHONETIC CHARACTER In the character 腐, 肉 (ròu, meat; flesh) suggests the meaning while 府 (fǔ) provides the pronunciation, meaning "to decay" or "rotten." Meat rots easily at normal temperature. Its extended meanings include "corrupt," "obsolete," and the abbreviated form for "tofu." In its ancient forms, 肉 is the pictograph of ribs with meat and means "meat." As a radical, 肉 is usually written as 月. 府 contains the shelter/roof radical 广 (yǎn) and the phonetic indicator 付 (fù, to pay), meaning "mansion," "government office," etc.

腐 形聲。從肉，府聲。本義指東西腐爛，引申義有腐敗、迂腐、豆腐的簡稱等。肉，象形。像切下的一塊帶骨頭的肉形。肉作為偏旁時寫作月。府，形聲。從广（簡易房），付聲。

篆 腐

腐蝕 fǔshí to erode; corrode
腐化 fǔhuà degenerate; corrupt

腐敗 fǔbài rotten; corruption
豆腐 dòufu tofu; bean curd

父

fù
father

PICTOGRAPH In its ancient forms, the character 父 shows a strong hand stretching out holding a stone ax—an important tool and weapon in primitive society—and is a vivid indication of the idea of "father." 父 has been extended to mean "male relative of a senior generation" or "a person who has invented or started something significant." 父親 （fùqin, father) is a rather formal word for father. When Chinese people address their fathers, they usually use 爸爸 (bàba, dad; father) instead of 父親.

父 象形。甲骨文、金文像手持斧做工形。因父親多是一家中辛苦勞作之人，故本義指父親，引申指男性長輩，尤指家族或親戚中的男性长者。也用來指在某一領域或偉業的開創者。

甲 ♂ 金 ♃ 篆 ♀

父親 fùqin father
父母 fùmǔ parents

祖父 zǔfù (paternal) grandfather
伯父 bófù father's brother; uncle

付

fù
to pay

ASSOCIATIVE COMPOUND In the Bronze Inscriptions, the character 付 consists of a person and a hand, signifying a person passing something to another. Therefore, 付 means "hand over," "turn over," or "pay." In Regular Script, 付 is comprised of the person radical 亻 and the character 寸 (cùn, inch). In Seal Script, 寸 combines 又 with 一. 又 means "right hand." 一 symbolizes the place on one's forearm an inch from the wrist, where a traditional Chinese doctor would feel a patient's pulse. Like 又, 寸 often signifies a hand when used within a character.

付 會意。金文從寸（手），從人，意指用手把物交與他人。

金 𠂤 篆 𬱖

付錢 fùqián to pay money
交付 jiāofù to handover; to deliver

付出 fùchū to pay; to invest (energy or time)
對付 duìfu to deal with; to cope

附

fù
to attach; near

PICTOPHONETIC CHARACTER The character 附 is comprised of the mound radical 阝 and the phonetic element 付 (fù), originally referring to "mound." Since a mound sits on the earth, 附 has been extended to mean "to rely on," "be dependent on," "to attach to," "to adhere to," "close to," "near."

附 形聲。從阜（左阝），付聲。本義為小土山，因土山依附于大地，引申為依附、附帶、靠近等。

篆 𨸏

附屬 fùshǔ affiliated with; attached to
附近 fùjìn nearby

附和 fùhé to go along with; to chime in with
附件 fùjiàn attachment

復/复

fù
to duplicate

PICTOPHONETIC CHARACTER 復 consists of the radical 彳 (walk slowly; left step) and the phonetic component 复 (fù). In the Oracle-Bone Inscriptions, 复 looks like a cave dwelling with two exits. There is a foot next to the lower exit, suggesting a person returning to the cave. The first meaning of 复, therefore, was "to return." Its extended meanings include "again," "duplicate," "recover," and "reply." Later the radical 彳 (walk slowly; left step) was added to 复, but the meaning did not change. The simplified character 复 uses the original form.

復 形聲。從彳，复聲，意為往返。复，會意。甲骨文上部像有兩個出口的洞穴，下部從止（腳），表示人出入洞穴，引申為重復。复是復字的古本字，後人加偏旁彳，簡體字恢復古本字的原貌。

甲 金 篆

復習 fùxí to review; revision
復活 fùhuó bring back to life

反復 fǎnfù repeatedly; over and over
復活節 fùhuójié Easter

傅

fù
tutor; instructor

PICTOPHONETIC CHARACTER 傅 is made up of the person radical 亻 and the phonetic symbol 尃 (fū). It originally referred to assisting a ruler in governing a country. Later it came to mean "to assist," "tutor," "teacher," or "instructor." 尃 is the combination of the semantic element 寸 (cùn, inch, though 寸 refers to a hand in 尃) and the phonetic 甫 (fǔ, begin; just now). 尃 is the old form of 敷, its original meaning being "to spread." It has been extended to mean "to apply (medicine)," "to state," or "to announce."

傅 形聲。從亻，尃（fū）聲。本義為輔佐，引申義有教導、老師或傳授技藝的人。尃，形聲。從寸，甫（fǔ，剛才、古代男子的美稱）聲，是敷的古字。敷本義是鋪開，引申義有搽、陳述、傳佈等。

篆

師傅 shīfù master; experienced worker; craftsman
麵包師傅 miànbāo shīfù baker (literally: bread master)

該/该

gāi
should; ought to

PICTOPHONETIC CHARACTER The character 該 consists of the speech radical 言 and the phonetic element 亥 (hài). Its original meaning was "military disciplines," and extended meanings include "should," "ought to," "obliged to," "fated to," "to deserve," or "be someone's turn." In the Oracle-Bone and Bronze Inscriptions, 亥 is a pictograph of a pig without a head and feet, meaning "to cut." In the simplified character 该, the speak radical is simplified.

該 形聲。從言，亥聲。本義指軍中戒律，引申為應當、注定、輪到等。亥，象形。甲骨文、金文像切掉頭、蹄的豬，是"刻"的本字，本義為切割。

篆

應該 yīnggāi ought to; should
活該 huógāi It serves them right!

不該 bùgāi should not; to owe nothing
該死 gāisǐ Damn it!; damned; wretched

乾／干

gān
dry

ASSOCIATIVE AND PICTOPHONETIC COMPOUND 乾 is the combination of the semantic and phonetic element 倝 (gàn, sunrise; dawn) and the signifying 乙 (yǐ, pictograph of a sprout), meaning "dry," "dried," "exhausted," since when the sun rises, sprouts begin to dry. 乾, when pronounced as qián, means "heaven," "sun," "sovereign," and "male." 乙 is a pictograph of a sprout and has been borrowed to mean "second heavenly stem" or "second." 干 (gān; gàn), in its ancient forms, depicts a fork-like weapon, meaning "to offend," "to invade," or "to interfere." 干 is used as the simplified form of 乾 because of their shared pronunciation.

乾 會意兼形聲。從乙，從倝(gàn)，倝亦聲。本義為乾燥，引申義有乾枯、加工製成乾的食品（牛肉乾）、拜認的親屬（乾爹）等。乾讀作qián時是八卦之一，代表天。干，象形。像原始的獵具或武器，引申義有冒犯、干預等。用干做乾的簡化字屬同音替代。

篆 乾　干甲 ⼲　金 ⼲　篆 ⼲

乾洗 gānxǐ dry clean
牛肉乾 niúròugān beef jerky
乾淨 gānjìng clean
乾杯 gānbēi cheers; bottoms up (literally: dry a glass)

感

gǎn
to feel;
to sense

PICTOPHONETIC CHARACTER The character 感 consists of the heart radical 心 (xīn) and the phonetic element 咸 (xián, all), meaning "to move or touch one's heart." Its meanings also include "to move," "to affect," "to sense," "to feel," "feeling," "emotion," "being affected," and "being grateful." In the Oracle-Bone Inscriptions, 咸 is the combination of 戌 (xū, pictograph of a kind of ax weapon) and 口 (mouth), suggesting the soldiers' roar in the battle. It is used to mean "together," "all," or "united" in classical Chinese. Today 咸 is used as the simplified character of 鹹 (xián, salty)

感 形聲。從心，咸聲。本義為感動，引申義有感覺、感情、感染、感謝等。咸，會意。甲骨文從戌（xū），從口，表示眾人在征戰時齊聲呼喊，意為全、都。因為聲音相同，咸現用為鹹的簡化字。

篆 感　咸甲 ⼝　金 咸　篆 咸

感謝 gǎnxiè thank; be grateful
感人 gǎnrén moving; touching
美感 měigǎn sense of beauty; aesthetic perception
感冒 gǎnmào to have a cold

趕／赶

gǎn
to rush for

PICTOPHONETIC CHARACTER The character 趕 is composed of the walk radical 走 and the phonetic element 旱 (hàn), meaning "to catch up with," "to pursue," "to overtake," "to rush for," "to drive away," or "to expel." 旱 combines the sun radical 日 with the phonetic component 干 (gān), meaning "drought." In the Oracle-Bone Inscriptions, 干 depicts a fork-like weapon, which means "to offend," "to invade," or "to interfere." Today 干 is also used as the simplified character of 乾 (gān, dry; waterless). The 日 part in 趕 is removed to form the simplified character 赶.

趕 形聲。從走，旱聲。本義為野獸、牲畜翹著尾巴奔跑，引申義有追趕、趕上、趕快去做、驅趕等。旱，形聲。從日，干聲，意指乾旱。干現在也用為乾的簡化字。簡化字赶去除趕字中的日。金元已見此字。

篆 趕

趕上 gǎnshàng to catch up with
趕走 gǎnzǒu to drive away; to kick away
趕快 gǎnkuài at once; quickly; to hurry up
追趕 zhuīgǎn to pursue; to chase after

剛／刚

gāng
just now

ASSOCIATIVE COMPOUND In the Oracle-Bone Inscriptions, the character 剛 depicts a knife (right part) next to a net (left part), indicating the act of cutting a net. Its original meaning was "sharp and solid," and extended meanings are "indomitable," "firm," and "strong." 剛 may also be an adverb meaning "just," "just now," "only," "barely," etc. In Seal Script, 剛 becomes a pictophonetic character, consisting of the knife radical 刂 and the phonetic component 岡 (gāng, the ridge of a mountain). The simplified version of 岡 is 冈, which is used to form the simplified character 刚.

剛 會意。甲骨文以刀斷網來表示物體堅硬。本義指堅硬、堅利，引申義有剛毅、旺盛、剛才、正好等。剛在篆文中變為形聲字，從刂，岡（gāng）聲。岡，會意。篆文從山從网，指山梁如網狀。意为山脊。岡的簡體字為冈，元代已見。簡化字剛左邊的冈簡化，右邊不變。

甲 𠚣 金 𠚣 篆 剛

剛健 gāngjiàn vigorous; robust
剛才 gāngcái just now

陽剛 yánggāng manly; masculine
剛好 gānghǎo just right; happen to be

港

gǎng
harbor

ASSOCIATIVE AND PICTOPHONETIC COMPOUND The character 港 consists of the water radical 氵 and the semantic and phonetic component 巷 (xiàng, alley; lane), originally referring to "tributary" or "small stream." Its extended meanings are "port," "harbor," or "bay." Today it is also used as the abbreviated term for Hong Kong. In Seal Script, 巷 contains 共 (gòng, common; share) on the top and 邑 (yì, city; district) at the bottom, conveying the meanings of "alley" or "lane," since they are shared by the residents of a city. In Regular Script, 邑 is simplified in 巷.

港 會意兼形聲。從氵，從巷，巷亦聲。本義指與江河湖泊相通的小河道，引申義有港口、港灣、香港的簡稱。巷，會意。意指較窄的街道、胡同。篆文上從共，下從邑，表示巷子是城中大家共用的道路。楷書巷字中邑簡化。

巷 篆 𦉶

海港 hǎigǎng seaport; harbor
香港 xiānggǎng Hong Kong

港口 gǎngkǒu port; harbor
港幣 gǎngbì Hong Kong dollar

高

gāo
tall; high

PICTOGRAPH In the Oracle-Bone and Bronze Inscriptions, the character 高 looks like a tall building with a tower above and walls with a gate underneath, conveying the meanings "tall," "high," and "above average." When you memorize the character, try to imagine a two-story building with a gate on each level. Don't forget the tower on the top!

高 象形。像高聳的樓臺。

甲 髙 金 髙 篆 高

高大 gāodà tall; lofty
提高 tígāo to raise; to increase

高興 gāoxìng happy; glad
高級 gāojí high level; high grade; advanced

糕

gāo
cake

PICTOPHONETIC CHARACTER 糕 consists of the rice radical 米 and the phonetic 羔 (gāo, lamb), meaning "cake." The character 羔 contains the goat/sheep component (羊 yáng) on top and the fire radical (灬) underneath, referring to a lamb being roasted over fire. Compare 羔 with the character 美 (měi, beautiful).

糕 形聲。從米，羔聲，本義指用米粉、麵粉或豆粉製成的糕餅。羔，甲骨文、金文上從羊，下從火，表示烤小羊。本義為小羊羔。

篆 糕 羔 甲 金 篆

蛋糕 dàngāo cake
糕點 gāodiǎn pastry; cake

年糕 niángāo rice cake
糟糕 zāogāo too bad; terrible

告

gào
to tell; to inform

ASSOCIATIVE COMPOUND In the Oracle-Bone Inscriptions, 告 is comprised of 牛 (niú, ox) and 口 (kǒu, mouth), referring to the sound an ox makes. Extended meanings include "inform," "tell," "notify," "declare," "sue," etc. In its ancient form, the character 牛 depicts an ox head as viewed from the front.

告 會意。甲骨文從口，從牛。本義為牛叫，引申為上報、告訴、佈告等。

甲 金 篆

告訴 gàosu to tell; to inform
廣告 guǎnggào advertisement

報告 bàogào to report; report; paper; lecture
警告 jǐnggào to warn; to admonish

哥

gē
elder brother

ASSOCIATIVE COMPOUND In the Oracle-Bone Inscriptions, 可 (kě) resembles a mouth exhaling, and meant "approve" or "okay." The character 哥 consists of two 可 characters, one on the top of the other, showing someone opening his or her mouth to sing. Therefore, the original meaning of 哥 was "to sing," but later came to mean "elder brother." For the word "sing," 欠 (qiàn, yawn; breathe) is added to the right part of 哥 (歌 gē, sing). Does anyone have a big brother who always opens his big mouth to sing?

哥 會意。從二可。可有歡樂的意思，表示聲聲相連歌不斷，樂在其中，是歌的本字。后稱兄為哥，遂加欠作歌。

篆 哥

哥哥 gēge older brother
大哥 dàgē eldest brother

哥們兒 gēmenr Brothers!; brethren; dude (colloquial)
二哥 èrgē second brother

歌

gē
song

PICTOPHONETIC CHARACTER The character 歌 is composed of the radical 欠 (qiàn, to yawn; breathe) and the phonetic component 哥 (gē, elder brother), meaning "song" or "sing." In the Oracle-Bone Inscriptions, 欠 looks like a kneeling person yawning or breathing with an open mouth. Characters containing 欠 often have something to do with the mouth, for instance, 吹 (chuī, blow), 歎/叹 (tàn, sigh).

歌 形聲。從欠（人張口出氣），哥聲。本義為高聲吟誦。

金  篆 

唱歌 chànggē to sing a song
歌手 gēshǒu singer; vocalist
歌劇 gējù opera
歌星 gēxīng singing star; famous singer

個/个

gè
(MW for general people/things)

PICTOPHONETIC CHARACTER 個 consists of the person radical 亻 and the phonetic element 固 (gù, solid; consolidate). 個 is a common measure word for people and other nouns. 固 has 囗 (wéi, enclose) outside and 古 (gǔ, ancient) inside, indicating an invincible city. 古 is the combination of 十 (shí, ten) and 口 (kǒu, mouth), suggesting the way in which ancient stories are passed down orally. Thus, 古 means "ancient." Many complex Chinese characters are combinations of a few simple characters, so you can learn several characters at once. 個 was originally written as 个, and the simplified character 个 restores this original form.

個 形聲。從人，固聲。固，從囗，從古，指城四周有墻保護，便可永固不破，引申為堅硬，牢固等。个 象形。竹像兩根並生的竹子，个為一根竹子，本用以指竹子的數量，擴大範圍以後用作量詞。後另造“個”字，簡化後仍為“个”。

篆 

這個 zhège this; this one
個性 gèxìng personality; individual character
個人 gèrén individual; personal
個子 gèzi height; stature; build

給/给

gěi
to give

PICTOPHONETIC CHARACTER 給 consists of the silk radical 糹 and the phonetic symbol 合 (hé, close). Since silk is considered a good gift, 給 is used to mean "to provide," "give," "grant," and "for the benefit of." In its ancient form, the character 合 resembled a container with a lid, meaning "to close," "shut," "get together," and "match." The simplified character 给 contains the simplified form of the silk radical.

給 形聲。從糸，合聲。本義為豐足，引申為供給、給与等。合，上像容器的蓋子，下像容器本身。蓋子蓋在容器上，意指合攏。簡體字给的部首簡化。

篆 

交給 jiāogěi to hand over; to turn in
借給 jiègěi to lend to someone
送給 sònggěi to send; to give as a present
給力 gěilì cool; nifty; awesome

跟

gēn
with; and

PICTOPHONETIC CHARACTER 跟 has the foot radical 足 and the phonetic component 艮 (gēn). 跟 originally referred to "heel," from which the meanings "follow," "with," and "and" derived. You can also see 艮 in the character 很 (hěn, very). In the Oracle-Bone and Bronze Inscriptions, the upper part of 艮 is a big eye and the lower part is a person, indicating someone turning back to stare. The meanings of 艮 are "disobey," "tough," "blunt," and "straightforward."

跟 形聲。從足，艮聲。本義為腳後跟，引申為跟隨，還可作連詞。

篆 跟　艮　甲 🧍　金 🧍　篆 艮

腳跟 jiǎogēn heel
跟隨 gēnsuí to follow

高跟鞋 gāogēnxié high- heeled shoes
跟蹤 gēnzōng to follow someone's tracks; to tail

更

gèng
even more

gēng
to alternate

ASSOCIATIVE COMPOUND In the Oracle-Bone Inscriptions, the character 更 resembles a hand using a spatula to turn a pancake over on a griddle, meaning "to change" or "to alternate" (pronounced gēng). 更 can be used as an adverb meaning "even more" and "furthermore" (pronounced gèng). You will also encounter 更 in the character 便 (biàn, convenient).

更 會意甲骨文從攴（手持鏟），從丙（餅鐺），意指持鏟翻餅。引申為改換、更加等。

甲 🖐　金 🖐　篆 🖐

更新 gēngxīn to update
更衣室 gēngyīshì fitting room; locker room

更正 gēngzhèng to correct
更加 gèngjiā even more

公

gōng
public

ASSOCIATIVE COMPOUND In the Oracle-Bone and Bronze Inscriptions, the upper part of 公 is 八 (bā, eight) and the lower part resembles a container. The original meaning of 八 was to divide something into two parts. Therefore, 公 means to evenly divide things in a container. The extended meanings of 公 are "fair," "impartial," "public," "collective," etc.

公 會意。篆文從八（分），從厶（sī 私）。甲骨文、金文從八，從口（指容器口），表示平均分配容器中的東西。

甲 公　金 公　篆 公

辦公 bàn'gōng to do office work
公園 gōngyuán park

公司 gōngsī company; firm; corporation
公寓 gōngyù apartment

The Way of Chinese Characters

69

G - K

功

gōng
skill

ASSOCIATIVE AND PICTOPHONETIC COMPOUND The character 功 consists of the radical and phonetic element 工 (gōng, work) and the signifying component 力 (lì, strength; power), suggesting one working with all one's strength. The meanings of 功 include "meritorious deed," "skill," "effect," and "success."

功 會意兼形聲。從力，
從工；工亦聲。力，
盡力；工，工作。盡力
工作必有功勞功績。

金 𢀖 篆 𠛥

用功 yònggōng diligent; to study hard
功課 gōngkè homework; classwork

功夫 gōngfu skill; kungfu
成功 chénggōng success; to succeed

共

gòng
altogether

ASSOCIATIVE COMPOUND In the Oracle-Bone and Bronze Inscriptions, the character 共 represents two hands holding a piece of jade, meaning to "present jade or offerings." Since one uses both hands to present a gift, 共 extends to mean "together," "altogether," "in company," "common," "share," etc.

共 會意。甲骨文、金文
像用雙手捧一塊碧玉形。
本義為供奉，供給，引
申義有拱手、環繞、
合計、共同等。

甲 𦥑 金 𦥑 篆 𦥑

一共 yígòng altogether
共同 gòngtóng common; jointly

公共 gōnggòng public
共和國 gònghéguó republic

狗

gǒu
dog

PICTOPHONETIC CHARACTER The character 狗 is made of the dog radical 犭 and the phonetic 句 (jù; gōu). 狗 originally meant "puppy," but later refers to all dogs. In ancient writing systems, 句 combines the mouth radical 口 and the phonetic 丩 (jiū, hook; entangled). Originally 句 referred to the rises and falls of intonation, from which the Chinese derived the meaning "sentence." The dog is a beloved animal in Western culture, but in Chinese culture it is often regarded as unpleasant. Thus 狗 (like other characters with the dog radical 犭) carries with it some negative connotations.

狗 形聲。篆文從犬
（犭），句（gōu）聲。
《说文》曰：大者為犬，
小者為狗。狗本義為狗
崽，後泛指犬。句，會意
兼形聲。古文字從口，丩
（jiū，曲折）聲。本義為
語調曲折，引申為句子。
中文中有不少對狗，
或像狗的行為的蔑稱，
如狗腿子、狗奴才。

篆 𤟥

狼狗 lánggǒu wolf dog; wolfhound
熱狗 règǒu hot dog

走狗 zǒugǒu running dog; lackey
狗腿子 gǒutuǐzi henchman; hired thug

夠/够
gòu
enough

PICTOPHONETIC CHARACTER 夠 consists of the signifying component 多 (duō, many; a lot) and the phonetic symbol 句 (gōu/jù), meaning "enough," "more than enough," etc. This character can be written in two ways: 夠 or 够. In its ancient forms, the character 多 looks like two pieces of meat, meaning "many," "a large amount," or "extra." In Regular Script, 多 became one 夕 (xī, sunset; evening) on top of another 夕. In ancient writing systems, 句 combines the mouth radical 口 and the phonetic 丩 (jiū, hook) to refer to rises and falls of intonation. Later 句 came to mean "sentence."

夠 形聲。從多，句聲。主要意思指從數量上滿足需要。多，會意。多字像兩塊肉形。古時祭祀用肉，用兩塊以表示多。句，會意兼形聲。古文字從口，丩（jiū 纏繞、曲折）聲。本義為語調曲折，引申為句子。

多 甲 金 篆

足夠 zúgòu enough; sufficient
夠吃 gòuchī enough to eat
夠用 gòuyòng enough to use/spend
夠本 gòuběn to break even

古
gǔ
ancient

ASSOCIATIVE COMPOUND The character 古 is the combination of 十 (shí, ten) and 口 (kǒu, mouth), suggesting an ancient time when stories were passed down orally from people to people. Thus, the meanings of 古 are "ancient," "age-old," "old," "classical," "paleo-," and "antiquity."

古 會意。從十，從口。十意指多，用很多人以口口相傳的事來表示年代遠久。在有文字之前，古代的事只能靠口口相傳。

金 古 篆 古

古代 gǔdài ancient times
古蹟 gǔjī historic site
古人 gǔrén the ancients
考古 kǎogǔ archaeology

顧/顾
gù
to look after;
to attend to

PICTOPHONETIC CHARACTER 顧 is composed of 頁 (yè, head; page) and the phonetic component 雇 (gù). Its original meaning was "to turn and look" or "to look back". The extended meanings include "to look at," "to look after," "to attend to," "to care for," "to visit," etc. In the Oracle-Bone Inscriptions, 頁 depicts a person with an oversized head and originally meant "head." 雇 combines 隹 (zhuī, short-tailed bird) and 戶 (hù, household), referring to a bird that flies to peasants' homes in Spring, when laborers are hired to work the fields. 雇 extended to mean "to hire." The simplified 顾 derives from the cursive style of 顧.

顧 形聲。從頁，雇聲。本義為回頭看。引申義有看、照顧、光顧等。頁，象形。甲骨文像頭部突出的人形，本義為頭，引申為書頁。雇，從隹，從戶，戶亦聲。本義是指一種飛到農戶家以示農耕季節開始的候鳥，引申為雇用。簡化字顾是顧字的草書楷化字。

篆 顧 草 顾 頁 甲 金 篆 草

顧問 gùwèn consultant
照顧 zhàogu to take care of
回顧 huígù to look back; to review
顧客 gùkè customer

瓜
guā
melon; gourd

PICTOGRAPH In the Bronze Inscriptions, the character 瓜 depicts a gourd under vines, representing the gourd family, which includes melon, squash, cucumber, and pumpkin. 瓜 can also be used for gourd-shaped things, such as "腦瓜 (nǎoguā, skull; head; brain)," "瓜皮帽 (guā pí mào, skullcap resembling half a melon)."

瓜 象形。金文像籐蔓上結的一個瓜形。本義為葫蘆類植物果實的統稱。種類很多，譬如西瓜、南瓜、冬瓜、黃瓜等。引申義有像瓜一樣的東西、分割等。

金 [金文] 篆 [篆文]

黃瓜 huángguā cucumber
南瓜 nánguā pumpkin

西瓜 xīguā watermelon
瓜果 guāguǒ melons and fruits

拐
guǎi
to turn

PICTOPHONETIC CHARACTER In Seal Script, the character 拐 is composed of the hand radical 扌 and the phonetic element 另 (咼 guǎ). 拐 originally meant "walking stick" and later came to mean "cripple," "swindle," "to abduct," "to turn," or "to change direction." In the Oracle-Bone Inscriptions, 咼 looks like a piece of bone without meat on it. It is used to mean "to cut off flesh from the bones." 另 was an alternative form of 咼 in ancient times.

拐 形聲。從扌，另（咼/另 guǎ）聲。本義為拐棍，引申義有瘸、跛行，騙走人或財物，轉變方向等。

篆 [篆文] 另 甲 [甲骨文] 篆 [篆文]

拐棍 guǎigùn walking stick
拐彎 guǎiwān to go round a curve; to turn

拐角 guǎijiǎo corner; turning
拐賣 guǎimài to abduct and sell

關/关
guān
to involve; to close

ASSOCIATIVE COMPOUND In the Bronze Inscriptions, the character 關 looks like a door with a bolt. In Seal Script, the component inside 關 resembles two strands of rope with which to tie the doors. The original meaning of 關 was "door bar," from which derived the meanings: "to close," "to shut," "frontier pass," "key point," "to concern," "to involve," "to be related," etc. 関 is a variant form of 關, and the simplified character 关 adopts only the part inside 関.

關 會意。金文從門，中間像門閂之形。篆文門內改為像以繩索把門繫住。本義為門閂，引申義有關閉、關卡、關鍵、關聯等。関是關的俗體字，簡化字关進一步去掉了門。

金 [金文] 篆 [篆文]

關燈 guāndēng to turn off the light
關係 guānxi relation

海關 hǎiguān customs
關心 guānxīn to care about

館／馆

guǎn
place; building

ASSOCIATIVE AND PICTOPHONETIC COMPOUND 館 consists of the food radical 飠 and the phonetic and signifying element 官 (guān, official), and means "accommodation for guests." In its ancient form, 官 is the combination of the roof radical 宀 and 𠂤 (duī, hill). Its original meaning was "government office," with the extended meanings of "public," "official," etc. In the simplified character 馆, the food radical is simplified.

館 會意兼形聲。從食，官聲，意指供人飲食住宿娛樂的地方。官，會意。從宀，從𠂤，本義為官府。簡體字馆的部首簡化。

官 甲  金 篆

飯館 fàn'guǎn restaurant
茶館 cháguǎn teahouse

圖書館 túshūguǎn library
旅館 lǚguǎn hotel

慣／惯

guàn
to be used to

PICTOPHONETIC CHARACTER The character 慣 consists of the vertical heart radical 忄 and the phonetic component 貫 (guàn), meaning "to be used to," or "indulge." 貫 combines 毌 (guàn, string; pierce) with 貝 (bèi, cowry shell), meaning "pass through," "link together," or "a string of 1,000 copper coins." In the simplified character 惯, only the shell part 貝 has been simplified.

慣 形聲。從忄，貫聲，意為習慣。貫，會意兼形聲。從毌（貫穿），從貝，表示把錢幣穿成一串。簡體字惯中的貝簡化為贝。

貫 篆

習慣 xíguàn habit; custom; be accustomed to   慣用語 guàn yòngyǔ commonly used phrase

---

廣／广

guǎng
wide; vast

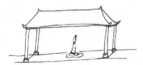

PICTOPHONETIC CHARACTER The character 廣 consists of 广 (yǎn, shelter; shed) and the phonetic component 黃 (huáng). Its original meaning was "a hall without walls," from which the Chinese derived the meanings "spacious," "wide," "vast," "extensive," "to expand," and "to broaden." In the Oracle-Bone Inscriptions, the character 黃 looks like a pendant with a knot above and tassels beneath, meaning "ring-shaped jade pendant." Since this kind of ornament was usually made of yellow jade, "yellow" is the extended meaning of 黃. 广 is used as the simplified form of 廣, although originally they were different characters.

廣 形聲。從广（yǎn），黃聲。本義為四周無壁的大屋，引申為廣闊、推廣、廣泛等。广（yǎn），象形。古文字像是依山崖建造的房屋，本義為寬大的房屋。有广字旁的字本義常與房屋、建築有關。广和廣原本不同義，是兩個字。現用广來作為廣的簡化字。

金 篆

廣大 guǎngdà vast; numerous
廣告 guǎnggào commercial; advertisement

廣場 guǎngchǎng square; plaza
廣東 guǎngdōng Guangdong Province

貴/贵

guì
honorable; expensive

ASSOCIATIVE COMPOUND In Seal Script, the top part of 貴 delineates two hands holding something and lower part is a cowry shell. Since cowry shells were used as money in ancient times, the basic meanings of 貴 are "valuable," "expensive," and "costly." Extended meanings include "noble," "honorable," etc. In the simplified version of the character 贵, the radical 贝 (bèi, cowry shell) is developed from the cursive style of 貝. As either radical or character, 貝 is written as 贝 in simplified characters.

貴 會意。篆文上像雙手捧物，下從貝。貝代表錢，凸顯出手捧之物十分貴重。簡體字贵下部的贝是繁體貝的草書楷化字。

篆

高貴 gāoguì noble; honorable
貴賓 guìbīn honored guest; VIP

可貴 kěguì valuable; precious
貴姓 guìxìng (honorable) surname

國/国

guó
country; nation

ASSOCIATIVE COMPOUND The character 國 represents its meaning in a concise and vivid way. Within the character 國, 囗 (wéi, enclose) stands for the boundary or moat surrounding a city, 一 represents the land, 口 (kǒu, mouth) the population, and 戈 (gē, dagger-axe) the weapon protecting the country. In the simplified character 国, the inside of the enclosure is replaced by the character 玉 (yù, jade), as an emperor's jade seal represents the highest authority of a country.

國 會意。囗像城池，一為土地，口指人口，戈用以守衛。簡體字將中間部分改為玉字。國有玉璽，是會意字。

甲 金 篆

國家 guójiā country; nation
國際 guójì international

中國 zhōngguó China
外國 wàiguó foreign country

果

guǒ
fruit; result

PICTOGRAPH In the Oracle-Bone Inscriptions, 果 is a pictograph of a tree with three fruits. In the Bronze Inscriptions, these three fruits become one large one. In Seal Script, this large fruit is replaced with the character 田 (tián, field), which deviates somewhat from the original meaning.

果 象形。像樹上結出的果實。甲骨文樹上有三個果子，金文變成一個大果子。在楷書中方形化則變成了田字。

甲 金 篆

水果 shuǐguǒ fruit
成果 chéngguǒ achievement; gain

蘋果 píngguǒ apple
如果 rúguǒ if; in case

過/过

guò
to pass

PICTOPHONETIC CHARACTER The character 過 is composed of the walk radical 辶 and the phonetic element 咼 (guō), meaning "pass," "cross," "spend," "go beyond," "go through," "to celebrate," " to live," etc. 咼 combines 口 (kǒu, mouth) and 冎 (guǎ, dismember; slit), meaning "mouth that goes awry." The simplified character 过 developed from the cursive style of 過 with 寸 replacing 咼.

過 形聲。從辶，咼聲。咼，形聲。從口，從冎（殘缺）；冎亦聲。咼本義指歪嘴。簡體字过用寸代替咼，是由繁體字過的草書楷化而來。

甲 金 篆 蝸 草 通

過來 guòlai to come over
過分 guòfèn excessive; undue

過去 guòqu to go over; to pass by
過年 guònián to celebrate Chinese New Year

孩

hái
child

PICTOPHONETIC CHARACTER 孩 consists of the radical 子 (zǐ, child; son) and the phonetic symbol 亥 (hài, cut). Its original meaning was children's laughter. Later it came to simply mean "child." In the Oracle-Bone and Bronze Inscriptions, 亥 is a pictograph of a pig without a head and feet, meaning "to cut." In Regular Script, the character 亥 still resembles a pig, but one with its head on the top and two legs and a tail as the lower part.

孩 形聲。從子，亥聲。本義為小兒笑聲，引申為兒童，孩子。亥，象形。甲骨文像切掉頭、蹄的豬，是"刻"的本字，本義為切割。

篆 孩 亥甲 丂 金 丏

孩子 háizi child
女孩 nǚhái girl

小孩 xiǎohái child; kid
男孩 nánhái boy

還/还

hái
still; yet

huán
to exchange

PICTOPHONETIC CHARACTER The character 還 consists of the walk radical 辶 and the phonetic component 瞏 (qióng/huán, look around with fear; lonely). The original meaning of 還 was "go back" or "return" (pronounced huán). Today it is also used as the adverb "still" (pronounced hái). In Seal Script, 瞏 is the combination of an eye 目 on the top and the phonetic symbol 袁 (yuán) underneath. 袁 looks like a garment with a jade ring in the middle, meaning "long garment." In the simplified character 还, 不 replaces 瞏.

還 形聲。從辶，瞏（qióng/huán）聲，返回、交還之意。亦用作副詞，表示持續。瞏，回首驚視之意。簡體字还用不取代瞏。元代已有此字。

金 瞏 篆 還

還是 háishi or; still; had better
還好 háihǎo not bad; fortunately

還有 háiyǒu furthermore; also
還給 huángěi return to

海

hǎi
sea

PICTOPHONETIC CHARACTER 海 consists of the water radical 氵 and the phonetic element 每 (měi), meaning "sea," "a great number of people or things coming together," "countless," "great capacity," etc. In the Oracle-Bone Inscriptions, the character 每 depicts a woman 女 with featherlike ornaments on her head, originally referring to female beauty.

海 形聲。金文從水，每聲。每，會意。甲骨文、金文均像婦女頭戴裝飾物，表示女子之美，後借用為每天的每。

金 㳟　篆 㴬

上海 Shànghǎi Shanghai
海軍 hǎijūn navy

海濱 hǎibīn beach
海關 hǎiguān costums

寒

hán
cold

ASSOCIATIVE COMPOUND In the Bronze Inscriptions, the character 寒 looks like a person covered in straw hiding inside a house, and the two strokes at the bottom stand for ice. The original meaning of 寒 was "cold," and extended meanings are "tremble," "poor," and "needy."

寒 會意。金文、篆文中像人躲在屋內草中取暖，下面兩橫代表冰，表示屋內極為寒冷。

金 㝱　篆 㝱

寒冷 hánlěng frigid; bitterly cold
寒假 hánjià winter vacation

寒冬 hándōng severe winter
寒風 hánfēng cold wind

漢/汉

hàn
Chinese ethnicity

PICTOPHONETIC character The character 漢 contains the water radical 氵 and the phonetic component 堇 (jǐn). Originally 漢 referred to a tributary of the Yangtze River. 漢 is also the character for the Han Dynasty (206 B.C.–220 A.D.), considered a golden age of ancient Chinese history. Of China's 56 ethnic groups, the Han (漢) has the largest population. 漢 also refers to the Chinese language of the Han people. In the simplified character 汉, 又 replaces 堇. The same simplification can be found in the character 難 (nán, difficult), with the simplified form 难.

漢 形聲。篆文從水，難聲。本義為水名，即漢水。又有漢朝、漢族、漢語等詞。簡體字汉的簡化方法與难（難）字相同，都是以又來替代堇。明清已見此字。

篆 㶏

漢語 hànyǔ Chinese language
漢學 hànxué sinology

漢字 hànzì Chinese characters
漢人 hànrén the Han people

航

háng
to navigate

PICTOPHONETIC CHARACTER The character 航 is formed by the signifying component 舟 (zhōu, boat) and the phonetic component 亢 (kàng), originally referring to large ark-like boats. Later extended meanings include "boat," "ship," "to navigate," "to sail," and "to fly." In its ancient forms, 舟 is the pictograph of a small boat. 亢 looks like a man standing erect, meaning "haughty," "high," "firm," and "excessive." For the evolution of 舟, see the entry for 搬 (bān, to move).

航 形聲。從舟，亢 (kàng) 聲。本義為方舟，引申義有船、航海或航空。舟，象形。像小船形。亢，象形，像人挺立形，意有高、高傲、強硬、過度等。

篆 航　亢 甲 金 篆 亢

航海 hánghǎi sailing; navigate; voyage
航班 hángbān flight

航空 hángkōng aviation; voyage
民航 mínháng civil aviation

好

hǎo
good; fine

hào
to like

ASSOCIATIVE COMPOUND In the Oracle-Bone and Bronze Inscriptions, the character 好 shows a woman holding a child. In traditional Chinese society, giving birth to children, especially sons, was a married woman's main responsibility. The inability to bear children was considered a legitimate reason for a husband to divorce his wife. Mencius said: "There are three major sins against filial piety, and the worst is to have no heir." It follows that women who had sons were considered good. The components 女 (nǚ, female) and 子 (zǐ, child) can both be found the **Basic Radicals** Section.

好 會意。從女、從子，以能生兒育女使家族興旺的婦女為好。

甲 好 金 篆

好吃 hǎochī tasty; delicious
好看 hǎokàn good-looking

友好 yǒuhǎo friendly; amicable
好像 hǎoxiàng as if; to seem like

G - K

號／号

hào
number

ASSOCIATIVE AND PICTOPHONETIC COMPOUND The character 號 is the combination of 号 (hào, cry) and 虎 (hǔ, tiger), indicating the roar of a tiger. The original meaning of 號 was "shout," and extended meanings include "command," "order," "mark," "number," and "date." The character 号 consists of 口 (kǒu, mouth) and 丂 (kǎo, breathe), meaning "to cry." In the Oracle-Bone Inscriptions the character 虎 vividly depicts a tiger. In Regular Script, 虎 is made up of 虍 (hū, tiger radical) and 几 (jī, small table). The simplified 号 only retains the left part of 號.

號 會意兼形聲。從号，從虎；号亦聲。本義為虎叫，引申為呼叫、日期等。号像口中出氣，意指呼喊。虎，象形。像老虎之形。簡體字号僅保留繁體的左邊一半。

篆 號　虎 甲 金 篆

號碼 hàomǎ number
口號 kǒuhào slogan

信號 xìnhào signal
挂號 guàhào to register (a letter etc.)

喝

hē
to drink

PICTOPHONETIC CHARACTER The character 喝 combines the mouth radical 口 and the phonetic component 曷 (hé, how; why; when), and means "to drink." 曷 is a pictophonetic character that consists of the radical 曰 (yuē, say) and the phonetic symbol 匃 (gài, beg; beggar).

喝 形聲。從口，曷聲，有呼喊，吸食液體等意。曷，形聲。從曰（説話），從匃（乞求），表示喝止、疑問等。

篆 喝

吃喝 chīhē food and drink; diet   喝酒 hējiǔ to drink (alcohol)

合

hé
to suit; to fit

ASSOCIATIVE COMPOUND In its ancient forms, the character 合 has a lid 亼 (jí) on top of a container, with 口 in the lower part, meaning "to close" or "shut." Extended meanings include "combine," "join," "suit," "agree," etc.

合 會意。下像盒子，上像盒蓋，合在一起表示合攏。

甲 〔合〕 金 〔合〕 篆 〔合〕

合適 héshì suitable; fitting   合作 hézuò to cooperate; to collaborate
聯合 liánhé unite; alliance   聯合國 liánhéguó United Nations

和

hé
and;
harmonious

huo
warm

PICTOPHONETIC CHARACTER 和 is a simplification of the character 龢. In its ancient form, 龢 has 龠 (yuè, the pictograph of a flute-like instrument) as the signifying component and 禾 (hé, a pictograph of a ripe rice plant) as the phonetic symbol, meaning "harmonious." Today it also means "echo," "and," "peace," "mild," etc. In Regular Script, 龠 is replaced by 口 (kǒu, mouth) since one uses one's mouth to play wind instruments (like flutes). 禾 remains part of the character today, but is found on the left side instead of the right.

和 形聲。甲骨文從龠，禾聲，意指樂聲和諧。引申為和諧、協調、和睦、和好等意，也可用作連詞。古文簡化，改龠為口。龠，像一由多條竹管做成的笙簫。禾，像一株禾形。上像禾穗，下像根部。

甲 〔龢〕 金 〔龢〕 篆 〔龢〕

和平 hépíng peace; peaceful   和尚 héshang Buddhist monk
和諧 héxié harmonious; harmony   暖和 nuǎnhuo warm

黑

hēi
black

ASSOCIATIVE COMPOUND In the Bronze Inscriptions, the character 黑 depicts a sweaty person with a smoke-blackened face. In Regular Script, the top part of 黑 resembles the blackened face, while the middle part is 土, which stands for the ground, and the bottom part is the fire radical 灬. You will also see 黑 in the character 點 (diǎn, dot; o'clock).

黑 會意。金文字形像被煙熏火烤，大汗淋漓、滿面污垢的人。

金 篆

黑色 hēisè black (colour)
黑板 hēibǎn blackboard

黑人 hēirén black people
天黑 tiānhēi to get dark

很

hěn
very

ASSOCIATIVE AND PICTOPHONETIC COMPOUND In the Oracle-Bone and Bronze Inscriptions, the upper part of 艮(gěn) is one large eye and the lower part a person, indicating someone turning back to stare at something. The meanings of 艮 include "disobey," "tough," "blunt," and "straightforward." The character 很 has the radical 彳 (left step; walk slowly) and the character 艮 (gěn) as both the phonetic and signifying component. 很 originally meant "defy," "violate," or "fierce," but today is used as the adverb "very" or "quite."

很 會意兼形聲。從彳（走路，道路），艮（gěn）聲，指人在走路時回頭瞪眼怒視。本義指不順從、凶狠，引申義為程度高。艮，會意。甲骨文從人，像人回首瞪視狀。

艮 甲 金 篆

很好 hěnhǎo very good
很多 hěnduō many

很少 hěnshǎo very little; seldom
Adj. 得很 Adj. dehěn very Adj.

紅／红

hóng
red

PICTOPHONETIC CHARACTER The character 紅 consists of the silk radical 糸 and the phonetic element 工 (gōng). The original meaning of 紅 was "pink silk," and later came to mean "red." 工 (gōng) resembles a carpenter's square and means "labor," "work," or "craft." The silk radical is simplified to form the character 红.

紅 形聲。從糸，工聲。本義為粉紅色的絲綢，後泛指紅色。顏色常用絲帛表示，故從糸。簡體字红的偏旁纟是由繁體糸簡化而來。

篆

紅酒 hóngjiǔ red wine
紅茶 hóngchá black tea

紅綠燈 hónglǜdēng traffic light
紅旗 hóngqí red flag

後／后

hòu
after; behind

ASSOCIATIVE COMPOUND The character 後 consists of 彳 (walk slowly; left step), 幺 (yāo, string; tiny), and 夊 (suī, left foot), suggesting someone walking behind another with one's left foot tied by a string or rope. The meanings of 後 include "behind," "back," "after," "later," and "last." Originally 后 (hòu) was used to mean empress. Today 后 is also used as the simplified form of the traditional character 後.

後 會意。從彳（半條街），從幺（繩），從夊（suī 腳）。表示足被繩系住，走在後面。簡體字用后（皇后的后）替代後，屬同音替代字。

甲 缓 金 後 篆 復

以後 yǐhòu after; later (in the future)	然後 ránhòu then; afterwards
後來 hòulái later (in the past)	最後 zuìhòu last; finally

候

hòu
time; season; await

PICTOPHONETIC CHARACTER In Seal Script, 候 consists of the person radical 亻 and the phonetic component 矦 (hóu, marquis), meaning "await" or "wait for," also extending to mean "time." In the Bronze Inscriptions, 矦 is comprised of 厂 (hǎn, target for archery) and 矢 (shǐ, arrow). The original meaning of 矦 was "target." Later it came to mean "marquis," "duke," or "prince under an emperor." In its ancient form, 矢 is represented by the drawing of an arrow. Notice how 候 has changed in its Regular Script form.

候 形聲。篆文從人，矦聲，本義是等候。矦，會意。從厂從矢（箭），厂像靶子，矢在靶上，本義為箭靶。

篆 儵

時候 shíhòu time; moment	等候 děnghòu to wait; to wait for
氣候 qìhòu climate	問候 wènhòu to send one's regards to; to say hello to

---

戶／户

hù
door; household

PICTOGRAPH In the Oracle-Bone Inscriptions, 戶 looks like a door with one panel (as opposed to a door with two panels, represented by 門/门). Its original meaning was "one-paneled door," and has been extended to mean "door," "family," "household," "family status," and "(bank) account," etc.

戶 象形。甲骨文像單扇門的形狀。（一扇為戶，兩扇為門）本義指單扇的門，引申義泛指門、人家、住戶、門第、帳戶等。

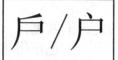

甲 日 篆 尸

住戶 zhùhù resident	用戶 yònghù user; subscriber
戶外 hùwài outdoor	個體戶 gètǐhù self-employed

護/护

hù
to protect

PICTOPHONETIC CHARACTER 護 is comprised of the word/speech radical 言 and the phonetic element 蒦 (huò), meaning "to defend," "to protect," "to be partial to," or "to shield." In its ancient forms, 蒦 looks like a right hand (又, yòu) holding an owl (萑, huán). 蒦 is the original form of 獲 (huò, to catch; to capture). Nowadays 蒦 is only used as the phonetic element in a character. In the simplified 护, the hand radical 扌 replaces 言, and the phonetic 户 (hù) replaces 蒦 (huò), indicating protecting a person with hands rather than words.

護 形聲。從言，蒦 (huò) 聲。本義為保護，引申為袒護、庇護等。蒦，會意。像手捉住一貓頭鷹。是獲的本字。獲字加一犬字旁。蒦後意指尺度、法度，現僅用於聲旁。簡化字护左邊以扌代替言，右邊聲旁用户代替蒦。元代已有此寫法。

篆 護　蒦甲  金　篆

保護 bǎohù to protect
護士 hùshi nurse

愛護 àihù to take good care of; to love and protect
護照 hùzhào passport

花

huā
to spend;
flower

PICTOPHONETIC CHARACTER The character 花 consists of the grass/plant 艹 radical and the phonetic 化 (huà), meaning "flower," "blossom," "flowery," "multicolored," etc. Today 花 also means "to spend." In the Oracle-Bone Inscriptions, 化 depicts two people heading in different directions, meaning "change," "turn," "convert," etc.

花 形聲。從艸，化聲。化，會意。甲骨文像兩人一正一倒形，意指變化。

甲　　金　　篆

花園 huāyuán garden
開花 kāihuā to bloom; to blossom

花錢 huāqián to spend money
花費 huāfèi expense; cost

滑

huá
slippery; to slide

PICTOPHONETIC CHARACTER The character 滑 consists of the water radical 氵 and the phonetic component 骨 (gǔ, bone). The original meanings of 滑 were "to slip," "to slide," "slippery," and its extended meanings include "cunning," "crafty," and "insincere." In its ancient forms, the top part of 骨 looks like a scapula and the bottom part flesh 月, indicating a bone with flesh. To memorize the character 滑, imagine someone slipping in a puddle and breaking a bone.

滑 形聲。從水，骨聲。本義為光滑或滑動。引申義有圓滑、狡猾等。骨，象形兼會意。甲骨文像骨節形狀。篆文上部是冎，冎意為占卜用的骨頭，下部為肉月，表示骨肉相連。

篆　　骨甲 之 篆 骨

滑冰 huábīng skating
滑板 huábǎn skateboard

滑雪 huáxuě skiing
圓滑 yuánhuá smooth and evasive; slick and sly

G - K

化

huà
to transform;
to influence

ASSOCIATIVE COMPOUND   In the Oracle-Bone Inscriptions, 化 is the drawing of two men with one standing upright and the other upside down. The original meaning of 化 was "change" or "to change," from which it has derived the meanings "to convert," "to transform," "to influence," "to melt," "to digest," "to beg alms," a shorter term for "chemistry," etc.

化 會意。甲骨文中字形
為一正一倒的兩個人。
本義為變化、使變化；
引申義有轉化、感化、
溶化、消化、化緣、
化學、使轉化等。

甲 𠤎   金 𠤎   篆 𠤎

變化 biànhuà change
文化 wénhuà culture

西化 xīhuà to westernize; westernization
化學 huàxué chemistry

話/话

huà
speech

ASSOCIATIVE COMPOUND   The character 話 consists of the word radical 言 and the character 舌 (shé, tongue), meaning "talk," or "spoken language." In the Oracle-Bone Inscriptions, 舌 is a pictograph of a tongue sticking out of a mouth. The speech radical is simplified in the simplified version of the character (话).

話 會意。從言，從舌，
意指交談、話語等。舌，
象形。下部像口，上部像
舌，表示舌頭伸出口外。
簡體字话的部首簡化。

篆 䚾

說話 shuōhuà to speak; to talk
對話 duìhuà dialogue

電話 diànhuà telephone; phone call
上海話 shànghǎihuà Shanghai dialect

劃/划

huà
to plan;
to divide

ASSOCIATIVE AND PICTOPHONETIC COMPOUND   劃 consists of the knife radical 刂 and the semantic and phonetic element 畫 (huà, to draw; painting), originally meaning "to cut apart." Extended meanings include "to divide," "to draw (a line)," "to mark," "to assign," and "plan." In the Oracle-Bone Inscriptions, the top part of 畫 looks like a hand holding a brush, and the bottom part a decorative pattern. 划 (huá) combines 戈 (gē, dagger-axe) with the knife radical 刂, originally meaning "to paddle," "scratch," and "profitable." Today 划 is used as the simplified character of 劃, and carries the meanings of both 划 and 劃.

劃 會意兼形聲。從刂，
從畫，畫亦聲。本義為用
刀把物體割開、分開，
引申義有劃分、劃綫、
撥給、籌劃、計劃等。
划（huá），會意。從戈，
從刂。繁體字中原本就
有划字，意思有撥水前
進、在物體表面刮或擦
過等。簡化字用划字來
替代劃，屬同音替代。

篆 劃

劃分 huàfēn to divide
規劃 guīhuà planning; program; to map out

計劃 jìhuà plan; to plan
劃綫 huàxiàn to draw a line

The Way of Chinese Characters

壞/坏

huài
bad

PICTOPHONETIC CHARACTER The character 壞 is made up of the radical 土 (tǔ, soil; earth) and the phonetic component 褱 (huái, surround). Its original meaning was "to collapse," from which the meanings "to break down," "broken," "bad," "spoiled," "awfully," or "extremely" have derived. 褱 is formed with a 罒 (dà) inserted in the middle of 衣 (yī, clothes), which looks like an eye shedding tears on clothes. 褱 is the variant form of 懷, meaning "to think of," "to yearn for," "bosom," and "mind." In the simplified character 坏, 不 (bù, no) replaces 褱.

壞 形聲。從土，褱 (huái) 聲。本義指牆壁倒塌，引申義有毀掉、崩潰、不好、變壞等。褱是懷的異體字，本義為思念，引申義有心存、胸部、胸懷、懷胎等。坏字本讀作 pī，指未燒過的磚瓦，後來此意改用坯字。簡化字用坏代替壞。

篆 坏 壞

壞蛋 huàidàn bad egg; bastard; scoundrel	壞事 huàishì a bad or evil thing; to ruin
壞話 huàihuà unpleasant words; malicious gossip	破壞 pòhuài to destroy; to ruin

---

歡/欢

huān
happy; joyous

PICTOPHONETIC CHARACTER The character 歡 consists of 欠 (qiàn, breathe; yawn) as the radical and the phonetic element 雚 (guàn), meaning "joyous," or "vigorously." The ancient form of 雚 looks like an owl with a large head and eyes, and also means "owl." In Regular Script, 雚 is the combination of 卝 (grass radical), two 口 (kǒu, mouth), and 隹 (zhuī, short-tailed bird). In the Oracle-Bone Inscriptions, 欠 looks like a person with a mouth open wide to breathe or yawn. In the simplified character 欢, 又 replaces 雚.

歡 形聲。從欠，雚 guàn 聲。雚，小雀或貓頭鷹。欠，象形。甲骨文中像人張口出气狀。人像鳥一般張口嘰嘰喳喳地說話，意為歡喜快樂。簡體欢字左邊以又取代雚。明清已有欢字。

篆 歡

喜歡 xǐhuan to like; to be fond of	歡迎 huānyíng to welcome; welcome
歡樂 huānlè happy; joyous; gay	聯歡 liánhuān to have a get-together

---

換/换

huàn
to exchange;
to change

PICTOPHONETIC CHARACTER The character 換 is comprised of the hand radical 扌 and the phonetic component 奐 (huàn), meaning "exchange," "barter," "change," and "convert." In Seal Script, 奐 depicts a person on top, a cave dwelling in the middle, and two hands at the bottom, possibly referring to people building a large dwelling with their hands. Meanings of 奐 include "magnificent," "abundant," and "bright-colored." The simplified character 换 derives from the cursive style of 換 and differs only slightly from the traditional form.

換 形聲。從手，奐聲，意為對換、變換等。奐，會意。篆文下有雙手，上有人站在高大的洞穴之上，本義指用手建造高大洞穴以為居所，引申為盛大。簡體字换是繁體字換的草書楷化字，字右部稍有改動。

篆 換 草 换

退換 tuìhuàn exchange a purchase	換錢 huànqián to change money
交換 jiāohuàn to exchange; interchange	替換 tìhuàn replace; substitute for

G - K

黃 / 黄
huáng
yellow

PICTOGRAPH In the Oracle-Bone Inscriptions, the character 黃 looks like a pendant with a knot above and tassels underneath, meaning "ring-shaped jade pendant." Since this kind of ornament was usually made with yellow jade, "yellow" is the extended meaning of 黃. The simplified version of 黃 is the variant form 黄.

黃 象形。甲骨文、金文像佩璜形。上為系带，中为佩璜，下為垂穗，本義為佩玉。因這種佩玉多為黃色，引申為黃顏色。黃是黃的異體字，後也用為黃的簡體字。

甲 𩽾 金 黃 篆 黃

黃色 huángsè yellow (color); pornographic
黃油 huángyóu butter

黃金 huángjīn gold
黃河 huánghé Yellow River

回
huí
to return

PICTOGRAPH In its ancient form, the character 回 represents a whirlpool or an eddy. The original meaning of 回 was "whirl" or "circle." Today it means "return," "go back," "turn around," "reply," "refuse," etc.

回 象形。甲骨文像水的漩渦。

甲 𠃌 金 𠁥 篆 𠁥

回來 huílai to come back
回家 huíjiā to return home

回去 huíqu to go back
回國 huíguó to return to one's home country

會 / 会
huì
meeting

ASSOCIATIVE COMPOUND In its ancient form, 會 is made up of three parts: the lower part represents a container; the middle is the food; the top is the container's lid, meaning, "to join together," "converge," and "assemble." Extended meanings of 會 include "to meet," "meeting," "gathering," "association," "to be able to," "to be likely to," etc. The simplified character 会 derives from the cursive style of the traditional character 會.

會 會意。甲骨文、金文字形下像容器，上像容器的蓋子，中間像盛放的食物。蓋上容器的蓋子，表示會合，引申為開會等。簡體字会是繁體字會的草書楷化字。

甲 𣂈 金 𣂈 篆 𣂈 草 会

開會 kāihuì to have a meeting
會話 huìhuà conversation

晚會 wǎnhuì evening party
機會 jīhuì opportunity; chance

The Way of Chinese Characters

活

huó
to live; living

ASSOCIATIVE AND PICTOPHONETIC COMPOUND In Regular Script, the character 活 consists of the water radical 氵 and the semantic and phonetic component 舌 (shé, tongue), meaning "to live," "to survive," "active," "lively," or "work." In its ancient forms, 舌 depicts a tongue sticking out of the mouth. The character 活 may indicate the fact that humans cannot live without water !

活 會意兼形聲。篆書楷書從水，舌聲。因為人要活離不開水，所以舌邊有水。舌，象形。像舌頭伸出口外。活本義為水流聲，引申為生存、存活、有生命力、工作等。

篆 𣴎 舌 甲 𠮳 金 𠮷 篆 舌

活著 huózhe to live; alive
生活 shēnghuó life; to live

活動 huódòng activity
活力 huólì vigor; energy

或

huò
or

ASSOCIATIVE COMPOUND In the character 或, 囗 (wéi, enclose) stands for the boundary or moat of a city, 一 for the land, and 戈 (gē, dagger-axe) for the weapon used to protect the country. The original meaning of 或 was "country" or "nation." However, "country" is now expressed with 國, while 或 means "or," "either," "perhaps," "maybe," etc.

或 會意。甲骨文從戈，從口（口像城的圍牆），表示以武器（戈）保衛城池。金文、篆文下部加一橫以示國土疆界。本義為邦國，假借義為或者。

甲 𢆶 金 或 篆 或

或者 huòzhě or
或多或少 huòduō huòshǎo more or less

或許 huòxǔ perhaps; maybe

貨/货

huò
merchandise

ASSOCIATIVE AND PICTOPHONETIC COMPOUND In Seal Script, the character 貨 is comprised of the radical 貝 (bèi, cowry shell) and the signifying and phonetic element 化 (huà, change). Since shells were used as money in ancient times, 貨 means "goods," "merchandise," "commodity," or "money." In the Oracle-Bone Inscriptions, the character 化 depicts two people heading in different directions, meaning "change," "turn," "convert," etc. The shell part 貝 is simplified to form the character 货.

貨 會意兼形聲。從化（變化），從貝（古時錢幣）；化亦聲。指用錢購買貨物。 化，會意。甲骨文中像一正立人形，一倒立人形，意為變化。簡體字货中的贝是繁體字貝的草書楷化字。

篆 貨 化 甲 𠤎

貨物 huòwù goods; commodity; merchandise
售貨員 shòuhuòyuán salesperson

貨幣 huòbì currency; monetary; money
百貨公司 bǎihuò gōngsī department store

G - K

機/机

jī
machine

金 𢆶 篆 𣛮

PICTOPHONETIC CHARACTER The character 機 is composed of the wood radical 木 and the phonetic element 幾 (jǐ), meaning "machine," "plane," or "chance." The character 幾 consists of two wisps of silk 幺 (yāo, tiny; small) on the top, and a person with a dagger-axe 戍 (shù, guard; defend) at the bottom. Originally 幾 referred to dangerous signs to ward against, and later came to mean "a few" and "how many." The simplified form of 幾 is 几, which also forms the right part of the simplified character 机.

機 形聲。從木，幾聲，指機器、機會、重要事務等。簡體字机的右部以几替代繁體的幾，属同音替代。

飛機 fēijī airplane
司機 sījī driver

機場 jīchǎng airport
洗衣機 xǐyījī washing machine

級/级

jí
grade; level

篆 絽 及甲 𠂤 金 𠂤 篆 𠂤

PICTOPHONETIC CHARACTER The character 級 consists of the silk radical 糸 and the phonetic element 及 (jí, to reach). The original meaning of 級 referred to the grade of silk specifically. Its extended meanings include: "grade," "level," "rank," and "step." In the Oracle-Bone and Bronze Inscriptions, 及 resembles a hand touching someone on the back, therefore meaning "to reach" or "come up to." The silk radical in the character 級 is in simplified form.

級 形聲。從糸，及聲。本義為絲的优劣次第，引申為等級。及，會意。甲骨文、金文從又（右手），從人，像一隻手從後抓住一個人狀。本義為逮捕，引申為趕上、追上、到達。级字部首簡化。

年級 niánjí grade; year (in school, college, etc.)
上級 shàngjí higher authorities; superiors

高級 gāojí high grade; advanced
下級 xiàjí low ranking; subordinate

極/极

jí
extremely; pole

篆 𣛮 亟 金 亟 篆 亟

PICTOPHONETIC CHARACTER The character 極 is formed with the wood radical 木 and the phonetic indicator 亟 (jí). Originally 極 referred to a ridgepole—the highest horizontal timber in a roof—from which derived the meanings "topmost," "extreme," "extremely," "farthest," and "pole." In Regular Script, 亟 combines 了, 口, 又, and 一, and means "urgent." In the simplified character 极, 及 (jí) is used to replace 亟 because it has the same pronunciation.

極 形聲。從木，亟聲。本義為房屋的正樑、脊檁（lǐn）。因為脊檁在房屋最高處，引申為頂點、極度、盡頭。金文亟是二（指天地）中有一人，人左有口，右是又（右手），像是人忙碌的狀態，本義為急迫。簡化字极把極字右邊的亟用及代替，屬於同音替代。

極好 jíhǎo excellent
太極 tàijí the Supreme Ultimate

北極 běijí North Pole
太極拳 tàijíquán shadowboxing; Tai Chi

jǐ
oneself

PICTOGRAPH In its ancient form, 己 resembled a large belly, meaning "oneself," "personal," etc. You can find 己 in the characters 起 (qǐ, rise) and 記 (jì, to record). Note the slight difference between 己 and 已 (yǐ, already).

己 象形。古文字中像人腹形，用作人稱代詞、自己、本身等。注意己 (jǐ) 和已 (yǐ) 的區別。(已 yǐ，象形。甲骨文、金文、篆文中本字像頭朝下的胎兒，引申為已經)。

甲 己　金 己　篆 己

自己 zìjǐ oneself; one's own
知己知彼 zhījǐ zhībǐ know yourself, know your enemy (idiom)

知己 zhījǐ intimate friend

幾 / 几

jǐ
how many;
a few

ASSOCIATIVE COMPOUND The character 幾 consists of two wisps of silk 幺幺 (yāo, tiny; small) on top, and a person with a dagger-axe 戍 (shù, guard; defend) at the bottom. Originally 幾 meant signs of danger to guard against. Later it came to mean "few" or "how many." Whether used in a statement or a question, 幾 refers only to a small number (between one and nine). Originally the character 几 (jǐ) meant a small table. In simplified characters, 几 is used to replace 幾 and means "how many" or "a few" because the pronunciations are very similar.

幾 會意。上部 "幺幺" 表示微小，下部 "戍" 意為防備。表示在發現細微跡象時就要警惕，加以防備。本義為細微跡象、先兆，後作為數詞、疑問詞。戍，會意。甲骨文、金文像人持戈。几字早已存在，如茶几。簡體字用几代替幾，屬同音替代字。

金 幾　篆 幾

幾個 jǐge a few; several; how many
幾年 jǐnián a few years; how many years

好幾 hǎojǐ several; quite a few
幾十 jǐshí tens of

計 / 计

jì
to count

ASSOCIATIVE COMPOUND The character 計 combines the speech/words radical 言 with 十 (shí, ten), meaning "to count (numbers)." Its extended meanings include "to calculate," "to plan," "a plan," "idea," "scheme," "stratagem," "a meter," or "a gauge." In the character 计, the speech radical 讠 is in its simplified form.

計 會意。從言，從十。十是數目字，本義為口數數目或計算。引申義有核算、計劃、策略、測量用的儀器（溫度計）等。計字的部首言 簡化為讠。

篆 計

計算 jìsuàn to calculate
計劃 jìhuà plan; to plan

計程車 jìchéngchē taxi; cab
會計 kuàijì accounting; accountant

記/记

jì
to remember; to
record

PICTOPHONETIC CHARACTER The character 記 consists of the words/speech radical 言(yán) and the phonetic element 己 (jǐ), meaning "to write down," "to record," "to remember," "to keep in mind," "mark," "sign," "notes," and "record." In its ancient forms, 己 looks like a large belly, meaning "oneself," "personal," etc. The words/speech radical is simplified in the character 记.

記 形聲。從言，己聲。本義為記錄，引申義有記住、記載人事的文字（傳記、遊記）、標誌等。己，象形。古文字中像人腹形，用作人稱代詞、自己、本身等。一說己像繩曲之形。言字旁簡化為讠，簡化字记屬偏旁類推簡化。

篆 記

記得 jìde to remember
記者 jìzhě reporter; journalist

忘記 wàngjì to forget
日記 rìjì diary

際/际

jì
border; boundary

PICTOPHONETIC CHARACTER 際 consists of the mound radical 阝 and the phonetic indicator 祭 (jì). It used to mean "the joint of two mud walls," and from this has derived the meanings "boundary," "edge," "between," "inside," "on occasion," etc. In the Bronze Inscriptions, 祭 consists of a piece of meat (upper left), a hand (upper right), and an altar (示, lower part), signifying the act of putting meat on an altar with a hand. 祭 means "to offer sacrifices," and "to worship." In its ancient forms, 示 looks like an altar upon which sacrificial offerings were placed. In the simplified 际, 示 replaces 祭.

際 形聲。從阜/阝（在此表示土墻），祭聲。本義為兩墻相交之處的縫，引申為分界處、彼此之間、裏邊、時候等。祭，會意。金文從肉，從又（右手），從示（祭臺），表示用手把肉放在祭臺上祭神。本義為祭祀。簡化字际右邊以示代替祭。

篆 際 祭 甲 金 篆

邊際 biānjì boundary; edge
交際 jiāojì to socialize; communication

國際 guójì international
實際 shíjì practical

蹟/迹

jì
remains; ruins

PICTOPHONETIC CHARACTER The character 蹟 is comprised of the foot radical 足 and the phonetic 責 (zé). Its original meaning was "footprint," and extended meanings are "mark," "trace," "track," "relics," "ruins," "remains." In its ancient forms, 責 consists of cowry shell 貝 and the phonetic element 朿 (cì), meaning "to demand (money)," "to blame," "duty," and "responsibility." 迹 was a variant of 蹟, and is used today as the simplified version of 蹟.

蹟 形聲。從足，責聲。本義為腳印，引申義為痕蹟，前人遺留的事物等。責，形聲。古文字從貝，朿（cì）聲。意思有索取（錢財）、責備、處分、責任等。迹、跡是蹟的異體字，現用迹作蹟的簡化字。

金 篆 迹 責 甲 金 責

古蹟 gǔjì historic sites
印蹟 yìnjì mark; trace

足蹟 zújì footprint; trail
奇蹟 qíjì miracle

加
jiā
to add

ASSOCIATIVE COMPOUND The character 加 consists of 力 (lì, power; strength) and 口 (kǒu, mouth), originally referring to "to slander," or "to calumniate." Today 加 means "to add," "plus," "to increase," "to append." Can you answer the following question in Chinese: 八十四 加十六是多少？

加　會意。從力，從口，本義指以語言誣陷他人、誇大，如"慾加之罪，何患無辭"。引申義有增加、加起來、加以等。

加油 jiāyóu cheer of support; to refuel
參加 cānjiā to participate

加速 jiāsù to speed up
加州 jiāzhōu California

家
jiā
family; home

ASSOCIATIVE COMPOUND In the Oracle-Bone and Bronze Inscriptions, the character 家 consists of the roof radical 宀 on top and a pig 豕 underneath. In China's ancient agricultural society, a household without pigs or other livestock would be considered poor. In its ancient forms, 豕 is the pictograph of a pig with a head, rounded body, legs, and a short tail. Notice the differences between 豕 and 亥 (hài), a pig without head and feet.

家　會意。從寶蓋頭，從豕，表示在家中養豬。農業社會中不養牲畜不像一個家。

家庭 jiātíng family; household
國家 guójiā country; nation

大家 dàjiā all; everyone
家長 jiāzhǎng head of a household

傢/家
jiā
furniture

PICTOPHONETIC CHARACTER The character 傢 consists of the person radical 亻 and the phonetic element 家 (jiā, family; home), referring to "furniture," "tool," or "fellow." 家 consists of the roof radical 宀 on top and a pig 豕 (shǐ) underneath. In an agricultural society, a household without pigs or other livestock would be considered incomplete. 家 is now used as the simplified form of 傢.

傢　形聲。從亻，家聲。意指器物或工具，亦指人或家畜（小傢伙）。家，會意。從宀，從豕，表現古時人在家中養豬的習慣。傢是家字的後來分化字。簡化字用家代替繁體字傢是恢復古本字。

傢俱 jiājù furniture
小傢伙 xiǎojiāhuo kid, little thing

傢伙 jiāhuo guy; tool (slang)

G - K

架

jià
shelf

ASSOCIATIVE AND PICTOPHONETIC COMPOUND The character 架 contains the wood radical 木 and the semantic and phonetic element 加 (jiā, add; plus), meaning "to put up," "to erect," or "to build." The extended meanings of 架 include "frame," "rack," "shelf," "to support," "to kidnap," and "to quarrel." 加 consists of 力 (lì, power; strength) and 口 (kǒu, mouth), originally meaning "to slander." Today 加 primarily means "to add," "plus," and "to increase."

架 會意兼形聲。從木，從加，加亦聲。表示把木頭加在一起，本義為搭建、構築，引申為架子、支撐、攙扶、綁架、爭吵等。加，會意。從力，從口，本義指以語言誣陷他人，引申為添加等。

書架 shūjià bookshelf
十字架 shízìjià cross

衣架 yījià hanger
打架 dǎjià to fight; scuffle

假

jiǎ
vacation; holiday

jiǎ
false; fake

PICTOPHONETIC CHARACTER The character 假 consists of the person radical 亻 and the phonetic component 叚 (jiǎ/jià), meaning "borrow," "in case," "assume," "false" (pronounced as jiǎ), "holiday," or "vacation" (pronounced as jià). In the Bronze Inscriptions, the left part 叚 represents a cliff and the right part represents two hands, suggesting a person climbing up a cliff. 叚 originally meant "lean against," or "rely on," but is now only used as a part within characters.

假 形聲。從人，叚聲，意為假期。叚，會意。金文左邊是山崖，右邊是兩隻手，意指用雙手攀崖。叚本義為憑借、借助。

寒假 hánjià winter vacation
放假 fàngjià to have a holiday or vacation

暑假 shǔjià summer vacation
虛假 xūjiǎ false; fake

間/间

jiān
(MW for rooms); between

ASSOCIATIVE COMPOUND In the Bronze Inscriptions and Seal Script 間 is the combination of 門 (mén, door) and 月 (yuè, moon), representing a sliver of moonlight seen through the panels of a door. In Regular Script, 月 is replaced with 日 (rì, sun). Meanings of 間 include "space in between," "opening," "separate," "between," "middle," "among," and "space," and it is also used as a measure word for rooms. The door radical in the character 间 is in simplified form.

間 會意。金文從門，從月，用門中可看見月光表示空隙之意。楷書門中改月為日。簡體字间的部首簡化。

金 門 篆 間

中間 zhōngjiān between; middle
時間 shíjiān time

房間 fángjiān room
空間 kōngjiān space

檢／检

jiǎn
to inspect

PICTOPHONETIC CHARACTER The character 檢 consists of the wood radical 木 and the phonetic component 僉 (qiān), originally referring to the seal on a box used to keep papers and letters. Later 檢 came to mean "to check," "to examine," "to inspect," or "restraint." 僉 has 亼 (jí, to gather together) on the top, two mouths (吅 xuān) in the middle, and two persons underneath (从 cóng), originally referring to many people speaking simultaneously and has been extended to mean "unanimous," "together," or "all." 僉 is simplified to 佥 in the character 检.

檢 形聲。從木，僉聲。本義為書匣上的封印，引申義有查檢、約束等。僉 (qiān)，會意。上從亼 (jí集合)，中從二口 (吅 xuān)，下從二人 (从)，本義為眾人同聲，引申為眾人、大家、都。佥源於僉的草書楷化字，是僉的簡化字。簡化字检屬於偏旁類推簡化。

篆 檢

檢查 jiǎnchá to check
檢票 jiǎnpiào to check a ticket
檢驗 jiǎnyàn to examine; to inspect
體檢 tǐjiǎn physical check-up

簡／简

jiǎn
simple

PICTOPHONETIC CHARACTER The character 簡 consists of the bamboo radical 竹 and the phonetic component 間 (jiān), originally referring to "bamboo strips used for writing." People in ancient China wrote on bamboo strips. The extended meanings of 簡 include "letter," "brief," "uncomplicated," "simple," and "to select." 間 is the combination of 門 (mén, door) and 日 (rì, sun), representing a sliver of a sunbeam shining through the door panels. The other meanings of 間 include "opening," "between," "middle," "among," and "space." The door part in the character 简 is in simplified form.

簡 形聲。從竹，間聲。本義為古代用於書寫的竹片。引申為簡單、信件、選擇等。間，會意。金文從門，從月，用門中可看見月光表示空隙之意。楷書門中改月為日。簡化字將間簡化為间，屬於偏旁類推簡化。

篆 簡

竹簡 zhújiǎn inscribed bamboo-slips
簡化 jiǎnhuà to simplify
簡單 jiǎndān simple
簡體字 jiǎntǐzì simplified characters

件

jiàn
(MW for items)

ASSOCIATIVE COMPOUND The character 件 consists of the person radical 亻 and the character 牛 (niú, ox), signifying a person butchering an ox. The original meaning of 件 therefore was "to cut apart" or "divide." Later, 件 came to mean "single item" and is used as a measure word for many things, including "matters," "clothing worn on top," "furniture," "luggage," etc. In the Oracle-Bone Inscriptions, 牛 depicts an ox head from the front.

件 會意。篆文從人，從牛，指人把牛分解成部分。本義為分解、分割，引申為量詞。牛，象形。像帶角的牛頭正面。

篆 件 牛 甲 金 篆 牛

文件 wénjiàn document; file
事件 shìjiàn event; happening; incident
證件 zhèngjiàn certificate; ID
條件 tiáojiàn condition; requirement

jiàn
healthy

PICTOPHONETIC CHARACTER The character 健 consists of the person radical 亻 and the phonetic component 建 (jiàn), meaning "strong," "healthy," "to strengthen," and "to be good at." The character 建 combines the radical 廴 (yǐn, to move on) with 聿 (yù, writing brush; then) originally meaning "to enact laws" and extended to mean "to establish," "to build," and "to propose." In the Oracle-Bone and Bronze Inscriptions, 聿 shows a hand holding a brush. 聿 is often used as a component in characters pertaining to brushwork, such as 書 (shū, book), 筆 (bǐ, pen), 畫 (huà, painting), and 律 (lǜ, law).

健 形聲。從亻，建聲。本義為健壯、強健，引申義有健康、使強壯、善於等。建，會意。從廴（長行），從聿，本義為建立朝廷的律法。引申為創立、建造、提出等。聿，象形。甲骨文像以手持筆狀，本義為筆。後用作文言助詞。

篆

健康 jiànkāng healthy
健身 jiànshēn to keep fit; body building

健美 jiànměi strong and handsome
健身房 jiànshēnfáng gym

教

jiāo
to teach

jiào
education

ASSOCIATIVE AND PICTOPHONETIC COMPOUND In its ancient forms, the left part of 教 consists of 爻 (yáo, counting sticks) and 子 (zǐ, child), indicating a child learning. The right part of 教 is a hand holding a stick, suggesting a tutor supervising the child. Physical forms of punishment were common practice in China's past. In Regular Script, the right part of 教 is simplified into the tap/rap radical 攵, and 爻 on the top left is replaced with 耂, which is also seen in 老 (lǎo, old) and 考 (kǎo, test). The lower left 子 remains the same.

教 會意兼形聲。甲骨文從攴 pū（手持棍狀），從子，從爻 yáo（算籌相交之形）。表示手持棍監督教導孩子學習計算。

A

甲 𣥂 金 𣥂 篆 𣪊

教室 jiàoshì classroom
教授 jiàoshòu professor

教材 jiàocái teaching materials
教育 jiàoyù to educate; to teach; education

腳/脚

jiǎo
foot

PICTOPHONETIC CHARACTER The character 腳 consists of the flesh radical 月 and the phonetic 卻 (què). Its original meaning was "shank," and extended meanings are "foot" and "base." 卻 is the combination of 谷 (gǔ, valley; gorge) and a keeling person 卩, meaning "to step back," "to retreat," "to withdraw," "to decline," and "but." 却 is a variant of 卻. In the simplified character 脚, 却 is used to replace 卻.

腳 形聲。從肉月，卻聲。本義為小腿，引申為足、物體的底部（山腳、褲腳）。卻，會意。從卩（跪人），從谷（在此表示困境），以示人臨困境而退縮。意思有後退、推卻、可是等。却過去是卻的俗體字，現在用為卻的簡化字。簡化字腳中的卻也改為却。

篆

腳步 jiǎobù footstep
腳心 jiǎoxīn arch (of the foot)

腳跟 jiǎogēn heel
山腳 shānjiǎo the foot of the mountain

餃/饺		
jiǎo dumpling	PICTOPHONETIC CHARACTER The character 餃 is made up of the food radical 飠 and the phonetic 交(jiāo), meaning "stuffed dumplings" or "ravioli." 交 is a pictograph of a figure with crossed legs. The original meaning of 交 is "to cross," and extended to mean "to hand over," "to make (friends)," "to pay (money)," etc. In the character 饺, the food radical is simplified.	**餃** 形聲。從飠，交聲。指半圓形内有餡兒的麵食。交，象形，像兩腿相交的正面人形。簡化字饺只是部首飠簡化為饣。

餃子 jiǎozi dumpling　　水餃 shuǐjiǎo boiled dumpling

叫		
jiào to be called; to call	PICTOPHONETIC CHARACTER The character 叫 consists of the mouth radical 口 and the phonetic element 丩 (jiū), meaning "call" or "shout." 丩 (jiū) is the phonetic indicator of the character 叫 (jiào) because the pronunciations of jiū and jiào are similar. In its ancient form, 丩 looks like tangled vines or silk, and means "entangle."	**叫** 形聲。從口，丩聲。丩意為糾纏，像籐蔓糾結狀。一說像絲綫纏繞。

丩 甲  金  篆 

叫做 jiàozuò to be called; to be known as　　叫好 jiàohǎo to applaud; to cheer
狗叫 gǒujiào dog bark　　貓叫 māojiào meow

接		
jiē to receive; to welcome	PICTOPHONETIC CHARACTER 接 contains the hand radical 扌 and the phonetic component 妾 (qiè). Its original meaning was "to touch with hands," and evolved to mean "to contact," "to receive," "to continue," and "to take over." In ancient writing, 妾 contains 辛 (xīn, pungent; suffering) above 女 (nǚ, female). In the Oracle-Bone and Bronze Inscriptions, 辛 is the pictograph of a knife used to tattoo the face of criminals or slaves. 妾 originally referred to "female slave," but came to mean "concubine." It was sometimes used by women as a self-deprecatory term. In Regular Script, 妾 combines 立 (lì, stand) and 女(nǚ, female).	**接** 形聲。從扌，妾聲。本義為接觸，引申義有連接、接受、迎接、連續、接替等。妾，會意。甲骨文從辛（刑刀），從女。表示受過刑的有罪女子，引申為女奴、小老婆，另外也是古代婦女的自謙之稱。楷書像是一個站立的女人，也表示地位低下。

篆  妾 甲  金  篆 

接近 jiējìn to approach; to get close to　　接受 jiēshòu to accept
接手 jiēshǒu to take over　　直接 zhíjiē direct

節/节

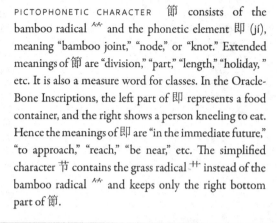

jié
(MW for classes);
holiday

PICTOPHONETIC CHARACTER 節 consists of the bamboo radical ⺮ and the phonetic element 即 (jí), meaning "bamboo joint," "node," or "knot." Extended meanings of 節 are "division," "part," "length," "holiday," etc. It is also a measure word for classes. In the Oracle-Bone Inscriptions, the left part of 即 represents a food container, and the right shows a person kneeling to eat. Hence the meanings of 即 are "in the immediate future," "to approach," "reach," "be near," etc. The simplified character 节 contains the grass radical 艹 instead of the bamboo radical ⺮ and keeps only the right bottom part of 節.

節 形聲。從竹，即聲。本義為竹節，引申為量詞、節日等。即，會意。甲骨文、金文中左邊像食器，右邊像一人跪坐，準備進食。本義為即將就食。簡體字节上部把竹字頭改為草字頭，下部保留即字的右部，十分近似節字的草體。

金 𥳑 篆 𥳑 草 节

兩節課 liǎngjié kè two classes
季節 jìjié season

節日 jiérì holiday; festival
節目 jiémù program; item (on a program)

姐

jiě
elder sister

PICTOPHONETIC CHARACTER The character 姐 contains 女 (nǚ, female) as the radical and 且 (qiě) as the phonetic element. This combination shows that the character relates to something female and is pronounced as, or similar to, the sound of 且 (qiě). In the Oracle-Bone and Bronze Inscriptions, the character 且 looks like a memorial tablet used in ancestral worship. The original meaning of 且 is "ancestor."

姐 形聲。從女，且聲。且在甲骨文、金文中像代表祖先之靈的牌位，供祭祀時用。

篆 姐

姐姐 jiějie older sister
姐妹 jiěmèi sisters

姐夫 jiěfu older sister's husband
大姐 dàjiě eldest sister; elder sister

介

jiè
to be between

ASSOCIATIVE COMPOUND In the Oracle-Bone Inscriptions, the character 介 resembles a man (人) wearing armor, as it originally meant "armor." Since this figure is shown between two pieces of a suit of armor, 介 has extended to mean "between" or "interpose."

介 會意。從八，從人。甲骨文字形從人，四短畫表示由一片片皮革串成的甲衣，本義指人穿甲衣，引申為介於中間等。

甲 𠆎 金 𠆎 篆 𠆎

介紹 jièshào introduce; introduction
簡介 jiǎnjiè summary; brief introduction

中介 zhōngjiè to act as intermediary
媒介 méijiè media; medium

今

jīn
today; now

PICTOGRAPH In the Oracle-Bone and Bronze Inscriptions, 今 looks like a figure with an open mouth, sticking out his or her tongue right at the moment of taking a drink. 今 therefore means "now" and "the present."

今 象形。像一人正張口喝下面罎子裏的酒，表示此時、現在的意思。

甲 金 篆 今

今天 jīntiān today
今晚 jīnwǎn tonight

今年 jīnnián this year
今後 jīnhòu from now on

緊/紧

jǐn
tense; tight

ASSOCIATIVE COMPOUND The character 緊 combines the vertical eye 臣, right hand 又, and silk 糸 characters, referring to the tightening of a silk string. 緊 originally meant "tighten" or "tight," and extended to mean "tense," "urgent," "strict," "short of money," etc. The simplified character 紧 derives from the cursive style of 緊. Just as in the character 蓝/藍 (lán), two vertical lines replace the eye part 臣.

緊 會意。上部左為豎著的眼睛，右是手，下部從絲（省為糸），本義指眼睛盯着，用手將絲弦調緊。 簡體字紧是繁體字緊的草書楷化字。如同藍字，將臣簡化為兩豎。

篆  草 紧

緊張 jǐnzhāng nervous; tense
要緊 yàojǐn important; urgent

趕緊 gǎnjǐn hurriedly; without delay
不要緊 búyàojǐn unimportant; not serious; it doesn't matter

近

jìn
close; near

PICTOPHONETIC CHARACTER The character 近 consists of the walk radical 辶 and the phonetic 斤 (jīn), meaning "near," "close," "intimate," and "approximately." In the Oracle-Bone Inscriptions, 斤 (jīn, ax; unit of weight) looks like an ax with a crooked handle.

近 形聲。從辶，斤聲。斤，象形。甲骨文中上像斧頭，下像斧柄。

篆 近

附近 fùjìn vicinity; nearby
近年 jìnnián recent year(s)

最近 zuìjìn recently; lately
近視 jìnshì myopia; nearsighted

G - K

進/进

jìn
to enter

ASSOCIATIVE COMPOUND The character 進 consists of the walk radical 辶 and the short-tailed bird character 隹 (zhuī). Since birds can only walk forwards, 進 means "move forward," "enter," or "into." In the simplified character 进, 井 (jǐng, well) replaces 隹 since the pronunciations of 井 and 進 (jìn) are similar.

進 會意從辶，隹聲。甲骨文從止（腳趾）從隹（短尾鳥）。因隹趾只能前進不能後退，本義為向前進。簡體字进用井替代隹，因井與進聲音相近。

甲 金 篆

前進 qiánjìn to go forward; to advance
進步 jìnbù progress; improvement; to improve

進去 jìnqu to go in
進口 jìnkǒu to import; imported; entrance

京

jīng
capital city

PICTOGRAPH In the Oracle-Bone and Bronze Inscriptions, 京 (jīng, capital) resembles a large grand building at the top of a hill or mountain. "Capital" is the extended meaning of 京. Compare 京 with 高 (gāo, tall) and 亮 (liàng, bright).

京 象形。像建于高丘之上的華屋大廈，引申為京城、首都。

甲 金 篆

京城 jīngchéng capital of a country
東京 dōngjīng Tokyo

北京 běijīng Beijing
京劇 jīngjù Beijing opera

睛

jīng
eyeball

PICTOPHONETIC CHARACTER The character 睛 consists of the eye radical 目 and the phonetic indicator 青. 睛 initially referred to "eyeball" or "pupil of the eye," and has been extended to mean "eye" or "sight." 青 as a phonetic component is also used in 情 (qíng, feeling; affection), 晴 (qíng, to clear up; sunny day), 精 (jīng, spirit; essence), 請 (qǐng, please; to invite), and 清 (qīng, pure; clear).

睛 形聲。從目，青聲。本義為眼珠，引申泛指眼睛。

篆 睛

眼睛 yǎnjīng eyes
畫龍點睛 huàlóng diǎnjīng to add the finishing touch (literally: to bring the painted dragon to life by drawing the pupils of its eyes)

目不轉睛 mù bùzhuǎnjīng to fix one's eyes on something

The Way of Chinese Characters

精

jīng
essence; refined

PICTOPHONETIC CHARACTER 精 is comprised of the rice radical 米 and the phonetic indicator 青(qīng) Originally 精 referred to "polished rice," from which derived the meanings of "essence," "exquisite," "refined," "proficient," "spirit," etc. In the Oracle-Bone Inscriptions, 米 resembles grains scattered around a rack. In the Bronze Inscriptions, the upper part of 青 is 生 (shēng, grow) and the lower part 丹 (dān, red color), indicating that the color of a growing plant is green. In Regular Script, the upper part of 青 is 生 without the downward left stroke, and the lower part changes from 丹 to 月 (yuè, moon; month).

精 形聲。從米，青聲。本義為優質純淨的上等細米，引申義為精華、精致、精細、精通、精神、妖精、精子等。米，象形，甲骨文字形像散落在地的米粒。青，會意兼形聲。金文從生，從丹，丹為紅色。用生長中的植物來表示綠色之意。後楷書寫作青。

篆 精 米甲 ⺌ 金 釆 青金 㫶

精力 jīnglì energy
精英 jīngyīng elite
精美 jīngměi exquisite; elegant
味精 wèijīng monosodium glutamate (MSG)

經/经

jīng
to pass through

ASSOCIATIVE AND PICTOPHONETIC COMPOUND In the Bronze Inscriptions, 巠 (jīng) is a pictograph of a loom with vertical strands of fabric, known as the "warp" (as opposed to the horizontal strands, called the "weft"). The character 經 consists of the silk radical 糸 and the signifying and phonetic element 巠 (jīng), meaning "warp," "through," "pass through," "undergo," "endure," etc. The simplified character 经 derives from the cursive form of the traditional character 經.

經 會意兼形聲。從糸，從巠（像繃在織布機上的三根經線；一說像水流至地面）；巠也兼表聲。經的本義是織物的縱綫，引申為經過、經歷。簡體字经是繁體字經的草書楷化字。

G - K

金 巠 篆 巠 草 经

已經 yǐjīng already
經驗 jīngyàn to experience; experience
經過 jīngguò to pass; to go through
經濟 jīngjì economy; economic

淨/净

jìng
clean; pure

PICTOPHONETIC CHARACTER The character 淨 consists of the water radical 氵 and the phonetic element 爭 (zhēng), meaning "clean," "pure," "to cleanse," "empty," "net (profit, income, etc.)," and "entirely." In Seal Script, the character 爭 looks like two hands—one up and the other down—fighting for the object in the middle, meaning "to fight for," "to compete," "to argue," etc. The simplified character 争 derives from the cursive version of 爭. In the simplified character 净, the water radical 氵 is replaced by the ice radical 冫 while 爭 takes its simplified form 争.

淨 形聲。從氵，爭聲。本義為清潔、乾淨，引申為洗乾淨、用完了（錢花淨了）、純粹等。爭，會意。篆文字形上下部分像兩隻手在爭中間的一物，本義為爭奪。争是爭的草書楷化字。淨的簡化字净左邊將氵改為冫，右邊將爭改為争。

金 淨 篆 淨 草 净 爭 篆 爭

清淨 qīngjìng at peace; pure (Buddhism)
白淨 báijìng (skin) fair and clean
乾淨 gānjìng clean
淨化 jìnghuà to purify

靜／静

jìng
quiet

PICTOPHONETIC CHARACTER The character 靜 consists of the radical 青 (qīng, green; blue; black) and the phonetic element 爭 (zhēng), originally referring to "bright color." It has been extended to mean "still," "motionless," "quiet," "silent," "serene," "virtuous," and "chaste." In the simplified character 静, 争 replaces 爭.

靜 形聲。從青，爭聲。本義為色彩鮮明，引申義有停止的、沒有聲響的、安詳、貞靜等。簡化字静中的爭簡化。

金 𤗅 篆 靜

安靜 ānjìng quiet
冷靜 lěngjìng sober; calm

文靜 wénjìng graceful and quiet
靜物 jìngwù still object

久

jiǔ
long time

PICTOGRAPH In Seal Script, 久 looks like a person lying down with a long moxa cone (a cylinder of cotton wool or other combustible material) burning on her or his back. The original meaning of 久 was "moxibustion" (a traditional treatment of Chinese medicine in which moxa cones are placed on the skin and ignited in order to treat disease or produce analgesia). Later the character 火 (huǒ, fire) was added under 久 to form a new character 灸 (jiǔ, meaning moxibustion). 久 then came to mean "a long time."

久 象形。篆文久字從人，背後一橫像以燃著的艾草在人背後薰灸之形，是灸的初文。

篆 𠃉

不久 bùjiǔ before too long; soon
好久不見 hǎojiǔ bújiàn long time no see

長久 chángjiǔ for a long time

酒

jiǔ
wine

ASSOCIATIVE AND PICTOPHONETIC COMPOUND 酒 is comprised of the water radical 氵 and the signifying and phonetic element 酉 (yǒu, wine jar), thereby meaning "alcoholic drink," "wine," "liquor," or "spirits." In its ancient form, 酉 is a pictograph of a wine jar. Later it was also borrowed to mean "the tenth of the twelve earthly branches" (see page 20).

酒 會意兼形聲。從氵，從酉；酉亦聲。指從酒壇中舀酒。酉，象形。像酒罎子形。后借為地支的第十位。

甲 酒 篆 酒 酉 甲 𠮷 金 酉

啤酒 píjiǔ beer
酒吧 jiǔbā bar; pub

酒精 jiǔjīng alcohol; ethanol
酒店 jiǔdiàn wine shop; hotel; restaurant

就
jiù
just

ASSOCIATIVE COMPOUND The character 就 is made up of 京 (jīng, capital) and 尤 (yóu, outstanding). The original meaning of 就 was "to reach the pinnacle," and extended meanings include "accomplish," "undertake," and "come near." 就 is also used as an adverb, meaning "just," "only," "right away," "as early as," "simply," "exactly," or "then." In the Oracle-Bone and Bronze Inscriptions, 京 (jīng, capital) resembles a building at the top of a hill or mountain. In the Oracle-Bone and Bronze Inscriptions, 尤 looks like a wart on a hand. Thus, its original meaning was "wart." Today, 尤 means "fault," "particularly," "especially," and "outstanding."

就 會意。從京，從尤。"京"為建于高丘之上的宮殿。"尤"為突出。"就"本義指達到至高處，引申為趨向、就要、隨即等。尤，象形。甲骨文從又（右手），一斜畫表示手上的贅疣，引申為突出、特別。

 篆

就是 jiùshì precisely; in the same way as
成就 chéngjiù accomplishment; achievement

早就 zǎojiù already at an earlier time
一···就··· yī... jiù... as soon as...

具
jù
tool; utensil

ASSOCIATIVE COMPOUND In the Oracle-Bone Inscriptions, the character 具 depicts two hands holding a tripod, meaning "to serve food and drinks." Its extended meanings are "utensil," "appliance," "tool," "to prepare," "to possess," etc. In Regular Script, the tripod and the two hands are simplified. Note that there are three lines inside the top part of 具.

具 會意。甲骨文像雙手奉鼎（一種食具）。本義為供上酒食，引申為器具、具有等。

 甲 　 金 　 篆

用具 yòngjù utensil; appliance
文具 wénjù stationery

家具 jiājù furniture
玩具 wánjù toy

覺/觉
jué
to feel; to think

jiào
to sleep

ASSOCIATIVE AND PICTOPHONETIC COMPOUND In Seal Script, 覺 consists of the radical 見 (jiàn, to see) and the signifying and phonetic element 學 (xué, to study), indicating someone studying with open eyes. 覺 means "awake," "sense," "feel," "reckon," (jué) "sleep" (the process from falling asleep to awakening, pronounced jiào), etc. Note that both 覺 and 學 have the same upper component, but their lower parts differ. The simplified character 觉 developed from the cursive form of 覺. The simplification of the top of 觉 (覺) is the same as that of 学 (學).

覺 會意兼形聲。篆文從見，學聲，表示睜大眼睛、聚精會神來學習領悟。本義為明白、醒悟。簡體字觉是繁體字覺的草書楷化字，上半部的簡化法與學字相同，下半部與見同。

篆 　 草

覺得 juéde to feel; to think
睡覺 shuìjiào to go to bed; to sleep

發覺 fājué to realize; to detect
午覺 wǔjiào siesta; afternoon nap

G - K

咖

kā
coffee

PICTOPHONETIC CHARACTER 咖 is comprised of the mouth radical 口 and the phonetic component 加 (jiā, plus). Originally 咖 was an onomatopoeic word for laughter. Later it was joined with 啡 (fēi) and came to mean "coffee" because it sounds similar to the English word "coffee." In the word 咖喱 (curry), 咖 is pronounced as gā. 加 consists of 力 (lì, power; strength) and 口 (kǒu, mouth), originally meaning "slander" or "calumniate." Today 加 means "to add" or "plus."

咖 形聲。象聲詞，模擬笑声。加，會意。從力，從口，本義指以語言誣陷他人。

加 金 篆 咖

咖啡 kāfēi coffee
咖啡館 kāfēiguǎn coffee shop

咖啡因 kāfēiyīn caffeine
咖喱 gālí curry

卡

kǎ
card

ASSOCIATIVE COMPOUND The character 卡 is the combination of 上 (up) and 下 (down), signifying something that is stuck in a particular position and cannot move upward or downward. The meanings of 卡 (pronounced qiǎ) include "wedge," "block," "clip," "outpost," etc. 卡 is now more commonly used to transliterate some English words because of similar pronunciations, such as "card" (卡 kǎ), "calorie" (卡路里 kǎlùlǐ), "cartoon" (卡通 kǎtōng), etc.

卡 會意。無古字。由上下二字合併而成，意指不上不下，卡在中間。也用作關卡，卡子等。因聲音近似，還用來音譯一些英文詞彙，如卡片 (card)，卡路里 (calorie)，卡通 (cartoon) 等。

卡片 kǎpiàn card
刷卡 shuākǎ to use a credit card; to swipe a card

信用卡 xìnyòngkǎ credit card
卡車 kǎchē truck

開/开

kāi
to open; to operate

ASSOCIATIVE COMPOUND In the Ancient Inscriptions, 開 looks like two hands removing a door bar. Its original meaning was "to open a door." Extended meanings include: "open," "start," "operate," etc. The simplified character 开 retains the hands part of the traditional character 開 but is without the door part.

開 會意。古文字形像雙手拿掉門閂開門狀。簡體字开僅保留繁體字開門的那部分。

篆 開

開門 kāimén to open a door
開會 kāihuì to have a meeting

開車 kāichē to drive a car
開始 kāishǐ to begin; beginning

看

kàn
to watch;
to read

ASSOCIATIVE COMPOUND The character 看 is the combination of 手 (shǒu, hand) and 目 (mù, eye), indicating the act of looking into the distance with a hand over one's eyes. Its original meaning was "look into the distance," and extended meanings include "to see," "look at," "read," "visit," etc.

看 會意。從手，從目。表示以手掌置於目上遮光遠望。

篆 看

看見 kànjiàn to see
好看 hǎokàn good-looking

看病 kànbìng to see a doctor
難看 nánkàn ugly

康

kāng
healthy; affluent

ASSOCIATIVE COMPOUND In the Oracle-Bone and Bronze Inscriptions, the character 康 is formed with two hands husking grain (禾) on the top and chaff (four dots) at the bottom, originally meaning "husk" or "bran." Later 康 has been borrowed to mean "peaceful and happy," "healthy," "affluent," and "abundant." A new character 糠 was later created to mean "husk" or "bran." In Regular Script, 康 becomes the combination of 广 (yǎn, shelter; shed) and 隶 (lì, subservient; attached to; scribe).

康 會意。甲骨文、金文上像用雙手搓稻穀上的皮殼，下像從稻穀子實上脫落下的皮殼，是糠的本字。本義為糠，後借用來表示安樂、健康、富裕（小康之家）、廣大（康莊大道）等。

甲 康 金 康 篆 康

健康 jiànkāng healthy; health
小康 xiǎokāng well-to-do; fairly well-off

安康 ānkāng good health
康復 kāngfù to recuperate

考

kǎo
test; to test

PICTOGRAPH In the Oracle-Bone and Bronze Inscriptions, 考 is written as 老, which looks like an elderly person with a walking stick in hand. The original meaning of 考 was "old" or "aged," but later came to mean "examine," "test," "inspect," "verify," etc. In ancient Chinese society, elders were considered more knowledgeable, and therefore in a position to test younger people. They might even have had the authority to use sticks to punish those who failed their tests!

考 象形。本義為老，引申為考試。甲骨文、金文老、考是同字，都像老人長髮弓背，扶着拐杖形。

甲 考 金 考 篆 考

考試 kǎoshì to take an exam; exam
小考 xiǎokǎo quiz

大考 dàkǎo final exam
期中考 qīzhōngkǎo midterm exam

烤

kǎo
to bake; to roast;
to grill

金

PICTOPHONETIC CHARACTER The character 烤 combines the fire radical 火 with the phonetic indicator 考 (kǎo), meaning to "to bake," "to roast," "to grill," and "to warm by fire." In the Oracle-Bone and Bronze Inscriptions, 考 looks like an elderly person with a walking stick in hand. In ancient Chinese society, elders were considered more knowledgeable, and therefore in a position to give younger people tests.

烤　形聲。從火，考聲。本義指用火烘乾或烘熟，引申為靠近火取暖、烹飪方法等。考，象形。像老人長髮弓背，扶着拐杖形。本義為老，引申為考試、檢察、考證等。

烤肉 kǎoròu barbeque
烤麵包 kǎo miànbāo toasted bread

烤鴨 kǎoyā roasted duck
烤箱 kǎoxiāng oven

靠

kào
to lean on; to rely on

PICTOPHONETIC CHARACTER 靠 consists of the semantic element 非 (fēi, not) and the phonetic 告 (gào), originally meaning "opposite to each other." In its ancient form, 非 resembles the two opposing wings of a flying bird, and originally meant "run counter to." Extended meanings are "not conform with," "wrong," "non-." Though the wings are opposite, they also support each other. Thus, extended meanings of 靠 are "to lean on/against," "alongside," "rely on," "come near to," and "trust." See the entry on 告 (gào) for more information on its origins.

靠　形聲。從非（兩翅相背），告聲。本義為兩物相違背，鳥翅相背而又相依，靠的引申義有倚著、依靠、挨近、信任等。非，象形。甲骨文、金文像鳥展開雙翅飛翔狀。由於兩翅相背，本義為違背，引申為不正確等。請見本書對告字的解釋。

篆 非甲 飛 篆 非

靠椅 kàoyǐ arm-chair
可靠 kěkào reliable

靠山 kàoshān patron; supporter
靠窗 kàochuāng by the window

可

kě
but;
to permit

ASSOCIATIVE AND PICTOPHONETIC COMPOUND In the Oracle-Bone Inscriptions, 可 resembles a mouth exhaling, and means "approve." The extended meanings of 可 include "fit," "okay," "may," "can," and "but."

可　會意兼形聲。從口，從丂(kǎo)；丂亦聲。丂，气欲舒出狀。本義為口中舒气以示認可，引申為許可、同意等。

甲 可 金 可 篆 可

可以 kěyǐ can; may
可是 kěshì but; however

可能 kěnéng probably; maybe
可愛 kě'ài cute; lovely

The Way of Chinese Characters

渴
kě
thirsty

PICTOPHONETIC CHARACTER 渴 is made up of the water radical 氵 and the phonetic element 曷 (hé). Its original and primary meaning is "thirst," and it has been extended to mean "to yearn for" or "to crave". 曷 is a pictophonetic character that consists of the radical 曰 (yuē, say) and the phonetic element 匃 (gài, beg; beggar), meaning "what," "how," "why not," and "when" in classical Chinese. You will also encounter 曷 in 喝 (hē, to drink)

渴 形聲。從氵，曷聲 (hé)，有口渴，渴望等意。曷，形聲。從曰 (說話)，從匃 (gài 同 丐，乞求)，意义與何相同，表示什麼、怎麼、為什麼不、何時、難道等。

篆

口渴 kǒukě thirsty
渴望 kěwàng to thirst for; to long for

解渴 jiěkě to quench thirst
渴求 kěqiú to crave

刻
kè
quarter (hour);
to carve

ASSOCIATIVE AND PICTOPHONETIC COMPOUND The character 刻 is composed of the knife radical 刂 and the phonetic and signifying component 亥 (hài), meaning "cut" or "carve." 刻 also extends to mean "quarter (of an hour)." In its ancient form, 亥 looks like a pig without a head or feet. Its original meaning was "cut," but later was borrowed to mean "the last of the twelve earthly branches" (see page 20). The character 刻 is a later character invented to cover the original meaning of 亥. 亥 is also in the character 孩 (hái, child).

刻 形聲兼會意。從刂，亥聲，本義為切割，後用於計時單位。亥，甲骨文中像割了頭蹄的豬形，是"刻"的本字。

篆

雕刻 diāokè to carve; to engrave; sculpture
立刻 lìkè immediately; right away

時刻 shíkè time; moment; constantly
刻苦 kèkǔ hardworking; assiduous

客
kè
guest

ASSOCIATIVE AND PICTOPHONETIC COMPOUND The character 客 consists of the roof radical 宀 and the character 各 (gè, arrive; each), suggesting someone arriving at a house. It follows that the meaning of 客 is "visitor," "guest," or "traveler." In the Oracle-Bone and Bronze Inscriptions, 各 is a combination of 夂 (zhǐ, a moving foot) and 口 (kǒu, the entrance of a dwelling). The original meaning of 各 was "arrive." Later it came to mean "each" or "every." Be careful not to confuse 各 and 名 (míng, name).

客 會意兼形聲。從宀，從各；各亦聲。指人自外面進屋之意。各，會意。甲骨文、金文中從止 (腳趾)，從口 (古人穴居洞口)，本義指來到，引申為每個。

金  篆

客人 kèrén guest
客氣 kèqi polite; courteous

請客 qǐngkè to invite to dinner; to entertain guests
客廳 kètīng living room

課/课

kè
class; lesson

PICTOPHONETIC CHARACTER The character 課 consists of the word radical 言 and the phonetic element 果 (guǒ, fruit), and means: "class," "lesson," or "course." In the Oracle-Bone Inscriptions, 果 is a pictograph of a tree with three fruits. In the Bronze Inscriptions, these three fruits become one large one. In Seal Script, this large fruit is replaced with the character 田 (tián, field), which deviates somewhat from the original meaning. A class or course should be fruitful, not fruitless! The speech radical in the character 课 is in its simplified form.

課 形聲。從言，果聲，意為考試、課時等。果，象形。像樹上結出的果實。簡體字课的部首簡化。

篆課 果甲 金果 篆果

上課 shàngkè to go to class; to attend class; to conduct a class
課文 kèwén text

下課 xiàkè to finish class
課本 kèběn textbook

空

kòng
free time

kōng
empty; sky

PICTOPHONETIC COMPOUND The character 空 consists of the radical 穴 (xué, cave) and the phonetic component 工 (gōng, work). The original meaning of 空 was "hole." It is used today to mean "empty," "hollow," "in vain," "sky" (pronounced kōng), or "unoccupied," "vacant," and "free time" (pronounced kòng). In Seal Script, 穴 is a pictograph of a cave dwelling.

空 形聲。從穴，工聲，本義為窟窿。穴，象形。像洞穴形。

金 篆宔

有空 yǒukòng have time; at one's leisure
空氣 kōngqì air

空間 kōngjiān space; room
航空 hángkōng aviation

哭

kū
to cry; to weep

ASSOCIATIVE COMPOUND The character 哭 is the combination of two mouths 吅 (xuān, shout; clamor; noise) and 犬 (quǎn, dog), meaning "wail," "cry," or "weep." Possibly the creator of this character sensed sorrow and pain in the barking of dogs or thought that when men cried they sounded like wailing dogs. In its ancient forms, 犬 resembles a dog. 犬 meant "a big dog" whereas 狗 indicated "a small dog" in ancient times.

哭 會意。從吅（xuān 呼叫、喧嚷），從犬，用眾犬哀號以示人哭。犬，象形。古時大狗稱犬，小狗稱狗。

金吅 篆哭 犬甲ʔ 金ʔ

哭聲 kūshēng sound of weeping
哭叫 kūjiào to cry and yell

大哭 dàkū to cry loudly
哭訴 kūsù to complain tearfully

The Way of Chinese Characters

酷

kù
cool; cruel

PICTOPHONETIC CHARACTER The character 酷 consists of the radical 酉 (wine jar) and the phonetic 告 (gào, tell). 酷 originally referred to the smell of strong alcoholic drinks and extended to mean "cruel," "extremely," etc. Since the pronunciation of 酷 is similar to "cool," it is also more recently used as a translation of the English word. In the Oracle-Bone Inscriptions, 告 is comprised of 牛 (niú, ox) and 口 (kǒu, mouth), originally referring to the sound an ox makes and extending to mean "inform," "tell," etc.

酷 形聲。從酉，告聲。本義為酒味濃烈，引申義有酷烈殘暴與表程度很深的意思。因音與英文cool 相似，所以用來直譯 cool 在俚語中表達時興並有吸引力的意思。告在甲骨文從口，從牛。本義為牛叫，引申為上報、告訴、佈告等。

篆 酷

殘酷 cánkù cruel; cruelty
酷暑 kùshǔ the intense heat of summer

冷酷 lěngkù unfeeling; callous; grim
酷愛 kù'ài ardent love

褲／裤

kù
pants

PICTOPHONETIC CHARACTER 褲 consists of the clothing radical 衤 and the phonetic component 庫 (kù), meaning "pants" or "trousers." The character 庫 is comprised of 广 (yǎn, shed; shelter) and 車 (chē, vehicle), originally meaning "garage," and later "warehouse." In the Oracle-Bone and Bronze Inscriptions, 車 depicts a chariot. In Seal Script, 車 is simplified to one wheel and its axle. Only the vehicle part 车 is simplified to form the simplified character 裤. The simplified character 车 derives from the cursive style of the traditional character 車.

褲 形聲。從衣，庫聲。庫，會意。從車，從广。广指大棚，本義指放兵車的大棚，引申為倉庫。簡體字库下部的车是繁體字車的草書楷化字。

草 裤 車 草 车

褲子 kùzi trousers; pants
短褲 duǎnkù short pants; shorts

褲腿 kùtuǐ trouser legs
牛仔褲 niúzǎikù jeans (literally: cowboy pants)

快

kuài
fast; quick

ASSOCIATIVE AND PICTOPHONETIC COMPOUND 快 is comprised of the vertical heart radical 忄 and the signifying and phonetic element 夬 (guài, archery), meaning "fast," "swift," "hurry up," or "soon." In the Oracle-Bone Inscriptions, 夬 resembles a hand and a bow, signifying the act of using a bow and arrow.

快 會意兼形聲。篆文從心，從夬(guài 鈎弦射箭)，夬亦聲。本義指心情順暢，痛快高興，如射出之箭。夬，會意。甲骨文像手拉射箭時所用的鈎弦器。

篆 快

快餐 kuàicān fast food
趕快 gǎnkuài at once; immediately

飛快 fēikuài very fast; at lightning speed
快樂 kuàilè happy; merry

塊/块

kuài
piece; dollar

PICTOPHONETIC CHARACTER 塊 consists of the earth/soil radical 土 and the phonetic element 鬼 (guǐ), originally meaning "lump of soil." Extended meanings of 塊 are "lump," "piece," "chunk," "gold or sliver dollar," and "dollar." In the Oracle-Bone Inscriptions, the character 鬼 resembles a monster with a huge head, meaning: "ghost," "spirit," "spooky," "sinister," etc. In Seal Script, a tail is added to the monster. 夬 replaces 鬼 to form the simplified character 块, as the pronunciation of 夬 (guài, archery) is similar to that of 塊 (kuài).

塊 形聲。從土，鬼聲。本義為土塊，引申為量詞。鬼，象形。在甲骨文、金文中均像大頭鬼。簡體字块用夬 (guài, archery) 替代鬼，因夬與塊聲音相似。

篆 𠙹 鬼 甲 𤾯 金 𩲡 篆 鬼

土塊 tǔkuài dirt clod
冰塊 bīngkuài ice cube

大塊頭 dàkuàitóu tall and bulky fellow; hefty man
一塊 yíkuài one block; one piece; one dollar; together

辣

là
spicy

PICTOPHONETIC CHARACTER The character 辣 consists of the semantic component 辛 (xīn, pungent) and the phonetic element 束 (shù), meaning "hot (spicy)," "peppery," "pungent," "sting," "vicious," and "ruthless." In the Oracle-Bone and Bronze Inscriptions, 辛 is a pictograph of a chiseled knife used to tattoo the faces of prisoners. The extended meanings of 辛 are "pungent," "laborious," and "suffering," In the Oracle-Bone Inscriptions, the character 束 looks like a sack tied on both ends with a cord, meaning "to tie," "to bind," "to control," "to restrain," "bundle," "bunch," etc. Some scholars think 束 looks like firewood tied together by rope.

辣 形聲。從辛，束聲。本義指辣椒、蒜等有刺激性的味道，引申義有兇狠、殘忍等。辛，象形，像在犯人臉上刺字的刑具。引申義有辛苦、辛辣等。束，會意。金文從口從木，像袋子的兩端被捆扎起來。也有人認為束像用繩子把木柴捆在一起。束本義為束縛。

辣椒 làjiāo chili; hot pepper
酸甜苦辣 suān tián kǔ là sour, sweet, bitter, and spicy; joys and sorrows of life

辣妹 làmèi sexy girl

來/来

lái
to come

PHONETIC LOAN CHARACTER In its ancient form, 來 looks like a wheat plant. The original meaning of 來 was "wheat," but later it came to mean "come." In Regular Script, 來 is the combination of 木 (mù, wood; tree) and two 人 (rén, man; person), suggesting two people coming together beneath a tree. The simplified character 来 derives from the cursive style of the traditional version 來.

來 假借。甲骨文中像一株有根杆葉穗的麥苗。本義為麥，後借用為來去的來，本義遂失。簡體字来是繁體字來的草書楷化字。

甲 來 金 來 篆 𣏟 草 来

回來 huílai to return; to come back
來自 láizì to come from (a place)

起來 qǐlai to stand up; to get up
將來 jiānglái in the future; future

The Way of Chinese Characters

藍/蓝

lán
blue

PICTOPHONETIC CHARACTER 藍 is composed of the grass radical ⺾ and the phonetic component 監 (jiān), meaning "indigo plant" and extending to mean "blue." In the Oracle-Bone and Bronze Inscriptions, the character 監 represents a girl kneeling next to a basin and gazing at her reflection in the water, meaning "watch," "oversee," "supervise," etc. In Regular Script, 臣 (chén, a vertical eye, extended to mean "official") and 皿 (mǐn, utensil) still carry traces of the original 監. The simplified character 蓝 derives from the cursive style of 藍 with two vertical lines replacing the component 臣.

藍 形聲。從艸，監聲。本義指蓼藍，葉子可用來提煉藍色染料。監，象形。甲骨文、金文中監字像人睜大眼用水盆照自己的容顏。簡體字蓝是繁體字藍的草書楷化字，將臣簡化為兩豎。

篆 藍 草 藍 監 甲 監 金 監

藍色 lánsè blue (color)
藍天 lántiān blue sky

深藍 shēnlán dark blue
藍圖 lántú blueprint

籃/篮

lán
basket

PICTOPHONETIC CHARACTER The character 籃 consists of the bamboo radical ⺮ and the phonetic element 監 (jiān), originally referring to "basket made of bamboo, vine, or willow twigs." Nowadays 籃 is also used to refer to basketball. For more about the origins of 監, see the entry for 藍 (lán, blue). The simplified character 监 derives from the cursive style of 監, in which two vertical lines replace 臣. 监 is in its simplified form in the character 篮.

籃 形聲。從竹，監聲。本義為竹籤或柳條編成的籃子，引申為籃球運動。监是監的草書簡化字，將監字中的臣簡化為兩豎。簡化字篮屬偏旁類推簡化。

篆 籃 監 甲 監 金 監 篆 監

籃子 lánzi basket
男籃 nánlán men's basketball

籃球 lánqiú basketball
女籃 nǚlán women's basketball

懶/懒

lǎn
lazy

PICTOPHONETIC CHARACTER In Seal Script, 嬾 consists of the female radical 女 and the phonetic component 賴 (lài), meaning "lazy," "idle," or "indolent" and reflecting ancient prejudice against women. In Regular Script, the female radical 女 is replaced by the heart radical ⺖, suggesting "laziness" is related to one's heart. In Seal Script, 賴 is formed with a shell 貝 (bèi) and the phonetic element 剌 (là, slash). 賴 originally meant "to profit" and extended to mean "to depend on," "to renege (on an agreement)," "to accuse falsely," "bad," or "poor." In the simplified 懒, only 貝 is simplified into 贝.

懶 形聲。篆文從女，賴聲。意為懶惰、不勤快、疲憊無力。楷書改女字旁為豎心旁。篆文嬾字表現了對女性的歧視與偏見。賴，形聲。篆文從貝，剌聲。本義為贏利、利益。引申義有依靠、耍賴等。簡化字懒字中貝字簡化為贝，属于偏旁類推简化。

篆 懶

懶人 lǎnrén lazy fellow
好吃懶做 hàochī lǎnzuò to like to eat but hate to work; to eat one's head off
懶得 lǎnde not wishing to do anything; disinclined

lǎo
old

PICTOGRAPH   In the Oracle-Bone and Bronze Inscriptions, the character 老 depicts an old man with long hair and a bent back, leaning on a walking stick. Although the character looks significantly different in its regular script form, one can still see evidence of the older forms. The extended meanings of 老 include "venerable," "experienced," "of long standing," "all the time," "of the past," and "outdated."

老　象形。像長髮長鬚老人弓腰扶拐杖之形。

甲 𦥑 金 𦥑 篆 耆

老人 lǎorén old man or woman; the elderly
老師 lǎoshī teacher

老年 lǎonián old age
老闆 lǎobǎn boss; proprietor

了

le
(particle for the completion of an action)

PICTOGRAPH In Seal Script, 了 looks like a baby who is wrapped in swaddling clothes. The original meaning of 了 was to finish wrapping a baby in a blanket or swaddling clothes. Now 了 is used to mean the end or completion of an event or action. Compare 了 with 子 (zǐ, son; child).

了　象形。從子，但無臂，像嬰兒在繈褓中束其兩臂。本義為收束、引申為完畢、了解、結束等。

篆 𠄌

算了 suànle forget about it
除了… 以外 chúle … yǐwài besides; apart from; in addition to; except for

為了 wèile in order to; for the sake of

累

lèi
tired

ASSOCIATIVE AND PICTOPHONETIC CHARACTER   In Seal Script, the character 累 is comprised of the semantic component 糸 (mì, silk thread) and the phonetic element 畾 (léi), originally meaning "rope." The extended meanings of 累 include "tie up," "bind," "detain," "get somebody into trouble," "toil," "tired," etc. In Regular Script, the character 累 is made up of 田 (tián, field) and 糸 (mì, silk string). In the past men worked in the field and women made silk. Both jobs were laborious and made people exhausted.

累　會意兼形聲。篆文從糸，畾聲，有纏繞、捆綁、牽連、拖累、勞累等意。正體字上為田，下為糸 (束絲)，可想為男耕女織都是使人勞累之事。

篆 𤳋 𤳋

累死了 lèisǐle to be exhausted

勞累 láolèi tired; exhausted; worn out; to toil

lěng
cold

PICTOPHONETIC CHARACTER The character 冷 is comprised of the ice radical 冫 and the phonetic element 令 (lìng, order; command), meaning "cold," "frosty," "deserted," etc. In the Oracle-Bone Inscriptions, 令 resembles a person sitting under a roof and opening his mouth to issue instructions. Be sure to distinguish 令 from 今 (jīn, today; now).

冷　形聲。從冫，令聲。本義為寒冷，引申義有冷淡、寂靜、不常見等。令，甲骨文中上像屋頂，下像一跪坐人形，指人于室內發號施令。

篆 冷　令 甲 弓　金 𠁥　篆 令

冰冷 bīnglěng ice cold
冷清 lěngqīng cold and cheerless; deserted

冷氣 lěngqì air conditioning
冷笑 lěngxiào sneer

lí
pear

PICTOPHONETIC CHARACTER The character 梨 contains the wood/tree radical 木 and the phonetic component 利, meaning "pear." 利 combines 禾 (hé, grain) and the knife radical 刂, signifying the act of reaping grain with a knife. The extended meanings of 利 include "sharp," "gain," "profit," "benefit," or "advantage." In its ancient forms, 禾 resembles ripe grain on a stalk.

梨　形聲。從木，利聲。意為梨樹或梨樹的果實。利，會意。從禾從刀（刂），指用鐮刀收割禾穀，本義為鋒利，引申為利益、有利等。禾在古文字中像成熟了的稻穀。

篆 梨

梨子 lízi pear
梨花 líhuā pear flower

梨樹 líshù pear tree
鳳梨 fènglí pineapple

lí
away from

ASSOCIATIVE AND PICTOPHONETIC COMPOUND In the Oracle-Bone Inscriptions, the character 離 depicts a bird in a net, indicating the act of catching a bird. Its original meaning was "oriole," and because the bird is caught in the net, its extended meanings include "to suffer," "to separate," "apart from," "distant from." You can find 隹 (zhuī), the pictograph of a short-tailed bird in the **Basic Radicals** section. The simplified character 离 retains only the left part of 離.

離　會意兼形聲。從隹，离聲。甲骨文像以網捕鳥形。原義為黃鸝（黃鶯）。因黃鸝遭到捕獲而引申為遭受、分開、相距等。隹，象形。意為短尾鳥。簡化字离僅用繁體字離的左邊。

甲 𪚗　篆 离　離

分離 fēnlí to separate
離婚 líhūn to divorce

離開 líkāi to leave; to depart from
離題 lítí to go off topic; to digress

李

lǐ
plum;
(surname)

ASSOCIATIVE AND PICTOPHONETIC COMPOUND The character 李 has 木 (mù, tree; wood) on the top and 子 (zǐ, child) underneath, meaning "plum." The character 李 resembles a child under a plum tree, trying to reach the fruit. Both 木 and 子 help to reveal the meaning of the character 李. 子 also functions as a phonetic symbol.

李 會意兼形聲。從木，子聲。本義為果木。孩子站在樹下看樹上的李子，考慮如何摘下。

篆

李子 lǐzi plum
老李 lǎolǐ Old Li

行李 xíngli luggage; baggage
李白 Lǐ Bái Li Bai (701-762), famous Tang Dynasty poet

理

lǐ
reason; in good order

PICTOPHONETIC CHARACTER The character 理 consists of the jade radical 王 (see 王 (wáng) in **Basic Radicals**) and the phonetic element 里 (lǐ), referring to "processing jade stone." The extended meanings of 理 are "texture," "inner essence," "reason," "logic," "truth," "theory," "natural science," "to operate," "to manage," "to put in order," "to tidy up," "to pay attention to," etc. 里 is the combination of 田 (tián, field) and 土 (tǔ, earth; soil), referring to "native place" or "neighborhood."

理 形聲。篆文從玉，里聲。本義為治玉，即按照紋理把玉從石裏剖出來。引申為紋理、事理、理論、自然科學、管理、整理等。王作為偏旁時意指玉，有王作偏旁的字本義多與玉有關。里，會意。從田，從土。表示人所居住的地方與長度單位，如故里、萬里等。

篆 理

整理 zhěnglǐ to organize; to sort
理科 lǐkē (subjects of) natural sciences

真理 zhēnlǐ truth
物理 wùlǐ physics

裏/裡/里

lǐ
inside

PICTOPHONETIC CHARACTER In **Basic Radicals**, you can find the character 衣 (yī, clothing) and its radical form 衤. The characters 裏/裡 consist of the radicals 衣/衤 and the phonetic element 里 (lǐ). 裏/裡 originally meant "lining" (of a garment), and extends to mean "inside" or "in." 里 is the combination of 田 (tián, field) and 土 (tǔ, earth; soil), referring to "native place" or "neighborhood." To form 裏, 里 was inserted into 衣, while 裡 combines 衤 and 里. 里 is the simplified form for both 裏 and 裡.

裏/裡 形聲。從衣，里聲。本義指衣服的裏層，引申為內部、裏面。里，會意。從田，從土。有田有土，表示人所居住的地方與長度單位，如故里、鄰里、萬里等。簡體字里的字意擴充，包含了繁體字裏/裡的所有意思。

篆 裏

裏邊 lǐbian inside
那裏 nàlǐ there

這裏 zhèlǐ here; inside
哪裏 nǎlǐ where; humble expression for denying compliments

The Way of Chinese Characters

禮 / 礼

lǐ
gift;
ceremony

ASSOCIATIVE AND PICTOPHONETIC COMPOUND In the Oracle-Bone and Bronze Inscriptions, 豊 depicts a high-legged plate with two strings of jade inside, referring to a ceremonial utensil. In Seal Script, a show/altar radical 礻/示 (shì, show) was added on the left. 禮 originally meant "offering sacrifices to gods" and later came to mean "rite," "ceremony," "etiquette," "courtesy," and "gift." In the Oracle-Bone Inscriptions, 示 represents a T-shaped stone table upon which sacrificial offerings were placed. When 示 (shì, show) functions as a radical, it is written as 礻. 礼 was a variant form of 禮 and is now its simplified version.

禮 會意兼形聲。禮原寫作豊(lǐ)。豊在甲骨文、金文上為兩串玉,下為豆(器皿),表示將玉放在器皿中,作為祭祀的供品。篆文給豊字左邊加義符示/礻(祭桌)而成為禮。本義為祭神以求福,引申為禮節、禮儀、禮貌、禮物等。簡化字礼的寫法古時已有。

甲 𧰨 金 豊 篆 禮

婚禮 hūnlǐ wedding, marriage ceremony
禮物 lǐwù gift

禮拜 lǐbài week; worship
送禮 sònglǐ to give someone a present

倆 / 俩

liǎ
(colloquial)
two

ASSOCIATIVE AND PICTOPHONETIC COMPOUND The character 倆 consists of the person radical 亻 and the semantic and phonetic component 兩 (liǎng, two; a couple), referring to two persons primarily. 倆 also means "both," "a pair," or "some" and is usually used colloquially in northern China. In the Bronze Inscriptions, the character 兩 depicts a chariot with two yokes, meaning "a couple" or "two." In the simplified character 两, the inside is composed of two 人, differing slightly from the traditional character 兩. In the character 俩, 兩 is simplified to 两.

倆 會意兼形聲。從亻,從兩。指兩個(夫妻倆),也指少量幾個(買倆饅頭帶著)。倆字主要用在華北一些地方的口語中。兩,會意。金文像一輛有兩個軛的戰車,引申為並列成雙之物。簡體字两去掉兩字中間一豎,並把中間的兩個入字改為兩個人字。

咱倆 zánliǎ we two
姐妹倆 jiěmèiliǎ the two sisters

他們倆 tāménliǎ the two of them
兄弟倆 xiōngdìliǎ the two brothers

連 / 连

lián
even; to link

ASSOCIATIVE COMPOUND The character 連 is made up of the walk radical 辶 and 車 (chē, vehicle; cart), originally meaning "to pull a cart." Its extended meanings are "to connect," "to link," "in succession," "continuously," "a company (of soldiers)," "including," "to involve," and "even." In the Oracle-Bone and Bronze Inscriptions, the character 車 depicts a chariot complete with frame, axle, wheels, and yokes. In Seal Script, 車 is simplified to one wheel on its axle. The simplified character 车 developed from the cursive style of 車. 車 is simplified in the character 连.

連 會意。從辶/辵,從車。本義表示拉車行走,引申為連接、連續、牽連、包括、甚至、以及軍隊的編制單位。車,象形。篆文像簡化了的車形,只有車架、一個輪子與軸。簡化字车是繁體字車的草書楷化字。簡化字连屬於偏旁類推簡化。

篆 連

連接 liánjiē to link; to connect
接二連三 jiē'èr liánsān one after another

連日 liánrì day after day
連... 都... lián... dōu... even...

臉/脸

liǎn
face

PICTOPHONETIC CHARACTER 臉 consists of the flesh radical 月 and the phonetic indicator 僉 (qiān), meaning "face" and extended to mean "dignity." Chinese people are traditionally concerned about not losing face (dignity) (丟臉 diū liǎn). 僉 has 亼 (jí, to gather together) on top, two mouths (吅 xuān) in the middle, and two persons underneath (从 cóng), originally referring to many people speaking simultaneously and extended to mean "unanimous," "together," or "all." The simplified 佥 derives from the cursive version of 僉 and is always written as 佥 when it is the phonetic indicator in a simplified character.

臉 形聲。從月（肉月），僉 (qiān) 聲。本義為臉頰、引申義有整個面部、情面等。僉 (qiān)，會意。上從亼(jí集合)，中從二口 (吅 xuān)，下從二人（从），本義為眾人同聲，引申為眾人、大家、都。簡化字佥源於僉的草書楷化字。簡化字脸屬於偏旁簡化。

草

長臉 chángliǎn long face
臉紅 liǎnhóng to blush

臉書 liǎnshū Facebook
不要臉 búyàoliǎn shameless

練/练

liàn
to practice;
to drill

PICTOPHONETIC CHARACTER The character 練 is comprised of the silk radical 糸 and the phonetic element 柬 (jiǎn). 練 originally meant "to boil and scour raw silk," and extends to mean "practice," "drill," or "train." In its ancient form, 柬 consists of 束 (shù, a bunch of bamboo pieces; firewood) and 八 (bā, to divide; eight). The original meaning of 柬 was "to choose" or "select." Later it came to mean "note" or "card." The silk radical is simplified to form 练, while the right part derives from the cursive style of the character 柬.

練 形聲。從糸，柬聲。本義指把生絲煮得柔軟潔白，引申為反復練習。柬，從束（一捆東西），從八（分別），意指打開一捆東西從中挑選，引申為信札書簡。簡體字练字左邊的部首由糸簡化為纟，右邊一半是柬字的草書楷化字。

篆 練 草 練

練習 liànxí exercise; drill; practice
教練 jiàoliàn sports coach; trainer

練字 liànzì to practice writing characters
熟練 shúliàn practiced; proficient; skilled

涼/凉

liáng
cool

PICTOPHONETIC CHARACTER The character 涼 consists of the water radical 氵 and the phonetic symbol 京 (jīng), meaning "cool", "cold," "chilly," and "discouraged." In the Oracle-Bone and Bronze Inscriptions, 京, which means "capital city," looks like a palace at the top of a hill or artificial mound. In the simplified character 凉, the ice radical 冫 replaces the water radical 氵.

涼 形聲。從水，京聲。本義為水溫較低，引申為溫度較低，使降溫、灰心失望等。京，象形。甲骨文、金文字形像在高丘上建造的宮殿。一說像人工筑成的高丘，引申為京城。涼過去為凉的俗寫字，現用作涼的簡體字。冫的意思是冰，例如用在冰、冷等字中。

篆 涼

涼菜 liángcài cold dish
涼快 liángkuài nice and cool

涼鞋 liángxié sandals
涼水 liángshuǐ cold water

兩/两

liǎng
two; a couple of

ASSOCIATIVE COMPOUND In the Bronze Inscriptions, the character 兩 resembles a chariot with two yokes, meaning "a couple" or "two." In Regular Script, 兩 retains the same basic structure as that of the Bronze Inscription form. In the simplified character 两, the inside is composed of two 人, differing slightly from the traditional character 兩.

兩　會意。金文像車衡上有兩個軛的戰車，引申為並列成雙之物。簡體字两去掉兩字中間一豎，並把中間的兩個入字改為兩個人字。這種寫法元代已見。

金 兩　篆 兩

兩旁 liǎngpáng　both sides　　　　兩國 liǎngguó　both countries
一舉兩得 yìjǔ liǎngdé　one move, two gains; kill two birds with one stone

---

亮

liàng
bright

ASSOCIATIVE COMPOUND In Seal Script, 亮 consists of 高 (gāo, tall; high) in the upper part and 人 in the lower part, suggesting a person standing in a high place, where it is presumably also bright. Take care to distinguish 亮 from 高.

亮　會意。篆文從高，從儿（人），表示人在高處則明亮。

篆 亮

明亮 míngliàng　bright; shining　　　天亮 tiānliàng　dawn; daybreak
亮點 liàngdiǎn　highlight; bright spot　　漂亮 piàoliang　pretty; beautiful

---

聊

liáo
to chat

ASSOCIATIVE AND PICTOPHONETIC COMPOUND The character 聊 is comprised of the ear radical 耳 (ěr) and the phonetic and signifying element 卯 (mǎo, mortise and tenon joint), suggesting that chatter and small talk can bring people closer to each other (like a mortise and tenon). In its ancient form, 卯 looks like an animal cut in half. The original meaning of 卯 was "slaughter" or "kill;" "mortise and tenon" is its extended meaning.

聊　會意兼形聲。從耳，卯聲，意為依賴、閒談等。卯，象形。甲骨文中像將一物從中間分開。本義為剖分，引申為榫眼等。

卯 甲 卯　金 卯　篆 卯

聊天 liáotiān　to chat　　　　聊聊 liáoliao　to chat
無聊 wúliáo　bored; boring; senseless　　閒聊 xiánliáo　to chat casually

料

liào
material

ASSOCIATIVE COMPOUND The character 料 is comprised of 米 (mǐ, rice) and 斗 (dǒu, Chinese peck; a measure for grain: 1斗=1 decalitre), indicating the act of measuring grains with a 斗. The original meaning of 料 was "to measure" or "to weigh" and has been extended to mean "to estimate," "to calculate," "to anticipate," "to guess," "to take care of," "material," "stuff," etc. In the Oracle-Bone Inscriptions, 斗 looks like a dipper for liquor, referring to "measuring device."

料 會意。左邊是米，右邊是斗，指用斗來量米，本義為稱量，引申為估計、料想、照料、原料等。斗，象形。甲骨文像舀酒的勺形，引申指量器。

金 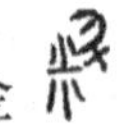 篆 

木料 mùliào lumber; timber
香料 xiāngliào spice
飲料 yǐnliào beverage
料理 liàolǐ to manage; cuisine

另

lìng
other; another

PICTOGRAPH In the Oracle-Bone Inscriptions, 另 is the variant form of 冎 (guǎ), which looks like a piece of ox scapula used for divination, meaning "to scrape meat off bones for divination." "To separate," "separately," "in addition," "other," and "another" are the extended meanings of 另. In Regular Script, 另 becomes the combination of 口 (kǒu, mouth) and 力 (lì, power; strength).

另 象形。甲骨文中與冎本為一字，像是一塊剔淨用來占卜的牛肩胛骨。本義為剔淨牛骨，引申為割開、分開、另外、別的。

甲  篆 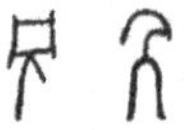

另外 lìngwài other; moreover
另行 lìngxíng separately; at some other time
另請高明 lìng qǐng gāomíng to find someone better qualified

樓/楼

lóu
multi-storied building; floor (of a building)

PICTOPHONETIC CHARACTER The character 樓 consists of the wood radical 木 and the phonetic element 婁 (lóu), referring to "a building of two or more stories" or "one of the stories of a building." In Seal Script, 婁 is the combination of 母 (mǔ, mother), 中 (zhōng, middle) and 女 (nǚ, female), possibly suggesting that it is difficult for a middle-aged woman to become a mother and therefore meaning "hollow," "physically weak," or "debilitated." The simplified character 娄 derives from the cursive style of 婁. Thus in the character 楼, 婁 is replaced by 娄.

樓 形聲。從木，婁聲。指兩層或兩層以上的房屋，也指房子的一層。婁（lóu），會意。從母、中、女，本義為中空，引申為身體虛弱。西瓜過熟而瓜瓤中空也稱作"婁了"。簡化字娄是婁的草書楷化字，宋元已有此字。楼字中娄簡化。

篆  **婁** 草 

樓房 lóufáng building
樓上 lóushàng upstairs
二樓 èrlóu second floor
樓下 lóuxià downstairs

路
lù
road; way

PICTOPHONETIC CHARACTER The character 路 is the combination of the foot radical 足 and the phonetic symbol 各 (gè), meaning "road," "path," "way," "route," etc. In the Oracle-Bone and Bronze Inscriptions, 各 combines 夂 (an approaching foot) and 口 (the entrance of a cave-dwelling). The original meaning of 各 was "to arrive" and later it came to mean "each" or "every."

路 形聲。從足，從各（到來），各亦聲。意指道路。

金 路 篆 路

公路 gōnglù highway; road
路燈 lùdēng street light

路上 lùshang on the road; on a journey
走路 zǒulù to walk; to go on foot

錄／录
lù
to record

PICTOPHONETIC CHARACTER In Seal Script, 錄 is comprised of the gold radical 金 and the phonetic component 录 (lù). The original meaning of 錄 was "golden color" and extended meanings include "to write down," "record," "copy," "hire," etc. In the Oracle-Bone and Bronze Inscriptions, 录 looks like water filtering through a hanging sack. 录 originally meant "filter" and extended to mean "record" and "copy." The simplified character 录 comes from the right part of 錄, which is a variant form of 錄.

錄 形聲。從金，录聲，記載、抄寫、錄用之意。录，會意。甲骨、金文像木架上吊了一個布袋，濾出裏面的水。录的本義為濾。繁體字錄的另一寫法是彔，簡體字录去掉錄的金字旁。

录 甲 [seal] 金 [seal] 篆 [seal]

錄音 lùyīn to record (sound); sound recording
錄取 lùqǔ to recruit; to enroll; to admit to

錄像 lùxiàng to videotape; video recording
錄用 lùyòng to hire (an employee)

亂／乱
luàn
randomly; messily

ASSOCIATIVE COMPOUND In the Bronze Inscriptions, the character 亂 looks like two hands unraveling entangled silk strings, meanings "messy," "disorder," "chaos," "riot," "confused," "perplexed," "arbitrarily," and "randomly." In later forms, 乚 is added to the right of the character. In the simplified character 乱, 舌 (shé, tongue) replaces the left part of 亂, since some people sometimes would 胡言亂語 (húyán luànyǔ, to speak at random; to talk nonsense).

亂 會意。篆文左邊上下像以兩手整理架上的亂絲。本義為整理亂絲，引申指無秩序、無條理、心緒不寧、混淆、男女之間不正當的關係、隨便任意等。簡化字把亂字左邊改為舌，有言語混亂之意。宋元已見此字。

篆 [seal]

忙亂 mángluàn rushed and muddled
亂七八糟 luànqī bāzāo at sixes and sevens; in a terrible mess

亂說 luànshuō to blabber; to make irresponsible remarks

倫/伦

lún
ethics;
moral principles

PICTOPHONETIC CHARACTER The character 倫 contains the person radical 亻 and the phonetic component 侖 (lún), meaning "normal human relationship," "ethics," "order," "match," "comparison," and "coherence." In ancient writing, 侖 consists of 亼 (jí, to gather together; to assemble) and 冊 (cè, book; volume), indicating the act of compiling documents and meaning "to arrange" or "logical order." 冊 resembles a set of bamboo slips stringed together into a book, a common bookmaking method in ancient China. In the simplified character 伦 the right part of 倫 has been replaced with the similarly pronounced 仑.

倫 形聲。從亻，侖聲。本義為人倫，引申為秩序、同類、匹敵等。侖，會意。從亼(jí 集合)，從冊。表示將竹簡按文理順序編成冊。意為順序、條理。冊在古文字中像被編串在一起的竹簡。簡化字仑是用匕替代侖字的下半部分。倫的簡化字是伦。

人倫 rénlún human relations; ethics
倫理 lúnlǐ ethics; morals

天倫 tiānlún family bonds
亂倫 luànlún incest

旅

lǚ
to travel

ASSOCIATIVE COMPOUND In the Oracle-Bone and Bronze Inscriptions, the character 旅 depicts two men under an army flag, meaning "a brigade." The extended meanings of 旅 include "troop," "force," "trip," and "travel." In Seal Script, 旅 combines 㫃 (yǎn, flags flying) with 从 (two persons, one following another). In Regular Script, 从 in the character 旅 looks different from that in Seal Script.

旅 會意。甲骨文、金文像二人在飄揚的軍旗下。本義是軍旅，古代軍隊的編制單位。引申義為軍隊、在外作客、旅行等。

旅館 lǚguǎn hotel
旅行 lǚxíng travel

旅客 lǚkè traveler
旅行社 lǚxíngshè travel agency

律

lǜ
law; rule

PICTOPHONETIC CHARACTER The character 律 combines the radical 彳 (left step; walk slowly) with 聿 (yù, pen; then) as the phonetic symbol, meaning "rule" or "law." In the Oracle-Bone and Bronze Inscriptions, 聿 shows a hand holding a brush. 聿 is often used in characters pertaining to brushwork, such as 書 (shū, book), 筆 (bǐ, pen), and 畫 (huà, painting).

律 形聲。從彳（左腳走半步為彳，一説彳為小步走走停停的樣子，一説指半條街），聿聲。意為法律、規則。聿，象形。甲骨文、金文像以手持筆狀，本義為筆。

法律 fǎlǜ law
紀律 jìlǜ discipline

律師 lǜshī lawyer
一律 yílǜ uniformly; without exception

綠 / 绿

lǜ
green

PICTOPHONETIC CHARACTER The character 綠 is composed of the silk radical 糸 and the phonetic component 录 (lù), meaning "green." In the Oracle-Bone and Bronze Inscriptions, the character 录 looks like water filtering through a hanging sack. 录 originally meant "filter" and extended to mean "record," or "copy." You can also find 录 in 錄 (lù, to record). 绿 is a variant form of 綠, of which the silk radical is simplified to 纟 to form the simplified character 绿.

綠 形聲。從糸，录聲，本義為綠色。绿是綠的異體字，部首簡化後變為簡體字。

篆

綠燈 lǜdēng green light
綠茶 lǜchá green tea
綠化 lǜhuà make green with plants; to reforest
綠豆 lǜdòu mung bean

媽 / 妈

mā
mother; mom

PICTOPHONETIC CHARACTER The character 媽 is composed of 女 (nǚ, female) and 馬 (mǎ, horse). 女 shows that the character's meaning relates to someone female and 馬 indicates the pronunciation. 媽 does not mean female horse, though! In the simplified character 妈, 马 derives from the cursive form of 馬.

媽 形聲。從女，馬聲。簡體字妈右邊的馬簡化為马。

媽媽 māma mommy; mother
大媽 dàmā father's elder brother's wife; aunty (term for an elderly woman)
奶媽 nǎimā wet nurse

麻

má
hemp; numb

ASSOCIATIVE COMPOUND The character 麻 combines 广 (yǎn, shed; shelter) and 枂 (pài, peel; hemp), referring to people working with hemp in a workshop. 麻 originally meant "hemp" or "flax." Since the surface of hemp is usually rough, extended meanings of 麻 include "rough," "coarse," "numb," etc.

麻 會意。篆文從广（敞屋），從 枂（pài 剝麻），表示人在屋下劈麻晾麻。麻是大麻、亞麻、黃麻等植物的統稱。

金 麻 篆 麻

大麻 dàmá hemp; marijuana
芝麻 zhīma sesame (seed)
麻煩 máfan troublesome; trouble; to trouble
麻木 mámù numb; insensitive

L-R

碼／码

mǎ
symbol indicating a
number

PICTOPHONETIC CHARACTER The character 碼 consists of the stone radical 石 (shí) and the phonetic element 馬 (mǎ), originally referring to "agate" in the combination "碼碯" (mǎnǎo). Today "agate" is expressed by 瑪瑙, while 碼 is borrowed to mean "a sign or symbol indicating a number," "code," "weight," "yard (a measure of length)," and "to pile up." In its ancient form, 石 looks like a rock under a cliff. In the simplified character 码, 马 is used to replace 馬.

碼 形聲。從石，馬聲。本義為瑪瑙，後此意用瑪瑙來表示，而碼借用為表示數目、文字的符號、計算數目的用具（籌碼、砝碼）、漢字編碼、堆疊，也作為英文長度單位yard的譯名。

石 甲 石 金 石 篆 石

號碼 hàomǎ number
數碼 shùmǎ digit

密碼 mìmǎ secret code; password
數碼相機 shùmǎ xiàngjī digital camera

嗎／吗

ma
question
particle

PICTOPHONETIC CHARACTER The character 嗎 combines the mouth radical 口 with a phonetic 馬 (mǎ, horse). 馬 is a pictograph of a horse. The mouth radical 口 is often used as a component of interrogatives and onomatopoeic words. In the simplified form of the character (吗), the 马 part derives from the cursive form of 馬.

嗎 形聲。部首"口"有時用於疑問詞或象聲詞。馬，象形字。簡體字右邊用了簡化的马字。

好嗎 hǎoma OK?
是嗎 shìma Is that so?

夠嗎 gòuma Is that enough?
不是嗎 búshìma Isn't that so?

買／买

mǎi
to buy

ASSOCIATIVE COMPOUND In the Oracle-Bone and Bronze Inscriptions, 買 is the combination of 网 (wǎng, net) and 貝 (bèi, cowry shell). These shells were used as money in ancient times. In the Oracle-Bone Inscriptions, the character 网 is the pictograph of a net. In Regular Script, the net radical is written as 罒. The character 買 contains 罒 and 貝. The simplified form 买 is developed from the cursive style of 買.

買 會意。甲骨文、金文從网，從貝，像用網撈貝。古時以貝殼做為貨幣換取物品，意為購買。簡體字买是繁體字買的草書楷化字。

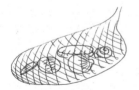

甲 罓 金 貝 篆 買 草 买

買菜 mǎicài to buy vegetables; do grocery shopping
買主 mǎizhǔ buyer

買單 mǎidān to pay a restaurant bill
購買力 gòumǎilì purchasing power

賣 / 卖

mài
to sell

ASSOCIATIVE COMPOUND In the Bronze Inscriptions, the top part of 賣 contains a big eye and a cowry shell, suggesting showing merchandise to a customer. In Seal Script, 賣 is the combination of 出 (chū, out) and 買 (mǎi, to buy), indicating that merchandise has been sold. In Regular Script, 出 is simplified to 士 (shì, man), possibly referring to a man who has bought the goods. The original meaning of 賣 was "to sell," and came to mean "to show off," "to spare no effort," "to betray," etc. The simplified form 卖 developed from the cursive style of 賣.

賣 會意。金文上為眼，像以貨物示人。篆文從出，從買，楷書上部改為士。本義為出售貨物換錢。引申義有賣弄、賣力、出賣等。買，會意。甲骨文、金文從网，從貝，像用網撈貝。古時曾以貝殼為貨幣，意為購買。簡體字卖是繁體字賣的草書楷化字。

金 𩫡 篆 𧶜 草 卖

買賣 mǎimài buying and selling; business	賣主 màizhǔ seller
拍賣 pāimài auction	專賣店 zhuānmàidiàn specialty store

慢

màn
slow

PICTOPHONETIC CHARACTER The character 慢 consists of the vertical heart radical ⺖ and the phonetic component 曼 (màn), meaning "slow." In the Oracle-Bone Inscriptions, 曼 depicts two hands holding an eye open. The original meaning of 曼 was "open eyes," with the extended meanings "prolonged" and "graceful." Later, the hands in the upper part changed to 曰, forming the Regular Script form of 曼.

慢 形聲。從心，曼聲，本義為惰怠。曼，會意。甲骨文、金文像看到美妙的人或事時，以兩手把眼睛撐得大大的，目不轉睛地看。本義為張目，引申為美好、嫵媚之意。

慢 慢 曼 甲 𤕣 金 𣋎 篆 𣋗

慢跑 mànpǎo jogging; to jog	慢慢 mànmàn slowly
慢慢吃 mànmàn chī Enjoy your meal	放慢 fàngmàn to slow

忙

máng
busy

PICTOPHONETIC CHARACTER The character 忙 has the vertical heart radical ⺖ and the phonetic component 亡 (wáng, to flee), meaning "busy" or "hurry," states which can affect one's heart. In its ancient form, the character 亡 looks like a person (the upper part) hiding in a corner (the lower part). Its original meaning is "run away," from which derived the meanings "lose," "perish," and "decease."

忙 形聲。從忄，亡聲。《說文》認為亡字從人，從乚。乚為隱蔽，意指人逃亡時躲在於隱蔽之處。

亡 甲 𠤣 金 𠤛 篆 𠤔

忙亂 mángluàn rushed and muddled	急忙 jímáng hastily
忙碌 mánglù busy; bustle about	幫忙 bāngmáng to help; to lend a hand; to do a favor

L - R

毛

máo
hair; dime

PICTOGRAPH In the Bronze Inscriptions, the character 毛 looks like a tuft of hair, originally meaning "fur." Extended meanings of 毛 are "hair," "wool," "rough," "*mao*" (a fractional unit of money in China), or "dime." Be sure to distinguish 毛 from 手 (shǒu, hand).

毛 象形。金文像皮上叢生的毛。

金 篆

毛筆 máobǐ writing brush
毛巾 máojīn towel

毛衣 máoyī woolen sweater; sweater
毛病 máobìng fault; defect; shortcoming

冒

mào
to belch;
to emit

ASSOCIATIVE COMPOUND In its ancient forms, 冒 is comprised of a hat 冃 (mào) placed over an eye 目 (mù). It originally meant "hat," and has been extended to mean "to cover," "to emit," "to give off," "to risk," "brave," "rash," "imprudent," "to pretend to be," etc. Later, a scarf radical 巾 was added to the left of 冒 to form the new character 帽 (mào) and refer to a "hat". Thus 冒 no longer carries its original meaning.

冒 會意。從冃（mào，帽子），從目，指頭上戴帽子。本義是帽子，此意現寫作帽。冒的引申義有覆蓋、向上升、頂著、不顧、冒失、冒充等。

金  篆

冒險 màoxiǎn to take a risk; to venture
冒名 màomíng to use someone else's name; imposter

冒死 màosǐ to risk one's life
感冒 gǎnmào to have a cold

麼／么

me
(interrogative
or exclamatory
particle)

PICTOPHONETIC CHARACTER The character 麼 consists of the phonetic indicator 麻 (má, hemp) and the component 幺 (yāo, tiny), functioning as an interrogative auxiliary. In the Oracle-Bone and Bronze Inscriptions, 幺 and 么 (me) are used interchangeably to mean a "wisp of silk." 麻 combines 广 (yǎn, shed; shelter) and 林 (pài, to peel hemp), suggesting people processing hemp in a workshop. 麻 originally meant "hemp" or "flax" and extended to mean "rough," "coarse," "numb," etc. The simplified character 么 is derived from the bottom part of the traditional 麼.

麼 形聲。用為助詞，語氣詞。從么，麻聲。甲骨文、金文中么同幺，像一把細絲。麻，像在敞屋下（或屋簷下）劈麻晾麻。簡體字么取繁體字麼的下半部。

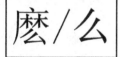

篆

什麼 shénme what
怎麼 zěnme how (Verb); how come

多麼 duōme how (Adj.); so
那麼 nàme like that; in that way; so

沒 / 没

méi
(have) not

mò
to sink

ASSOCIATIVE COMPOUND In Seal Script, 沒 consists of a circle or whirlpool 回 on top, and a right hand 又 at the bottom, indicating a person sinking in a whirlpool with one hand sticking out. It makes sense that the original meaning of 沒 was "to sink" or "disappear" (pronounced mò). Current meanings include "disappear," "end," and "to not have." In Regular Script, a water radical 氵 is added to the left of the character and the component 回 on the top has been simplified to 几 or 勹. The simplified form is 没.

没 會意。從水。篆文像
人淹沒在漩渦中，水面
上只能看見一隻手狀。
本義為淹沒，引申為沒
有。没是沒的異體字，
也用為沒的簡化字。

篆

沒有 méiyǒu not have; have not
沒意思 méiyìsi boring; of no interest

沒關係 méi guānxi it doesn't matter
沒用 méiyòng useless

美

měi
beautiful

ASSOCIATIVE COMPOUND In the Oracle-Bone Inscriptions, the top part of 美 shows the front view of a goat's head with horns (羊), and the bottom part the front view of a person (大). In ancient times, men often wore horns or feathers on their heads as part of decorative costumes in celebrations or dances, which were considered beautiful. Hence, the meaning of 美 is "beautiful." In Regular Script, the character 美 is still a combination of 羊 (yáng, goat; sheep) and 大 (dà, big).

美 會意。從羊，從大。
男子頭戴羊角作裝飾，是
男性健美的表現。一説
是羊肥大則肉味鮮美。

甲  金 美 篆 美

健美 jiànměi healthy and beautiful
美國 měiguó United States

完美 wánměi perfect
美元 měiyuán US dollar

每

měi
every; each

ASSOCIATIVE COMPOUND In the Oracle-Bone Inscriptions, the character 每 represents a woman with featherlike ornaments on her head, originally referring to female beauty. In the Bronze Inscriptions, two dots are added to the woman's chest to indicate her breasts. The character 美 (měi, beautiful), which represents a person wearing goat horns for decoration, originally referred to male beauty and later came to encompass all kinds of beauty. 每 is now used to mean "every," "each," "each time," "often," etc.

每 會意。甲骨文、金文
像婦女頭上戴有裝飾物。
本義表示女子之美，後
借用為每天的每。

甲 金 篆

每天 měitiān everyday
每次 měicì every time

每年 měinián every year
每(個)人 měi(ge)rén everybody

妹

mèi
younger sister

PICTOPHONETIC character The character 妹 is made up of the female radical 女 and the phonetic element 未 (wèi, future). In its ancient form, 未 is a pictograph of a tree with many leaves. (Compare 未 with 木 mù, wood; tree.) 未 originally meant "luxuriant," and later came to mean "future." "Younger sister," therefore, is a young girl with bounteous future.

妹 形聲。從女，未聲。未，甲骨文像樹木生长旺盛，枝葉繁茂状。本義為繁茂，引申義為將來。

甲 𣎳 金 𣎳 篆 𣎼

妹妹 mèimei younger sister
表妹 biǎomèi younger female cousin

姐妹 jiěmèi sisters
兄妹 xiōngmèi brother(s) and sister(s)

悶／闷

mēn
stuffy

mèn
depressed

ASSOCIATIVE AND PICTOPHONETIC COMPOUND The character 悶 is composed of the radical and phonetic element 門 (mén, door) and the signifying component 心 (xīn, heart), meaning "shut oneself or somebody else indoors," "cover tightly," "stuffy," "muggy," "keep silent," "depressed," etc. The radical 門 is simplified to form the character 闷.

悶 會意兼形聲。從心，從門（表示關閉），意指人關在屋内，心中憋悶。門也兼表聲。簡體字闷的部首簡化。

篆 悶

悶熱 mēnrè hot and stuffy; muggy
鬱悶 yùmèn gloomy; depressed

煩悶 fánmèn moody; worried
納悶 nàmèn puzzled; bewildered

們／们

mén
(plural suffix)

PICTOPHONETIC COMPOUND 們 is the plural marker for people. It consists of the person radical 亻 and the phonetic component 門 (mén; door). 門 is always written as 门 in simplified form.

們 形聲。從人，門聲。簡體字中，門皆簡化為门。

我們 wǒmen we; us
他們 tāmen they; them

你們 nǐmen you (plural)
她們 tāmen they; them (for females)

miàn
face; side

PICTOGRAPH In the Oracle-Bone Inscriptions, the character 面 delineates the contour of a face with an huge, exaggerated eye, since eyes are the most striking part of one's face. The meanings of 面 include: "face," "to face," "side," "aspect," surface," etc.

面 象形。甲骨文像是臉形。外似面部輪廓，中是一誇大了的眼睛，因眼睛為臉部最為醒目、最為傳神之處。本義為面孔，引申為面向、方面、表面、臉面等。

甲 篆

見面 jiànmiàn to meet; to see each other
前面 qiánmiàn ahead; in front

面對 miànduì to confront; to face
方面 fāngmiàn respect; aspect

---

mín
the people;
folk

PICTOGRAPH In the Bronze Inscriptions, the character 民 looks like an eye stabbed by an awl, exhibiting a kind of cruel punishment. The original meaning of 民 was "slave" and has been extended to mean "the people," "populace," "civilians," "a member of a nationality," "folk," "a person of certain occupation," and "civil."

民 象形。金文像以銳物刺人眼。本義為奴隸，引申為民眾、民族、民間的、從事某種職業的人、非軍事的。

金 篆

人民 rénmín people
民主 mínzhǔ democracy

網民 wǎngmín netizen
民航 mínháng civil aviation

---

mǐn
nimble;
agile

ASSOCIATIVE AND PICTOPHONETIC COMPOUND In the Oracle-Bone Inscriptions, the character 敏 looks like a woman and a hand, indicating being quick at jobs done by hand, as women were good at needlework which requires nimble fingers. The extended meanings of 敏 are "quick," "agile," "nimble," "clever," "smart," and "diligent." In Seal Script, 敏 becomes the combination of the semantic and phonetic element 每 (měi) and the tap/rap radical 攵.

敏 會意兼形聲。從攵，每聲。本義為動作快捷靈活。引申義有聰明靈活、腦子反應快、勤勉等。

甲 金 篆

機敏 jīmǐn alert and resourceful
敏感 mǐngǎn sensitive

聰敏 cōngmǐn sagacity
過敏 guòmǐn to be allergic

míng
name

ASSOCIATIVE COMPOUND The character 名 has 夕 (xī, sunset; evening) on the top and 口 (kǒu, mouth) at the bottom, suggesting a person calling someone's name in the dark. Hence, 名 means "name," and also extends to mean "given name," "excuse," "reputation," "famous," etc. (See both 夕 and 口 in **Basic Radicals**.)

名 會意。從口，從夕。夕，夜裏。夜色昏暗，相互看不見，只好叫名字。

甲 叩 金 召 篆 名

姓名 xìngmíng name and surname
有名 yǒumíng famous; well-known
名單 míngdān list (of names)
名勝 míngshèng famous scenic or historical spot

明

míng
bright

ASSOCIATIVE COMPOUND The character 明 is a combination of the sun 日 (rì, sun) and the moon 月 (yuè, moon). Since both the sun and moon are luminous, the original meaning of 明 is "bright." Extended meanings of 明 include "daybreak," "clear," "wise," and "next." (See both 日 and 月 in **Basic Radicals**.)

明 會意。從日，從月。日月皆明亮之物，所以用來表示明亮。

甲 叨 叨 金 叨 篆 叨

明亮 míngliàng bright; shining
明年 míngnián next year
明天 míngtiān tomorrow
文明 wénmíng civilization; civilized

末

mò
end

EXPLICIT CHARACTER The character 末 consists of the radical 木 (mù, wood; tree), with a horizontal stroke on the top, indicating the tip of a tree. The extended meanings of 末 include "top," "end," "last stage," etc. Do not confuse 末 with the character 未 (wèi, future). In 末 (mò, end), the top line is longer than the lower line, suggesting that there is no space for development; whereas in 未 (wèi, future), the top line is shorter, indicating that there is room for growth. It is 未 (wèi) that appears in the character 妹 (mèi, younger sister).

末 指事。從木，木上一橫表示樹梢所在的位置。

金 末 篆 末

周末 zhōumò weekend
年末 niánmò end of the year
期末 qīmò end of term/semester
末日 mòrì last day; final days; doomsday

mǔ
mother

PICTOGRAPH In its ancient forms, the character 母 is the same as 女 (nǔ, female; woman) except for the two dots added to her bosom to indicate her breasts and to imply that she is nursing a baby. The original meaning of 母 is mother, and its extended meanings include "one's elderly female relatives," "female (animal)," "origin," or "source." As in the case of 父 (fù, father), when Chinese people address or refer to their mothers, they usually use 媽媽 (māma, mom; mother) instead of 母親.

母 象形。古文字從女，胸前加兩點表示乳房，以示母親要給孩子餵奶。本義為母親，引申義有女性長輩(尤指家族、親戚中的女性長輩，如祖母、伯母、姨母等)、雌性動物（母雞、母牛）、最初的、能滋生其他事物的本體（母語、酵母）。

甲  金 篆

母親 mǔqīn mother
母校 mǔxiào alma mater

母馬 mǔmǎ mare
母語 mǔyǔ mother tongue; native language

---

mǔ
housemaid

ASSOCIATIVE AND PICTOPHONETIC COMPOUND The character 姆 is made up of the female radical 女 and the semantic and phonetic element 母 (mǔ, mother; female), referring to "the governess of girls in a noble family," "wet nurse," or "housemaid." In its ancient forms, the character 母 looks like a woman on her knees, and two dots are added to the her chest to represent her breasts, signifying that she has her baby and is feeding it. Today 姆 is also used to transliterate many foreign words and names.

姆 會意兼形聲。從女，從母，母亦聲。本義為中國古代教未出嫁女子婦道的女教師，後又指乳母，保姆。姆也用於一些英文詞彙的音譯。

母 甲 金 篆

保姆 bǎomǔ nanny; housekeeper
湯姆 tāngmǔ Tom

朗姆 lǎngmǔ rum
山姆大叔 shānmǔ dàshū Uncle Sam

L-R

---

ná
to take; to get

ASSOCIATIVE COMPOUND The character 拿 combines 手 (shǒu, hand) with 合 (hé, to close; to unite; to collect), suggesting the action of taking or holding something with one's hands. Its meanings include "to take," "to hold," "to grasp," "to bring," "to use," or "to capture." In its ancient forms, the character 合 has a lid 亼 (jí) on top and 口 (which suggests a box) in the lower part, meaning "to close" or "to shut." Its extended meanings include "to combine," "to join," "to gather," "to suit," "to agree," etc.

拿 會意。楷書從合，從手，表示合手相持。本義為用手取或握住，引申義有捉拿、掌握、用、把等。合，會意。下像盒子，上像盒蓋，合在一起表示合攏。

篆

拿筆 nábǐ to hold a brush/pen
拿走 názǒu to take away

拿住 názhù to hold firmly
拿手 náshǒu expert in; to be good at

哪

nǎ/něi
which

PICTOPHONETIC CHARACTER 哪 is made up of the radical 口 and the phonetic 那 (nà), and means "which" or "where." Interrogatives often include the mouth radical 口, as in 嗎 and 呢.

哪 形聲。從口，那聲，用作疑問代詞。

哪裏 nǎli where; humble expression for denying compliments
哪些 nǎxiē which ones?

哪兒 nǎr where
哪位 nǎwèi which person?

那

nà/nèi
that

ASSOCIATIVE AND PICTOPHONETIC COMPOUND In Seal Script, 那 is the combination of 冄 (rǎn, whiskers) and 邑 (yì, town; city), referring to foreigners with long beards and hair who lived west of ancient China. Later 冄邑 came to mean "that," and was simplified to 那. 阝 is a common radical. When 阝 appears on the right, it means "town" or "city," derived from the character 邑. When 阝 appears on the left, it signifies "mound" or "plenty," derived from the character 阜 (fù, mound; plenty), such as in 郊 (jiāo, suburbs), or 陡 (dǒu, steep).

那 會意兼形聲。篆文從邑（城邑），冄 rǎn 聲，本義指留有長髮長鬚的西夷國人。楷書寫作那。

篆 [seal character]

那裏 nàli there
那些 nàxiē those

那兒 nàr there
那麼 nàme like that; in that way; in that case

奶

nǎi
milk; (paternal) grandmother

ASSOCIATIVE AND PICTOPHONETIC COMPOUND The character 奶 is composed of the female radical 女 and the semantic and phonetic component 乃 (nǎi). In its ancient forms, 乃 looks like the breasts of a woman. 乃 originally meant "breast," and was borrowed to mean "to be," "your," "so," and "then" in classical Chinese. 奶 is a character that was invented later. Its original meaning is "breast," and extended meanings include "milk," "to breast-feed," and "grandmother," etc.

奶 會意兼形聲。奶，從女，從乃，乃亦聲。本義指乳房，引申義為乳汁、餵奶、祖母等。乃，象形。古文字像女性的乳房。是奶的本字，後借用為代詞"你"，"你的"；係詞"是"，副詞"於是"等。

乃 甲 [character] 金 [character] 篆 [character]

牛奶 niúnǎi milk (cow)
奶油 nǎiyóu cream

奶酪 nǎilào cheese
奶奶 nǎinai grandma

男
nán
male

ASSOCIATIVE COMPOUND The character 男 consists of 田 (tián, field) and 力 (lì, plow; physical strength or power). In ancient agricultural societies, men provided most of the manpower in the fields, and it was the men's duty to plow the fields.

男 會意。從田，從力（甲骨文像犁形），借用犁耕田來代表男子。"男耕女織"在田裏耕種主要是男人的事。

甲  金 篆

男人 nánrén man
男生 nánshēng male student; young male

男孩(子) nánhái(zi) boy
男朋友 nánpéngyou boyfriend

南
nán
south

PICTOGRAPH In the Oracle-Bone Inscriptions, 南 is the pictograph of a musical bell, referring to an ancient percussion instrument. Later 南 was borrowed to mean "south," "southern part," or "southward," probably because 南 was an instrument played in Southern China in ancient times. In Regular Script, 南 still somewhat resembles a large bell that can be hanged from a high place by the noose on its top.

南 象形。甲骨文像懸挂著鎛鐘一類的敲擊樂器，本義為敲擊樂器，後借用為南北的南。

甲 金 篆

南方 nánfāng south, the South (of a state)
南京 nánjīng Nanjing

南極 nánjí the South Pole
南瓜 nánguā pumpkin

難／难
nán
difficult; hard

PICTOPHONETIC CHARACTER In its ancient form, the character 難 consists of the phonetic component 堇 (jǐn) and the radical 隹 (zhuī, short-tailed bird), originally meaning a particular species of bird. In the Oracle-Bone Inscriptions, 堇 looks like a shackled person in flames. Since 堇 contains the meanings of "suffering" and "disaster," later the character 難 came to mean "difficult," "hard," or "troublesome." Note the difference between 堇 and the left part of 難. In the simplified form 难, 又 replaces 堇.

難 形聲。金文從隹，堇（jǐn）聲，本義指一種鳥，因從"堇"（焚燒人牲祭天求雨）而借用來表示艱難困苦。堇，甲骨文像用火焚燒捆綁的人牲，意指以人牲祭祀求雨，引申為乾旱、災難等。簡體字难左邊用又替代，屬符號替代字。明清已見此字。

金 篆 堇 甲

難受 nánshòu difficult to bear; to feel unwell
難過 nán'guò to feel sad

難看 nánkàn ugly
困難 kùnnan difficulty; difficult

腦/脑

nǎo
brain

篆 腦

PICTOGRAPH The right part of the character 腦 is the pictograph of a baby's head with a few hairs on the scalp. The left part contains the flesh radical 月, which also serves to indicate the meaning of the character. Current meanings of 腦 include "brain," "mind," "head," and "essence." In the simplified character 脑, the right part is simplified, but the flesh radical 月 of the traditional character is still retained.

腦 象形。左為肉月旁，右部像囟門與頭髮。簡體字脑的右邊簡化，但保留了繁體字腦的輪廓。舊時已有此字。

腦子 nǎozi brains; mind
電腦 diànnǎo computer

腦門 nǎomén forehead
首腦 shǒunǎo head (of state); leader

呢

ne
(question
particle)

尼 篆 尼

ASSOCIATIVE AND PICTOPHONETIC CHARACTER 呢 is made up of the mouth radical 口 (kǒu, mouth) and the phonetic element 尼 (ní). In its ancient form, 尼 looks like two people close to each other, therefore meaning "close" or "intimate." In Chinese, question markers sometimes contain the radical 口, since one needs to open one's mouth to ask a question. 嗎 (ma) is another example of a question marker.

呢 語氣詞。會意兼形聲。從口，尼聲。尼，像二人相近之形，意為二人親昵，後作"昵"。

能

néng
can; to be
able to

甲 能 篆 能

PICTOGRAPH In the Oracle-Bone Inscriptions, 能 depicts a bear, complete with head, claws, body, and tail. Originally 能 referred to a "bear." Since bears are strong and can withstand low temperatures, 能 extended to mean "ability," "capability," and "to be able." Later, the fire radical 灬 was added under 能 to make the character 熊 (xióng) for "bear."

能 象形。甲骨文像有頭、背、尾、掌的熊形。本義為熊，因熊兇猛力大，後被借為能字。而後另造熊字。

能力 nénglì ability; capability
功能 gōngnéng function

才能 cáinéng talent; aptitude
能幹 nénggàn capable; competent

nǐ
you

PHONETIC LOAN CHARACTER   The character 你 is derived from 爾 (ěr). In its ancient form, 爾 looks like silkworms spinning silk to make cocoons. Later this character was borrowed to represent the pronoun "you" since the pronunciation of "you" was similar to that of 爾. In Regular Script 爾 is simplified to 尔 with the person radical 亻 added on the left.

你 假借。古時寫作爾，像蠶吐絲結繭。一説像花枝垂下之形。假借為第二人稱的代詞。楷書加人字旁。

甲 金 篆

你們 nǐmen you (plural)
我愛你 wǒ ài nǐ I love you

你好 nǐhǎo Hello!; Hi!; How are you?
迷你 mínǐ mini

---

nián
year

ASSOCIATIVE COMPOUND   In the Oracle-Bone and Bronze Inscriptions, the character 年 depicts a figure carrying crops on his or her back. The original meaning of 年 was "harvest." Since a harvest is the result of a year's hard work, 年 extended to mean "year."

年 意。從禾，從人。甲骨文、金文像人背禾形，表示五穀成熟是一年勞作的成果，引申為一年。

甲 金 篆

今年 jīnnián this year
明年 míngnián next year

去年 qùnián last year
年級 niánjí grade; year (in school, college, etc.)

---

niàn
to read aloud

PICTOPHONETIC CHARACTER   The character 念 combines the heart radical 心 and the phonetic element 今 (jīn), meaning "to read aloud," "to think of," "to miss," "thought," "idea," "study," "to read aloud," etc.

念 形聲。從心，今聲，意為大聲誦讀、想念、想法、學習等。

甲 金 篆

念經 niànjīng to recite Buddhist scripture
想念 xiǎngniàn to miss; remember with longing

念書 niànshū to read; to study
紀念 jìniàn to commemorate; to remember

您

nín
you (polite)

ASSOCIATIVE COMPOUND The character 您 was first seen in writing from the Jin and Yuan Dynasties (1115–1368). 您 consists of 你 (nǐ, you) on the top and 心 (xīn, heart) at the bottom, signifying a heartfelt respect toward "you."

您 會意。你的敬稱。

您好 nínhǎo hello (polite)　　　　您的 nínde your; yours (polite)
您貴姓 nín guìxìng What's your (honorable) surname?

紐/纽

niǔ
knob; button

ASSOCIATIVE AND PICTOPHONETIC COMPOUND The character 紐 consists of the silk radical 糸 and 丑 (chǒu) as both the phonetic and signifying component. Its original meaning was "to tie a knot." In its ancient form, 丑 looks like a hand twisting an object and its original meaning was "twist" or "wrench," but later was borrowed to mean "the second of the twelve earthly branches" (see page 20).

紐 會意兼形聲。從糸，丑聲。本義為打結，紐扣為其引申義。丑，古字像以手用力扭曲一物，本義為擰扭，后借用表示地支的第二位而另造"扭"字表示擰扭之意。丑現也是繁體字醜的簡化字。

篆

紐帶 niǔdài tie; link; bond　　　　紐扣 niǔkòu button
電鈕 diànniǔ push button (electric switch)　　　紐約 niǔyuē New York

---

暖

nuǎn
warm

PICTOPHONETIC CHARACTER 暖 consists of the sun radical 日 and the phonetic element 爰 (yuán), meaning "warm," "genial," and "to warm up." In the Oracle-Bone Inscriptions, 爰 depicts a hand (on the top) holding a stick (in the middle) and passing it to another hand (on the bottom), meaning "to pull by hand" or "to hand over."

暖 形聲。篆文從火，爰聲，意思為暖和、使溫暖。楷書改火為日。爰，會意。甲骨文上方像一隻手持物，讓下方的另一隻手（又）抓住，本義為援助，借用為何處、於是等。

篆 爓　爰 甲 金 篆

暖和 nuǎnhuo warm　　　　　　暖氣 nuǎnqì heater
保暖 bǎonuǎn to keep warm　　　暖水瓶 nuǎnshuǐpíng thermos bottle

pà
to fear;
to be afraid of

PICTOPHONETIC CHARACTER The character 怕 is made up of the vertical heart radical 忄 and the phonetic component 白 (bái), meaning "to fear," "to dread," "to be afraid of," or "perhaps." The ancient forms of 白 may be an indication of bright rays spreading from the sun or it could be referring to a grain of white rice—scholars differ on the explanation of it. The original meaning of 白 is "white." Its extended meanings include "bright," "pure," and "in vain."

怕 形聲。從忄，白聲。本義為害怕，引申義有擔憂、疑慮等。白，象形。像太陽初升、光芒四射狀。另一說像一顆白米粒。本義為白色。

篆

可怕 kěpà fearful; frightening
怕生 pàshēng to be shy with strangers

怕死 pàsǐ to be afraid of death
恐怕 kǒngpà I'm afraid; perhaps

拍

pāi
to clap; racket

PICTOPHONETIC CHARACTER The character 拍 combines the hand radical 扌 with the phonetic 白 (bái), originally meaning "to pat with a hand." Its extended meanings are "to strike," "to clap," "to slap," "flap," "racket," "time or beat (of music)," "to shoot (photo; film)," and "to flatter."

拍 形聲。從扌，白聲。本義為用手掌拍打，引申為敲擊、拍子（球拍、蒼蠅拍）、音樂的節奏、拍攝（拍照片、拍電影）、奉承（拍馬屁）等。

拍打 pāidǎ to pat; to flap
球拍 qiúpāi racket

拍手 pāishǒu to clap hands
拍電影 pāi diànyǐng to shoot a film

牌

pái
plate; card; brand

PICTOPHONETIC CHARACTER The character 牌 consists of 片 (piàn, a flat/thin piece) and the phonetic component 卑 (bēi), originally referring to "a piece of wood with words on it." The meanings of 牌 include "signboard," "bulletin board," "plate," "tablet," "trademark," "brand," "cards," etc. In Seal Script, 片 represents the right half of a split tree and indicates the act of splitting wood into pieces. In the Bronze Inscriptions, 卑 depicts a serving container held in the left hand, meaning "low," "inferior," "humble," "contemptible," "mean," etc.

牌 形聲。從片（木片），卑聲。本義指作為標誌的木板，引申為作為標誌的物品、產品商標、作為娛樂用的骨牌紙牌等。片，指事。從半木，是樹木劈開后右邊的一半。卑，會意。金文從又（手），從申（指酒器），表示以手托酒器伺奉人，意為卑賤。

卑 金 篆

路牌 lùpái street sign
名牌 míngpái famous brand

牌照 páizhào license plate
打牌 dǎpái to play cards

盤 / 盘

pán
plate; dish

PICTOPHONETIC CHARACTER The character 盤 consists of 皿 (mǐn, dish; vessel) as the signifying component and 般 (bān) as the phonetic. The original and primary meaning of 盤 is "tray" or "plate," and the extended meanings include "to circle around," "to entwine," "to cross-examine," "to interrogate," "to check," and "a measure word for plate-like objects." In its ancient forms, 皿 is a pictograph of a vessel for food or drinks while 般 is the combination of 舟 (zhōu, boat) and 殳 (shū, spear), meaning "sort" or "kind." The simplified 盘 takes off the 殳 from 盤.

盤 形声。從皿，般聲。本義為平而淺的器皿，引申义有像盤子的東西、盤旋、盤起來、盤問、盤點，也可作為量詞。皿，象形，像盛飲食的器皿。般，會意。從舟，從殳(shū 古代一種用竹木製成的武器)，意為種類。簡化字盘去掉繁體盤中的殳。

甲 𥁋 金 𥂦 篆 𥇧 皿 甲 𦥑 金 𦥑 篆 𥁑

盤子 pánzi tray; plate; dish
鍵盤 jiànpán keyboard
光盤 guāngpán compact disc; CD or DVD
算盤 suànpán abacus

旁

páng
side; edge

ASSOCIATIVE AND PICTOPHONETIC COMPOUND In the Oracle-Bone Inscriptions, 旁 is made up of the signifying component 凡 (fán, all; ordinary) and the semantic and phonetic element 方 (fāng, square; side), suggesting all sides that surround one. 旁 also means "side," "nearby," "close by," "other," or "heterodox." In the Oracle-Bone Inscriptions, 方 portrays a shovel for lifting or moving earth and extended to mean "cubic meter," "square," "area," or "side." In Regular Script, the top part of 旁 resembles 立 (lì, stand) with two additional hooks under the bottom line.

旁 會意兼形聲。甲骨文從凡，從方，方亦聲。本義為四方，即旁邊，引申為附近、其它的、偏旁、不正等。方，象形。像劂土的工具。甲骨文上短橫像手握的橫柄，中間一長橫是腳踩的地方，下為分叉的鍤。本義為土鍤，引申義正方形、方面、地方等。

甲 𣃘 金 𣃙 篆 𣃚

旁邊 pángbiān side
身旁 shēnpáng by the side of someone
路旁 lùpáng roadside
旁聽 pángtīng to audit

胖

pàng
fat

ASSOCIATIVE AND PICTOPHONETIC COMPOUND The character 胖 consists of the flesh/meat radical 月 and the semantic and phonetic element 半 (bàn, half). In its ancient forms, 半 consists of 八 (bā, to divide; eight) and 牛 (niú, cow), indicating the act of cutting an ox in half. Originally 胖 referred to "half an animal used as sacrifice," from which the meanings "stout," "fat," and "corpulent" derived.

胖 會意兼形聲。從肉月旁，從半(半頭牛)，半亦聲。本義為古時祭祀時用的半邊牲畜，肥胖是其引申義。半，會意。上從八(分開)，下從牛。表示將牛從中切為兩半，意為事物的二分之一。

篆 𦙢

胖子 pàngzi fat person; fatty
肥胖 féipàng obese
發胖 fāpàng to put on weight; get fat
矮胖 ǎipàng short and stout; dumpy

pǎo
to run

PICTOPHONETIC CHARACTER The character 跑 is built with the foot radical 𧾷 and the phonetic 包 (bāo), meaning "to run," "to flee," "to escape," "to run errands," and "to leak." In its ancient forms, 包 looks like a fetus in the womb, originally referring to the afterbirth. Its extended meanings are "to wrap," "to surround," "to contain," "package," "bag," "lump," etc.

跑　形聲。從足，包聲。意為奔跑、逃跑、為某種事奔忙（跑買賣）、漏出等。包，象形。甲金篆像腹中胎兒形狀。本義為胎衣，引申為把東西包起、包或像包的東西（書包、錢包、紅包、包子）、包含、腫起的疙瘩等。

跑步　pǎobù　to run
跑鞋　pǎoxié　running shoes

長跑　chángpǎo　long-distance running/race
跑車　pǎochē　sports car

---

péng
friend

PICTOGRAPH In the Oracle-Bone and Bronze Inscriptions, the character 朋 represents two strings of cowry shells, suggesting a monetary unit. Later 朋 extended to mean "friend" because the strings of shells are together. In Regular Script, the two strings of shells are replaced by two moons 月.

朋　象形。甲骨文、金文像兩串貝殼形，本義為古代貨幣單位，後引申為朋友。楷書寫作朋。

甲 　金

朋友　péngyou　friend
親朋　qīnpéng　relatives and friends

女朋友　nǚpéngyou　girlfriend
交朋友　jiāo péngyou　to make friends

L - R

---

pí
beer

PICTOPHONETIC CHARACTER The character 啤 consists of the mouth radical 口 and the phonetic symbol 卑 (bēi, contemptible). 啤 is a more recent character, created to translate the word "beer" (啤酒 píjiǔ). In the Bronze Inscriptions, 卑 depicted a serving container held in the left hand, and meant "low," "inferior," "contemptible," "mean," etc.

啤　形聲。從口，卑聲。卑，會意。金文從又（手），從申（指酒器），表示以手托酒器伺奉人，意為卑賤。啤為新造字，用於德文的音譯及意譯。

卑 金 　 篆

啤酒　píjiǔ　beer
啤酒廠　píjiǔ chǎng　brewery

生啤　shēngpí　draft beer
啤酒節　píjiǔ jié　Beer Festival

篇

piān
(MW for articles)

PICTOPHONETIC CHARACTER The character 篇 is comprised of the bamboo radical 𥫗 and the phonetic component 扁 (biǎn). Since the Chinese wrote on pieces of bamboo before paper was invented, 篇 means "chapter," "a piece of writing," or a "measure word for articles." In Seal Script, 扁 is the combination of 戶 (hù, household) and 冊 (cè, volume; copy), and originally referred to the horizontally inscribed board hung in a family's house. Today, 扁 usually means "flat." In the Oracle-Bone Inscriptions, 戶 is the pictograph of a door with one panel. In ancient writing, 冊 represented a bound scroll of bamboo.

篇 形聲。篆文從竹，扁聲，意為典籍、著作、文章，也可用做文章的量詞。扁，會意。篆文從戶，從冊。本義為匾，引申為平薄物體等。

扁 篆 扁

詩篇 shīpiān poem; epic
短篇 duǎnpiān short (article etc.)

長篇 chángpiān lengthy (article; report etc.); full-length
短篇小説 duǎnpiān xiǎoshuō short story

片

piàn
(MW for tablets, films); slice

EXPLICIT CHARACTER In Seal Script, 片 stands for the right part of 木 (mù, wood), signifying the act of splitting wood into pieces and meaning "wood chip." The extended meanings of 片 include "a flat and thin piece," "a slice," "partial," "incomplete," and "one-sided." It is also a measure word for films, slices, tablets, tracts of land, etc.

片 指事。從半木，是木塊劈開後右邊的一半。本義是木片，引申義為平而薄的東西、不全的等，亦用作一些物體的量詞。

甲 𠂢 篆 片

名片 míngpiàn business card
刀片 dāopiàn razor

相片 xiàngpiàn photo
片面 piànmiàn one-sided

票

piào
ticket

ASSOCIATIVE COMPOUND In Seal Script, the upper part of 票 means "to rise," or "leap up," and the lower part is a fire radical, referring to "flame" or "blaze." Today 票 means "ticket," "ballot," "bank note," etc. In Regular Script, 票 is rather different from its earlier form. The upper part is similar to 西 (xī, west) while the character 示 (shì, show) comprises the lower part.

票 會意。篆文中下部從火，上部意指升高，本義指火焰騰起。

篆 票

機票 jīpiào plane ticket
支票 zhīpiào check; cheque

郵票 yóupiào stamp
票房 piàofáng box office

The Way of Chinese Characters

漂

piào
pretty

piāo
to float

篆

PICTOPHONETIC CHARACTER The character 漂 consists of the water radical 氵 and the phonetic element 票 (piào, ticket). The primary meanings of 漂 include "float," "drift" (pronounced piāo), and "bleach" (pronounced piǎo). Since cloth looks nice after being bleached, 漂 also extends to mean "pretty" (pronounced piào).

漂 形聲。從水，票聲，有漂浮、沖洗、漂白之意。票，會意。篆文下部從火，本義是火焰騰起。

漂流 piāoliú float on the current; rafting
漂白 piǎobái to bleach; to whiten

漂泊 piāobó drift aimlessly; to lead a wandering life
漂亮 piàoliang pretty; beautiful

平

píng
level; even

PICTOGRAPH The character 平 looks like a balance or scale that is equally weighted on both sides, meaning "even," "flat," "impartial," "equal," "fair," etc. Some scholars believe 平 looks like floating duckweed. Since the surface of duckweed is flat, 平 means "flat" or "even."

平 象形。一説像天平形，意為公平、不向一方傾斜。一説平字似水面浮萍。

金 平 篆

水平 shuǐpíng level; standard
平等 píngděng equal; equality

公平 gōngpíng fair; impartial
和平 hépíng peace; peaceful

瓶

píng
bottle

PICTOPHONETIC CHARACTER 瓶 is comprised of the radical 瓦 (wǎ, tile) and the phonetic element 并 (bìng, side by side; merge), meaning "bottle," "vase," "jar," or "flask." In Seal Script, the character 瓦 resembles two roof tiles. In the Oracle-Bone Inscriptions, 并 consists of two people 人人 and the character 二 (èr, two), indicating two people standing side by side.

瓶 形聲。從瓦，并聲，古代用來汲水的容器。并，會意。古文字中皆像二人並立。瓦，象形。像房上兩片瓦相扣的形狀。

金 篆 瓶

瓶子 píngzi bottle
熱水瓶 rèshuǐpíng thermos bottle

花瓶 huāpíng flower vase
瓶裝 píngzhuāng bottled

蘋/苹

píng
component in
蘋果/苹果

PICTOPHONETIC CHARACTER The character 蘋 is formed by grass radical 艹 and the phonetic symbol 頻 (pín), originally referring to "duckweed." In modern Chinese, 蘋 means "apple" when used with 果 (guǒ, fruit). 頻 combines 步 (bù, step) and 頁 (yè, head; page), meaning "frequency," or "rate." In its ancient form, 步 consists of two footprints one ahead of the other, indicating the act of walking. In the Oracle-Bone Inscriptions, 頁 resembles a person with an oversized head. In the simplified character 苹, 平 (píng) replaces 頻 (pín) in 蘋 since their pronunciations are similar.

蘋　形聲。從艸，頻聲。指一種水生植物，亦稱為"大萍"或"田字草"。後借用來指蘋果。頻，會意。從步從頁。意指頻繁、頻率。步，會意。像一前一後邁步行走的兩腳。頁，象形。像人突出的頭部，引申為頁數。簡體字苹用平取代蘋字中的頻，屬同音替代。

蘋果 píngguǒ apple
蘋果派 píngguǒpài apple pie

蘋果汁 píngguǒzhī apple juice
蘋果酒 píngguǒjiǔ cider

期

qī
period (of time)

PICTOPHONETIC CHARACTER The character 期 is composed of the moon radical 月 and the phonetic element 其 (qí), meaning "period of time," "expectation," or "appointment." Since people observe the cycles of the sun or the moon to tell time, in Chinese 日 (rì, sun; day) and 月 (yuè, moon; month) are used as radicals in characters pertaining to time, such as 朝 (zhāo, early morning) and 晚 (wǎn; evening; late). In the Oracle-Bone Inscriptions, the character 其 is a pictograph of a dustpan or winnowing pan (used to sift grain), meaning "dustpan." Later 其 became primarily used as a third-person pronoun in Classical Chinese.

期　形聲。從月，其聲。其，象形。甲骨文像簸箕形，本義為簸箕。後因用為人稱代詞，遂另造箕字。

篆

星期 xīngqī week
學期 xuéqī term; semester

星期日 xīngqīrì Sunday
時期 shíqī period; phase

起

qǐ
to rise

PICTOPHONETIC CHARACTER 起 is the combination of the walk radical 走 (zǒu) and the phonetic element 己 (jǐ, oneself), meaning "up," "rise," "get up," "start" or "establish." In its ancient form, 己 resembles the large belly of a person and means "oneself."

起　形聲。從走，己聲。意為立起。走，象形兼會意。金文上像一人甩開雙臂跑步狀，下從止（腳），意指奔跑。己，象形。甲骨文像人腹之形。

篆 起

起床 qǐchuáng to get up
一起 yìqǐ together

起飛 qǐfēi (of aircraft) to take off
對不起 duìbuqǐ I'm sorry; excuse me

qì
steam; gas

ASSOCIATIVE AND PICTOPHONETIC COMPOUND The character 汽 combines the water radical 氵 and the signifying and phonetic element 气 (qì), meaning "vapor" or "steam." In the Oracle-Bone and Bronze Inscriptions, 气 looks like three thin clouds in the sky, meaning "air," "gas," or "weather."

汽 會意兼形聲。從水，從气；气亦聲。意為水蒸氣、氣體。气，象形。甲骨文、金文像雲气升騰浮動狀。

篆 〔气〕 气 甲 三 金 乁 篆 乁

汽水 qìshuǐ soda; pop
汽車 qìchē car; automobile

公共汽車 gōnggòng qìchē bus
汽油 qìyóu gasoline

---

qì
air

ASSOCIATIVE COMPOUND The character 氣 combines 气 (qì, air) and 米 (mǐ, rice). In the Oracle-Bone and Bronze Inscriptions, 气 looks like three thin clouds in the sky, meaning "air," "gas," or "weather." 米 was added under 气 later. In the Oracle-Bone Inscriptions, 米 resembles grains scattered around a rack. 米 and 气 were combined to form 氣, meaning "mood," "breath," and "human energy/spirit," in addition to "air," "gas," and "weather." The simplified character 气 uses the original form of 氣.

氣 會意。甲骨文、金文為三橫，像天上雲氣流動狀。後人在气下加米字以示人體內之氣或能量。簡體字气去掉了氣下面的米字，從而恢復了古本字的原貌。

篆 乁 米 甲 ⁖⁘ 金 釆 篆 釆

天氣 tiānqì weather
空氣 kōngqì air

氣候 qìhòu climate
氣功 qìgōng *qigong*, a system of deep breathing exercises

---

qiān
to sign

PICTOPHONETIC CHARACTER The character 簽 combines the bamboo radical ⺮ and the phonetic 僉 (qiān), meaning "to sign one's name." 簽 also refers to "bamboo slips used for divination or drawing lots," "label," and "sticker." 僉 has 亼 (jí, gather together) on top, two mouths (吅 xuān) in the middle, and two persons underneath (从 cóng), originally referring to many speaking simultaneously, and has been extended to mean "unanimous," "together," or "all." The simplified 佥 derives from the cursive version of 僉, and is always written as 佥 when it is the phonetic component of a simplified character.

簽 形聲。從竹，僉 (qiān) 聲。意為署名、畫押、簽署。也指有專門用途的竹片或紙片（書簽）、尖細的小棍（牙簽）等。僉，會意。上從亼(jí 集合)，中從二口(吅 xuān)，下從二人(从)，本義為眾人同聲，引申為眾人、都。佥是僉的草書楷化字，也用作簡化字。

篆 〔簽〕

簽名 qiānmíng signature; to sign one's name
書簽 shūqiān bookmark

簽證 qiānzhèng visa
牙簽 yáqiān toothpick

前

qián
front; before

ASSOCIATIVE COMPOUND In its ancient form, the character 前 combines 止 (zhǐ, foot) in the upper part and 舟 (zhōu, boat) in the lower part, suggesting the action of moving forward by boat. Meanings of 前 include "forward," "ahead," "front," "before," "formerly," etc. In Regular Script, the upper part of 前 resembles two feet on a horizontal line, 月 replaces 舟, and a knife radical 刂 is added to the right.

前　會意。金文從止（足），從舟，表示人乘船而行。

篆

前進 qiánjìn go forward; forge ahead
前天 qiántiān the day before yesterday

以前 yǐqián before; ago
前年 qiánnián the year before last

錢/钱

qián
money

PICTOPHONETIC CHARACTER 錢 contains the gold/ metal radical 金 and the phonetic element 戔 (jiān), meaning "metal currency," "money," "cash," or "fund." Since the character 戔 consists of two dagger-axes, meaning "to kill" or "murder," 錢 possibly refers to the fact that disputes involving money can generate jealousy and strife. The left part simplifies from 金 to 钅, and the right part from 戔 to 戋, to form the simplified character 钱.

錢　形聲。從金，戔聲。戔，會意。從二戈，本義為殘殺，是殘的古字。簡體字钱左邊部首由金簡化為钅，右邊戔簡化為戋。

篆 錢

找錢 zhǎoqián to give change
有錢 yǒuqián well-off; wealthy

錢包 qiánbāo purse; wallet
價錢 jiàqián price

且

qiě
(conjunction)

PICTOGRAPH In the Oracle-Bone and Bronze Inscriptions, the character 且 looks like a memorial tablet used in ancestral worship, originally meaning "ancestor." Later, the meaning of "ancestor" came to be expressed with the new character 祖, and 且 has been used instead as an adverb or conjunction to mean "just," "for the time being," "moreover," "even," "both... and...," etc. You can find 且 in 姐 (jiě, elder sister), 助 (zhù, to assist), and 宜 (yí, suitable).

且　象形。甲骨文、金文像用來祭祀祖先的牌位。一說像男性生殖器，本義是祖。意思有並且、而且、暫且、尚且、將要等。

甲 且　金 且　篆 且

不但...而且... búdàn... érqiě... not only... but also
且不說 qiěbùshuō let alone; not to mention

而且 érqiě moreover; in addition
且慢 qiěmàn hold on

青 qīng — green; blue

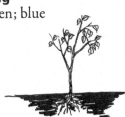

ASSOCIATIVE AND PICTOPHONETIC COMPOUND In the Bronze Inscriptions, the upper part of 青 is 生 (shēng, grow) and the lower part 丹 (dān, red color), indicating the color of a growing plant. 生 also serves as the phonetic indicator. In Regular Script, the upper part of 青 is 生 without the downward left stroke and the lower part changes from 丹 to 月 (yuè, moon; month). The original meaning of 青 is "green." However, it originally referred to many colors in a blue-green spectrum, thus it can also mean "blue," "black," and "youth." One can usually figure out what color it refers to from the context or its position in fixed combinations.

青 會意兼形聲。金文從生，從丹，丹為紅色。用生長中植物的顏色來表示綠色之意。後楷書寫作青或靑。丹，象形。四周像丹砂井，中間一點像丹砂形。一說青字指生長在井邊的植物是青色的。青的本義為像植物一樣的綠色。有時也指藍色、黑色。

金 篆 青

青菜 qīngcài green vegetable
青年 qīngnián youth; youngster

青春 qīngchūn youth
年青 niánqīng youthful

清 qīng — clear; clean; pure

PICTOPHONETIC CHARACTER The character 清 consists of the water radical 氵 and the phonetic 青 (qīng, green). Originally 清 referred to "clear water" and has extended to mean "clear," "pure," "clean," "clarified," etc. 青 is used as a phonetic symbol in a number of characters, such as 情 (qíng, feeling; affection), 晴 (qíng, clear up; sunny day), 精 (jīng, spirit; energy), and 睛 (jīng, eyeball).

清 形聲。篆文從水，青聲，本義指水清澈透明。引申義有純淨、單純、寂靜、明晰、清潔、廉潔等。

篆

清涼 qīngliáng cool and refreshing
清楚 qīngchǔ clear; to be clear about

冷清 lěngqīng deserted; desolate
清早 qīngzǎo early morning

請／请 qǐng — please; to invite

PICTOPHONETIC CHARACTER In the character 請, 言 (yán, word) is the radical and 青 (qīng, green) is the phonetic element, meaning "to ask," "please," and "to invite." In the simplified character 请, the radical 讠 is derived from the cursive form of the radical 言. As a radical, 言 is always written as 讠 in simplified characters.

請 形聲。從言，青聲。青，會意兼形聲。簡體字请的部首讠是由繁体部首言 的草书楷化而来。

金 請 篆 請 草 请

請問 qǐngwèn excuse me; may I ask
請假 qǐngjià request leave of absence

請客 qǐngkè invite to dinner; entertain guests
申請 shēnqǐng to apply for

秋

qiū
autumn; fall

ASSOCIATIVE COMPOUND The character 秋 combines 禾 (hé, growing grain) and 火 (huǒ, fire), indicating the fire-like colors of the crops when they are ripe in the fall. 秋 originally meant "harvest time" and has been extended to mean "autumn," "time," "period," "year," etc. In the Oracle-Bone and Bronze Inscriptions, 禾 resembles a ripe rice plant with hanging ears.

秋　會意。從禾，從火。秋天穀物成熟顏色變深，似火灼，如紅高粱，故加義符火。本義為莊稼成熟的季節，即秋天，引申義有年、時期等。禾，象形。甲骨文、金文中像禾苗形。

篆 烌

秋天 qiūtiān autumn; fall
中秋 zhōngqiū mid-autumn; the Moon Festival

秋收 qiūshōu fall harvest
千秋 qiānqiū thousand years

球

qiú
ball

PICTOPHONETIC CHARACTER The character 球 consists of the jade radical 王 and the phonetic component 求 (qiú, request). Its original meaning was "beautiful jade." Later it came to mean "ball." In the Oracle-Bone Inscriptions, 求 is a pictograph of a fur coat. Since a fur coat represents warmth, shelter, and material comfort as things that people seek, later 求 came to mean "seek," "request," "beg," etc.

球　形聲。從玉，求聲，意為美玉或球形的物體。求，象形。像毛翻在外的皮裘。後求加衣字為裘。"求"引申為尋求、乞求等。

篆 球　求 甲

足球 zúqiú soccer
地球 dìqiú the earth

籃球 lánqiú basketball
球賽 qiúsài sports match; ballgame

去

qù
to go

ASSOCIATIVE COMPOUND In the Oracle-Bone and Bronze Inscriptions, the character 去 consists of 大 on top and 口 at the bottom, indicating a person (大) leaving her or his cave (口). In Regular Script, the upper part of the character is 土 (tǔ, earth; soil) and the lower part is 厶 (sī, private).

去　會意。甲骨文、金文從大（人），從口（洞穴出口），表示人離開洞穴。

甲 　 金 　 篆

出去 chūqu to go out
去年 qùnián last year

進去 jìnqu to go in
失去 shīqù to lose

趣

qù
interest; interesting

PICTOPHONETIC CHARACTER The character 趣 consists of the walk radical 走 and the phonetic element 取 (qǔ). The original meaning of 趣 was "walk swiftly" while extended meanings include "inclination," "delight," "interest," and "interesting." 取 is made up of 耳 (ěr, ear) and 又 (yòu, right hand; again), suggesting a right hand holding an ear. In ancient times, soldiers cut off the left ears of enemies as proof of victory. 取 therefore means to "capture," "get," "take," or "fetch."

趣　形聲。從走，取聲。本義指快步行走，引申為志趣、愉悅、興趣、有趣等。取，會意。　甲骨文從耳，從又（手），指古代割戰俘左耳以計戰功。

篆 𧺴

興趣 xìngqù interest; hobby
風趣 fēngqù humor; humorous; witty

有趣 yǒuqù interesting; fascinating; amusing
趣味 qùwèi taste; liking

然

rán
like that; so

ASSOCIATIVE AND PICTOPHONETIC COMPOUND In the Bronze Inscriptions, the character 然 consists of the fire radical 灬 and the signifying and phonetic element 肰 (rán, dog meat), referring to the roasting of a dog over fire. The original meaning of 然 was "burn" or "ignite." Later a fire radical 火 was added to the left of 然 (燃) to mean "burn" or "ignite." Now 然 means "right," "so," "like that," "but," "nevertheless," etc. In Seal Script, 肰 combines the flesh radical 月 with the character 犬 (quǎn, dog). 犬 depicts a large dog in the Oracle-Bone and Bronze Inscriptions.

然　會意兼形聲。金文從火，從肰（狗肉）；肰亦聲。意指用火烤狗肉。犬，象形。甲骨文、金文中像一條大狗形，本義為大狗。

金 𤋱　篆 然

雖然 suīrán although; even though
當然 dāngrán of course

然後 ránhòu then; afterwards
自然 zìrán nature; natural; naturally

讓／让

ràng
to allow;
to cause;
to let

PICTOPHONETIC CHARACTER The character 讓 consists of the word radical 言 and the phonetic element 襄 (xiāng), originally meaning "blame." Today 讓 means "yield," "let," "allow," "make," etc. In the Bronze Inscriptions, 襄 consists of mouths (suggesting weeping), twigs (used in funerals), and clothes, referring to the removal of mourning apparel after a funeral. Therefore, 襄 means "to get rid of," "finish," "assist," etc. The characters 襄, 裏 (lǐ, inside) and 還 (hái, still; yet), all contain the character/radical 衣. In the simplified 让, the speech radical is simplified while 上 (shàng) replaces 襄 (xiāng), as their pronunciations are similar.

讓　形聲。從言，襄聲，本義為責備。襄，從衣，其中兩口表示哭聲，意指辦完喪事脫去喪服去耕地。襄本義為解衣耕地，借用為升高、輔助等。簡體字让用上代替襄，屬於近音替代字。

篆 讓

讓座 ràngzuò to give up one's seat for sb.
讓位 ràngwèi to abdicate

讓步 ràngbù to concede; to give in
忍讓 rěnràng to exercise forbearance

L-R

熱 / 热

rè
hot

PICTOPHONETIC CHARACTER 熱 consists of the fire radical 灬 and the phonetic symbol 埶 (yì), meaning "heat," "hot," "to heat up," "to warm up," "fever," "craze," "ardent," "passionate," etc. In the Oracle-Bone Inscriptions, 埶 resembles a person planting a sapling with his or her hands, meaning "to plant," In the Bronze Inscriptions, 土 (tǔ, earth; soil) is added under the sapling. The simplified character 热 derives from the cursive style of the character 熱, with 扌 on the top left instead of 坴 (lù).

熱 形聲。從火，埶聲。本義為溫度高。引申義有加熱、情意熾烈、發燒、急盼得到等。埶，會義。甲骨文中像一人手持樹苗栽種狀，本義為種植。簡體字热是繁體字熱的草書楷化字，左上方以扌 代替。

金 𤋳 篆 𤏆 草 热 埶 甲 𡍃 金 𡑍

熱身 rèshēn warm-up
熱情 rèqíng enthusiastic; enthusiasm

熱心 rèxīn warm-hearted
熱門 rèmén in great demand; hot topic of discussion

認 / 认

rèn
to recognize;
to know

PICTOPHONETIC CHARACTER The character 認 consists of the word radical 言 and the phonetic component 忍 (rěn, tolerate), meaning "recognize," "know," or "identify." The character 忍 is the combination of 心 (xīn, heart) and 刃 (rèn, the edge of a knife; blade), suggesting that tolerating or enduring something is like having a knife in one's heart. 刀 (dāo) depicts a knife, and in 刃, the dot points to the cutting edge of a knife. In the simplified 认, the speech radical is simplified and 人 replaces 忍, since their pronunciations are similar.

認 形聲。從言，忍聲。忍，會意兼形聲，從心，刃聲。忍的滋味就像一把刀插在心上。刃 指事。從刀，一點指向刀刃處。簡體认字部首由言 簡化為讠，聲旁由人替代忍。

忍 金 𢛳 篆 𢖒

認識 rènshi to know; to recognize; to be familiar with
認真 rènzhēn conscientious; earnest

認字 rènzì literate
認為 rènwéi to think; to consider

容

róng
to hold;
to contain

ASSOCIATIVE COMPOUND The character 容 is comprised of the roof radical 宀 and the character 谷 (gǔ, valley; gorge). Since both houses and valleys have the capacity to hold people and/or things, 容 means "to contain," "hold," "allow," or "tolerate." In the Oracle-Bone Inscriptions, the upper part of 谷 looks like flowing water, while the bottom part resembles a mountain pass.

容 會意。從宀，從谷，意指房屋、山谷都有容納人或物的空間。谷，象形。甲骨文中像水從山谷中流出。

甲 𧮫 篆 𡧍

內容 nèiróng content; substance
容易 róngyì easy

容許 róngxǔ to permit; to allow
形容 xíngróng to describe; description

肉

ròu
meat; flesh

PICTOGRAPH In its ancient forms, 肉 is the pictograph of the ribs of an animal and meant "animal meat." It was used later to mean all kinds of meat, flesh, and pulp of fruits. 肉 is written as 月 when used as a radical. For example, the characters 腿 (tuǐ, leg), 臉/脸 (liǎn, face), 腦/脑 (nǎo, brain), and 腳/脚 (jiǎo, foot) all contain the flesh radical 月.

肉 象形。像切下的一塊帶骨頭的肉。本義指動物的肉，引申指人肉、某些果實內可食用的部分等。

甲 𠕋 金 𠕋 篆 𠕋

牛肉 niúròu beef
瘦肉 shòuròu lean meat

羊肉 yángròu mutton
烤肉 kǎoròu barbeque

如

rú
as; if

ASSOCIATIVE COMPOUND The character 如 consists of 女 (nǔ, female) and 口 (kǒu, mouth), meaning "obey," or "in compliance with" because traditionally women were to listen to men's words. One of the Confucian classics lists the three rules women must obey: obeying her father before marriage, her husband after marriage, and her son if her husband dies. The extended meanings of 如 include "according to," "as if," "as," "if," etc.

如 會意。從女，從口。按照傳統的價值觀念，女人應該柔順，聽從男人的話。《儀禮‧喪服‧子夏傳》道：〝未嫁從父，既嫁從夫，夫死從子〞。如本義為順從、遵照。引申為如同、例如、假如等。

甲 𠤳 金 𠤳 篆 𠤳

如果 rúguǒ if; in case
不如 bùrú not equal to; not as good as

比如 bǐrú for example; for instance
如下 rúxià as follows

賽/赛

sài
game;
competition

PICTOPHONETIC CHARACTER The character 賽 contains the cowry shell radical 貝 (bèi) at the bottom and phonetic component 宷 (sè) on top, originally meaning "to offer sacrifices to gods." The extended meanings of 賽 include "contest," "game," "race," "match," "competition," and "to surpass," possibly because some ancient sacrifices also included games and competitions in the ceremony. In the character 赛, 贝 is in its simplified form.

賽 形聲。從貝，宷聲。本義為舉行祭祀以酬謝神明，引申為比賽活動、比勝負、勝過等。

篆 𥩙

比賽 bǐsài competition
賽車 sàichē car race

賽馬 sàimǎ horse race
籃球賽 lánqiúsài basketball game

掃/扫

sǎo
to sweep

ASSOCIATIVE COMPOUND The character 掃 is the combination of the hand radical 扌 and semantic element 帚 (zhǒu, broom), suggesting "to sweep with a broom." The meanings of 掃 include "to sweep," "to clear away," "to wipe out," or "to go quickly through." In its ancient form, 帚 depicts a broom placed upside down: the top part is the broom and the lower part the handle. The simplified character 扫 consists of only the hand radical 扌 and the top part of 帚.

掃 會意。從扌，從帚，表示用掃帚來打掃，引申義有清除、很快地掠過等。帚，象形。像頭朝下的掃帚之形。簡化字扫把帚的有下半部去掉，十分近似掃字的草書。

草 扫 帚 甲 金 篆

掃地 sǎodì to sweep the floor
掃描 sǎomiáo to scan

打掃 dǎsǎo to clean
掃興 sǎoxìng to have one's spirits dampened

色

sè
color

ASSOCIATIVE COMPOUND In Seal Script, the upper part of 色 is a standing person, and the lower part is a kneeling person, suggesting someone angrily rebuking another. The original meaning of 色 was "an angry look," and later came to mean: "color," "look," "expression," "appearance," "feminine charms," etc. In Regular Script, the lower part of 色 has changed to 巴, which you can also see in the character 吧 (ba, a particle).

色 會意。篆文上是站立之人，下為下跪之人，前者訓斥後者。本義為怒色，引申為顏色、姿色、臉色、景色等。

篆

臉色 liǎnsè complexion; look
黃色 huángsè yellow (color); pornographic

顏色 yánsè color
彩色 cǎisè multi-colored

沙

shā
sand

ASSOCIATIVE COMPOUND The character 沙 combines the water radical 氵 with 少 (shǎo, few; little; less; short of). In the Oracle-Bone Inscriptions, 少 depicts four grains of sand. The original meaning of 沙 is "sand" and its extended meanings include "granule," "powder," and "hoarse."

沙 會意。從氵，從少。水少則沙現。本義為沙粒；引申為細碎如沙之物、不響亮。少，象形。少在甲骨文中為四點細小的沙粒。

金 篆

沙子 shāzi sand
豆沙 dòushā bean paste

沙漠 shāmò desert
沙發 shāfā sofa; couch

shān
shirt

PICTOPHONETIC CHARACTER The character 衫 is comprised of the clothes radical 衤 and the phonetic element 彡 (shān), meaning "unlined upper garment" or "short-sleeved shirt." 彡 may also refer to a decorative pattern, tassel, ribbon, hair, beard, carving, or shadow. You will also encounter 彡 in the character 影 (yǐng, shadow).

衫　形聲。篆文從衣，三 (sān)聲，意為單衣。

篆

襯衫 chènshān shirt; blouse
套衫 tàoshān pullover

長衫 chángshān long gown; traditional Chinese dress for men
T恤衫 T xùshān T-shirt

商

shāng
commerce;
business

PICTOGRAPH In its ancient form, the character 商 looks like a wine container, which was its original meaning. The wine container had a measuring function, so 商 extended to mean "measurement," "consult," "discuss," and "negotiate." Since business involves a lot of negotiation, 商 came to mean "commerce," "business," and "trade."

商　象形。甲骨文、金文 像古代盛酒的容器。酒 器有量度，故引申為估 量、商量。做生意重在 雙方商議，因此又引申 為經商、做買賣。

甲 金 篆

商店 shāngdiàn store; shop
商品 shāngpǐn goods; commodities; merchandise

商人 shāngrén merchant; businessman
商場 shāngchǎng shopping center

S - W

上

shàng
above; top

EXPLICIT CHARACTER In the Oracle-Bone and Bronze Inscriptions, 上 consists of two horizontal lines. The longer line on the bottom represents the horizon; the short line on top represents something above the horizon. In Regular Script, a vertical line is added on top of the longer horizontal line. The primary meaning of 上 is "above," "upper" or "top." Extended meanings of 上 include: "up," "on," "go to," and "last."

上　指事。表示在一物在 另一物之上。

甲 二 金 二 篆

樓上 lóushàng upstairs
晚上 wǎnshang evening; night

上午 shàngwǔ morning
上學 shàngxué to go to school; to attend school

燒/烧

shāo
to burn

PICTOPHONETIC CHARACTER The character 燒 is comprised of the fire radical 火 (huǒ) and the phonetic symbol 堯 (yáo), meaning "to burn." Its extended meanings include "to cook," "to roast," "to boil," "to heat," and "fever." 堯 is the combination of 垚 (yáo, mountain high) and 兀 (wù, high and flat on the top), referring to "high and far." 堯 is also the name of a legendary emperor-sage in ancient China. The simplified form 尧 derives from the cursive style of 堯. In the simplified character 烧, 尧 is used to take the place of 堯.

燒 形聲。從火，堯聲。本義為使物體着火，引申義有加熱、烘烤、發燒等。堯，會意。從垚（yáo，三土山重疊，意指山高），在兀（wù，一橫在人上，表示高而平）上，意指高遠。堯也是傳說中上古帝王。簡體字尧是堯字的草書簡化字。烧字中堯簡化為尧。

篆 燒 堯 草

燒水 shāoshuǐ to boil water
紅燒 hóngshāo braised with soy sauce
燒香 shāoxiāng to burn incense
發燒 fāshāo to have a fever

少

shǎo
few; little

shào
young

PICTOGRAPH The character 少 (shǎo, few; little; less; be short) derives from 小 (xiǎo, small; petty; minor; young). In the Oracle-Bone Inscriptions, both 小 and 少 depict a few grains of sand. In Regular Script, a downward left stroke is added under 小 to create 少. 少 is often used for the quantity of things, whereas 小 is used for size or age.

少 象形。少是由小字分化而來，古時小、少常通用。小在甲骨文、金文中為三點，像是細小的沙粒。少為四點。

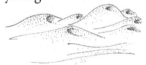

甲 ⼩ 金 少 篆 少

多少 duōshǎo how much; how many
少有 shǎoyǒu rare; seldom
不少 bùshǎo many; a lot; not few
少年 shàonián young adult; juvenile

紹/绍

shào
to introduce;
to continue

PICTOPHONETIC CHARACTER 紹 consists of the silk radical 糸 and the phonetic element 召 (zhāo, summon), meaning "continue" or "carry on." Extended meanings include "to introduce" and "to refer." The character 召 is the combination of 刀 (dāo, knife) and 口 (kǒu, mouth). The simplified silk radical 纟 is derived from the cursive of the traditional radical 糸. Only the radical is simplified in the character 绍.

紹 形聲。從糸，召聲。本義為繼續、繼承，引申為介紹、引薦等。簡體字部首纟是由糸的草書楷化而來。绍字的部首纟簡化。

甲 紹 篆 紹 草 紹

介紹 jièshào to introduce; introduction
紹興 shàoxīng Shaoxing, prefecture-level city in Zhejiang
紹興料酒 Shàoxīng liàojiǔ cooking wine

The Way of Chinese Characters

社

shè
organized body

ASSOCIATIVE COMPOUND　The character 社 is comprised of the show/altar radical ネ/示 and 土 (tǔ, soil; earth; land), originally referring to "the god of land." Its extended meanings are "sacrifices to the god of land," "the site to offer sacrifices to the god of land," "organized body," "association," "agency," "club," and "society." In its ancient forms, 示 resembles an altar and means "to show." The radical 示 is often written as ネ, which usually appears in characters related to religious ritual.

社　會意。從ネ/示（祭臺），從土，本義為土地神，引申為祭祀土地神、祭祀土地神的地方、一些團體、機構等。

甲 ⌂ 金 祉 篆 社

社會 shèhuì society
報社 bàoshè newspaper publisher

社交 shèjiāo interaction; social contact
旅行社 lǚxíngshè travel agency

舍

shè
house; residence

PICTOGRAPH　In the character 舍, 人 (jí) represents the roof, 十 the pillar, and 口 the wall, creating a combined meaning of "hut," "shed," or "house."

舍　象形。舍字上部人像房頂，中間是支撐房屋的柱子，下面的口代表牆。

金 舍 篆 舍

宿舍 sùshè dormitory

校舍 xiàoshè school building

誰/谁

shéi
who

PICTOPHONETIC CHARACTER　The character 誰 is the combination of the word/speech radical 言 and the phonetic element 隹 (zhuī, short-tailed bird). 誰 does not mean the speech of a bird, but the personal interrogative pronoun "who." In the simplified character 谁, the speech radical is simplified.

誰　形聲。從言，隹聲。簡體字偏旁簡化。

金 誰 篆 誰

誰的 shéide whose
誰知 shéizhī who would have thought; unexpectedly (literally: who knows)

誰都/也 shéidōu/yě everybody

身

shēn
body

PICTOGRAPH In its ancient forms, 身 is a pictograph of a woman with a child in her womb. Its original meaning was "pregnant," from which derived the meanings "body," "life," "oneself," "personally," "one's morality and conduct," "the main part of a structure or body," etc.

身 象形。甲骨文像一懷
有身孕的大肚子婦女。
本義為懷孕，引申為身
體、親身、人的品德、
地位、物體的主幹。

身體 shēntǐ body; health
身教 shēnjiào to teach by one's own example

身高 shēngāo height
出身 chūshēn family background

什

shén
what

PHONETIC LOAN CHARACTER The character 什 is the combination of the person radical 亻and 十 (shí, ten). In ancient times, a group of ten soldiers or ten households was named 什. Later 什 came to represent an interrogative without any change in form. 什 also means "assorted," "miscellaneous" (pronounced shí).

什 假借。從人，從十。
古代戶籍十家為什，兵
制十人為什。"什" 後
借用為疑問代詞。

什麼 shénme what
沒什麼 méishénme it doesn't matter

為什麼 wèishénme why; for what reason
什麼的 shénmede and so on; and the likes

生

shēng
to be born; to grow

ASSOCIATIVE COMPOUND In the Oracle-Bone inscriptions the character 生 looks like a seedling growing out of the ground. Hence the original meaning of 生 is "the growth of plants." It can also mean "grow," "life," "give birth to," "unripe," "student," etc. In Regular Script the bottom part of 生 is 土 (tǔ, soil; earth), and the upper part resembles grass or plants growing above.

生 會意。像地面上剛長
出的一株幼苗，本義指
草木生長。

生日 shēngrì birthday
生詞 shēngcí new word

生活 shēnghuó life; activity; to live; livelihood
留學生 liúxuéshēng student studying abroad

勝 / 胜

shèng
victory; wonderful

PICTOPHONETIC CHARACTER The character 勝 consists of 力 (lì, power, strength) and the phonetic component 朕 (zhèn), meaning "to be able to bear," "to win," "to surpass," "victory," "success," "wonderful," and "scenic spots and historical sites." In its ancient forms, 朕 consists of a boat and two hands holding a pole meaning "seam." Later, 朕 was exclusively used by the emperors of China to mean "I." The character 胜 (xīng) is composed of the flesh radical and 生 (shēng, to be born), which originally meant "raw meat," "smell of fish," etc. 胜 is used as the simplified form of 勝 since their pronunciations are similar.

勝 形聲。從力，朕聲。意思為能承受、勝過等。朕，會意。古文字像是雙手在填船縫。本義為船縫，自秦始皇起，專用為皇帝自稱。胜，形聲。從肉月旁，生聲。原本讀作 xīng，本義為生肉腥臭，同腥。因聲音相近，胜現作為勝的簡化字，但兩字原本互不相關。

篆 胜 朕 甲 金 篆 勝

勝利 shènglì victory
勝訴 shèngsù to win a lawsuit

得勝 déshèng to win a victory
名勝 míngshèng famous scenic spot

師 / 师

shī
teacher

ASSOCIATIVE COMPOUND The character 師 consists of 自 (duī, hill) on the left and 帀 (zā, circle; surround) on the right, suggesting numerous people gathered on a hill. The original meaning of 師 was "mass" or "army," and later came to mean "study," "teacher," etc. The simplified character 师 derives from the cursive style of the traditional character 師, and 自 is replaced by two vertical strokes.

師 會意。師字左邊 自 (duī) 意為小土山，右部帀 (zā) 是環繞的意思，意指眾人環繞在土山旁。本義指眾人、軍隊、都邑，引申為學習、老師等。师是師字的草書楷化字。

金 篆 師 草 师

老師 lǎoshī teacher
導師 dǎoshī academic advisor; supervisor

律師 lùshī lawyer
師傅 shīfu master worker

時 / 时

shí
time

PICTOPHONETIC CHARACTER The character 時 combines the radical 日 (rì, sun) and the phonetic element 寺 (sì, temple), meaning "season," "time," or "often." In the Bronze Inscriptions, 寺 consists of 止 (zhǐ, stop) and 又 (yòu, hand), meaning "hold," "handle," or "manage." Later 寺 came to mean "temple" or "monastery." The simplified character 时 is developed from the cursive style of the traditional character 時, with 寸 replacing 寺 on the left.

時 形聲。從日，寺聲。寺，形聲。金文從又 (手)，從止。手之所止為持，本義為持有。簡體字时是繁體字時的草書楷化字，右邊以寸代替寺。

甲 金 篆 時 草 时

時間 shíjiān time
同時 tóngshí at the same time; simultaneously

時候 shíhou time; moment
小時 xiǎoshí hour

實/实

shí
solid; reality

ASSOCIATIVE COMPOUND In the Bronze Inscriptions, the character 實 consists of the radicals 宀 (roof), 田 (field), and 貝 (cowry shell; money), meaning "well-off" or "substantial." Its extended meanings include "solid," "true," "reality," "honest," and "fruit." In Seal Script, 實 becomes the combination of the roof radical 宀 and 貫 (guàn). 貫 is made up of 毌 (guàn, string; pierce) and 貝 (bèi, cowry shell), meaning "to link together" or "a string of 1,000 copper coins." The simplified character 实 derives from the cursive style of 實.

實　會意。金文從宀（房屋），從田，從貝，指有房屋、良田、錢財。篆文宀下改為貫（錢串），意指家裏有錢。實本義為殷實，富有，引申義有充實、真實、實際、誠實、果實等。簡化字实是繁體字實的草書楷化字。把實下部的貫改為头。

金 實　篆 實　草 实

老實 lǎoshi honest; truthful
現實 xiànshí reality

實習 shíxí internship; field work
實力 shílì actual strength

識/识

shí
to recognize

PICTOPHONETIC CHARACTER 識 is made up of the word radical 言 and the phonetic symbol 戠 (zhī, sign), meaning "to recognize," "know," or "knowledge." 戠 is the combination of 音 (yīn, sound) and 戈 (gē, dagger-axe), suggesting the sound of a small bell attached to a weapon, from which the meaning "sign" is derived. 音 and 言 are cognate characters that both resembled tongues sticking out of mouths in their ancient forms, indicating mouth sounds. Later, their meanings diverged. In the simplified 识, the speech radical is simplified and 只 (zhǐ) replaces 戠 (zhī), as the two are similarly pronounced.

識　形聲。從言，從戠（zhī）；戠也兼表聲。戠，甲骨文像戈上挂有鈴、環之類的飾物，本義為標誌、記住。音，會意。表示口舌發出的聲音。戈，象形。是一種長柄橫刃的兵器。簡體字识左邊部首簡化，右邊聲旁用只替代戠，屬于近音替代。

戠 甲 戠　金 戠　篆 戠

認識 rènshi to know; to recognize
知識 zhīshi knowledge

常識 chángshí common sense; general knowledge
意識 yìshi be aware; to realize; consciousness

始

shǐ
to begin

ASSOCIATIVE AND PICTOPHONETIC COMPOUND In the Oracle-Bone Inscriptions, 台 looks like a fetus with its head facing down toward the birth canal, and originally meant "pregnant." The character 始 consists of the female radical 女 and the signifying and phonetic element 台 (tái), originally referring to the beginning stages of pregnancy. Extended meanings of 始 include "to begin," "start," and "just."

始　會意兼形聲。從女，從台（胎兒）；台也兼表聲。本義為剛開始受孕懷胎，引申泛指開始。台，甲骨文像頭朝下的胎兒。

台 甲 台　金 台　篆 台

開始 kāishǐ to begin; beginning
始末 shǐmò the whole story

原始 yuánshǐ primitive; original
始祖 shǐzǔ earliest ancestor

shì
city; market

ASSOCIATIVE AND PICTOPHONETIC COMPOUND In its ancient form, the character 市 has 之 (zhī, go) on the top and 冂 (jiǒng, designed market area) at the bottom, meaning "go to the market". Since every city had a market, 市 extended to mean "city." In the ancient form of the character 市, 之 also functions as the phonetic element.

市 會意兼形聲。甲骨文從之（去，前往），從冂（jiǒng，劃出的集市範圍），之亦表聲。本義指集市、市場。因有城即有市場，故有城市一詞。

 甲

市場 shìchǎng marketplace; market
城市 chéngshì city; town

夜市 yèshì night market
市長 shìzhǎng mayor

式

shì
type; style

PICTOPHONETIC CHARACTER The character 式 combines 工 (gōng, tool; work) with the phonetic element 弋 (yì). Its original meaning is "construction rules," from which it has derived the meanings "rule," "regulation," "style," "type," "formula," "pattern," and "ceremony." In its ancient forms, 弋 is the pictograph of a stake/pile driven into the ground, and later was borrowed to mean "a retrievable arrow with a string attached" and "to shoot (birds) with a bow."

式 形聲。從工，弋聲。本義為建築的規則法度，引申為規格、樣式、格式、儀式等。弋，象形。甲骨文像打進地裏的木樁形，本義指小木樁。後也借來指射鳥用的帶有繩子的短箭，這種箭可以回收。

篆

樣式 yàngshì style; pattern
中式 zhōngshì Chinese style

新式 xīnshì new style
西式 xīshì Western style

事

shì
affair; matter

ASSOCIATIVE COMPOUND In the Oracle-Bone Inscriptions, the character 事 looks like a hand holding a hunting fork to catch a wild animal. Hunting was an essential part of primitive society, so the character 事 became used to mean "matter," "affair," or "event." In Regular Script, the animal is simplified to a horizontal stroke on top; the square in the middle and the vertical hook stand for the fork, while the component in the lower part refers to a hand.

事 會意。在甲骨文中像一手持獵叉狀。因古代狩獵是經常發生的事，故以此來泛指做事。

甲 金 事 篆 事

事情 shìqíng affair; matter; thing
事件 shìjiàn event; happening; incident

做事 zuòshì to work; to handle matters
軍事 jūnshì military affairs

是

shì
to be

ASSOCIATIVE COMPOUND In its ancient form, the character 是 is a combination of 日 (rì, sun) and 正 (zhèng, straight), indicating high noon. 是 originally meant "straight," and has evolved to mean "correct," "yes," "to be," etc. In Regular Script, the lower part of 是 is no longer 正, but instead like the lower part of 足 (zú, foot) and 走 (zǒu, to walk).

是 會意。金文從日，從正，表示日正當午。本義為正、直，引申義有正確、是非、肯定等。

甲 𤴓 金 𤴓 篆 是

但是 dànshì but; however
總是 zǒngshì always

可是 kěshì but; however
只是 zhǐshì merely; simply; only

室

shì
room

ASSOCIATIVE AND PICTOPHONETIC COMPOUND The character 室 consists of the roof radical 宀 and the signifying and phonetic element 至 (zhì, to arrive), meaning "room." 至 also appears in the character 到 (dào, arrive).

室 會意兼形聲。從宀，從至；至亦聲。指人歇息居住的地方。

甲 𡩀 金 室 篆 𡨈

教室 jiàoshì classroom
室友 shìyǒu roommate

辦公室 bàn'gōngshì office
室外 shìwài outdoors

視／视

shì
to view; to look at

ASSOCIATIVE COMPOUND The character 視 consists of the radical 礻 (shì, show; altar) and 見 (jiàn, see), suggesting acts of predicting future events according to astronomical phenomena. Therefore it means "to view," "look at," "regard," "treat," etc. 礻 is derived from the character 示. In the Oracle-Bone Inscriptions, 示 resembles a stone altar upon which sacrifices are offered. Hence, characters with the 礻 radical are often associated with religious ceremonies or divination activities. In the simplified version (视), the 见 part is in its simplified form.

視 會意。甲骨文從示，從目，指用眼觀看天象。示也兼表聲。示，象形。甲骨文字形像用石塊搭起來的祭臺。視字右邊簡化。

甲 𥄎 篆 視

注視 zhùshì to watch attentively; to gaze
重視 zhòngshì to attach importance to; think highly of

視力 shìlì vision; eyesight
電視 diànshì television; TV

試/试

shì
test; to try

PICTOPHONETIC CHARACTER The character 試 is comprised of the word radical 言 and the phonetic 式 (shì), meaning "to try," "test," or "examination." 式 combines 弋 (yì, arrow with rope) and 工 (gōng, tool; work). Its original meaning was "rule" or "regulation." Today it is used to mean "style," "type," or "ceremony." The speech radical in 试 is in its simplified form.

試 形聲。從言，式聲，意指任用、嘗試、考試等。式，形聲。從工，弋聲，本義為建築的規則法度。簡體字试的部首簡化。

篆

考試 kǎoshì to take an exam; exam
口試 kǒushì oral examination

筆試 bǐshì written examination
試驗 shìyàn experiment

適/适

shì
to suit; appropriate

PICTOPHONETIC CHARACTER The character 適 consists of the walk radical 辶 and the phonetic element 商 (dì, screech; scream). The primary meanings of 適 are "to go to" (a place), "follow," and "pursue." Extended meanings include "right," "well," "comfortable," "fit," "suitable," "proper," etc. In Regular Script, 商 shows ten mouths (十 and 口) screaming inside a building. In the simplified character 适, 舌 (shé, tongue) replaces 商, as the pronunciation of 舌 is similar to that of 適 (shì).

適 形聲。從辶，商聲。本義指前往、來到，引申為舒適、適合、適宜等。商，甲骨文、金文、篆文中從口，從帝，意為高聲。簡體字适以舌代替商，因舌與適聲音相似，屬近音替代字。

合適 héshì suitable; appropriate
舒適 shūshì cozy; snug

適合 shìhé to fit; to suit
適應 shìyìng to adapt

收

shōu
to receive; to accept

PICTOPHONETIC CHARACTER In Seal Script, the character 收 consists of the signifying element 攴 (pū, hit with stick) on the right and the phonetic element 丩 (jiū) on the left, originally meaning "arrest." The extended meanings are "take in," "collect," "receive," "gather in," "harvest," etc. In Regular Script, in the character 收, 攴 is replaced by the tap/rap radical 攵, for the meaning of 攵 is the same as 攴. 攵 is also seen in the character 教 (jiāo, to teach).

收 形聲。篆文從攴(pū 手持杖擊打)，丩聲。本義為逮捕，收監，引申為收容、收集、收到、收復、收獲等。部首攵與攴意思相同。

篆

收拾 shōushi to put in order; to tidy up
回收 huíshōu to recycle

收入 shōurù income; revenue
收音機 shōuyīnjī radio

首
shǒu
head

PICTOGRAPH In its ancient forms, 首 looks like a head with a few hairs on the top and an eye underneath. The original meaning of 首 is "head," from which it derived the meanings "leader," "chief," "supreme," "first," "beginning," "to inform against somebody," "a measure word for poems or songs," etc.

首　象形。甲骨文像有頭髮、眼睛突出的人頭，本義為頭，引申為首領、最高的、第一、開始、告發、詩歌、歌曲的量詞等。

甲 金 篆

首飾 shǒushì jewelry
首先 shǒuxiān first of all

首都 shǒudū capital city
一首歌 yìshǒu gē a song

受
shòu
to bear

ASSOCIATIVE COMPOUND In the Oracle-Bone and Bronze Inscriptions, the character 受 looks like one hand (top part) passing something (middle part) to another hand (bottom part), originally referring to "giving and receiving." The extended meanings of 受 include "to receive," "to accept," "to suffer," "to bear," "to endure," and "to tolerate." It is also used as an indicator of passive voice.

受　會意。甲骨文、金文上從爪（手），下從手，中為一物，表示一人接受另一人給與的贈物。本義為給與和接受，引申義有接受、遭受、忍耐、受到等。

甲 金 篆

接受 jiēshòu to accept; to receive
難受 nánshòu feel unwell; feel bad

忍受 rěnshòu to tolerate
受傷 shòushāng injured; wounded

售
shòu
sale; to sell

ASSOCIATIVE COMPOUND The character 售 consists of 隹 (zhuī, short-tailed bird) and 口 (kǒu, mouth), referring to the shouting of peddlers, as it resembles the chirping of birds.

售　會意。從口，隹聲，指像鳥鳴一樣的叫賣聲。

篆

售貨 shòuhuò sell goods
售完 shòuwán sell out

售貨員 shòuhuòyuán salesperson
零售 língshòu retail

The Way of Chinese Characters

瘦

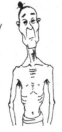

shòu
thin; slim
(of a person/
animal)

PICTOPHONETIC CHARACTER The character 瘦 is formed with the sick radical 疒 and the phonetic component 叟 (sǒu), meaning "thin," "lean," "slim," "emaciated," "meager," "to lose weight," "tight (of clothes)," "infertile," etc. 瘦 used to be regarded as unhealthy, as opposed to modern trends. In Seal Script, 叟 was written as 㝢 (sǒu), which shows a hand 又 holding a torch 火, searching inside a house 宀. Its original meaning is "to search" and has been extended to mean "old man," probably because an old man with poor eyesight cannot see things clearly without a torch.

瘦 形聲。篆文從疒，叜(sǒu)聲。楷書改為瘦。本義指肌肉不豐滿，脂肪少。引申義有使消瘦、細小、貧瘠等。叜，會意。篆文寫作㝢，從手（又），似手持火把（火），在房（宀）內搜索。本義為搜索，後引申指老年男子，而另造搜字以示搜索之意。

篆 [seal forms] 甲 [oracle form] 篆 [seal form]

瘦子 shòuzi skinny person
瘦小 shòuxiǎo skinny and petite

瘦肉 shòuròu lean meat
瘦高 shòugāo tall and thin

叔

shū
uncle

ASSOCIATIVE AND PICTOPHONETIC COMPOUND In the Bronze Inscriptions, the character 叔 consists of a right hand 又 and the semantic and phonetic component 尗 (shú, collective name for beans and peas), suggesting the action of picking up beans and meaning "to pick up" originally. In its ancient forms, 尗 looks like a bean stalk on the ground with beans growing underneath. 叔 has long been borrowed to mean "father's younger brother," "husband's younger brother," "uncle," etc.

叔 會意兼形聲。從尗（shú 豆類的總稱），從又（右手），尗亦聲。表示用手拾取豆類，本義為拾取，後借用來指父親的弟弟、丈夫的弟弟、或與父親同輩兒年齡較小的男性等。尗，象形。上像豆杆，中間一橫表示土地，下面三畫表示豆類，是菽的本字。

金 [bronze form] 篆 [seal form]

叔叔 shūshu father's younger brother; uncle
叔母 shūmǔ wife of father's younger brother; aunt

叔父 shūfù father's younger brother; uncle
大叔 dàshū uncle; an elderly male

書/书

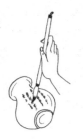

shū
book

ASSOCIATIVE COMPOUND In the Oracle-Bone Inscriptions, the upper part of 書 shows a hand holding a brush (聿 yù) and the lower part resembles a box (口), indicating the act of writing on something. Besides "write," 書 also means "script," "book," or "letter." The simplified character 书 derives from the cursive style of the traditional character 書.

書 會意。甲骨文上是手持筆形，下為一器物，指手持筆在器物上書寫。书是書字的草書楷化字。

甲 [oracle form] 金 [bronze form] 篆 [seal form] 草 [cursive form]

書店 shūdiàn bookstore
書包 shūbāo schoolbag; satchel

書架 shūjià bookshelf
念書 niànshū to read; to study

舒

shū
to stretch; to
smooth out

ASSOCIATIVE COMPOUND The character 舒 consists of
舍 (shè, house; shě, give alms) and 予 (yǔ, give; grant;
bestow). Since both 舍 and 予 carry the meaning of
"to open and give," 舒 means "to unfold," "to spread,"
"to stretch," "to smooth out," "to relax," "leisurely," etc.
舍 is a pictograph wherein 亼 (jí) represents the roof,
十 the pillar, and 口 the wall, creating a combined
meaning of "house." In Seal Script, 予 looks like a hand
pushing something to others.

舒 會意。從舍，從予。
舍和予都有給與、放開之
意，故舒本義為伸展，
緩解。舍，象形。像房
舍形，引申為施与，放
棄等。予，像以手把物
推給他人。

篆 舒

舒服 shūfu comfortable; feeling well
舒心 shūxīn pleased

舒適 shūshì cozy; snug
舒暢 shūchàng happy; entirely free from worry

暑

shǔ
heat; summer

ASSOCIATIVE AND PICTOPHONETIC COMPOUND The
character 暑 is comprised of the sun radical 日　(rì)
and the semantic and phonetic component 者 (zhě,
originally meaning "to burn"), meaning "heat," "hot,"
"hot weather," or "summer heat." In the Oracle-Bone
and Bronze Inscriptions, 者 depicts food being cooked
in a wok, meaning "to burn," "to boil," or "to kindle."
Later 者 came to be used primarily as an auxiliary word
after a verb or adjective to indicate a class of persons or
things.

暑 會意兼形聲。從日，
從者，者亦聲。本義為炎
熱，引申為熱天、夏季。
者，會意。甲骨文、金
文中上像架起的木架與
水蒸氣，下從火，本義
是燒煮，後借用在形容
詞、動詞後表示某類人
或事物。者在暑字中以
燒煮表現夏日的炎熱。

篆 暑

暑假 shǔjià summer vacation
酷暑 kùshǔ the severe heat of summer

暑期 shǔqī summer vacation time
中暑 zhòngshǔ sunstroke; heatstroke

屬/属

shǔ
to belong to

ASSOCIATIVE AND PICTOPHONETIC COUMPOUND
In Seal Script, 屬 combines 尾 (wěi, tail) with the
semantic and phonetic component 蜀 (shǔ, silkworm),
indicating that the tail is connected to the worm's
body. Its original meaning was "to connect" and later
came to mean to "to belong to," "to be subordinate to,"
"category," "genus," "relatives," and "to be born in the
year of (a zodiac sign)." In its ancient forms, 蜀 looks
like a silkworm with a prominent head. It is also the
abbreviated name of Sichuan province. 属 is a variant
form of 屬 and is also used today as the simplified
version of 屬.

屬 會意兼形聲。篆文從
尾，蜀聲。本義為連接，
引申義有跟從、從屬、
類別、親屬、屬相等。
蜀，象形。像頭部突出
的蠶。蠶叢是昔時蜀國
開國的先王。蜀也是四
川省的簡稱。簡化字把
屬字下部改為禹，漢代
已有此字。

篆 屬 蜀 甲 金 篆

金屬 jīnshǔ metal
屬相 shǔxiàng symbolic animal of one's birth year, sign of the Chinese Zodiac

家屬 jiāshǔ family members

The Way of Chinese Characters

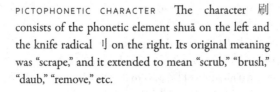

shuā
to brush; to swipe

PICTOPHONETIC CHARACTER The character 刷 consists of the phonetic element shuā on the left and the knife radical 刂 on the right. Its original meaning was "scrape," and it extended to mean "scrub," "brush," "daub," "remove," etc.

刷 形聲。左半邊為聲旁，右從刂。本義為用刀刮，引申為用刷子清洗、梳理、塗抹、划過、刷子等。

篆 刷

牙刷 yáshuā toothbrush
刷卡 shuākǎ use a credit card (or swipe card)

刷牙 shuāyá brush one's teeth
印刷 yìnshuā to print; printing

---

shuài
handsome; smart

ASSOCIATIVE COMPOUND In the Oracle-Bone Inscriptions, the character 帥 resembles two hands (the left part) holding a flag or scarf (the right part), and originally meaning "commander-in-chief." Since such commanders often have a commanding presence and impressive bearing, "handsome" became one of the extended meanings of 帥. Be sure to distinguish 帥 from 師 (shī, teacher). If you are lucky, you may have 很帥的老師 (a handsome teacher)! The simplified 帅 derives from the cursive style of the traditional 帥. The same simplification can be found in 師, with the simplified form 师.

帥 會意。甲骨文字形右似佩巾，左為伸出的雙手，像用兩手展開佩巾狀。本義為佩巾，借用為軍中統帥，引申為英俊、有風度等。簡體字帅是繁體字帥的草書楷化字，簡化方法與師字相同。

甲 帥 金 帥 篆 帥

元帥 yuánshuài marshal (in the army)
帥哥 shuàigē handsome guy; lady-killer

主帥 zhǔshuài command; commander-in-chief
帥氣 shuàiqi handsome; dashing

---

shuāng
pair

ASSOCIATIVE COMPOUND In Seal Script, 雙 resembles a person holding a pair of birds in one hand. Consequently, meanings of 雙 include "pair," "two," "twin," "both," and "dual." In Regular Script, 雙 consists of two short-tailed birds 隹隹 and a right hand 又. Two hands replace the one hand holding two birds to form the simplified character 双.

雙 會意。從又（右手），從雙佳（短尾鳥），表示一隻手抓兩隻鳥。簡體字双把繁體字雙改為兩個又字，意為雙手，屬會意詞。宋元時期已見双字。

篆 雙

雙手 shuāngshǒu both hands
雙打 shuāngdǎ doubles (in sports)

雙方 shuāngfāng bilateral; both sides
雙胞胎 shuāngbāotāi twins

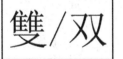

睡

shuì
to sleep

ASSOCIATIVE AND PICTOPHONETIC COMPOUND The character 睡 consists of the eye radical 目 and the character 垂 (chuí, hang down; droop), representing a person with his or her head bowed and eyes closed. The original meaning of 睡 was "to doze while seated." Today 睡 means "to sleep." The lower part of 垂 is 土 (tǔ, earth; soil). The upper part represents a plant with drooping branches and blossoms.

睡 會意兼形聲。從目從垂；垂亦聲。本義為坐寐。

篆 睡

睡覺 shuìjiào to go to bed; to sleep
午睡 wǔshuì a nap afer lunch

睡着 shuìzháo fall asleep
睡衣 shuìyī night clothes; pajamas

說／说

shuō
to speak

ASSOCIATIVE COMPOUND The character 說 combines the word radical 言 and the character 兌 (duì, exchange), meaning "to speak," "talk," "say," or "explain." In the Oracle-Bone Inscriptions, 兌 combines 人 (rén, person), 口 (kǒu, mouth), and 八 (bā, divide), symbolizing a grinning person. The original meaning of 兌 was "joyous," while extended meanings include "exchange," "convert," and "add." The speech radical in 说 is in its simplified form.

说 會意。從言，從兌 (duì)。本義為言語中有喜悅之情，引申為言辭、陳述、勸說等。兌，從人，從口，從八（分開）。人笑則口開，本義為喜悅。说字部首簡化。

兌 甲 ⅄ 金 ⅄ 篆 兌

說話 shuōhuà to speak; to say; to talk
小説 xiǎoshuō novel; fiction

聽説 tīngshuō hear of; be told
説謊 shuōhuǎng to lie

司

sī
to take charge of

ASSOCIATIVE COMPOUND In the Oracle-Bone and Bronze Inscriptions, the character 司 depicts a hand placed over a mouth, symbolizing a person issuing orders. Therefore, the meanings of 司 are "to take charge of," "to manage," "department," etc.

司 會意。甲骨文、金文像把手遮在嘴上發號施令。另一說司字上像人，下為口，表示人用口發號施令。引申義有主持、掌管、行政部門。

甲 司 金 司

司法 sīfǎ judicial; (administration of) justice
公司 gōngsī company; firm; corporation

司機 sījī driver
上司 shàngsi superior; boss

思

sī
to think

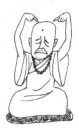

ASSOCIATIVE COMPOUND In Seal Script, 思 is a combination of 囟 (xìn, top of head) and 心 (xīn, heart), implying that thinking is done with one's mind and heart. 思 means "to think," "consider," "think of," or "long for." In Regular Script, the upper part 囟 has changed into 田 (tián, field), which is unrelated to the original meaning.

思 會意。篆文從心，從
囟。囟指人的腦門。古
人以為大腦與心都有思
考的功能，故以二者來
表示思考、思想、思念
等意。

篆

思考 sīkǎo reflect on; ponder over
思念 sīniàn to long for; to miss

思想 sīxiǎng thought; thinking; ideology
意思 yìsi meaning

死

sǐ
to die; (complement indicating extreme degree)

ASSOCIATIVE COMPOUND In its ancient forms, 死 presents a person kneeling beside the skeleton (歹 dǎi) of a person who has died, mourning over him. Its original and primary meaning is "to die," "dead," "death," and the extended meanings are "to risk one's life," "implacable," "rigid," "inflexible," "impassable," and "extremely." 歹 is the pictograph of a skeleton. Its original meaning was "skeleton," and has been transferred to mean "bad," "vicious," or "depraved."

死 會意。甲骨文從歺
(dǎi 殘骨、枯骨。歺是歹
的古體字)，從人，像人
在枯骨邊悼念死者。本
義為死亡，引申義有不顧
生死、拼命（死戰）、
不可調和（死敵）、不
靈活（死板）、不通
（死胡同）、極度（難
受死了）等。

甲 𠕋 金 𣦵 篆 𣦳

死人 sǐrén dead person
死路 sǐlù dead end

死心 sǐxīn to give up hope
餓死了 èsǐle to be starved to death; extremely hungry

送

sòng
to see off; to deliver

ASSOCIATIVE COMPOUND In the Oracle-Bone and Bronze Inscriptions, the character 送 depicts a boat, two hands, and a punt-pole, referring to someone poling a boat to deliver passengers or goods. Meanings of 送 include "send," "deliver," "carry," "see somebody off," "escort," and "give as a present." In Regular Script, 送 combines the walk radical 辶 with 丷 and 天.

送 會意。從辶，從
关。"送"字在甲骨文、
金文中左像船形，右像
雙手持篙，本義指以船
運送。

甲 𣥂 金 𦥔

送行 sòngxíng to see sb. off; to give a send-off party
雪中送炭 xuězhōng sòngtàn provide help when most needed (literally: send coal during snow)

送禮 sònglǐ to give a present

素

sù
vegetarian; made
from vegetables

ASSOCIATIVE COMPOUND In the Bronze Inscriptions, the character 素 looks like two hands holding a silk string. In Seal Script, the top part of 素 is 垂 (chuí, droop) and the bottom part 糸 (mì, silk), indicating soft silk sagging down. The original meaning of 素 was "raw silk," from which derived the meanings of "plain," "white," "nature," "essence," "elements," and "vegetarian (food)." Do you think vegetarian food is the purest food for mankind?

素 會意。金文像兩手持一束絲。篆文上從垂，下從糸。表示柔軟自然下垂的絲綢。本義為沒有染色的生絹，引申義有本色、白色、顏色單純淡雅、樸素、本質、構成事物的基本成分、素菜等。

金 𧘇 篆 𧗣

素菜 sùcài vegetarian dish; vegetables
因素 yīnsù factor; element

吃素 chīsù to be a vegetarian
素淨 sùjìng plain and neat

速

sù
speed

PICTOPHONETIC CHARACTER The character 速 is comprised of the walk radical 辶 and the phonetic element 束 (shù), meaning "swift," "rapid," "speedy," "speed," or "velocity." In the Oracle-Bone Inscriptions, the character 束 looks like a sack tied on both ends with cord, meaning: "tie," "bind," "control," "restrain," "bundle," "bunch," etc. Some scholars think 束 looks like a bunch of bamboo pieces or firewood.

速 形聲。從辶，束聲，本義指迅速。束，會意。金文從口從木，像袋子的兩端被捆扎起來。本義為束縛。

甲 𣎵 金 𧗵 篆 𧗜

速度 sùdù speed
高速 gāosù high speed

加速 jiāsù accelerate
高速公路 gāosù gōnglù highway; freeway

宿

sù
to stay; to lodge

ASSOCIATIVE COMPOUND In the Oracle-Bone Inscriptions, the character 宿 consists of a person lying on a mat beneath the roof radical 宀, meaning "to stay overnight." In Regular Script, the character 百 (bǎi, hundred) replaces the mat part of 宿, which could suggest a lot of people lodging in a guesthouse.

宿 會意。甲骨文從宀，從人，從𠕁 (tiàn 席)，像人在屋裏的席子上休息。

甲 𠕦 金 𠕧 篆 𡩃

宿舍 sùshè dormitory
住宿 zhùsù to stay at; lodging; accommodation

宿舍樓 sùshèlóu dormitory building
歸宿 guīsù place to return to; final destination

訴／诉

sù
to tell; to relate

PICTOPHONETIC CHARACTER The character 訴 consists of the word radical 言 and the phonetic component 斥 (chì), meaning "tell," "relate," "complain," "accuse," and "appeal to." In the Oracle-Bone Inscriptions, 斤 looks like an ax with a crooked handle. When you add a short stroke to the middle of 斤, it becomes the character 斥 (chì, oust; reprimand). The speech radical is simplified to form the character 诉.

訴 形聲。從言，斥聲，告訴、控訴之意。斥，斤字加一點，意為指責、責備。簡體字诉的部首簡化。

篆

告訴 gàosu to tell; to inform
訴訟 sùsòng lawsuit

起訴 qǐsù to sue; to bring a lawsuit against
訴苦 sùkǔ vent one's grievance; to complain

酸

suān
sour

PICTOPHONETIC CHARACTER The character 酸 combines the wine jar radical 酉 (yǒu) with the phonetic 夋 (qūn). Its original meaning was "vinegar", and came to mean "sour," "acid," "tingle," "sad," "pedantic," etc. In its ancient forms, 酉 outlines a wine jar. Though later 酉 was borrowed to mean "the tenth of the twelve earthly branches" (see page 20), characters with 酉 as the radical still often have something to do with wine or fermentation. 夋 originally meant to walk slowly and solemnly. Today 夋 usually serves as the phonetic indicator in a character.

酸 形聲。從酉(yǒu)，夋(qūn)聲。本義為醋，引申為酸味。另外還有微痛、無力、傷心、迂腐等意。酉，象形，像酒罈子形。與釀酒發酵有關的字，常用酉字做部首，因為都要用罈子，如酥、酪、酶、釀。夋，形聲。意指行走遲緩而莊重，現主要用作字的聲旁。

篆 醱　酉 甲　酉 金　酉 篆 酉

酸菜 suāncài pickled vegetable
心酸 xīnsuān to feel sad

酸奶 suānnǎi yogurt
寒酸 hánsuān miserable and shabby; stinginess

算

suàn
to calculate

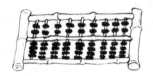

ASSOCIATIVE COMPOUND In Seal Script, 算 combines the bamboo radical ⺮ and the character 具 (jù, tool), signifying the use of a bamboo tool, such as an abacus, used to make calculations. In its ancient form, the character 竹 (zhú) is a pictograph of two bamboo branches with leaves (note the difference between the bamboo character 竹 and the radical ⺮). 具 resembles two hands holding a three-legged vessel. In Regular Script, the upper part of 算 is ⺮, and the bottom part is 廾 (gǒng, two hands holding something), but the middle changes to 目.

算 會意。從竹，從具，表示計算時使用的竹製器具，即算盤。具，會意。甲骨文從雙手，從鼎（食具），指雙手舉鼎以供酒食。

篆 算

算盤 suànpán abacus
計算 jìsuàn to count; to calculate

算術 suànshù arithmetic; sums
打算 dǎsuàn to plan; plan

雖/虽

suī
although

PICTOPHONETIC CHARACTER The character 雖 consists of 虫 (chóng, worm; insect), and phoneic element 唯 (wěi), originally referring to a particular kind of reptile, similar to a lizard. Today 雖 is used as conjunction, meaning "although," and "even if." In its ancient form, the character 虫 looks like a kind of snake, meaning "venomous snake." Its extended meanings are "insect," "worm," and "reptile." The simplified character 虽 retains only the left part of the traditional character 雖.

雖 形聲。從虫，唯聲。本義指一種似蜥蜴的爬蟲，今用作連詞，表示轉折。唯，甲骨文從口，從佳（短尾鳥），意指恭敬的應答。簡體字虽僅取繁體字雖的右部，舊時已有此字。

虫 甲 乙 金 乙 篆 乙　　雖然 suīrán although; even though　　雖説 suīshuō though; although

---

歲/岁

suì
age

ASSOCIATIVE COMPOUND In the Oracle-Bone and Bronze Inscriptions, the character 歲 contains a tool with a long shaft and two footprints, meaning "step forward to harvest." Since crops are harvested once a year, 歲 extended to mean "year" and "age." In Regular Script, 歲 consists of an ax-type tool 戌 (xū), with a footprint 止 (zhǐ) on the top and another under 戌. The two footprints together become the character 步 (bù, step). A variant form of 歲 is 崴. The simplified character 岁 replaces the bottom part of 崴 with 夕.

歲 會意。甲骨文、金文從戉（yuè 斧形），從步，指在田裏邁步向前，用斧形鐮刀之類農具收割莊稼。戉兼表聲。歲本義為收割，引申為一年的收成、年齡等。篆文改戉為戌（xū 斧形兵器）。歲有異體字崴，簡體岁字保留了崴字上部的山，而下部改為夕字。

甲 金 篆　　歲數 suìshu age　　十歲 shísuì ten years old
歲月 suìyuè years; time　　萬歲 wànsuì Long live (someone)!

所

suǒ
so; place

PICTOPHONETIC CHARACTER In the Bronze Inscriptions and Seal Script, 所 consists of the radical 斤 (jīn, ax; unit of weight) and the phonetic component 戶 (hù, door; household). The original meaning of 所 was the sound of wood being cut. Later it came to mean "place" or "so." In the Oracle-Bone Inscriptions, 斤 looks like an ax with a crooked handle, and 戶 looks like a door with one panel (as opposed to a door with two panels, represented by 門/门).

所 形聲。從斤，戶聲，本義為伐木的聲音。引申義為處所、助詞等。斤，象形。上像斧頭，下像斧柄。戶，指單扇的門。一扇為戶，兩扇為門。

金 篆　　所以 suǒyǐ therefore; so　　住所 zhùsuǒ dwelling place; residence
厠所 cèsuǒ toilet; lavatory　　研究所 yánjiūsuǒ research institute; graduate school

tā
it

PICTOGRAPH In its ancient form, the character 它 looks like a snake moving in a zigzag way, and its original meaning was "snake." Later 它 was borrowed to mean "other," or "it," and a worm radical 虫 was added the left of 它 to make a new character 蛇 (snake).

它　象形。古字像一頭部突出、身體彎曲的蛇形。本義為蛇，後借為別的、另外等意。近代用它來指代事物、動物。而蛇的意思則由它字左邊加部首虫來表示。

甲 篆

它們 tāmen they (for animals or inanimate objects)
其它 qítā other (something); the others; else

---

tā
he

他

PICTOPHONETIC CHARACTER 他 is built with the person radical 亻 and the phonetic component 也 (yě, also). 他 is a variant form of 佗. It originally meant "other" and is used today as the third person pronoun for males. In the Bronze Inscriptions and Seal Script, 也 looks like a snake with a large head, and its original meaning was "snake." Later 也 was borrowed to mean "also" or "too".

他　形聲。第三人稱代詞。是佗的異體字。在金文中"也"是一條拖著尾巴、頭部突出的蛇形。本義為蛇，后被借為語氣詞、助詞與副詞。

篆

他們 tāmen they
他人 tārén somebody else; other people

其他 qítā other; (something or somebody) else
吉他 jítā guitar

---

tā
she

她

PICTOPHONETIC CHARACTER 她 consists of the female radical 女 and the phonetic component 也 (yě, also). It is used as the third person pronoun for females. Both 他 (tā, he) and 她 (tā, she) have the component 也 in the right part, but the character 他 has the person radical 亻 while 她 has the female radical 女.

她　形聲。從女，從也。女性第三人稱代詞。

她們 tāmen they; them (for females)　　她自己 tā zìjǐ herself

臺/台

tái
platform;
deck

ASSOCIATIVE COMPOUND In Seal Script, 臺 looks like a high platform. Its original meanings are "platform" and "stage," and it has been extended to mean "things shaped like a platform," "stand (for holding things)," "deck," "(broadcast) station," etc. In its ancient forms, 台 looks like a fetus upside down in its mother's womb, and originally meant "pregnant." Since being pregnant is a happy event, 台 extended to mean "joyful." Today 台 is often used in both traditional and simplified characters instead of 臺, as they are pronounced the same. However, the traditional 臺 is still used in formal written language.

臺/台 會意。篆字整體像是高臺：上部像高臺上的建築，中間是高字的省略，下部為至（到達），意指人可到高臺上眺望四方。早在金元時期台已作為臺字的簡化字使用，屬於同音替代。現今民間多用"台灣"，而在官方文件中則使用正式的"臺灣"。

篆 臺 台 甲 𠃋 金 㠯 篆 㠯

台灣 táiwān Taiwan
新臺幣 xīntái bì Taiwan dollar

陽台 yángtái balcony
電視台 diànshìtái TV station

太

tài
too; extremely

EXPLICIT CHARACTER The character 大 means "big." A dot is added under 大 to emphasize the large size or scale. Consequently, 太 means "too," "excessively," or "extremely."

太 指事。為強調事物過大，在大字下再加一點。

甲 㚘 大 金 大 篆 㚖

太陽 tàiyáng sun
太極拳 tàijí quán shadowboxing; Tai Chi

太空 tàikōng outer space
太太 tàitai Mrs.; Madam; wife

湯/汤

tāng
soup

PICTOPHONETIC CHARACTER The character 湯 is formed with the water radical 氵 and the phonetic 昜 (yáng). Its original meaning was hot water and extended to mean "soup," "decoction of medical ingredients," and "hot spring." In the Oracle-Bone Inscriptions, the upper part of 昜 is 日 (rì, sun), while the lower part resembles sunlight piercing through the clouds. 昜 means "sun" or "sunshine." The simplified character 汤 derives from the cursive style of the traditional character 湯.

湯 形聲。從水，昜（yáng）聲。本義為熱水，引申義有肉或菜做的湯、湯藥、溫泉等。昜，會意。昜，從日，從勿（像陽光穿過雲層射出狀），意指日出、太陽、明亮等。簡化字汤是由繁體字湯的草書楷化而來。

金 湯 篆 湯 草 汤

雞湯 jītāng chicken soup
湯麵 tāngmiàn noodles in soup

清湯 qīngtāng broth
湯勺 tāngsháo soup spoon

The Way of Chinese Characters

táng
sugar; candy

PICTOPHONETIC CHARACTER The character 糖 consists of the rice/grain radical 米 (mǐ) and the phonetic component 唐 (táng). It originally referred to malt sugar and later extended to mean "sugar," "candy," and "sweets." In the Oracle-Bone and Bronze Inscriptions, 唐 contains 庚 (gēng, 庚 looks like a bell, and extends to mean "age") on top and 口 (kǒu, mouth) at the bottom, suggesting a person talking with a voice like a bell and meaning "to boast" or "to exaggerate." 唐 is also the name of the Tang Dynasty (618–907), a golden age in Chinese history.

糖 形聲。從米，唐聲。本義為米麥製成的飴糖，引申為食糖、糖果。唐，會意。甲骨文、金文從口，庚（甲骨文像響鈴類樂器，引申為年齡、天干的第七位）聲，表示說話如響鈴一般大聲。本義為說大話，虛而不實。唐也是中國一个古朝代的名稱。

 篆 糖

白糖 báitáng white sugar
糖果 tángguǒ candy

紅糖 hóngtáng brown sugar
糖精 tángjīng sweetener

---

tǎng
to lie (down)

PICTOPHONETIC CHARACTER The character 躺 is comprised of the body radical 身 (shēn) and the phonetic element 尚 (shàng), meaning "to lie down" or "to recline." In its ancient forms, 身 depicts a pregnant woman. Its original meaning was "pregnant" and came to mean "body." 尚 looks like a drinking vessel in ancient writing. Since people show respect to each other when they propose a toast, 尚 means "to value," "esteem," etc.

躺 形聲。從身，尚聲。意為身體仰臥或側臥。身，象形。本義指身孕，引申泛指人與動物的軀體。尚，象形。像酒器形。本義當為酒器，因飲酒相互舉杯敬酒，引申為尊敬、崇尚。尚也用作副詞，表示還、仍然。

躺椅 tǎngyǐ deck chair
躺在床上 tǎng zài chuángshàng to lie in bed

躺下 tǎngxià to lie down

---

tào
(MW for suite or set)

ASSOCIATIVE COMPOUND The character 套 is the combination of 大 (dà, big) and 镸 (cháng, long). 镸 was an old variant form of 長. 套 means "a cover" or "a sheath," since a cover or a sheath is bigger and longer than the content under or inside it. The extended meanings of 套 include "to cover," "to loop," "snare," "to imitate blindly," "set," and "a set of."

套 會意。從大，從镸（镸，古時同長），因又大又長，本義為罩在物體外的東西。引申義有套住、圈套、模仿、同類事物組成的整體（套房、套餐）。也可作為搭配成組的事物的量詞，如一套家具、一套書。

篆

套子 tàozi cover; cap
客套 kètào polite formulas; civilities

外套 wàitào coat
套餐 tàocān combo; set meal

特
tè
special

PICTOPHONETIC CHARACTERS The character 特 consists of the ox radical 牛 and the phonetic element 寺 (sì, temple), and it originally meant "bull," "ox," "calf" or "small livestock." Since ox horns are striking, 特 extended to mean "outstanding," "special," "unusual," "exceptional," etc. In its ancient form, 牛 is the front view of an ox head.

特 形聲。從牛，寺聲。本義指公牛。因牛角突出醒目，引申為獨特、特別、特點、特色等。

篆 特

特別 tèbié especially; special; particular
奇特 qítè peculiar; queer

特點 tèdiǎn characteristic; distinguishing feature
模特 mótè (fashion) model

疼
téng
to be painful

PICTOPHONETIC CHARACTER The character 疼 is made up of the sick radical 疒 and the phonetic component 冬 (dōng), meaning "ache," "pain," "sore," or "to hurt." 疼 also means "to love dearly" or "to dote on," since love is a strong feeling that touches one's heart to cause a sense of ache. The character 冬 consists of 夂 (zhōng, end) on top and 冫 (bīng, ice) at the bottom, referring to winter—the cold period at the end of a year.

疼 形聲。從疒，冬聲。本義為疼痛，引申義為特別喜愛、憐愛。如：她的父母最疼她。冬，會意。上部的夂為古文終字，下部兩點水冫代表冰，意指冬天是年終天寒結冰的日子。

頭疼 tóuténg headache
疼愛 téngài to love dearly

牙疼 yáténg toothache
疼死了 téngsǐle really hurt

踢
tī
to kick

PICTOPHONETIC CHARACTER The character 踢 is composed of the foot radical 足 and the phonetic element 易 (yì), meaning "to kick." In the Oracle-Bone Inscriptions, 易 depicts the act of pouring water from one vessel to another, meaning "to change," "to exchange," "easy," etc.

踢 形聲。從足，易聲。意指用腳踢物，如踢球、踢毽子。易，會意。甲骨文像把水從一個容器中倒入另一容器中。本義為給予，引申為改變、容易等。

篆 踢

踢(足)球 tī (zú)qiú to play soccer
拳打腳踢 quándǎ jiǎotī to punch and kick; to beat

踢毽子 tī jiànzi to kick shuttlecock

提

tí
to lift

PICTOPHONETIC CHARACTER The character 提 consists of the hand radical 扌 and the phonetic component 是 (shì). Its original meaning is "to carry in one's hand with the arm hanging down," from which it has derived the meanings "to lift," "to raise," "to promote," "to advance," "to shift to an earlier date," "to bring up, "to draw out," "to extract," "to put forward," "to mention," etc.

提 形聲。從扌，是聲。本義為拎著（垂手拿著），引申義有把東西位置由下往上升、時間上提前、指出、提取、提煉等。

篆 提

手提包 shǒutíbāo handbag
提問 tíwèn to ask; to raise a question

提高 tígāo to improve; to get better
提名 tímíng to nominate

題/题

tí
topic;
question

ASSOCIATIVE AND PICTOPHONETIC COMPOUND The character 題 consists of the radical 頁 (yè, head; page) and the signifying and phonetic element 是 (shì, to be), meaning: "headline," "topic," "title," "subject," "inscribe," or "question." In the Oracle-Bone Inscriptions, 頁 depicts a person with an oversized head. Its original meaning was "head." Today it is used to mean "page." In the simplified character 题, the component 页 is in its simplified form, derived from its cursive form.

題 會意兼形聲。從頁（頭），從是，是亦聲。本義為額頭，引申為物體的前端、題目、書寫有特殊意義的文字等。頁，象形。甲骨文中像一個頭部極為突出的人形。本義為頭，引申為書頁的一張等。簡體字题右部的頁字簡化。

篆 題 頁甲 金 草

問題 wèntí question; problem; issue
題目 tímù subject; title; topic

沒問題 méiwèntí no problem
話題 huàtí topic of conversation

體/体

tǐ
body

PICTOPHONETIC CHARACTER The character 體 combines the bone radical 骨 (gǔ) with the phonetic element 豊 (lǐ), meaning "body." The extended meanings of 體 are "entity," "shape," "form," "style," "system," etc. In its ancient forms, the top of 骨 looks like a scapula and the bottom is flesh 月. In the Oracle-Bone and Bronze Inscriptions, 豊 depicts a high-legged plate with two strings of jade inside, referring to an ancient ceremonial utensil. The simplified 体 combines the person radical 亻 with 本 (běn, basis), indicating that one's body is fundamental.

體 形聲。從骨，豊聲。本義為身體，引申為物體、形狀等。篆文中骨字從冎 guǎ，從肉月，本義為卜骨。豊在甲骨文、金文上為兩串玉，下為豆（器皿），將玉放在器皿中作為祭祀供品。豊是禮的本字。体，會意。從亻，從本。本是基礎，人的身體是人一生事業的基礎。

篆 體

身體 shēntǐ body
體檢 tǐjiǎn physical check-up

體重 tǐzhòng body weight
體育 tǐyù sports; physical education|

天

tiān
sky; day

EXPLICIT CHARACTER As explained in the **Basic Radicals** section, the character 大 (dà, big) represents the front view of a figure. In the character 天, the horizontal stroke above 大 symbolizes "sky" or "heaven." 天 is also used to mean "God," "weather," or "day."

天　指事。從一、大。
"大"為正面人形，
"一"指頭上有天。

甲 金 篆 天

天空 tiānkōng sky
天氣 tiānqì weather

天堂 tiāntáng paradise; heaven
天下 tiānxià land under heaven; China or the world

甜

tián
sweet

ASSOCIATIVE COMPOUND The character 甜 is the combination of 舌 (shé, tongue) and 甘 (gān, sweet; delicious food; willing). By depicting a tongue tasting something sweet, it originally meant "the taste of candy or honey." The extended meanings of 甜 include "sweet (in taste, appearance, and words)," "luscious," and "pleasant." In ancient forms, 舌 is a pictograph of a tongue sticking out of a mouth and 甘 a mouth with something sweet or tasty in it. In classical Chinese, 甘 is more frequently used than 甜 when referring to "sweet" or "sweetness," but the case is reversed in modern times.

甜　會意。從舌，從甘，
指舌頭嘗到了甜味。本義
指糖或蜜的味道，引申
義有長相甜美，甜言蜜
語，睡得香甜等。舌，
象形。像舌頭伸出口外。
甘，指事。篆文從口，從
一，像口含甜美的食物。
古時多用甘字表示甜。

篆 甘 甲 篆

甜食 tiánshí sweets, dessert
甜美 tiánměi sweetness; sweet and beautiful

甜菜 tiáncài beet
嘴甜 zuǐtián honey-tongued

條/条

tiáo
(MW for long, thin objects)

PICTOPHONETIC COMPOUND The character 條 consists of the signifying part 木 (mù, wood) and the phonetic component 攸 (yōu), meaning "twig." 條 is also used as a measure word for long, narrow, or thin objects. In the Bronze Inscriptions, 攸 resembles a person paddling a boat in a river, meaning "flowing water," "long," etc. The simplified character 条 retains only the right part of 條.

條　形聲。從木，攸(yōu)
聲。本義為小樹枝，引
申為量詞。簡體字条僅
採用繁體字條的右邊。
元明已有此字。

篆

麵條 miàntiáo noodles
條件 tiáojiàn condition; term; requirement

條子 tiáozi short note; slip of paper
條約 tiáoyuē treaty; pact

The Way of Chinese Characters

跳

tiào
to jump

PICTOPHONETIC CHARACTER The character 跳 consists of the foot radical 足 and the phonetic component 兆 (zhào, omen; foretell). In its ancient form, 兆 resembles the cracks on an ox bone or tortoise shell after baking. Since a diviner would tell fortunes by reading crack marks on such shells, 兆 means "portend" or "omen."

跳　形聲。從足，兆聲。兆，象形。古文像龜甲燒裂後出現的紋路，意為徵兆。

篆

跳舞 tiàowǔ to dance
跳水 tiàoshuǐ to dive; diving (athletics)

跳高 tiàogāo high jump (athletics)
心跳 xīntiào heartbeat

鐵／铁

tiě
iron

PICTOPHONETIC CHARACTER The character 鐵 consists of the gold/metal radical 金 on the left and the phonetic symbol 戠 (zhì) on the right, meaning "iron." Extended meanings of 鐵 include "arms," "weapon," "hard and strong as iron," "indisputable," "unalterable," etc. In Regular Script 鐵 is comprised of five components: 金, 土, 口, 王, and 戈. In the simplified character 铁, 失 (shī) replaces 戠 (zhì) because of their similar pronunciations.

鐵　形聲。從金，戠（zhì）聲，意為鐵製的用具。簡體字铁左邊部首簡化，右邊以失（shī）代替戠（zhì），屬近音替代。元明時已見簡化了的鉄字。

篆 鐵

鐵路 tiělù railroad; railway
鋼鐵 gāngtiě steel

地鐵 dìtiě subway; metro
鐵飯碗 tiěfànwǎn secure employment (literally: iron rice bowl)

聽／听

tīng
to listen

ASSOCIATIVE COMPOUND In the Oracle-Bone Inscriptions, the character 聽 consists of only an ear and a mouth. Later the character became more complex. In Regular Script, one can see the radicals 耳 (ěr, ear), 王 (wáng, king), 十 (shí, ten), 目 (mù, eye), 一 (yī, one), and 心 (xīn, heart) within the character 聽. Perhaps you should listen to every Chinese word wholeheartedly eleven times in order to become a master at understanding Chinese! In the simplified character 听, the mouth radical 口 suggests the meaning, while the component 斤 (jīn) indicates the pronunciation.

聽　會意。甲骨文中從耳、從口，表示用耳聽別人說話。後加悳 dé。悳，真誠。直，會意。甲骨文字形像用眼睛正對標杆以測量物體是否直正。聽字強調要認真用心領悟所聞之事。簡體听字左邊口字表意，右邊斤字表聲。

甲 𦔻 金 𦔻 篆 聽

聽見 tīngjiàn to hear
聽話 tīnghuà to do what one is told; obedient

聽寫 tīngxiě to dictate; dictation
好聽 hǎotīng pleasant to hear

廳/厅

tīng
hall

PICTOPHONETIC CHARACTER The character 廳 consists of the radical 广 (yǎn, shed; shelter) and the phonetic element 聽, referring to a hall for holding meetings and/or receiving guests. In the simplified character 厅, 广 changes to 厂 (hǎn, cliff) and 聽 (tīng) is replaced with 丁 (dīng), as the two are similarly pronounced.

廳 會意兼形聲。從广（yǎn，敞屋），聽聲。簡體字厅將广改為厂，聽改為丁，因聽丁聲音近似。古時已有此字。

餐廳 cāntīng dining hall
舞廳 wǔtīng dance hall; ballroom

客廳 kètīng living room
大廳 dàtīng big hall; lobby

挺

tǐng
very; rather

PICTOPHONETIC CHARACTER The character 挺 consists of the hand radical 扌 and the phonetic element 廷, and it originally meant "pull out," "pull up," or "draw." Its extended meanings include "straight," "erect," "stick out," "straighten up," "quite," "very," etc. In the Bronze Inscriptions, the character 廷 looks like a man standing in front of the steps of a court, and means "royal court."

挺 形聲。從扌，廷聲。本義為拔出，引申為挺立、挺拔、筆挺、突出、相當等。廷，象形。金文像一人立於宮廷臺階前，本義為朝廷。

篆

挺立 tǐnglì to stand erect; to stand upright
挺住 tǐngzhù to stand firm; to stand one's ground

力挺 lìtǐng to support; to back
挺好 tǐnghǎo quite good

同

tóng
same

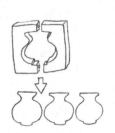

ASSOCIATIVE COMPOUND In its ancient form, the upper part of 同 depicts a mold and the lower part 口 resembles a casting from the mold. Castings made from a mold are all the same, so 同 therefore means "same" or "alike."

同 會意。上像模子，下像模子製出的產品。指用同一個模子製造相同的東西。

甲 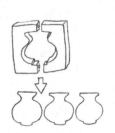 金 篆

同時 tóngshí at the same time; simultaneously
同屋 tóngwū roommate

同學 tóngxué classmate
同意 tóngyì to agree; to consent

頭/头

tóu
head; top

PICTOPHONETIC CHARACTER The character 頭 is composed of the radical 頁 (yè, head; page) and the phonetic element 豆 (dòu, bean; pea), meaning "head." Its extended meanings include "top," "first," "leading," "chief," "beginning or end," "side," and "measure word for some livestock." The simplified character 头 derives from the cursive style of 頭.

頭 形聲。從頁（人首），豆聲。本義為頭部，引申為頭等、為首的人、頂端、起點、終點、詞尾（石頭、木頭）等。頁，象形。像頭部突出的人形。（見預、題、顏。）豆，象形。甲骨文像古代高足食器，引申為豆類植物。簡體字头來自繁體字頭的草書。

篆 頭 草 头 頁 甲 金

頭腦 tóunǎo brain
帶頭 dàitóu to take the lead

頭疼 tóuténg headache
頭等 tóuděng first-class

圖/图

tú
picture; drawing

ASSOCIATIVE COMPOUND The character 圖 looks like a drawing of a map in which 囗 (wéi, enclosure) represents the border, while 啚 (bǐ) refers to a small administrative district (a unit of 500 households). In Regular Script, the character 啚 is comprised of 口, 十, and 回. The simplified version 图 derives from the cursive form of the traditional character 圖; the character 冬 (dōng, winter) is inside 囗.

圖 會意。從囗，從啚（bǐ）。囗像一張紙，啚指城邑都鄙。將城邑繪在紙上，即是地圖。图是由圖字的草書楷化而來，內為冬字。

金 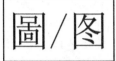 篆 圖 草

地圖 dìtú map
圖像 túxiàng image; picture; graphic

圖書館 túshūguǎn library
圖畫 túhuà drawing; painting

S - W

托

tuō
to entrust

ASSOCIATIVE AND PICTOPHONETIC COMPOUND The character 托 consists of the hand radical 扌 and the semantic and phonetic indicator 乇 (tuō, to depend on), meaning "to hold up something with one's palm." Its extended meanings are "to support (from under)," "a base," "a prop," "set-off," "to entrust," "to rely on," etc. In its ancient forms, 乇 looks like a blade of grass coming out of the ground (represented by the horizontal stroke). Since grass grows on the ground and has to depend on it to survive, 乇 has come to mean "to depend on" and "to entrust with."

托 會意兼形聲。從言，乇（tuō）聲。本義為用手掌托舉東西，引申為托舉東西的器具、陪襯、托付、依賴等。乇，象形。像長出地面的草葉形（一橫像地面，地下為草根，上為草葉）。草依大地而生，故乇有依賴、寄托之意。

篆 托 乇 甲 金 篆

托運 tuōyùn to consign for shipment; to check in one's luggage
襯托 chèntuō to serve as a foil to; to set off

托兒所 tuōérsuǒ nursery
摩托車 mótuōchē motorcycle

外

wài
outside; foreign

ASSOCIATIVE COMPOUND The character 外 is made up of 夕 (xī, sunset; evening) and 卜 (bǔ, fortune telling). The original meaning of 外 is "outside," but it can also mean "other" or "foreign." In the Oracle-Bone Inscriptions, 卜 resembles a crack on an oracle bone. It can be found in several characters pertaining to divination. For example, 占 (zhàn, divine) is the combination of 卜 and 口. 兆 (zhào, omen) represents more cracks on an oracle bone or shell. (See 跳 tiào, to jump.)

外 會意。從夕，從卜。古人在早上占卜。晚上占卜，則不在常規之內了。

金  篆 外

外國 wàiguó foreign country
外交 wàijiāo diplomacy; foreign affairs

外語 wàiyǔ foreign language
另外 lìngwài in addition; moreover; other

灣／湾

wān
strait; bay

ASSOCIATIVE AND PICTOPHONETIC COMPOUND The character 灣 consists of the water radical 氵 and the signifying and phonetic element 彎 (wān, bend; tortuous), meaning "a bend in a stream," "gulf," or "bay." The top part of 彎 contains 言 between two 糸, and 弓 in the lower part, originally meaning "to draw a bow." "Curved," "tortuous," "bend," and "turn" are the extended meanings of 彎. The simplified character 湾 developed from the cursive style of 灣.

灣 會意兼形聲。從水，從彎（彎曲）；彎亦聲。意為水流彎曲之處、港灣、海灣等。彎，形聲。從弓，䜌（luán）聲。本義為拉開弓，引申為彎曲。簡體字湾是繁體字灣的草書楷化字。

篆 䜌 草 湾

港灣 gǎngwān bay serving as harbor
臺灣 táiwān Taiwan

海灣 hǎiwān gulf; bay
綠灣 lùwān Green Bay

完

wán
finished

PICTOPHONETIC CHARACTER 完 combines the roof radical 宀 and the phonetic 元 (yuán). Originally 完 meant a house in perfect condition, from which evolved the meanings of "whole," "intact," "perfect," "complete," and "finished." In its ancient forms, the character 元 depicts two horizontal strokes on top of a person, meaning "head" (of a person). The extended meanings of 元 include "first," "primary," "chief," "monetary unit," and "the Yuan Dynasty (1271–1368)."

完 形聲。從宀，元聲。本義指房屋完好無缺，引申義為完整、完全、完美、完成等。元，指事。從一，從兀（wù）。本義為人頭，引申為第一、最初、為首的等。元也用作貨幣單位以及元朝的朝代名。

篆 完

吃完 chīwán to finish eating
完美 wánměi perfect; perfection

完成 wánchéng to complete; to accomplish
完蛋 wándàn to be ruined; to go bust

The Way of Chinese Characters

玩

wán
to play; to have fun

PICTOPHONETIC CHARACTER 玩 has the jade radical 王 (as a radical, the meaning of 王 is not "king" but "jade;" see the entry for 王 wáng in **Basic Radicals**) and the phonetic component 元 (yuán), suggesting jade or something like jade for people to enjoy and play with. The primary meaning of 玩 is "play," "have fun," or "enjoy." "To visit" is one of its extended meanings.

玩 形聲。從玉，元聲，指供玩賞之物或玩耍。玉作為偏旁時寫作王。

篆

玩具 wánjù plaything; toy
玩笑 wánxiào joke; jest

好玩兒 hǎowánr amusing; fun
開玩笑 kāi wánxiào to play a joke; to make fun of

晚

wǎn
evening; late

PICTOPHONETIC CHARACTER The character 晚 combines the sun radical 日 with the phonetic 免 (miǎn), meaning "evening" or "late." In its ancient form, 免 looks like a person with a big hat, meaning "take off," "remove," or "exempt" (even though the hat is still on the person's head).

晚 形聲。從日，免聲。免，會意。像人帶著冠冕形，意為脫去、赦免等。

免 金

晚上 wǎnshang evening, night
晚會 wǎnhuì evening party

晚飯 wǎnfàn evening meal; dinner
晚安 wǎn'ān Good night!

碗

wǎn
bowl

PICTOPHONETIC CHARACTER 碗 contains the stone radical 石 and the phonetic 宛 (wǎn), meaning "bowl" or the measure word for a bowl of something. Bowls were made of stone in primitive times. In its ancient forms, 石 looks like a rock under a cliff. 宛 consists of the roof radical 宀 and the phonetic symbol 夗 (yuàn). It originally referred to a palace with deep and winding paths, and has been extended to mean "tortuous," "winding," "to seem," and "as if."

碗 形聲。篆文從皿，夗 (yuàn) 聲。指圓形敞口的食器。后改為從石，宛聲。中國有以石製碗的傳統，尤其是玉石。碗也可作量詞。石，象形，像山崖下的大石塊。宛，會意兼形聲，從宀 (房屋)，夗 (彎曲) 聲。本義指宮室建筑幽深曲折回環，引申為曲折、好像等。

篆

飯碗 fànwǎn rice bowl
鐵飯碗 tiěfànwǎn iron bowl; a secure job

洗碗 xǐwǎn wash dishes
金飯碗 jīnfànwǎn golden bowl; a well-paid job

往

wǎng
toward; past

ASSOCIATIVE AND PICTOPHONETIC COMPOUND In its ancient forms, the character 往 consists of the signifying component 彳 (walk slowly; left step), 止 (zhǐ, foot; stop) and the phonetic symbol 王 (wáng), meaning to go toward a direction. In Regular Script, 止 is replaced by a dot on top of 王. "To depart," "past," "formerly," and "gone" are the extended meanings of 往. Note the differences between 往 and 住 (zhù, to live).

往　會意兼形聲。金文、篆文往字從彳，從止，王聲。楷書中止被一點取代。本義為前往、去、到，引申指過去。作為介詞有朝、向的意思。

甲 𧾷 金 徉 篆 𨓹

往北走 wǎngběi zǒu to go north
交往 jiāowǎng to make contacts with; association

往事 wǎngshì past events
往往 wǎngwǎng often; frequently

網／网

wǎng
net

PICTOGRAPH In its ancient form, the character 網 resembles the contour of a net. In Regular Script, the silk radical 糸 is added to indicate a net is made from ropes and 亡 (wáng) suggests the pronunciation. The simplified character 网 restores the original form.

網　象形。甲骨文、金文、篆文皆像一張網形。楷書加糸字旁表意，加亡字表聲。簡體字网恢復了古體字的本來形狀。

甲 ⽹ 金 ⽹ 篆 ⽹

網球 wǎngqiú tennis
網址 wǎngzhǐ web address

上網 shàngwǎng to be on the Internet
網站 wǎngzhàn website; network station

忘

wàng
to forget

ASSOCIATIVE AND PICTOPHONETIC COMPOUND The character 忘 is comprised of the heart radical 心 and the semantic and phonetic component 亡 (wáng, flee; lose; die), meaning "to forget," "to neglect," "to miss," and "to omit" something because it has fled from one's heart (mind). In its ancient form, the character 亡 looks like a person (the upper part) hiding in a corner (the lower part). Its original meaning was "to run away," from which derived the meanings "to lose," "to perish," and "to decease." You will also see 亡 in the character 忙 (máng, busy).

忘　會意兼形聲。從心，從亡（亡有佚失之意）。指心有所失而忘記。亡也兼表聲。忘本義為不記得，引申義有遺失、遺漏等。《說文》認為亡字從人，從乚。乚為隱蔽，意指人逃亡時躲於隱蔽之处。

金 𢗜 篆 忘

忘記 wàngjì to forget
難忘 nánwàng unforgettable

忘我 wàngwǒ to forget about oneself; selflessness
健忘 jiànwàng amnesia; to have a bad memory

望

wàng
to hope;
to gaze

ASSOCIATIVE COMPOUND In the Bronze Inscriptions, the character 望 looks like a person with large eyes looking up at the moon, and it means "gaze into the distance." Extended meanings of 望 include "wish," "hope," "to call on," "reputation," etc. In Regular Script, 望 combines the signifying part 月 (yuè, moon) and the phonetic elements 亡 (wáng, run away) and 王 (wáng, king).

望 會意。金文像人睜大眼睛望月狀。後加王字以表聲。

金 篆

希望 xīwàng to wish for; to hope
願望 yuànwàng desire; wish

失望 shīwàng disappointed; to lose hope
渴望 kěwàng to thirst for; to be eager for

危

wēi
danger

ASSOCIATIVE AND PICTOPHONETIC COMPOUND In Seal Script, the character 危 combines 人 (rén, person) with the signifying and phonetic element 厄 (è, strategic point; adversity), meaning "danger," "peril," "to endanger," "to jeopardize," "dangerous," "dying," "high," and "precipitous." 厄 looks like a man kneeling (㔾) on a cliff/rock (厂), meaning "strategic point," "disaster," "adversity," "hardship," "difficulty," "distress," and "cramped."

危 會意兼形聲。從人，從厄，厄亦聲。甲骨文像人站在山崖上，本義為人因身處高處而恐懼。引申義有不安全、傷害、人將死、高等。厄，會意。從厂（山崖），從㔾（像跪著的人），像人蜷縮在山崖上。本義為險要的地方，引申為災難、困苦等。

篆

危險 wēixiǎn dangerous; danger
病危 bìngwēi to be terminally ill

危機 wēijī crisis
安危 ānwēi safety and danger; safety

位

wèi
(MW for a
person [polite])

ASSOCIATIVE COMPOUND 位 combines the person radical 亻 and the character 立 (lì, stand) to mean the location, position, or place where a person stands. 位 is also used as the polite measure word for people. In the Oracle-Bone and Bronze Inscriptions, the upper part of 立 is the front view of a person (大), while the bottom stroke (一) stands for the ground, meaning "stand," "erect," or "upright."

位 會意。從人，從立，指人站立的位置，也用作量詞。立，會意。甲骨文、金文從大（正面人形），從一（地），表示人站立于地上。

篆   立 甲 金

位子 wèizi seat; place
地位 dìwèi position; status

座位 zuòwèi seat
單位 dānwèi a unit; work unit (one's workplace)

味

wèi
flavor; taste

PICTOPHONETIC CHARACTER The character 味 consists of the mouth radical 口 and the phonetic element 未 (wèi), meaning "taste" or "flavor," which has to do with one's mouth. Its extended meanings include "smell," "odor," "delicacy," "interest," etc. In its ancient forms, 未 is a pictograph of a tree with luxuriant leaves. (Compare 未 with 木.) 未 originally meant "luxuriant" and later came to mean "future," for everybody's future will grow into a "luxuriant" big tree!

味 形聲。從口，未聲。本義為滋味，即舌頭嘗到的味道。引申義有鼻子聞到的氣味、菜肴、趣味等。未，象形。甲骨文像樹木生長旺盛、枝葉繁茂狀。本義為繁茂，引申義為將來。

篆 味

氣味 qìwèi odor; scent
味道 wèidào taste; flavor

美味 měiwèi delicious; delicious food
味精 wèijīng monosodium glutamate (MSG)

為 / 为

wèi/wéi
for

ASSOCIATIVE COMPOUND In the Oracle-Bone Inscriptions, the character 為 delineates a hand (the upper part) leading an elephant (the lower part), suggesting a man using an elephant to help with his work. Therefore, 為 means "to do," "to do something for someone," or "for the sake of." In Regular Script, 為 becomes more simplified and abstract, but one can still see traces of the elephant's trunk and body (with its four legs underneath). The simplified character 为 derives from the cursive style of the traditional form 為.

為 會意。甲古文中像一隻手牽象鼻形。因古代用大象為人做事，故本義為做。簡體字为是繁體字為的草書楷化字。

甲 金 篆 草 为

因為 yīnwèi because
認為 rènwéi to think; to consider

為了 wèile in order to; for the sake of
成為 chéngwéi to become; to turn into

喂

wèi
hello; hey

PICTOPHONETIC CHARACTER The character 喂 consists of the mouth radical 口 and the phonetic element 畏 (wèi, fear). 喂 means "to feed," "hello," or "hey," often used over the phone. In the Oracle-Bone and Bronze Inscriptions, 畏 looks like a large-headed monster holding a stick in its hands, ready to attack. The primary meanings of 畏 are "fear" or "frightening," but it can also mean "respect with awe."

喂 形聲。從口，畏聲，意為喂養或用於打招呼。畏，會意。甲骨文、金文中像大頭鬼持杖欲打人狀，意為可畏。

畏 甲 金 篆

喂奶 wèinǎi to breast-feed
喂馬 wèimǎ to feed horses

喂食 wèishí to feed
喂雞 wèijī to feed chickens

衛 / 卫

wèi
to guard; to protect

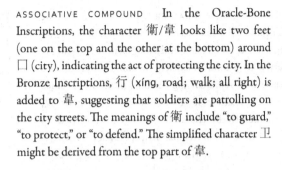

ASSOCIATIVE COMPOUND In the Oracle-Bone Inscriptions, the character 衛/韋 looks like two feet (one on the top and the other at the bottom) around 囗 (city), indicating the act of protecting the city. In the Bronze Inscriptions, 行 (xíng, road; walk; all right) is added to 韋, suggesting that soldiers are patrolling on the city streets. The meanings of 衛 include "to guard," "to protect," or "to defend." The simplified character 卫 might be derived from the top part of 韋.

衛 會意。甲骨文是兩足（有的四足，代表人）圍繞城邑（囗）而守衛著它。篆文從韋，從行（道路），以示眾人在四方路上巡衛城池。本義為保衛、防守。韋，會意。甲骨文像兩足環繞城邑，與衛同。後借用來表示加工鞣製過的獸皮。簡化字卫可能來源於韋字的上部。

保衛 bǎowèi to guard; to protect
衛星 wèixīng satellite
自衛 zìwèi self-defense
衛生 wèishēng sanitation; hygiene

文

wén
written language; script

PICTOGRAPH In the Oracle-Bone and Bronze Inscriptions, the character 文 shows a man with a tattoo on his chest. The original meaning of 文 was "tattoo" or "pattern." Later it came to mean "script," "language," "writing," "culture," "literary," etc. In Regular Script, the character 文 still looks like a man with a broad chest, but without the tattoo.

文 象形。甲骨文、金文像一正面站立、胸有刺青的人形。

作文 zuòwén to write an essay; composition
文人 wénrén scholar; literati
文學 wénxué literature
文化 wénhuà culture

問 / 问

wèn
to ask

ASSOCIATIVE AND PICTOPHONETIC COMPOUND In the character 問, 口 (kǒu, mouth) suggests the meaning and 門 (mén, door) the pronunciation. 門 also helps to reveal the meaning, as it indicates someone at the door, opening her/his mouth to ask a question. In the simplified character 问, the radical 门 derives from the cursive style of the character 門. As a radical or character, 門 is always written as 门 in simplified characters.

問 會意兼形聲。從口，門聲。像人到門下張口問事。簡體字问的部首门是繁體字門的草书楷化字。

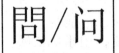

問路 wènlù ask for directions
問好 wènhǎo to say hello to; to send one's regards
問題 wèntí question; problem; issue
學問 xuéwèn learning; knowledge

S - W

我

wǒ
I; me

PHONETIC LOAN CHARACTER   In the Oracle-Bone Inscriptions, the character 我 is the sketch of a weapon with a saw-toothed blade and a long shaft and originally referred to a kind of ancient weapon. Later 我 was borrowed to represent the personal pronoun "I" since the pronunciation of "I" was similar to that of 我. Consequently the character 我 no longer carried its original meaning, In Regular Script, the left part of 我 is 手 (shǒu, hand) and the right part 戈 (gē, dagger-axe), representing a hand holding a dagger to protect oneself.

我 假借。甲骨文像兵器之形。後借為第一人稱，遂失本義。從手，像手執戈以自衛。

甲 𢦟 金 𢦠 篆 𢦐   我們 wǒmen we; us
自我 zìwǒ self-; ego (psychology)

我方 wǒfāng our side
自我中心 zìwǒ zhōngxīn self-centered

臥／卧

wò
to lie (down)

ASSOCIATIVE COMPOUND   The character 臥 is composed of a vertical eye 臣 and a person 人, suggesting "to lie down," "sleeping," or "to crouch." 臣 is the pictograph of a vertical eye, which refers to a person putting his head on the desk sideways. When people bow their heads and look at those in front of them, their eyes are vertical. You may try it in front a mirror. Originally 臣 meant "male slave" and has been extended to mean "state official or subject in dynastic China." In the simplified character 卧, 卜 replaces 人.

臥 會意。從人，從臣（豎目）。本義為人伏案休息，引申為躺下、躺著、供睡覺所用的（臥室、臥具、臥鋪）。臣，象形。甲骨文像人低頭眼睛向上看時的狀態（即眼睛處于豎立的位置），表示俯首屈從之意。本義為男性奴隸，引申為君主時代的官吏。簡化字卧將繁體字臥右部的人改為卜。

甲 𣦵 金 𦥑 篆 𦣞 臣 甲 𦥑   臥室 wòshì bedroom
臥虎藏龍 wòhǔ cánglóng undiscovered talents (literally: crouching tiger, hidden dragon)

臥鋪 wòpù sleeper; a sleeping berth

午

wǔ
noon

PICTOGRAPH   In the Oracle-Bone and Bronze Inscriptions, 午 resembles a wooden pestle, hence "pestle" was the original meaning. Later, 午 came to mean "disobedient," "offend," etc. Today 午 is used to mark the period of time between 11:00 a.m. and 1:00 p.m., the period generally considered to be "noon" by the Chinese.

午 象形。甲骨文、金文像舂米用的棒杵，是杵的初文，引申為抵觸、違逆等。後借用為午時，相當於白天十一時至十三時。

甲 𠦃 金 𠦄 篆 午   上午 shàngwǔ morning
中午 zhōngwǔ noon; midday

下午 xiàwǔ afternoon; p.m.
午飯 wǔfàn lunch

The Way of Chinese Characters

舞

wǔ
to dance; dance

PICTOGRAPH In the Oracle-Bone Inscriptions, the character 舞 looks like a person dancing with ox tails or ribbons in both hands. In Seal Script, 舛 (chuǎn, two feet) was added to the bottom of the character, indicating dancing with both hands and feet. In the Bronze Inscriptions and Seal Script, 舛 is a pictograph of a pair of feet, meaning "opposite" or "run counter to."

舞　象形。甲骨文中像一人雙手持物起舞。

甲 𣎻 金 𣎻 篆 舞

跳舞 tiàowǔ to dance
舞廳 wǔtīng dance hall; ballroom
舞會 wǔhuì dance; ball; party
芭蕾舞 bālěiwǔ ballet

物

wù
thing; matter

PICTOPHONETIC CHARACTER The character 物 consists of the ox/cow radical 牛 and the phonetic 勿 (wù), originally referring to vari-colored oxen/cows. Later 物 developed the meanings of "the material world," "thing," "matter," "goods," "substance," "content," etc. In the Oracle-Bone and Bronze Inscriptions, 勿 looks like a knife with drops of blood or falling pieces, meaning "don't" or "must not."

物　形聲。從牛，勿聲。本義為雜毛牛，引申為所有客觀的物體、物品、事物、内容等。勿，象形。甲骨文、金文像一把刀與血滴或砍下物體的碎片。一說像雲層中射出的陽光。意為不要，如"請勿隨地吐痰"、"請勿吸煙"等。

篆 物 勿 甲 弓 金 弓 篆 勿

動物 dòngwù animal
食物 shíwù food
生物 shēngwù organism; living creature; biology
禮物 lǐwù gift

務／务

wù
affair; task

PICTOPHONETIC CHARACTER The character 務 consists of 力 (lì, power; strength) and the phonetic element 敄 (wù), meaning "to devote to," "to be engaged in," or "to strive after." Its extended meanings include "affair," "business," "duty," "must", and "should." The character 敄 combines a lance 矛 with a hand 攵, meaning "strong" or "valiant." In its ancient forms, 矛 is the pictograph of a lance. The simplified character 务 uses only the right part of the traditional 務.

務　形聲。從力，敄(wù)聲。意指致力、從事，引申義有從事的事情、職業、工作、必需、一定等。敄，會意。像右邊一隻手握住左邊的矛，本義為強。簡化字务去掉繁體字務右邊的矛，元代已見。

篆 務 矛 金 矛 篆 矛

事務 shìwù affair
家務 jiāwù housework
服務 fúwù to serve; service
特務 tèwu secret agent; spy

西

xī
west

ASSOCIATIVE COMPOUND In the Oracle-Bone and Bronze Inscriptions, 西 resembles a bird's nest. In Seal Script, a bird is drawn at the top of the nest. Since birds return to their nests at dusk while the sun sets in the west, 西 means "west." Note the similarities and differences between 西 and 四 (sì, four).

西 會意。甲骨文、金文像鳥巢形，篆字則進一步在鳥巢上添一隻鳥。鳥類多半在日落時回巢，而日在西邊落下，故引申為西。

甲 金 篆

西邊 xībiān west; west side; western part
西方 xīfāng the West; the Occident; Western countries
西部 xībù western part
東西 dōngxi thing; stuff

希

xī
to hope

ASSOCIATIVE COMPOUND In Seal Script, 希 consists of 木 (mù, wood), 爻 (yáo, a wooden or bamboo fence) and 布 (bù, cloth), representing loosely woven cloth. The original meanings of 希 were "sparse" and "scarce," while "hope" is its extended meaning. In its ancient form, 乂 is shaped like a pair of scissors and 布 resembles a hand holding a scarf (巾 jīn). You will also see 巾 in the character 帥 (shuài, handsome).

希 會意。篆文從爻（籬笆交織狀），從巾，指織得像籬笆一樣稀疏的布或網，是"稀"的本字，引申為企求、希望。

篆

希望 xīwàng to wish for; hope
希臘 xīlà Greece

息

xī
to cease; to rest

ASSOCIATIVE AND PICTOPHONETIC COMPOUND The character 息 is the combination of 心 (xīn, heart) and the semantic and phonetic element 自 (zì). In the Oracle-Bone Inscriptions, 自 takes the shape of a nose. Originally 自 meant "nose," and later came to mean "self," "one's own," "from," "since," etc. 息 referred to "the air in one's heart (which should be "lungs," as modern science has proved) breathed through the nose" and originally meant "breath." The extended meanings of 息 include "to cease," "to rest," "news," "(financial) interest," "multiply," and "one's child."

息 會意兼形聲。從心，從自（鼻子），自亦聲。表示心氣從鼻出。本義為氣息、呼吸，引申為停止、休息、消息、利息、繁衍、子女等。自，象形。甲骨文像鼻形。本義為鼻子，後引申為自己，而鼻子則寫作"鼻"。

金 篆

氣息 qìxī breath; flavor
安息 ānxī to rest in peace
休息 xiūxi to rest
信息 xìnxī information; message

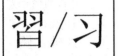

習/习

xí
to practice

ASSOCIATIVE COMPOUND In its ancient form, the character 習 combined 羽 (yǔ, feather) and 日 (rì, sun) to symbolize birds practicing flying during the day. Meanings of 習 include "to practice," "to study," "exercise," "review," "habit," etc. In Regular Script, the 日 in the lower part of 習 is replaced with 白 (bái, white), which also refers to daytime. In the Oracle-Bone Inscriptions, 羽 is a pictograph of the two wings of a bird. The simplified character 习 uses only one part of the traditional character 習.

習 會意。甲骨文、金文從羽，從日，表示小鳥在陽光中展翅學習飛翔。簡體字习僅保留了繁體字習的一部分。

甲 𦏵 篆 習

學習 xuéxí to learn; to study
復習 fùxí to review; revision

練習 liànxí exercise; drill; practice
習慣 xíguàn habit; custom

喜

xǐ
to like; happy

ASSOCIATIVE COMPOUND The character 喜 is the combination of 壴 (zhù, drum) and 口 (kǒu, mouth), indicating laughing while beating a drum. In its ancient form, 壴 looks like a drum with decorations on top and a stand underneath. 喜 means "happy," "happy event," "to be fond of," or "to like."

喜 會意。從壴(zhù 鼓)，從口，意指張口笑着，歡樂击鼓。

甲 𠺞 金 𠺞 篆 喜

喜歡 xǐhuan to like; to be fond of
喜樂 xǐlè joy

喜愛 xǐ'ài to be keen on; to love; to be fond of
恭喜 gōngxǐ congratulations

洗

xǐ
to wash

ASSOCIATIVE AND PICTOPHONETIC COMPOUND The character 洗 consists of the water radical 氵 and the signifying and phonetic element 先 (xiān, first; ahead of). In its ancient form, the top part of 先 represents a foot and the lower part a person. Since 先 includes foot, the character 洗 originally meant "to wash one's feet" and later came to mean "to wash," "bathe," etc.

洗 形聲兼會意。從水，從先（人腳向前伸），本義為洗腳。先也兼表聲。

篆 洗

洗澡 xǐzǎo to bathe; to take a shower
洗手間 xǐshǒujiān toilet; lavatory

洗衣機 xǐyījī washing machine
受洗 shòuxǐ to receive baptism; baptized

係 / 系

xì
to relate to

ASSOCIATIVE COMPOUND   In the Oracle-Bone Inscriptions, the character 係 looks like a kneeling person (left part) tied by a rope (right part), referring to "to tie" or "to bind". Its extended meanings include "to tie up," "to connect," "relationship," or "(literary) to be." In Regular Script, 係 became the combination of the person radical 亻 and 系 (xì). In the Oracle-Bone Inscriptions, 系 represents a hand holding two strings of silk, meaning "link," "system," "lineage," or "department." Today 系 is used as the simplified form of 係 and covers all the meanings of 係.

係 會意。係字在甲骨文中的字形似用繩捆住一跪著的人。意為捆綁、關聯、關係等。楷書係字從亻，從系。系字在甲骨文中為一隻手懸握兩束絲。有體系、世系、派系、直系、系統、科系等用法。簡化字用系代替係，並囊括了係字的全部用法。

甲 篆

關係 guānxi relationship; connection
公共關係 gōnggòng guānxi public relations

國際關係 guójì guānxi international relations
沒關係 méiguānxi it doesn't matter

下

xià
below; under

EXPLICIT CHARACTER   The character 下 is formed following the same principle that governs the formation of 上. In the Oracle-Bone and Bronze Inscriptions, 下 consists of two horizontal lines. The longer line on the top represents the horizon and the shorter one underneath refers to something below the horizon. In Regular Script, a vertical line is added beneath the longer horizontal line. The primary meaning of 下 is "below," "under," or "lower." Its extended meanings include "downward," "fall," "next," and "a short while."

下 指事。古文為指示符號，表示一物在另一物之下。

甲 二 金 二 篆 下

下雨 xiàyǔ to rain; rainy
下課 xiàkè to finish class; to get out of class

樓下 lóuxià downstairs
下班 xiàbān to finish work; to be off duty

夏

xià
summer

PICTOGRAPH   In the Bronze Inscriptions, the character 夏 represents a robust man standing with strong arms akimbo. 夏 is the name of the first dynasty in recorded Chinese history (ca. 2100–ca. 1600 B.C.) as well as an ancient name for China. Today, 夏 is used to mean "summer." Some scholars believe the character refers to a man with limbs exposed because of the hot summer weather.

夏 象形。金文中像人形，有頭（頁）、身、手、足，像個四肢發達、高大強壯的人。是古代中原漢民的自稱，也是中國歷史上第一個朝代。也用來指夏季。一說其字形暗示夏季天熱，人的手足都露在外面。

金 篆

夏天 xiàtiān summer
夏日 xiàrì summer day

初夏 chūxià early summer
夏令營 xiàlìngyíng summer camp

先

xiān
first

ASSOCIATIVE COMPOUND In its ancient form, the upper part of 先 is a foot and the lower part is a person, indicating one person walking ahead of another. In Regular Script, the upper part is 土 (tǔ, soil; earth), with a stroke on the left, and the lower part still resembles a person.

先 會意。甲骨文從之（足），在 儿（人）前，本義為走在他人前面。

甲 金 篆 先

先進 xiānjìn advanced
事先 shìxiān in advance; beforehand

先生 xiānsheng Mister; sir; husband; teacher
祖先 zǔxiān ancestor; ancestry

險/险

xiǎn
risk; danger

PICTOPHONETIC CHARACTER The character 險 consists of the mound radical 阝 and the phonetic element 僉 (qiān), suggesting "difficult to access," "a strategic pass," or "dangerously steep." The extended meanings of 險 include "dangerous," "danger," "sinister," and "almost." You can also see 僉 in the characters 臉 (liǎn, face) and 檢 (jiǎn, to check; to examine). 僉 is simplified to 佥 in the character 险.

險 形聲。篆文從阜（阝在字左邊意為阜[土山]；阝在字右邊意為邑[城市]），僉（qiān）聲。本義為地勢險峻，引申為危險、陰險等。作為副詞，意思是幾乎、差一點，如險勝。簡化字险中的僉簡化。

篆 險

危險 wēixiǎn dangerous
風險 fēngxiǎn risk

冒險 màoxiǎn to take a risk; adventure
保險 bǎoxiǎn insurance

現/现

xiàn
now; present

PICTOPHONETIC CHARACTER The character 現 combines the radical 王 (wáng, king) with the phonetic element 見 (jiàn, to see). As a radical, the meaning of 王 is "jade" rather than "king." In Chinese there is also an independent character for "jade:" 玉 (yù). In the Oracle-Bone Inscriptions, 玉 looks like a cluster of jade pieces. Since 現 consists of "jade" and "see," it originally meant "the revealing of jade by its light." Extended meanings include "appear," "existing," "present," and "now." In the simplified character 现, 见 is derived from the cursive form of 見.

現 形聲。從玉，見聲，本義指玉光外射，引申為顯露、出現、此刻之意。玉，象形。甲骨文像一串玉。金文和篆文改為三片玉。玉作為偏旁寫作王。簡體字现的右部簡化。

玉 甲 现

現在 xiànzài now; at present
發現 fāxiàn to discover

出現 chūxiàn to appear; to emerge
現實 xiànshí reality; realistic

線/线

xiàn
line; route

PICTOPHONETIC CHARACTER The character 線 consists of the silk radical 糸 and the phonetic element 泉 (quán), meaning "thread," "string," "wire," "line," etc. In the Oracle-Bone Inscriptions, 泉 (spring) looks like water gushing out of a mountain springhead. In Regular Script, 泉 combines 白 (bái, white) and 水 (shuǐ, water). 綫 is a variant form of 線. In the simplified character 线, both 糸 and 戔 are simplified. See also the character 钱 (錢) (qián).

線 形聲。從糸，泉聲。泉，象形。甲骨文像水從泉眼流出。綫是線的異體字。簡體字线是將繁體字綫左邊的部首簡化為纟，右邊戔簡化為戋。參見錢字的簡化法。

泉 甲 𜈖 篆 𜈖

線路 xiànlù line; circuit; bus route
光線 guāngxiàn light ray; light

天線 tiānxiàn antenna
電線 diànxiàn electric wire

香

xiāng
fragrant

ASSOCIATIVE COMPOUND In its ancient forms, the character 香 is the combination of 黍 (shǔ, millet) and 甘 (gān, sweet; tasty). 黍 is the pictograph of a millet plant and 甘 looks like something in the mouth. In Regular Script, 黍 is replaced by 禾 (hé, growing grain) and 甘 by 日 to form the character 香. The original meaning of 香 is the fragrance of grain or cereal, from which the meanings "fragrant," "aromatic," "sweet-smelling," "delicious," "tasty," "soundly," "popular," and "incense" have derived.

香 會意。篆文從黍，從甘，本義為穀物的香味。引申為氣味芬芳、香甜、食物味道好、吃得好、睡得好、受歡迎、香料等。楷書簡化寫作香。

甲 𜈖 篆 𜈖

香味 xiāngwèi fragrance; scent
香草 xiāngcǎo vanilla

香水 xiāngshuǐ perfume; cologne
香港 xiānggǎng Hong Kong

箱

xiāng
box; case

PICTOPHONETIC CHARACTER The character 箱 consists of the bamboo radical 竹 and the phonetic element 相 (xiāng), originally referring to boxes made of bamboo or wood. 箱 has been extended to mean "box," "case," or "trunk" of any material, and used as a measure word for boxes. It also refers to box-like things, for example 冰箱 (bīngxiāng, refrigerator). 相 combines 木 (mù, wood; tree) with 目 (mù, eye), indicating the act of looking closely at a tree. Hence the primary meaning of 相 is "to look at and appraise." Extended meanings of 相 include "appearance," "posture," "photograph," etc.

箱 形聲。從竹，相聲。指用竹木製成收藏衣物的器具，也泛指形狀象箱子的東西（冰箱、集裝箱）。另外箱也可作為量詞（一箱書，一箱衣服）。相，會意。從目，從木。表示用眼觀察樹木。本義為查看、審視。

篆 𜈖

箱子 xiāngzi box; case; chest
信箱 xìnxiāng mailbox

冰箱 bīngxiāng fridge
烤箱 kǎoxiāng oven

xiǎng
to want;
to think

PICTOPHONETIC CHARACTER   The character 想 is comprised of the radical 心 (xīn, heart) and the phonetic element 相 (xiàng, appearance), meaning "to think," "to ponder," "to recall," or "to want to." The character 相 combines 木 (mù, wood; tree) with 目 (mù, eye), indicating the act of looking closely at a tree. Hence the primary meaning of 相 is "to look at and appraise." Extended meanings include "appearance," "posture," "photograph," etc.

想　形聲。從心，相聲，本義為思考。相，會意。從目，從木，表示用眼睛觀察樹木。

篆

想法 xiǎngfǎ idea; opinion; notion
思想 sīxiǎng thought; thinking; ideology

想念 xiǎngniàn to miss; to remember with longing
理想 lǐxiǎng a dream; ideal

象

xiàng
elephant;
appearance; shape

PICTOGRAPH   In the Oracle-Bone Inscriptions, the character 象 is the sketch of an elephant. In Regular Script, the upper part of 象 delineates an elephant's head and tusks, while the lower part its body, legs, and tail. The original and primary meaning of 象 is "elephant," and its extended meanings include "image," "shape," "appearance," "form," "to imitate," and "phenomenon." In modern Chinese, 象 is used to refer to images out of nature, while 像 refers to those made to resemble the appearance of a person or man-made objects.

象　象形。甲骨文字形勾畫出大象的輪廓。本義為大象，引申為形狀、樣子、模擬等。一般用來指自然界或人物的形態。而像字多指用比較、模仿的方法製成的人或物的樣子，如畫像、雕像、圖像、音像等。

甲 金 篆 象

大象 dàxiàng elephant
想象 xiǎngxiàng to imagine; imagination

氣象 qìxiàng meteorological phenomena
現象 xiànxiàng phenomenon; appearance (of things)

像

xiàng
likeness;
portrait

PICTOPHONETIC CHARACTER   The character 像 is composed of the person radical 亻 and the phonetic element 象 (xiàng), meaning "to resemble," "to take after," "seem," "to portray," "picture," "image," "such as," etc. In the Oracle-Bone Inscriptions, the character 象 outlines an elephant. In Regular Script, the upper part of 象 represents the elephant's head and trunk, while the lower part indicates the body, legs and tail. In modern Chinese, 像 is used to refer to images made to resemble the appearance of a person or man-made objects, while 象 refers to images from nature.

像　形聲。從人，象聲，意指比照人物繪成的圖形、相像、好像、比如等。象，象形。甲骨文簡要勾畫出大象的輪廓。

篆 像 象 甲 金 篆 象

畫像 huàxiàng portrait
錄像 lùxiàng to record video; video recording

偶像 ǒuxiàng idol
好像 hǎoxiàng as if; to seem like

X - Z

校

xiào
school

ASSOCIATIVE AND PICTOPHONETIC COMPOUND 校 contains the radical 木 (mù, wood) and 交 (jiāo, cross) as both a phonetic and semantic component. 校 originally referred to the crossbar that latched the neck and hands of a criminal together. Today, 校 is used to mean "school." In its ancient form, 交 is a pictograph of a figure with crossed legs.

校 會意兼形聲。從木，從交；交亦聲。指用兩木相交製作的刑具。交，象形。像兩腿相交的正面人形。

篆 校

學校 xuéxiào school
校長 xiàozhǎng (school) president

校園 xiàoyuán campus
校友 xiàoyǒu schoolmate; alumni

笑

xiào
to laugh; to smile

ASSOCIATIVE COMPOUND The character 笑 consists of the bamboo radical ⺮ and the character 夭 (yāo). In the Oracle-Bone and Bronze Inscriptions, 夭 resembles a person dancing with one arm up and one arm down, suggesting lithe and graceful movement. 夭 is also used to describe luxuriant and gorgeous plants. A person's laughter may be compared to bamboo dancing in the wind, so the character 笑 means "laugh," "smile," or "to laugh at." In Seal Script, the character 夭 resembles a person with his or her head tilted to one side, meaning "to die young."

笑 會意。從竹，從夭（彎曲）。李陽冰勘定《說文》中解釋說"竹得風，其體夭曲，如人之笑。"夭，甲骨文、金文像人兩手搖擺起舞狀。有嬌媚、艷麗、茂盛、夭折等意。

篆 笑 夭 甲 大 金 大 篆 夭

可笑 kěxiào funny; ridiculous
笑話 xiàohua joke; jest

笑容 xiàoróng smile; smiling expression
開玩笑 kāi wánxiào to play a joke; to make fun of; to joke

些

xiē
(MW for indefinite amount); some

ASSOCIATIVE COMPOUND 些 is built with 此 (cǐ, this; these) on top and 二 (èr, two; a couple of) underneath, indicating that an amount is not much (though greater than one). Thus its meaning is "small amount or number," "a little," "a few," "some," and "measure word for an indefinite amount." In the Oracle-Bone Inscriptions, 此 contains a foot 止 (zhǐ, foot; stop) and a person on the right, indicating the place one stops and meaning "here," "this," "in this case," etc. In Regular Script, the person in 此 is replaced by 匕 (bǐ, ladle). Compare 此 with 比 (bǐ, compare).

些 會意。從此，從二，意指少許、一點兒、不深的程度。此，會意。從止，從匕（甲骨文像人形，楷書寫作匕；匕現今意指匕首），表示人止步之處。意為這、這個、這兒等。請把此字與比字加以比較。

篆 些 此 甲 些 金 些 篆 此

這些 zhèxiē these
哪些 nǎxiē which

那些 nàxiē those
一些 yìxiē some; a few; a little

鞋

xié
shoes

ASSOCIATIVE COMPOUND The character 鞋 consists of 革 (gé, leather) and two 土 (tǔ, earth; soil), referring to shoes (being leather products which touch the ground). In the Bronze Inscriptions, the character 革 looks like an animal skin, meaning "leather," "hide," "remove," etc.

鞋 會意。從革，從雙土。革，本義為剝去動物的皮毛，引申為皮革。

革 甲 𦰩 金 𦰩 篆 革

球鞋 qiúxié sneakers; athletic shoes
拖鞋 tuōxié slippers; sandals

皮鞋 píxié leather shoes
高跟鞋 gāogēnxié high-heeled shoes

寫／写

xiě
to write

PICTOPHONETIC CHARACTER The character 寫 contains the roof radical 宀 and the phonetic element 舃 (xì). The original meaning of 寫 was "to move things into a room," with the extended meaning "to write." In its ancient form, 舃 is a pictograph of a chattering bird (symbolized by an open beak in the upper part, and wings and claws in the lower part). 舃 originally meant "magpie." The simplified character 写 developed from the cursive form of 寫.

寫 形聲。從宀，舃(xì)聲。本義為移置，引申為傾吐、摹畫、書寫等。舃，象形。金文像一隻張開大嘴喳喳叫的喜鵲，本義為喜鵲。簡體字写是繁體字寫的草書楷化字，但草書写字上面多帶一點。

篆 𪚾 草 写 鳥 金 𦉥 篆 𦉤

寫字 xiězì to write a letter
寫作 xiězuò to compose; writing

寫信 xiěxìn to write a letter
聽寫 tīngxiě to dictate; dictation

謝／谢

xiè
to thank

PICTOPHONETIC CHARACTER The character 謝 consists of the word radical 言 and the phonetic symbol 射 (shè). The original meaning of 謝 was "resign." Its extended meanings are "decline," "apologize," and "thank." In the Bronze Inscriptions, the character 射 depicts a hand drawing a bow, meaning "to shoot." In Seal Script, the bow is replaced by a human body 身 (shēn). In its ancient form 身 was a pictograph of a pregnant woman. In Regular Script, 謝 is the combination of three characters: 言 (yán, word), 身 (shēn, body), and 寸 (cùn, inch). As a radical, 言 is always simplified as 讠.

謝 形聲。從言，射聲。射，會意。甲骨文像張弓射箭形。金文加手。篆文將弓改為身，從寸。寸有手意，指用手張弓射箭始于身而及于遠。身，像人腹有身孕形。簡體字中，作為字左邊部首的言 一律簡化為讠。

射 甲 𢎺 金 𢎺 篆 𦥔

謝謝 xièxie thanks; thank you
多謝 duōxiè many thanks; thanks a lot

不謝 búxiè don't mention it; not at all
感謝 gǎnxiè gratitude; be grateful

新

xīn
new

ASSOCIATIVE AND PICTOPHONETIC COMPOUND 新 consists of the signifying parts 木 (mù, wood) and 斤 (jīn, axe), and the phonetic component 辛 (xīn), originally meaning "cut firewood" or "firewood." Since people in primitive societies made fire by creating friction on wood, 新 extended to mean "new," "fresh," "newly," "recently," "unused," etc. In the Oracle-Bone Inscriptions, 斤 looks like an ax with a crooked handle, meaning "ax," and later a traditional unit of weight. In the Oracle-Bone and Bronze Inscriptions, 辛 is the pictograph of a chisel-like instrument used to tattoo prisoners. Extended meanings of 辛 are "pungent," "laborious," and "suffering."

新 會意兼形聲。從木，從斤(斧)，辛聲。本義為用斧頭砍柴，是薪的本字，後用作新舊的新。辛，象形。甲骨文、金文中像鑿子一類的刑具，用來在犯人臉上刺字。

甲 金 新 篆 新

新式 xīnshì new-style
新聞 xīnwén news

新年 xīnnián New Year
新鮮 xīnxiān fresh; novel; uncommon

信

xìn
letter; to believe

ASSOCIATIVE COMPOUND The character 信 consists of the vertical person radical 亻 and the character 言 (yán, word; speak), implying that a person's words should be trustworthy. Therefore, the meanings of 信 are "true," "trust," "faith," and "believe." 信 is also used to mean "message" or "letter," which also might connote that one's written word should be true.

信 會意。從人，從言，本義指人要言而有信，引申為書信。

金 㐰 篆 信

信封 xìnfēng envelope
信心 xìnxīn confidence; faith

信箱 xìnxiāng mailbox
相信 xiāngxìn to believe; to trust

星

xīng
star

PICTOPHONETIC CHARACTER In the Oracle-Bone Inscriptions, the character 星 looks like a pictograph of light shining out from a cluster of stars. In the Bronze Inscriptions, it consists of three 日 shaped stars in the upper part and the phonetic indicator 生 (shēng, born) in the lower part. In Regular Script, 星 has only one star on top of 生.

星 形聲。從日，生聲。甲骨文像光芒閃耀的群星，金文改成三顆星，下加聲旁，楷書減為一顆星。

甲 金 篆 星

行星 xíngxīng planet
明星 míngxīng star; celebrity

星期 xīngqī week; day of the week
歌星 gēxīng singing star; famous singer

行

xíng
to walk; okay

háng
bank; firm

PICTOGRAPH   In the Oracle-Bone and Bronze Inscriptions, the character 行 delineates two streets intersecting. The original meaning of 行 was "intersection," and extended meanings include "road," "go," "walk," "carry out," "all right," and "will do." In Regular Script, 行 is comprised of 彳 (walk slowly; left step) and 亍 (chù, small step). You can also see 彳 in the characters 律 (lù, law; rule) and 後 (hòu, after). 行 is also pronounced as háng and means "bank," "line of business," "business firm," etc.

行　象形。甲骨文、金文像四通八達的道路。本義指十字路，引申為行走、走得通、可以等。

甲 艸 金 光 篆 行

行動 xíngdòng action; take action; mobile
自行車 zìxíngchē bicycle; bike

旅行 lǚxíng to travel; journey; trip
銀行 yínháng bank

姓

xìng
surname

ASSOCIATIVE AND PICTOPHONETIC COMPOUND   The character 姓 consists of 女 (nǚ, female) and 生 (shēng, give birth), meaning "surname." In the matrilineal society of ancient times, children adopted their mothers' surnames since women were considered superior to men. In the character 姓, 生 also functions as the phonetic element.

姓　會意兼形聲。從女，從生；生亦聲。姓是母系社會的反映。上古姓是族號，隨母系。

甲 𡛷 篆 姓

姓名 xìngmíng name and surname
百姓 bǎixìng common people

貴姓 guìxìng What is your name?
老百姓 lǎobǎixìng folk(s); ordinary people

興／兴

xìng
mood; interest

ASSOCIATIVE COMPOUND   In the Oracle-Bone and Bronze Inscriptions, 興 depicts four hands lifting a mold, and meant "to lift" or "raise" (pronounced xīng). Extended meanings of 興 include "start," "prosper" (xīng), "mood," and "interest" (xìng). In Regular Script, the four hands are still visible in the character 興, though the lower two have been simplified. The part the four hands are lifting is 同 (tóng, same). 同 refers to castings made out of the same mold. The simplified 兴 developed from the cursive style of the traditional 興. Notice that the top parts of the two characters are different.

興　會意。甲骨文、金文字形像四隻手同力共舉一幅模具。簡體字兴是由繁體字興的草書楷化而來。

甲 𦥑 金 𦥑 篆 𦥑 草

高興 gāoxìng happy; glad
興起 xīngqǐ to rise; to spring up

興趣 xìngqù interest; hobby
新興 xīnxīng newly developing; rising; burgeoning

休

xiū
to cease; to rest

ASSOCIATIVE COMPOUND The character 休 is the combination of the person radical 亻 and 木 (mù, wood; tree), indicating that a man is taking a rest under a tree. Its meanings include "to rest," "to stop," "to cease," "to cast off one's wife and send her to her parents," and "don't."

休　會意。從亻，從木，像人在樹下休息。本義是休息，引申義有停止、不要、舊時丈夫將妻子趕回娘家、斷絕夫妻關係等。

甲 休 金 休 篆 休

休息 xiūxi to rest
休學 xiūxué to suspend one's schooling

休假 xiūjià to take a vacation
退休 tuìxiū to retire

學／学

xué
to study

ASSOCIATIVE COMPOUND In the Bronze Inscriptions, the upper part of 學 represents two hands playing with four sticks, and the lower part shows a child under a roof, thereby representing a child learning math at home. You will find that only the tops are different if you compare the character 學 with 字 (zì, character). The simplified character 学 is derived from the cursive form of the traditional 學.

學　會意。金文像屋裏一個孩子雙手擺佈小木棍，學習計算。簡體学字是繁體學字的草書楷化字。

甲 學 金 學 篆 學 草 学

學習 xuéxí to learn; to study
學校 xuéxiào school

學生 xuésheng student
上學 shàngxué to go to school; to attend school

雪

xuě
snow

ASSOCIATIVE COMPOUND In Seal Script, the upper part of 雪 is 雨 (yǔ, rain), and the lower part 彗 (huì, broom; comet). 彗 looks like a hand (bottom part) holding a broom made of a couple of branches (top part). Therefore, 雪 literally means the rain that can be swept away. In Regular Script 雪 loses the broom part, and only the rain and hand remain. The extended meanings of 雪 include "snow-like," "to wipe out (shame; insult; humiliation)," and even "to avenge (a wrong)," since snow can cover all injustice, and unfairness and wrongdoing can be wiped away.

雪　會意。篆文上為雨，下為彗，彗意指手持掃把。中國人也管彗星 comet 叫掃把星，因彗星劃過天空的形狀像掃把。楷書雪去掉彗字的上部。雪字描摹人用掃帚掃雪，本義為天上降落的水的白色結晶體；引申義有像雪一般的、洗刷掉等。

甲 雪 篆 雪 彗甲 彗 篆 彗

滑雪 huáxuě to ski; skiing
雪人 xuěrén snowman

雪花 xuěhuā snowflake
雪白 xuěbái snow-white

押

yā
to give as security

PICTOPHONETIC CHARACTER The character 押 is comprised of the hand radical 扌 and the phonetic element 甲 (jiǎ). Its original meaning is to "to sign" or "to mark in lieu of signature," from which the meanings "to give as security," "to mortgage," "to pawn," "to detain," "to take into custody," and "to escort" have derived. In its ancient forms, 甲 looks like a spitted husk after the seed sprouts. Hence, its original meaning is "husk." It has been extended to mean "shell," "nail," "armor," "the first of the ten heavenly stems" (see page 20), and "the first (in order)."

押 形聲。從扌，甲聲。本義為在公文、契約上簽字或畫符號，引申義有以財物作擔保（押金）、拘禁扣留、監督護衛等。甲，象形。在甲骨文像種子發芽時裂開的皮殼，本義是種子的外殼，引申指一些動物身上的硬殼、盔甲、指甲等。甲也指順序或等級中的第一。

押金 yājīn deposit
關押 guānyā to imprison

押送 yāsòng to escort (prisoners, goods, etc)
在押 zàiyā under detention; in custody

鴨／鸭

yā
duck

PICTOPHONETIC CHARACTER The character 鴨 is made up of the signifying component 鳥 (niǎo, bird) and the phonetic element 甲 (jiǎ), meaning "duck." In its ancient forms, 甲 looks like a spitted husk after the seed sprouts. Hence, its original meaning is "husk," and its extended meanings include "shell," "nail," "armor," "the first of the ten heavenly stems" (see page 20), and "first in order." 鳥 is the pictograph of a bird, and is used to mean "bird." The simplified character 鸟 is derived from the cursive style of 鳥. In the character 鸭, 鸟 is in its simplified form.

鴨 形聲。從鳥，甲聲。意為鴨子。甲，象形。甲骨文像植物初生時種子殼裂開形，引申指動物身上的硬殼、用皮革或金屬做成的盔甲、指甲等。鳥，象形。本義指長尾鳥，隹指短尾鳥。後用來泛指鳥類。簡化字鸟來源於鳥的草體。簡化字鸭屬於偏旁類推簡化。

篆 鴨 鳥甲 金 草

鴨子 yāzi duck
烤鴨 kǎoyā roasted duck

鴨蛋 yādàn duck's egg
野鴨（子）yěyā(zi) wild duck

壓／压

yā
to press; to weigh down

ASSOCIATIVE AND PICTOPHONETIC COMPOUND 壓 combines the earth radical 土 (tǔ) with the phonetic/semantic component 厭 (yàn). Originally 壓 meant "to collapse," and extended to mean "to press," and "to suppress," etc. 厭 consists of 厂 (hǎn, cliff) and the phonetic 猒 (yàn). 厭 is actually the original form of 壓 but since its original meanings were taken by 壓, 厭 came to mean "be satisfied" and "be fed up with." In its ancient forms, 猒 combines 甘 (gān, tasty) and 肰 (rán, dog meat), meaning "be satisfied with tasty dog meat." The simplified 压 replaces 猒 in 壓 with a dot.

壓 會意兼形聲。從土，從厭，厭亦聲。本義為土受壓而崩塌。引申義有向下施力、壓住、壓制、壓力等。厭字的本義為壓迫，是壓的本字。因造壓字，厭用來表示滿足、因過多而不喜歡、厭煩、厭惡之意。簡化字压去掉壓字中的猒，而在土字中加一點。

篆 壓

壓力 yālì pressure; stress
氣壓 qìyā air pressure

電壓 diànyā voltage
血壓 xuèyā blood pressure

呀

ya
(exclamation particle)

PICTOPHONETIC CHARACTER 呀 consists of the mouth radical 口 and the phonetic element 牙 (yá, tooth), suggesting a person with an open mouth. 呀 can be used as an exclamation, onomatopoeic word, or an auxiliary. The character 牙 is a pictograph; in Seal Script, 牙 looks like a pair of jaws with two large teeth in the upper part.

呀 形聲。從口，牙聲。本義指張口狀，引申為嘆詞、象聲詞等。牙，象形。像口中牙齒上下相錯形。

牙 金 篆

啊呀 āyā interjection of surprise; Oh my!
天呀 tiānya Heavens!; My God!

哎呀 āiyā interjection of wonder, Ah! Dear me!
我的媽呀 wǒde māyā Oh my gosh!

淹

yān
to submerge; to drown

ASSOCIATIVE AND PICTOPHONETIC CHARACTER The character 淹 is comprised of the water radical 氵 and the phonetic 奄 (yǎn), meaning "to submerge," "to drown," "to flood," "to soak," etc. In the Bronze Inscriptions, 奄 has lightning on the top (电) and a person (大) underneath, signaling that the person is submerged in lightning. Its original meaning is "to cover," and has been extended to mean "suddenly," "abruptly," and "feeble and dying." In Seal Script and Regular Script, the positions of 大 and 电 are switched.

淹 會意兼形聲。從氵，從奄，奄亦聲。意為淹沒、浸泡等。奄，會意。從大，從申（閃電），意指人處於閃電之下，本義為覆蓋，引申為突然、氣息微弱等。

篆  奄 金 篆

淹沒 yānmò to submerge; to overwhelm; to flood

淹死 yānsǐ to drown

顔

yán
face; countenance

PICTOPHONETIC CHARACTER The character 顔 consists of the radical 頁 (yè, head; page) and the phonetic component 彥 (yàn), meaning "forehead." Extended meanings of 顔 include "face," "countenance," and "color." In the Oracle-Bone Inscriptions, 頁 resembles a person with a large head. You can also see 頁 in 題 (tí, topic) and 預 (yù, prepare). In the Bronze Inscriptions, 彥 combines 文 (wén, writing; language) and 弓 (gōng, bow), referring to those who are skilled at both literary and martial arts. In Regular Script, 彡 replaces the lower part of 彥 (弓). 頁 is simplified in 颜.

顔 形聲。篆文從頁，彥聲。意指額頭、面容、色彩等。頁像人頭形。彥，會意兼形聲。金文從文，從弓，指文武雙全、德才兼備的人。簡體字颜中的页字簡化。

篆 彥 金 篆 彥

顔面 yánmiàn face; prestige
顔色 yánsè color

容顔 róngyán mien; complexion
顔料 yánliào pigment; paint

鹽／盐

yán
salt

PICTOPHONETIC CHARACTER The character 鹽 contains the signifying component 鹵 (lǔ, natural salt) and the phonetic symbol 監 (jiān), meaning "salt." 鹵 looks like a salt pot with four enlarged salt particles in it. Its original meaning was "natural salt," and has been extended to mean "saline soil" or "thick gravy." For the origins of 監, see 藍 (lán, blue). 鹽 is one of the most complicated traditional characters; therefore the simplified 盐 changed the top of 鹽 to 土 and 卜, making the character much easier to write and memorize.

鹽　形聲。篆文從鹵，監聲。意指食鹽。鹵，象形，像盛着鹽的鹽罐。本義為鹽鹵，即鹵水，引申為鹽鹹地、濃汁等。監，象形。本義為照鏡，引申為監視、檢查、借鑑等。請參見藍字。簡化字盐將鹽字的上部改為土與卜。鹽字筆畫繁多，很早就有此簡化字。

篆 鹽　鹵金 ⊗　篆 鹵

食鹽 shíyán edible salt
鹽湖城 yánhúchéng Salt Lake City

鹽湖 yánhú salt lake
鹽酸 yánsuān hydrochloric acid

眼

yǎn
eye

ASSOCIATIVE AND PICTOPHONETIC COMPOUND The character 眼 contains the eye radical 目 and the phonetic and signifying part 艮 (gěn), meaning "eye." The extended meanings of 眼 are "field of vision," "small hole," and "crux (of a matter)." In the Oracle-Bone and Bronze Inscriptions, the upper part of 艮 is a big eye and the lower part a person, showing a man turning back to stare at something. The meanings of 艮 include "disobey," "tough," "blunt," and "straightforward." You will also encounter 艮 as a component in 很 (hěn, very) and 跟 (gēn, with).

眼　會意兼形聲。從目，艮 (gěn) 聲。本義為眼睛，引申為眼光、見識、孔穴、關鍵等。艮，會意。甲骨文、金文從人，像一人作回首瞪視狀。

篆 眼　艮甲　金　篆 艮

眼睛 yǎnjīng eyes
眼淚 yǎnlèi tears

眼鏡 yǎnjìng eyeglasses
近視眼 jìnshìyǎn myopia; nearsighted

演

yǎn
to show (a film);
to perform

PICTOPHONETIC CHARACTER The character 演 consists of the water radical 氵 and the phonetic component 寅 (yín), originally meaning "to flow (like a long, slow river)." Its extended meanings are "to evolve," "to develop," "to deduce," "to practice," "to perform," "to play," and "to act." In Seal Script, 寅 depicts the act of taking out an arrow inside a house with both hands, suggesting "reverence" or "respectfully." 寅 has been borrowed to mean "the third earthly branch" (see page 20) and "3–5 a.m."

演　形聲。從氵，寅 (yín) 聲。本義為水流漫長，引申義有擴展、演變、推理、演習、表演等。寅，會意。篆文像在房內以雙手取出箭形。原意為恭敬，後借為地支第三位，十二時辰中天亮前三至五時為寅時。

篆 演

演出 yǎnchū performance; to perform
導演 dǎoyǎn director (of a play, film, etc.)

演員 yǎnyuán actor or actress
演電影 yǎn diànyǐng to act in a movie

Z - X

養/养

yǎng
to raise

ASSOCIATIVE COMPOUND In the Oracle-Bone and Bronze Inscriptions, the character 養 depicts a hand holding a whip herding a sheep. In Seal Script, 養 is made up of 羊 (yáng, sheep; goat) and 食 (shí, food). The original meaning of 養 is "to raise," which has been extended to mean "to bring up," "to keep (pets)," "to support," "to train," "to foster," "to give birth," "to nourish," "to cultivate," etc. The simplified character 养 is derived from the cursive form of 養.

養 會意。甲骨文、金文像拿鞭子趕羊。篆文從羊，從食，表示以食喂羊。本義為飼養，引申為供養、培養、領養、生育、保養、修養等。簡化字养是養字的草書楷化字。

甲 𦊱 金 𤕦 篆 養 草 养

養狗 yǎnggǒu to keep a dog; to breed dogs
養家 yǎngjiā to support a family

養花 yǎnghuā to grow flowers; floriculture
養老 yǎnglǎo to live a retired life

癢/痒

yǎng
itchy

PICTOPHONETIC CHARACTER The character 癢 consists of the sick radical 疒 and the phonetic indicator 養 (yǎng), meaning "itchy" or "to have an itch to do something." 養 is made up of 羊 (yáng, goat) and 食 (shí, food), conveying the meanings "to raise (animals)," "to bring up (children)," "to keep (pets)," "to support," "to train," etc. In the Oracle-Bone and Bronze Inscriptions, 羊 depicts the front view of a goat head and 食 resembles a high-legged container full of food. 痒 is a variant form of 癢 and is now used as the simplified form of 癢.

癢 形聲。從疒，養聲。本義為癢，引申為受某種原因引起的強烈願望，想躍躍欲試，如心癢、手癢。養，會意，從羊，從食，表示以食喂羊。本義為飼養、引申為撫養、供養、培養、保養、生育等。痒是癢的異體字，現用作癢的簡化字。

篆 𤶇 癢

發癢 fāyǎng itch; itchy
抓癢 zhuāyǎng to scratch an itch

怕癢 pàyǎng to be ticklish
手癢 shǒuyǎng to have an itch to do something

樣/样

yàng
kind; appearance

PICTOPHONETIC CHARACTER The character 樣 combines the wood radical 木 and the phonetic element 羕 (yàng). Its original meaning was "acorn." Later it came to mean "shape," "kind," or "type." The character 羕 is made up of the phonetic part 羊 (yáng, goat) and the signifying part 永 (yǒng, originally swim, now meaning forever), meaning "undulate." The ancient form of 羊 depicts a goat head and the character 永 to show a figure swimming. In the simplified character 样, 羊 replaces 羕 since their pronunciations are similar.

樣 形聲。從木，羕聲。羕，形聲。從永，羊聲，形容水長。永，會意。甲骨文從人，像人在水流中游泳狀。本義指游泳，是泳的本字。後加水旁作泳，而以永為永久意。羊，象形。像羊頭之形。簡體字样把繁體右部的聲旁羕改為羊。

篆 樣

一樣 yíyàng the same; equally
樣品 yàngpǐn sample; specimen

樣子 yàngzi appearance; manner
樣式 yàngshì type; style

要

yào
to want

ASSOCIATIVE COMPOUND In its ancient form, the character 要 delineates a woman placing both hands on her waist. The original meaning of 要 was "waist," and its meanings now include "coerce," "demand," "must," "want," "ask for," and "important." People often stand with their arms akimbo when demanding something of someone. Later, a flesh radical 月 was added to the left of 要 to create a new character for waist 腰.

要 會意。像一人雙手叉腰形，是腰的本字。

金 𤴐 篆 𦥑

主要 zhǔyào main; principal; major
只要 zhǐyào so long as; provided

重要 zhòngyào important; significant
要不然 yàobùrán otherwise; or else

藥 / 药

yào
medicine

PICTOPHONETIC CHARACTER The character 藥 contains the grass radical ⁺⁺ and the phonetic element 樂 (yuè; lè). Originally 藥 referred to medicinal herbs, and extended to mean "medicine," "drug," "chemicals," "to cure," or "to poison." In its ancient forms, 樂 consists of two strings (幺幺), a pick (白), and wood (木), indicating its original meaning of a stringed musical instrument. Extended meanings are "music (yuè)," "happy (lè)," or "to take delight in." The character 葯 (yào) was a variant form of 藥. The simplified 药 derives from 葯 with the simplified silk radical 纟.

藥 形聲：從艸（⁺⁺），樂聲。本義指能夠治病的植物，引申為能治病的藥材、藥物以及一些化學藥物（農藥、炸藥）。樂，象形。甲骨文從絲，從木。表示將絲弦繃于木上，意指琴瑟之類的樂器。葯與藥音相同意相近，舊時可通用。簡化字药只是將葯的糸 簡化為纟。

金 𣡛 篆 藥

中藥 zhōngyào Chinese medicine
藥店 yàodiàn drugstore

西藥 xīyào Western medicine
火藥 huǒyào gunpowder

爺 / 爷

yé
grandpa; (respectful address for an elderly men)

PICTOPHONETIC CHARACTER The character 爺 contains the signifying component 父 (fù, father) and the phonetic indicator 耶 (yé/yē), originally referring to "father." Later 爺 extended to refer to an old gentleman, "master," "god," or "grandfather." 耶 consists of 耳 (ěr, ear) and the radical 阝 (town; city [when at right of characters]). In classical Chinese, 耶 (yé) functions as an interrogative particle. Nowadays, 耶 (yē) is often used in transliteration, as in 耶路撒冷 (yēlùsālěng, Jerusalem). The simplified character 爷 replaces 耶 with 卩 (jié).

爺 形聲。從父，耶（yé/yē）聲。本義是父親，引申為對長輩或年長男子的尊稱、對神佛的稱呼、祖父等。耶，會意。在古文中用作疑問詞，相當於嗎、呢，讀作 yé。而耶字用來翻譯時讀作 yē，如耶穌，耶和華，耶路撒冷。簡化字爺把爺字的下部改為 卩（jié）。

篆 爺

爺爺 yéye paternal grandfather
大爺 dàye father's older brother; uncle

姥爺 lǎoye maternal grandfather
老天爺 lǎotiān yé God; Heavens

Z - X

yě
also; too

PHONETIC LOAN CHARACTER In the Bronze Inscriptions and Seal Script, 也 looks like a snake with a large head, and its original meaning was "snake." Later 也 was borrowed to mean "also" or "too," but the character still looks like a snake with a big head, a cobra perhaps.

也 假借。在金文中 "也" 是一條拖著尾巴、頭部突出的蛇形。本義為蛇，後被借為語氣詞、助詞與副詞。

金 篆

也許 yěxǔ perhaps; maybe

也好 yěhǎo It may not be a bad idea; may as well

---

yè
night

PICTOPHONETIC CHARACTER In its ancient forms, the character 夜 consists of the radical 夕 (xī, sunset; evening) and the phonetic element 亦 (yì), referring to "evening," "night," or "nighttime." In the Oracle-Bone Inscriptions, 亦 depicts a person (大) with two dots under his or her armpits, originally referring to "armpit." Later it was borrowed to mean "also" in classical Chinese. In Regular Script, 夜 looks like a person (亻) under a roof (宀) with the lower right part symbolizing open eyes.

夜 形聲。金文、篆文從夕，亦聲。指從天黑到天亮的這段時間。亦，甲骨文從大（人的正面），旁邊兩點表示人的腋窩。亦本義是腋窩，後借用為副詞也。

金 篆

日夜 rìyè day and night
過夜 guòyè to stay overnight

半夜 bànyè midnight; in the middle of the night
夜市 yèshì night market

葉/叶

yè
leaf

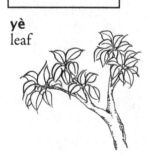

PICTOGRAPH In the Oracle-Bone Inscriptions, the character 葉 depicts a tree with three large leaves on its branches. In Regular Script, 葉 consists of the grass/plant radical 艹 on top, 世 in the middle, and 木 (mù, wood) at the bottom. In its ancient form, 世 (shì) looks like leaves, meaning "lifetime" or "the world." The character 叶 (the original pronunciation was xié, meaning "harmonious") became used as the simplified character for 葉 (yè), because they are now similarly pronounced.

葉 象形。甲骨文中像長着三片樹葉的樹枝。楷書加草字頭。叶字本讀作 xié，是協的異體字，現用來作為葉的簡體字，屬近音替代。

甲 金 篆

樹葉 shùyè tree leaves
葉子 yèzi foliage; leaf

紅葉 hóngyè red autumnal leaves
茶葉 cháyè tea; tea-leaves

業/业
yè
profession

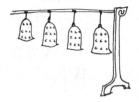

PICTOGRAPH In the Bronze Inscriptions, the character 業 resembles a wooden frame with bars on top from which musical instruments such as bells or drums are hung. Since playing musical instruments is a type of profession, extended meanings of 業 include "profession," "career," "employment," "school studies," "occupation," "line of business," "industry," etc. In Regular Script, the top of 業 still looks like the bars of the frame and the bottom contains the wood radical 木. The simplified character 业 retains only the top part of the traditional 業.

業 象形。金文中像懸挂鐘鼓樂器帶齒的木架，引申為事業、家業、學業等。簡體字业僅取業字的上半部。

金 業 篆 業

作業 zuòyè school assignment; homework
畢業 bìyè graduation; to graduate
專業 zhuānyè specialized field; major
工業 gōngyè industry

醫/医
yī
doctor; medicine

ASSOCIATIVE COMPOUND The character 醫 combines 医 (yī, an arrow 矢 in a quiver 匸) with 殳 (shū, an ancient weapon) and 酉 (yǒu, a wine jar), indicating the use of alcohol to heal a wound. Both 矢 and 酉 are pictographs in the Oracle-Bone and Bronze Inscriptions. 殳 looks like a hand holding a weapon. The simplified character 医 retains only the left top of the traditional character 醫.

醫 會意。医，古時盛箭的器具。殳 shū，會意。甲骨文像一隻手拿一件圓頭兵器，意指一種古代兵器。酉，象形。像一個尖底的酒罎子酒可以用以治病。醫指受到箭傷或兵器的傷害，可以用酒來消毒治病。簡體字医僅保留醫字左上方的部分。

篆 醫

醫生 yīshēng doctor
醫院 yīyuàn hospital
醫學 yīxué medical science; medicine
中醫 zhōngyī traditional Chinese medicine; doctor of Chinese medicine

宜
yí
suitable

ASSOCIATIVE COMPOUND In the Oracle-Bone and Bronze Inscriptions, the character 且 (qiě) looks like a memorial tablet used in ancestral worship, originally meaning "ancestor." You can also find 且 in the characters 姐 (jiě, elder sister) and 助 (zhù, to assist). The character 宜 consists of the roof radical 宀 and the character 且, referring to the act of placing ancestral offerings on a memorial tablet in a room. The original meaning of 宜 was "to offer sacrifices to ancestors or gods." Since this ritual was considered obligatory, 宜 extended to mean "should," "ought to," "suitable," and "appropriate."

宜 會意。從宀，從且（祖宗的牌位）。把祖宗的牌位放在室內，本義為祭祀，引申為合適、應當。

篆

適宜 shìyí suitable; appropriate
宜人 yírén pleasant; delightful
便宜 piányi cheap; inexpensive
不宜 bùyí not suitable; inappropriate

姨

yí
aunt

PICTOPHONETIC CHARACTER The character 姨 is comprised of the female radical 女 and the phonetic element 夷 (yí), referring to "the sisters of one's wife," "the sisters of one's mother," "aunt," and "concubine." 夷 is the combination of 大 (dà, big) and 弓 (gōng, bow). In its ancient forms 大 is the front view of a man, and 弓 the outline of a bow. 夷 shows a man carrying a bow on his shoulder and referred to the ancient non-Han people in Eastern China. Its extended meanings are "barbarian," "foreigner," "to eliminate," "to wipe out," "safe," "smooth," etc.

姨 形聲。從女，夷聲。本義為妻子的姊妹（大姨子、小姨子），引申也指母親的姊妹（姨母、姨夫），與母親年齡相仿但無親屬關係的女性（阿姨）或妾（姨太太）。夷，會意。從大（正面人形），從弓，像人背弓箭形。指古代中原以外的少數民族。

篆

阿姨 āyí aunt; auntie
姨父 yífù husband of mother's sister

姨母 yímǔ mother's sister; maternal aunt
大姨 dàyí mother's eldest sister; aunt

已

yǐ
already

PICTOGRAPH In the Oracle-Bone Inscriptions, 已 looks like a fetus in a head-down position, meaning "to stop," "to cease," "end," and "already." 已, 台, and 以 are cognate characters; in the Oracle-Bone Inscriptions the same character was used to mean 已, 台, and 以, and the three different characters evolved later. Note the slight difference between 已 and 己 (jǐ, oneself).

已 象形。甲骨文、金文、篆文均像頭朝下要出生的胎兒形，引申為已經。

甲 金 ♂ 篆 ♂

已經 yǐjīng already
已故 yǐgù the late; deceased

早已 zǎoyǐ long ago; for a long time
已婚 yǐhūn married

以

yǐ
with

ASSOCIATIVE COMPOUND In the Bronze Inscriptions, the right side of 以 is a person 人 and the left side is a fetus, therefore meaning "rely on." 以 can also mean "according to," "by means of," "with," or "because of."

以 會意。金文字形像頭朝下、快要降生的胎兒，旁邊站著一人。本義指已成形的胎兒，引申為憑藉、原因等。

甲 ♂ 金 이 篆 이

可以 kěyǐ can; may
以前 yǐqián before; ago

所以 suǒyǐ therefore; so
以後 yǐhòu after; later

椅

yǐ
chair

PICTOPHONETIC CHARACTER The character 椅 is made up of the wood radical 木 and the phonetic element 奇 (qí). Originally 椅 meant a kind of tree—idesia—and has been extended to mean "chair." In the Oracle-Bone Inscriptions, 奇 looks like a man riding on a horse. It originally meant "to ride" and has been extended to mean "rare," "strange," "uncanny." The original meaning of 奇, "to ride," has now been taken by 騎 (qí).

椅 形聲。從木，奇聲。本義指一種叫山桐子的樹，引申為椅子，例如籐椅、躺椅、轉椅等。奇，會意。甲骨文像人騎在馬背上，是騎的本字。引申義為奇異的、特殊的等。也有學者認為奇字像一人拄拐單腳站立。

篆 椅

椅子 yǐzi chair
轉椅 zhuànyǐ swivel chair

躺椅 tǎngyǐ reclining chair; deck chair
輪椅 lúnyǐ wheelchair

易

yì
easy

ASSOCIATIVE COMPOUND In the Oracle-Bone Inscriptions, the character 易 looks like pouring water from one vessel to another, meaning "change," "exchange," "easy," etc. In Regular Script, 易 differs greatly from its original Oracle-Bone form. The upper part of 易 is instead the vessel, with the lower part representing the pouring water.

易 會意。甲骨文像把水從一個容器中倒入另一容器中。本義為給予，引申為改變、容易等。

甲 〔金〕 金 〔篆〕 篆 易

容易 róngyì easy
交易 jiāoyì (business) transaction; deal

易學 yìxué easy to learn
貿易 màoyì (commercial) trade

意

yì
meaning

ASSOCIATIVE COMPOUND The character 意 consists of 音 (yīn, sound; music) and 心 (xīn, heart), signifying the sound of one's heart beating. 意 can also mean "desire," "intention," "will," "thought," "meaning," "expect," etc.

意 會意。從心，從音；音亦聲。用心音指心裏的想法。

篆 意

意思 yìsi meaning
意見 yìjiàn idea; opinion; objection

同意 tóngyì to agree; to consent
注意 zhùyì to pay attention to

X - Z

yīn
because

ASSOCIATIVE COMPOUND The character 因 looks like a figure (大) laying on a mat (囗), meaning "rely on," "on the basis of," or "in accordance with." It also extends to mean "cause," "reason," or "because."

因 會意。從囗，從大。像人仰臥於席上。意為憑藉、依靠等。

甲 因 金 因 篆 因

因為 yīnwèi because
原因 yuányīn cause; reason

因此 yīncǐ therefore; thus; consequently
基因 jīyīn gene

yīn
sound; music

ASSOCIATIVE COMPOUND 音 and 言 (yán) are cognate characters. In their ancient forms, both resemble a tongue sticking out from a mouth, representing a sound made by the mouth. Later the two characters diverged in usage. 言 refers to words or speech, while 音 means (musical) sound. In Regular Script, 音 is the combination of 立 (lì, stand) and 曰 (yuē, speak; say). In the Oracle-Bone and Bronze Inscriptions, the character 立 depicts a person standing on the ground, and 曰 signifies the sound coming out of the mouth. 音 also appears in 識/识 (shí, to recognize).

音 會意。音与言同源，是由同一個甲骨文字演變來的。金文在口中加一橫，表示發音時舌頭的位置。

甲 音 金 音 篆 音

聲音 shēngyīn voice; sound
音樂 yīnyuè music

發音 fāyīn pronunciation; to emit sound
拼音 pīnyīn *pinyin* (Chinese romanization)

yǐn
to drink

ASSOCIATIVE COMPOUND In Seal Script, 飲 portrays a person with his hands around a wine jar from which he is about to drink. The original meaning of 飲 is "to drink" and has been extended to mean "beverage." In Regular Script, 飲 is the combination of the food radical 食 and 欠 (qiàn). In the Oracle-Bone Inscriptions, 欠 looks like a kneeling person breathing with mouth wide open, meaning "to inhale," "to yawn," or "to lack." Characters containing 欠 often have something to do with the mouth. In the simplified 饮, the food radical 食 is simplified to 饣.

飲 會意。甲骨文像人手扶酒壜，俯首張口飲酒狀。篆文從食，從欠。本義為喝，引申為飲料（冷飲、飲食）等。欠，象形。像人張口出氣形。欠在飲字中像人張口飲酒。在簡化字饮中食字旁簡化為饣，屬於偏旁類推簡化。

篆 飲

飲茶 yǐnchá to drink tea
冷飲 lěngyǐn cold drink

飲料 yǐnliào beverage
飲食 yǐnshí diet; food and drink

印

yìn
to print

ASSOCIATIVE COMPOUND In the Oracle-Bone and Bronze Inscriptions, the character 印 depicts a hand (top left part) over a kneeling person (bottom right part), indicating the act of "pressing." The extended meanings of 印 include "imprint," "trace," "seal," "mark," "to print" "tally," and "to conform with."

印 會意。古文字上從手，下有一人跪在地上，像一人以手按壓另一人而使其跪著。本義為按壓，引申為印記、痕跡、圖章、印刷（印書、印報）、符合（心心相印）等。

甲 𣢮 金 𡲬 篆 𡲬

印象 yìnxiàng impression
打印 dǎyìn to print

手印 shǒuyìn handprint
複印 fùyìn to copy; to photocopy

英

yīng
flower; hero;
England

PICTOGRAPH 英 is the combination of the grass radical ⺾ and the phonetic 央 (yāng, center). Its original meaning was "flower" and extended meanings include "hero" and "outstanding." Additionally, in Chinese "England" is translated as 英國/国 (yīngguó) based on its English pronunciation. The grass radical ⺾ derives from the character 艸 (cǎo, grass). In the Oracle-Bone Inscriptions, 央 looks like a figure carrying something on a shoulder pole. Since the figure stands in the middle, 央 means "middle" or "center." In Regular Script, 央 resembles a figure from the front (dà, 大) with something on its shoulders.

英 形聲。從⺾，央聲。本義指花，引申為美好、傑出、才能出眾。央，古文像一人挑擔，意為正中、中心。

篆 𦳅

英雄 yīngxióng hero
精英 jīngyīng elite

英俊 yīngjùn handsome
英明 yīngmíng wise; brilliant

應/应

yīng
should

yìng
to respond

PICTOPHONETIC CHARACTER The character 應 consists of the heart radical 心 and phonetic element 雁 (yīng), meaning "should," "ought to," "need," or "agree to." When 應 is pronounced as yìng, it means "to respond to," "to answer," "to echo," or "to cope with." 雁 is an associative character, referring to eagles, hawks, or falcons. One can find the short-tailed bird radical 隹 in the character. The simplified character 应 is derived from the cursive version of the character 應.

應 形聲。從心，雁聲，應字第一聲時意為應當、應允等。第四聲時為回答、呼應、配合等。雁，會意。指一群獵鷹或魚鷹之類。簡體字应是繁體字應的草書楷化字。

金 � 篆 𥓲 草 应

應該 yīnggāi ought to; should
適應 shìyìng to adapt; to fit; to suit

應有 yīngyǒu due; proper; deserved
反應 fǎnyìng to react; to respond; reaction

The Way of Chinese Characters

yíng
to welcome

ASSOCIATIVE AND PICTOPHONETIC COMPOUND The character 迎 consists of the walk radical 辶 and the semantic and phonetic component 卬 (áng, to hold one's head high), meaning "to see somebody face to face," "to move toward," "to go and meet," "to greet," "to receive," "to welcome," and "to pander to." In Seal Script, the left part of 卬 is a man standing, and the right part is a man kneeling, meaning "to raise one's head," "to lift," "to hold high," "high," "soaring," and "high-priced."

迎 會意兼形聲。從辵（辶），從卬（áng，仰著、擡起），卬亦聲。迎本義為對面相逢，引申義有對著、向著、迎接、逢迎等。卬，會意。篆文像一人站著，一人跪著，意思有擡起、仰著、高漲、昂貴等。古時是昂的異體字。

歡迎 huānyíng to welcome (happily)   迎合 yínghé to cater to; to fawn over
迎新 yíngxīn to see in the New Year; to welcome new arrivals; to receive new students

---

yǐng
shadow

ASSOCIATIVE AND PICTOPHONETIC COMPOUND The character 影 consists of the radical 彡 (彡 can indicate decorative patterns; hair; beards; carvings; shadows) and 景 (jǐng, sunlight; view) as both the phonetic and signifying element, meaning "shadow," "reflection," and "film." 景 consists of 日 (rì, sun) and 京 (jīng, capital). In the Oracle-Bone and Bronze Inscriptions, 京 looks like a palatial structure built on a terrace. 京 originally meant "man-made highland." Later it came to mean "national capital."

影 形聲兼會意。三撇意為飾紋、光影等。景（日光），有影子就有光，景也兼表聲。景，形聲。從日，從京（高）。表示太陽高照。京，指事。甲骨文、金文中像在高丘上建宮觀之形，有高大、國都之意。

京 甲  金 篆 京

影子 yǐngzi shadow; reflection   攝影 shèyǐng take a photograph; photography; shoot a film
電影 diànyǐng movie; film   合影 héyǐng group photo; to have a group photo taken

---

yǒng
swimming

ASSOCIATIVE AND PICTOPHONETIC COMPOUND The character 泳 consists of the water radical 氵 and the semantic and phonetic element 永 (yǒng, long), meaning "swimming" or "types of swimming." In its ancient forms, 永 represents a person swimming in water. Originally 永 meant "swimming," and later came to mean "long stream," "long in time," "forever," "perpetual," and "permanent." 泳 is a later invention used to represent the original meaning of 永.

泳 會意兼形聲。從氵，從永，永亦兼表聲。泳是永字的加旁分化字。本義是在水中游泳。永，會意。甲骨文從人，像人在水流中游泳狀。本義為游泳，引申為水流長，時間永久、永遠等。本義游泳則加義符氵而寫作泳。

游泳 yóuyǒng swimming; to swim   蛙泳 wāyǒng breaststroke
自由泳 zìyóuyǒng freestyle   仰泳 yǎngyǒng backstroke

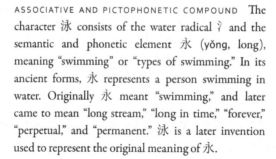

用
yòng
to use

PICTOGRAPH In its ancient forms, the character 用 resembles a wooden tub or bucket. Since tubs and buckets are often used in daily life, 用 extended to mean "use," "operate," "need," and "with."

用　象形。甲骨文、金文均像木桶形狀。因古人日常生活中常使用木桶，引申為使用。

甲 凵 金 用 篆 用

用法 yòngfǎ usage
不用 búyòng need not

有用 yǒuyòng useful
用功 yònggōng diligent; study hard

游
yóu
to swim

ASSOCIATIVE AND PICTOPHONETIC COMPOUND In the Oracle-Bone and Bronze Inscriptions, the character 斿 (yóu) is the combination of 㫃 (yǎn, flags flying) and 子 (zǐ, person; son; child), referring to "streamer" or "marching under a flag." In Seal Script, the water radical 氵 is added to the left of 斿 to refer to touring on water. The meanings of 游 include "to float," "to swim," "to drift," "to wander about," "roving," "itinerant," "to associate with," and "part of a river." In the past 斿 was used as an alternative of 游. Please compare 斿 with 旅 (lǚ, to travel).

游　會意兼形聲。在甲骨文、金文中，斿（yóu）從㫃（旌旗飄揚），從子。意指旌旗的垂飾物或持旗巡行。篆文在斿字左邊加氵成游，本義為在水中巡游，引申為游泳、閒逛、不固定的、交際、河流的一段等。古時斿也作為游的異體字。

甲 斿 金 斿 篆 游

游泳池 yóuyǒngchí swimming pool
中游 zhōngyóu middle reaches; middling state

上游 shàngyóu upriver; advanced position
下游 xiàyóu downriver; backward position

遊／游
yóu
to roam; to travel

ASSOCIATIVE AND PICTOPHONETIC COMPOUND In the Oracle-Bone Inscriptions, the character 斿 (yóu) is the combination of 㫃 and 子. Later, a walk radical 辶 was added to 斿, resulting in a combination that refers to moving/walking on the ground. The meanings of 遊 include "to travel," "to roam, "to stroll," "to make friends," "to lobby," etc. The primary meaning of 游 is "to swim" (see its entry above). Today 游 is also used as the simplified form of 遊, and in simplified characters conveys the meanings of both 遊 and 游.

遊　會意兼形聲。在甲骨文、金文中，斿（yóu）從㫃，從子。後在斿字下加止（表示腳），楷書改為辶，本義為在陸地上行走，引申義有遊歷、遊玩、遊逛、交遊、遊說等。游字意為游泳、河流的一段等。現在用為遊的簡化字，包含了遊、游兩字的意思。

甲 斿 金 斿

旅遊 lǚyóu to travel
遊行 yóuxíng parade; demonstration

導遊 dǎoyóu tour guide
遊客 yóukè tourist

yóu
post; mail

ASSOCIATIVE COMPOUND In Seal Script, the character 郵 is the combination of 垂 (chuí, hang down; frontier) and 邑 (yì, town; city), originally referring to the inns for couriers who carried mail on horseback and extending to mean "post," "mail," "postal," "postman," etc.

郵 會意。從阝（阝 指 邑，即居住區域），從 垂（在此義為邊陲）。 郵本義指古代供信差食 宿的驛站。引申義為郵 遞、郵差等。

篆 𨜂

郵局 yóujú post office
郵件 yóujiàn mail; post

郵票 yóupiào (postage) stamp
郵遞員 yóudìyuán mail carrier

友

yǒu
friend

ASSOCIATIVE COMPOUND In its ancient form, the character 友 delineates two right hands together, to represent two people shaking hands, as friends would. As you can find in the **Basic Radicals** Section, 又 (yòu) means "right hand." In Regular Script, the right hand in the upper part of 友 looks slightly different, but the one underneath remains the same as the radical. In ancient times, people used 朋 (péng, friend) and 友 separately. Although they both mean "friend," 友 refers to a closer friend than 朋.

友 會意。甲骨文以兩人 右手握在一起來指志同 道合的朋友。

甲 𠬶 金 𠂇𠂇 篆 𢓊

朋友 péngyou friend
交友 jiāoyǒu to make friends

友好 yǒuhǎo friendly; amicable
網友 wǎngyǒu online friend

有

yǒu
to have;
to exist

ASSOCIATIVE AND PICTOPHONETIC COMPOUND In the Bronze Inscriptions and Seal Script, the character 有 delineates a right hand (yòu, 又) holding a piece of meat (yuè, 月), meaning "to possess" or "to have." 又 also serves as the phonetic component of the character. The character 月 means moon, but when used as a radical often means "flesh," as in the characters 腿 (tuǐ, leg), 臉/脸 (liǎn, face), 腦/脑 (nǎo, brain), and 腳/脚 (jiǎo, foot). Be careful not to confuse 有 (yǒu, to have) and 友 (yǒu, friend).

有 會意兼形聲。金文、 篆文從又（右手）持肉 （肉月旁），意為持有。

金 𠧪 篆 𠂇

有錢 yǒuqián rich; wealthy
有意思 yǒu yìsi interesting; enjoyable; fun

有名 yǒumíng famous; well-known
有時候 yǒushíhou sometimes

The Way of Chinese Characters

右

yòu
right

ASSOCIATIVE COMPOUND In the Bronze Inscriptions, the character 右 depicts a hand stretching toward the right with a mouth underneath, signifying that one's mouth and hands are ready to help. Its original meanings were "to assist," "to protect," and "to bless," but now it is used to mean "the right side," "the west side," "right-wing," "the Right," and "precedence."

右 會意。從又（右手），從口，表示手口相助，本義為佑助，此意後由佑字取代，右則用為右邊、西、右翼、保守或反動、重要等。

金 𠂇 篆 𠂇

右手 yòushǒu right hand
往右拐 wǎngyòu guǎi to turn right

右邊 yòubiān the right-hand side
右派 yòupài the right wing

語/语

yǔ
language

PICTOPHONETIC CHARACTER The character 語 combines the word radical 言 and the phonetic component 吾 (wú), meaning "words," "to say," or "language." 吾 consists of the phonetic component 五 (wǔ, five) and the mouth radical 口. In classical Chinese 吾 is used to mean "I" or "my." The character 語 looks like five people opening their mouths to speak five different languages! The speech radical is simplified to form 语.

語 形聲。從言，吾聲，意為談論、談話等。吾，金文從口，五聲，用作第一人稱。簡體字语的部首簡化。

篆 𧩻

語言 yǔyán language
口語 kǒuyǔ colloquial speech; spoken language

漢語 hànyǔ Chinese language
語法 yǔfǎ grammar

寓

yù
residence

PICTOPHONETIC CHARACTER The character 寓 consists of the roof radical 宀 and the phonetic component 禺 (yú), meaning "to dwell," "to reside," "residence," and "to imply." In the Bronze Inscriptions, 禺 depicts a big-headed ghost-like ape, referring to a kind of monkey.

寓 形聲。從宀（房屋），禺（yú）聲。本義為寄居、居住，引申為住所、寄託（寓言—指有所寄託的話）。禺，象形。像頭部似鬼的一種大猩猩。現多用為字中表音的一部分，如遇、愚、寓、偶等。

金 禺 古 寓 篆 寓

公寓 gōngyù apartment
寓言 yùyán fable

寓所 yùsuǒ place of residence
寓意 yùyì implied meaning; moral

Z - X

預 / 预

yù
in advance; beforehand

ASSOCIAIVE AND PICTOPHONETIC CHARACTER   The character 預 consists of the radical 頁 (yè, page; head) and the phonetic component 予 (yǔ, give; push forward), originally meaning "a head thrusting forward." Its extended meanings include "beforehand," "in advance," and "to prepare." In the Oracle-Bone Inscriptions, 頁 resembles a person with an oversized head. The original meaning of 頁 was "head" with the extended meaning "page." In Seal Script, 予 resembles a hand pushing something to others, meaning "to give" or "grant." 頁, the right part of the simplified character 预, derives from the cursive style of 頁.

預 會意兼形聲。篆文從頁（人頭），從予（此處有前伸意），表示把頭伸到前面，引申為預先、參預等。予，象形。篆文像以手推物給他人狀，本義為給予。簡體字预右邊的页是由繁體字頁的草書楷化而來。

篆 𩑺

預備 yùbèi to prepare; to get ready
預報 yùbào forecast

預習 yùxí to prepare a lesson before class
預言 yùyán to predict; prophecy

元

yuán
yuan (Chinese monetary unit)

EXPLICIT CHARACTER   In its ancient forms, the character 元 depicts two horizontal strokes on the top of a person, meaning "head (of a person)." The extended meanings of 元 include "the beginning," "the first," "primary," "principal," "chief," "fundamental," "component," "element," "monetary unit," and "the Yuan Dynasty (1279–1368)."

元 指事。從一，從兀，本義為人頭，引申為生命萬物存在的根本因素、開始的、為首的、主要的、貨幣單位、元朝（1206-1368）等。兀（wù），指事。從一在人字上，本義為高而平，引申為高聳、光禿。

甲 ⋎ 金 ⋎ 篆 𣅏

元首 yuánshǒu head of state
美元 měiyuán U.S. dollar

元音 yuányīn vowel
日元 rìyuán Japanese yen

員 / 员

yuán
personnel

ASSOCIATIVE COMPOUND   In its ancient forms, 員 resembles a tripod with a round mouth on top, meaning "round" or "circular." Later 員 was used to mean "member," "personnel," or "a person engaged in some field of activity," and 圓 was created to mean "round" or "circle." In Regular Script, 員 combines 口 (kǒu, mouth) and 貝 (bèi, cowry shell), suggesting a person conducting business by talking with others. 貝 is simplified to form the character 员.

員 會意。甲骨文、金文中貝像鼎形，口是鼎口。本義指圓形，引申為人的數額以及從事某種職業的人。簡體字员中的贝字簡化。

甲 𪔅 金 𪔅 篆 員

員工 yuán'gōng staff; personnel; employee
售貨員 shòuhuòyuán salesperson

服務員 fúwùyuán waiter; waitress; attendant
演員 yǎnyuán actor or actress; performer

The Way of Chinese Characters

圓/圆

yuán
round

ASSOCIATIVE AND PICTOPHONETIC COMPOUND The character 圓 combines the enclosure radical 囗 and the semantic and phonetic element 員 (yuán). In its ancient form, 員 resembles a tripod with a round mouth on top, thereby meaning "round" or "circle." Later 員 came to mean "personnel" (see previous entry) and 圓 was created to mean "round" or "circle." The extended meanings of 圓 include "spherical," "full," "complete," "satisfactory," "tactful," and "a monetary unit." The simplified character 贝 (bèi, cowry shell) derives from the cursive style of the traditional 貝 and is always written as 贝 in simplified characters, such as 圆.

圓　會意兼形聲。 從囗，從員，員亦聲。本義為圓型，引申為球形、周全、使圓滿、靈活變通等。員，指事。甲骨文、金文中貝像鼎形，口是鼎口。本義指圓形，後借用為人的數額以及從事某種職業的人。員是圓的本字。貝字簡化為贝，簡化字圆屬偏旁類推簡化。

 篆

湯圓 tāngyuán glutinous rice ball
圓滑 yuánhuá cunning; slick

圓心 yuánxīn the center of a circle
圓珠筆 yuánzhūbǐ ballpoint pen

園/园

yuán
garden

PICTOPHONETIC CHARACTER The character 園 consists of an enclosure radical 囗 and the phonetic element 袁 (yuán), meaning "garden" or "park." In Seal Script, the bottom part of 袁 is 衣 (yī), a garment; the middle part resembles a ring and the top part the ring's band, meaning "quartz ring" or "long garment." Today 袁 is only used as a surname. In the simplified character 园, 元 (yuán, first; basic) replaces 袁 (yuán), for the two have the same pronunciation.

園　形聲。從囗，袁聲。本義為種果木、花草、菜蔬的地方，引申義又指供人休憩、遊覽、娛樂的地方。袁，會意。篆文上像系帶，中為玉佩，下乃衣服，意指胸前挂玉。本義為環玉，引申為環繞、長袍等，而現只用作姓。簡體字园以元代替袁，屬同音替代字。

 篆

花園 huāyuán garden
校園 xiàoyuán school campus

公園 gōngyuán park
園丁 yuándīng gardener

遠/远

yuǎn
far

PICTOPHONETIC CHARACTER The character 遠 contains the walk radical 辶 (辵) and the phonetic element 袁 (yuán) and refers to a long distance one needs to walk. The meanings of 遠 include "far," "distant," "remote," "profound," or "to keep at a distance." In the simplified character 远, 元 (yuán, first; basic) replaces 袁 (yuán) as the phonetic element since their pronunciations are the same.

遠　形聲。從辶（辵），袁聲。本義為要走很長距離的路，引申義有距離長、時間久、關係疏、差別大等。簡體字远把聲旁袁改為元，屬於同音替代。清代已有此寫法。

 金　篆

遠方 yuǎnfāng distant place
長遠 chángyuǎn long-term

遠見 yuǎnjiàn foresight
望遠鏡 wàngyuǎnjìng telescope

yuàn
yard

PICTOPHONETIC CHARACTER The character 院 consists of the mound radical 阝 and the phonetic 完 (wán), referring to "courtyard," "yard," or "compound." 院 is also used to designate institutes, colleges, hospitals, and certain government offices and public places. 完 combines the roof radical 宀 and the phonetic element 元 (yuán). It originally meant "a house that is nice and intact," from which the ancient Chinese derived the meanings "whole," "intact," "perfect," "complete," and "to finish."

院　形聲。從阝（阝 在字左意為阜，常與土、建築有關），完聲。本義指有圍牆的空地，引申為院子，也指某些學術、政府機構與公共場所。完，　形聲。　從宀，元聲。本義指房屋完好無缺，引申義為完整、完全、完美、完成等。

金 🖋 篆 🖋

院子 yuànzi courtyard
學院 xuéyuàn college; institute
醫院 yīyuàn hospital
電影院 diànyǐngyuàn cinema; movie theater

---

yuàn
wish; hope

PICTOPHONETIC CHARACTER Originally 願 and 愿 were two different characters. 願 combines 頁 (yè, head; page) with the phonetic element 原 (yuán). Its original meaning was "big head," and was later borrowed to mean "wish," "hope," "desire," and "ambition." 愿 is the combination of 心 (xīn, heart) and the phonetic 原 (yuán), meaning "honest" and "respectful and cautious." Today 愿 is used as the simplified form of 願. In the Bronze Inscriptions, 原 consists of 厂 (hǎn, cliff) and 泉 (quán, spring), depicting a spring coming out of a cliff and originally meaning "river's source." Extended meanings include "primary," "original," etc.

願　形聲。願與愿原本意思不同。願，從頁，原聲。本義為大頭，引申為願望、願意等。愿，形聲。從心，原聲。意為老實、恭謹。簡化字用愿替代願，屬同音替代。原，會意。從厂（hǎn 山崖），從泉。像泉水從山間流出。本義為水的源頭，引申為最初、原來等。

金 🖋 篆 🖋 🖋

願望 yuànwàng desire; wish; aspiration
願意 yuànyì to be willing to
許願 xǔyuàn to make a wish
自願 zìyuàn voluntary

yuē
agreement;
appointment

PICTOPHONETIC CHARACTER The character 約 is composed of the silk radical 糸 and the phonetic symbol 勺 (sháo), meaning "to tie" or "bundle up." The extended meanings of 約 include "keep within bounds," "restrain," "agreement," "to make an appointment," "ask or invite in advance," etc. In the Bronze Inscriptions, 勺 is the pictograph of a ladle. You will also see 勺 in the character 的 (de, a possessive or modifying particle). The silk radical is simplified to form the character 约.

約　形聲。從糸，勺聲。本義為捆縛，引申為約束、預先約定等。勺，象形，金文中像勺瓢形。簡體字约的部首簡化。

篆 🖋

約會 yuēhuì appointment; engagement; date
條約 tiáoyuē treaty; pact
大約 dàyuē approximately
節約 jiéyuē to economize; frugal

越

yuè
to exceed

PICTOPHONETIC CHARACTER The character 越 consists of the walk radical 走 and the phonetic element 戉 (yuè), meaning "to cross over," "to climb over," "to exceed," "vehement," and "the more... the more...." In its ancient forms 戉 is the pictograph of an ancient weapon similar to a big broad axe, meaning "battle-ax" or "halberd."

越　形聲。從走，戉（yuè）聲。本義為越過，引申義有超出、激昂，作為副詞意思是愈、更加。戉，象形。像一種形似大斧的古代兵器。

篆 越

越過 yuèguò to cross over; to transcend
越來越 yuèláiyuè more and more

越…越… yuè... yuè... the more... the more...
越南 Yuènán Vietnam

樂/乐

yuè
music

lè
happy

PICTOGRAPH In the Oracle-Bone Inscriptions, the character 樂 consists of 幺幺 (two strings) as the upper part and 木 (mù, wood) in the lower half, indicating a stringed musical instrument. In the Bronze Inscriptions, the representation of a "pick (for playing string instruments)" (白) is added between the strings. The original meaning of 樂 is musical instrument. Extended meanings are "music" (yuè), and "happy" (lè). The simplified character 乐 is derived from the cursive form of 樂.

樂　象形。甲骨文從絲，從木。表示將絲弦絣于木上，意指琴瑟之類的樂器。簡體字乐字是繁體字樂的草書楷化字。

甲 樂　金 樂　篆 樂　草 乐

音樂 yīnyuè music
快樂 kuàilè happy; joful

樂器 yuèqì musical instrument
可樂 kělè Cola; amusing; entertaining

運/运

yùn
to move

PICTOPHONETIC CHARACTER The character 運 contains the walk radical 辶 and the phonetic component 軍 (jūn), meaning "to move." Its extended meanings are "to transport," "to ship," "to utilize," "to apply," "fate," and "luck." In Seal Script, 軍 is the combination of 車 (chē, vehicle) and 勹 (bāo, to wrap), representing an encampment of troops and meaning "army," "military," or "arms." In the Oracle-Bone and Bronze Inscriptions, 車 depicts a complete chariot. In Seal Script and Regular Script, 車 is simplified to one wheel on its axle. In the simplified character 运, 云 (yún) replaces 軍 (jūn) in 運 since their pronunciations are similar.

運　形聲。從辶，軍聲。本義為移動，引申義為運輸、運用、運氣等。軍，會意，篆文從車，從勹，本義為駐扎（以車圍住扎營），引申為軍隊，士兵等。簡體字运把繁體運的聲旁軍改為云字。

篆 運　車甲 　金 車　篆 車

搬運 bānyùn to transport; to carry
運動 yùndòng sports; to exercise

托運 tuōyùn consign for shipment; to check (baggage)
運氣 yùnqi fortune; luck

在

zài
at; in; on

ASSOCIATIVE AND PICTOPHONETIC COMPOUND The character 在 consists of 土 (tǔ, earth; soil) as the radical and 才 (cái, just) as both a phonetic and signifying element. In its ancient form, 才 is the pictograph of a seed just sprouting from the ground, therefore meaning "just," "ability," etc. The character 在 uses the sprout breaking through the soil to indicate the existence of something. Therefore, 在 means "existence," "present," or may be used to mean "at," "in," or "on."

在 形聲兼會意。從土，從才；才亦聲。像草木從土中長出，以此表示存在。才，象形。像小苗破土而出，本義指才長出的草木。

甲 金 篆 在

存在 cúnzài to exist; to be; existence
現在 xiànzài now; at present

所在 suǒzài place; location; whereabouts
正在 zhèngzài in the process of (doing something)

再

zài
again

ASSOCIATIVE COMPOUND In its ancient form, the character 再 looks like two fish in a basket, meaning "twice" or "once again." In Regular Script, the upper part of 再 resembles the handle of the basket, the middle part resembles the bodies of two fish, and the lower part resembles the fish tails.

再 會意。甲骨文中其上下橫為二，當中像簍中的魚形，意指提兩條魚。本義為第二次，兩次。一説像兩魚相遇狀。

甲 金 篆 再

再見 zàijiàn goodbye; see you again later
不再 búzài no more; no longer

再三 zàisān over and over again
再説 zàishuō put off until later; moreover

糟

zāo
messy

PICTOPHONETIC CHARACTER The character 糟 is comprised of the rice radical 米 and the phonetic 曹 (cáo), meaning "distiller's grains" or "pickled with grains or wine." The extended meanings of 糟 are "rotten" and "messy." In the Oracle-Bone Inscriptions, 米 resembles grains scattered around a rack. You will also encounter 米 in the character 氣 (qì, air). In its ancient form, 曹 looks like two lanterns hanging over a doorway, originally meaning "pair" or "twin." Now it is primarily used as a family name.

糟 形聲。從米，曹聲，本義為酒渣、酒糟，引申義為糟粕、腐爛、壞了、浪費等。米，象形，甲骨文中像散落的米粒。曹，會意。甲骨文從二東，從口，像門口挂著兩個燈籠。本義為雙、偶。現通常用作姓。

篆 糟

酒糟 jiǔzāo distillers' grains
亂七八糟 luànqī bāzāo everything in disorder

糟糕 zāogāo oh no; too bad; how terrible
糟蹋 zāotà to waste; to ruin; to spoil

The Way of Chinese Characters

早
zǎo
early

ASSOCIATIVE COMPOUND 早 looks like the sun rising to the top of a crossed column, an instrument for solar observation (sun dial). The meanings of 早 include "morning," "early," "long ago," etc.

早 會意。篆文從日，從甲（原為測量日光的儀器），表示太陽升到甲之上，意為早晨。

金 ♀ 篆 ♀

早上 zǎoshang early morning	早飯 zǎofàn breakfast
提早 tízǎo ahead of schedule	早晚 zǎowǎn morning and evening; sooner or later

---

澡
zǎo
bath

PICTOPHONETIC CHARACTER The character 澡 consists of the water radical 氵 and the phonetic element 喿 (zào). It originally meant "to wash one's hands" but now is used to mean "bath." In the Bronze Inscriptions and Seal Script, 喿 delineates a tree with three mouths, signifying birds chirping in a tree. The original meaning of 喿 was the sound of birds or insects; "clamorous," "noisy," and "a confusion of voices" are its extended meanings.

澡 形聲。從水，喿（zào）聲。喿，會意。金文從三口，從木，指群鳥在樹上鳴叫。引申為嘈雜。

篆 澡

洗澡 xǐzǎo to bathe; to take a shower	澡盆 zǎopén bath tub
澡堂 zǎotáng public baths	沖澡 chōngzǎo to take a shower

怎
zěn
how

PICTOPHONETIC CHARACTER The character 怎 consists of the heart radical 心 and the phonetic symbol 乍 (zhà/zuò), meaning "why" or "how." In the Oracle-Bone and Bronze Inscriptions, 乍 looks like the stitching of a collar. The original meaning of 乍 was "to make" or "to do," and later it extended to mean "for the first time," "spread," or "abruptly."

怎 形聲。代詞，表示疑問。從心，乍聲。乍，甲骨文、金文像用針縫製衣領。

怎麼 zěnme how?; what?	怎麼樣 zěnmeyàng how about?; how are things?
怎麼辦 zěnme bàn What's to be done?	不怎麼樣 bù zěnmeyàng not up to much

站

zhàn
stand; station

PICTOPHONETIC CHARACTER 站 combines the radical 立 (lì, stand) and the phonetic element 占 (zhàn, divination), meaning "stand," "halt," "stop," "station," etc. In the Oracle-Bone and Bronze Inscriptions, the upper part of 立 is the front view of a person (大), while the bottom stroke represents the ground. 立 is also used in 位 (wèi, a polite measure word for people). The character 占 consists of 卜 (bǔ, a crack on an oracle bone) and 口 (kǒu, mouth), referring to the interpretation of oracle-bone cracks for divination. 占 is also the right part of 點 (diǎn, dot; o'clock).

站 形聲。從立，占聲。
立，會意。甲骨文、金
文從大（正面人形），
從一(指地面)，表示人
站在地上。占，會意。
上從卜（龜甲燒裂后之
兆紋），下從口，意指
觀察兆紋解說兇吉。

站住 zhànzhù Stop!; stand firmly
加油站 jiāyóuzhàn gas station

車站 chēzhàn rail station; bus stop
網站 wǎngzhàn website

張/张

zhāng
(MW for flat objects);
(surname)

PICTOPHONETIC CHARACTER The character 張 consists of the bow radical 弓 (see 弓 gōng in **Basic Radicals**) and the phonetic element 長 (cháng, long). Its original meaning was "to draw a bow," and extended meanings include "open up," "spread," and "display." 張 is also used as a measure word for things with flat surfaces. In ancient writing, the character 長 looks similar to 老, as it also resembles an old figure with long hair and a walking stick. In the simplified character 张, the right part 长 is derived from the cursive version of the traditional character 長.

張 形聲。從弓，長聲。
本義指把弦綳在弓上，
引申為拉開弓。引申義
有張開、擴張等。長，
象形。甲骨文中像一長
髮長鬚的老人弓腰拄拐
形。簡體字张的右部长
是由繁體字長的草書楷
化而來。

篆 𢎥 長甲 𠃌 金 𠃌 草 长

張開 zhāngkāi to open up; to spread; to extend
主張 zhǔzhāng to advocate; proposal

紙張 zhǐzhāng paper
緊張 jǐnzhāng nervous; intense; tense

找

zhǎo
to look for; to seek

ASSOCIATIVE COMPOUND The character 找 consists of the hand radical 扌 and the character 戈 (gē, dagger-axe), which may suggest searching for a dagger-axe with one's hand. The primary meaning of 找 is "to look for" or "to seek." 找 can also mean "to give (a customer) change."

找 形聲。從扌，戈聲，
像用手找戈。

找到 zhǎodào to find
找錢 zhǎoqián to give change

找出 zhǎochū to find out; to search out
自找 zìzhǎo to suffer from one's own actions

The Way of Chinese Characters

照

zhào
photograph; to
shine

ASSOCIATIVE AND PICTOPHONETIC COMPOUND The
character 照 consists of the signifying parts 日 (rì,
sun) and 灬 (fire radical), and the phonetic element 召
(zhāo, call), meaning "shine," "illuminate," "reflect," etc.
The character 召 combines 口 (kǒu, mouth) and the
phonetic component 刀 (dāo, knife), meaning "to call,"
and "to summon."

照 會意兼形聲。金文左
邊像手持火把狀，右邊
召是聲旁。篆文改為火
字旁，昭聲，昭也有日
光明亮之意。

金 𤐫 篆 𤌩

照明 zhàomíng lighting; illumination
照片 zhàopiàn photograph; picture

照相 zhàoxiàng to take a photograph
護照 hùzhào passport

折

zhé
to fold

ASSOCIATIVE COMPOUND In the Oracle-Bone
Inscriptions, the character 折 depicts an axe 斤 (left
part) and a tree hacked in the middle (right part),
meaning "to break" or "to fracture." In Regular Script,
the hand radical 扌 replaces the broken tree in 折. The
extended meanings of 折 are "to bend," "to fold," "to
suffer loss," "convinced," "discount," "accounts book,"
etc. In its ancient forms, 斤 looks like an axe with a
crooked handle, and later became a unit of weight in
traditional Chinese measurements. 斤 is also in 所
(suǒ, place), 近 (jìn, near) and 新 (xīn, new).

折 會意。甲骨文像以斤
（斧頭）將木砍斷。楷
書左邊改為扌旁，表示以
手持斧將物砍斷。本義為
折斷、弄斷，引申義有折
疊、彎曲、損失、信服、
折扣等。斤，象形。甲骨
文像一把橫刃斧頭。本義
為斧，引申為重量單位。
以斤作為意符的字本義往
往與斧頭有關。

甲 𣂒 金 𣂤 篆 𣂢

骨折 gǔzhé bone fracture
折扣 zhékòu discount

轉折點 zhuǎnzhédiǎn turning point
打折 dǎzhé to give a discount

者

zhě
(auxiliary
verb)

ASSOCIATIVE COMPOUND In the Oracle-Bone and
Bronze Inscriptions, the character 者 represents food
cooking in a wok, and meant "burn" or "kindle." Later
者 became primarily used as an auxiliary word after a
verb or adjective to indicate a class of persons or things,
such as in 讀/读者(dúzhě, reader) and 老者 (lǎozhě,
old person). In Regular Script, the upper part of 者 is
the same as that of 老, and the bottom part is 曰. 者 is
also part of 都 (dōu, all).

者 會意。甲骨文、金文
中上像架起的木架與水
蒸汽，下從火。本義為
燒、煮，後常用在形容
詞、動詞後以表示某類
人或事物。

甲 𦓀 金 𦓁 篆 𦓂

或者 huòzhě or; eiher... or...
學者 xuézhě scholar

記者 jìzhě reporter; journalist
讀者 dúzhě reader

這/这

zhè/zhèi
this

PICTOPHONETIC CHARACTER The character 這 is a combination of the walk radical 辶 and 言 (yán, word; to speak), indicating the action of walking somewhere to speak. 這 originally meant to "go to a certain place," "meet and welcome with words," and came to mean "here" and "this." The walk radical 辶 is often used in characters pertaining to movement with the feet, e.g., 進/进 (jìn, enter), 過/过 (guò, pass), and 逛 (guàng, stroll). In the simplified character 这, 文 replaces 言.

這 形聲。從辶，表示前去；從言，表示以言語相迎。本義為前往、迎接。簡體字这以文取代言，屬符號替代字。清代已見此字。

篆 𨑰

這裏/裡 zhèlǐ here
這些 zhèxiē these

這個 zhège this; this one
這麼 zhème so; this way; like this

針/针

zhēn
needle

ASSOCIATIVE COMPOUND The character 針 is composed of the gold/metal radical 金 and the semantic component 十 that resembles the shape of a pin. In addition to "pin," "needle," or "tack," 針 refers to needle-like objects and acupuncture. In the simplified character 针, the gold/metal radical is simplified from 金 to 钅.

針 會意。從金，從十，十像針頭突出的針形。本義為縫衣用的針。引申為像針一樣的東西、針灸等。簡化字针的部首簡化。

篆 鍼

針線 zhēnxiàn needle and thread
針灸 zhēnjiǔ acupuncture

打針 dǎzhēn injection
指南針 zhǐnánzhēn compass

真

zhēn
true; real; really

ASSOCIATIVE COMPOUND In the Oracle-Bone Inscriptions, the lower part of 真 is a bronze vessel on a tripod and the upper part a person, thus signifying someone savoring the delicacy in the vessel. The original meaning of 真 was "delicacy," and extended meanings include "true," "real," "truly," "indeed," etc. Be sure to remember that there are *three* lines inside the middle part of 真 in Regular Script.

真 會意。甲骨文從鼎，從人，指人到鼎邊拿美食吃。本義為美食，引申為真實等。

甲 𤮻 金 𤯠 篆 眞

真理 zhēnlǐ truth
認真 rènzhēn conscientious; earnest; serious

真心 zhēnxīn sincere; heartfelt
天真 tiānzhēn naive; innocent; artless

整

zhěng
to put in order

ASSOCIATIVE AND PICTOPHONETIC COMPOUND The character 整 combines the signifying components 束 (shù, to tie; to restrain) and 攵 (pū, rap/tap) with the semantic and phonetic element 正 (zhèng, straight; strengthen), suggesting "to straighten something with restraint and rap." The meanings of 整 include "to rectify," "to put in order," "orderly," "neat," "tidy," "to repair," "whole," and "to punish." In the Oracle-Bone Inscriptions, the character 束 looks like a sack tied on both ends with a cord, meaning "to tie," "to bind," "to control," "to restrain," "bundle," etc.

整 會意兼形聲。從束（束縛），從攵（敲打），從正，正亦聲。指用敲打（攵）、約束（束）的方法使之歸于正，本義為整理、整頓。引申義有整齊、完整的、修理、美化等。束，象形。像袋子的兩端被捆扎起來。一說像一捆木柴。本義為捆綁、束縛。

篆

整理 zhěnglǐ to organize; to sort
整體 zhěngtǐ whole entity; entire body

完整 wánzhěng complete; intact
整容 zhěngróng plastic surgery

正

zhèng
just; upright

ASSOCIATIVE COMPOUND In the Oracle-Bone Inscriptions, the character 正 is the combination of a 囗 (wéi, enclosure, here standing for a city) on top and a foot 止 underneath, suggesting people marching toward enemy territory. The extended meanings of 正 are "righteous" "correct," "upright," "straight," "precisely," "just now," etc. In Regular Script, the 囗 in the upper part of 正 has been simplified into 一, and the foot in the lower part has become 止 (zhǐ, foot; stop).

正 會意。從一，從止（足）。甲骨文、金文中像人足抵達一城邑，與"征"本為同一字。引申為端正、正面、正義等。

甲 ♂ 金 止 篆 正

正面 zhèngmiàn front; obverse side; positive
正式 zhèngshì formal; official

真正 zhēnzhèng genuine; true; genuinely
正常 zhèngcháng normal; regular

政

zhèng
politics

ASSOCIATIVE AND PICTOPHONETIC COMPOUND The character 政 is built with the tap/rap radical 攵 and the semantic and phonetic element 正 (zhèng, straight; to strengthen), representing the idea of rectifying something with force. Its original meaning is "to rectify" or "to correct" and its extended meanings include "political affairs," "politics," "administration," "government," and "affairs of a family or an organization."

政 會意兼形聲。從正，從攵（手持棍敲擊狀），正亦聲。本義為用力糾正、匡正，引申義有政務、政治、政策、政府、家政等。

甲  金 政 篆 政

政府 zhèngfǔ government
政策 zhèngcè policy

政治 zhèngzhì politics
專政 zhuānzhèng dictatorship

Z - X

證/证

zhèng
proof; certificate

PICTOPHONETIC CHARACTER The character 證 is made up of the word radical 言 and the phonetic component 登 (dēng), originally meaning "to testify" or "to give evidence." Extended meanings are "to prove," "to confirm," "evidence," "certificate," or "card." In its ancient forms, 登 consists of two hands (bottom part) carrying a high-legged vessel 豆 (middle part) and two feet ᛯ (top part), suggesting someone ascending to a higher stage with an offering. 登 means "to ascend," "ripe," and "to register." 証 originally meant "to expostulate with." Today 証 is used as the simplified form of 證 with the simplified 讠.

證 形聲。從言，登聲。本義是作證、證實，引申義包括證明、證據、證件等。登，會意。甲骨文、金文下是雙手捧豆（器皿），上是雙足向上（ᛯ bō），表示升階進獻新穀。引申義為登高、記載、登記等。証原意為諫，言字旁簡化後用作證的簡化字。

篆 ㄓ 政 登甲 ㄓ 金 ㄓ

證明 zhèngmíng to prove; proof
證件 zhèngjiàn identification

保證 bǎozhèng warranty; to guarantee
證書 zhèngshū certificate

知

zhī
to know

ASSOCIATIVE COMPOUND The character 知 combines 矢 (shǐ, arrow) and 口 (kǒu, mouth), suggesting one speaking as fast as an arrow flies. Extended meanings of 知 include "realize," "know," and "knowledge." In the Oracle-Bone and Bronze Inscriptions, 矢 depicts an arrow 矢 is also used in the character 醫 (yī, medicine).

知 會意。從矢（箭），從口，表示開口講話的速度如射箭一般快。本義為言詞敏捷，引申為了解知道等。

篆 ㄓ

知道 zhīdào to know; to become aware of
知識 zhīshi knowledge

通知 tōngzhī to notify; notice; notification
知音 zhīyīn intimate friend; soul mate

枝

zhī
branch; (MW for long, thin objects)

PICTOPHONETIC CHARACTER The character 枝 consists of the wood/tree radical 木 and the phonetic element 支 (zhī). The primary meaning of 枝 is "branch," or "twig." It is also used as a measure word for something long and narrow, such as a pen, candle, rifle, etc.

枝 形聲。從木，支聲。本義為樹枝，引申為一些狹長條形物體的量詞。支，古字像手持折斷的竹枝，本義為枝條，引申為分支、支撐、支援等。

篆 ㄓ

樹枝 shùzhī branch; twig
枝節 zhījié branches and knots; minor matters

剪枝 jiǎnzhī to prune
荔枝 lìzhī lychee fruit

zhí
straight

ASSOCIATIVE COMPOUND   In the Oracle-Bone Inscriptions, the character 直 outlines the shape of an eye with a straight line above it, indicating the act of looking straight ahead. The meanings of 直 are "straight," "to straighten," "upright," "straightforward," "fair and impartial," "frank," "stiff," "directly," "vertical," or "continuously." In Regular Script, its top becomes 十, but one still can see the traces of the eye at the bottom. Note that there are three lines inside the bottom part.

直 會意。甲骨文從目、從｜（標干），指用眼對準標杆測量是否是直綫。楷書有所改動。本義為不彎曲，引申義有伸直、跟地面垂直、公正、坦率、一直等。

甲 金 篆 直

直綫 zhíxiàn straight line
一直 yìzhí all along; always

正直 zhèngzhí upright; upstanding
簡直 jiǎnzhí simply; at all; virtually

---

zhǐ
only

EXPLICIT CHARACTER   只 is comprised of 口 (kǒu, mouth) with two strokes underneath, suggesting the action of breathing out of one's mouth. 只 originally functioned as an auxiliary word to indicate mood. Later it came to mean "only," "just," or "merely."

只 指事。從口，下有兩道，像人口説話時氣呼出狀。本義是語氣助詞。

篆 只

只有 zhǐyǒu only
只要 zhǐyào if only; so long as

不只 bùzhǐ not only; not merely
只好 zhǐhǎo have to; to be forced to

---

zhǐ
paper

PICTOPHONETIC CHARACTER   The character 紙 is comprised of the silk radical 糸 and the phonetic element 氏 (shì), meaning "paper." Before paper was invented, rich people sometimes wrote on silk. Therefore, 紙 contains the silk radical. In its ancient form, 氏 resembles a root underground, and its original meanings were "fundamental" and "foundation." It extended to mean "clan or branch of ancient nobility," "characters in legend," and "maiden name."

紙 形聲。從糸，氏聲。本義為紙張。古時未造紙之前寫文于絲竹上，故用糸做部首。氏，古文像根在地下形，本義為根本，根柢，引申為古代貴族的分支、傳説中的人物、已婚婦女等。

篆 紙

報紙 bàozhǐ newspaper
衛生紙 wèishēngzhǐ toilet paper

圖紙 túzhǐ blueprint; drawing; graph paper
造紙 zàozhǐ paper-making

Z - X

治

zhì
to govern; to manage

PICTOPHONETIC CHARACTER   The character 治 combines the water radical 氵 and the phonetic element 台 (tái), originally meaning "to regulate rivers and watercourses." Its extended meanings are "to regulate," "to control," "to govern," "to manage," "to cure," "to research," "to punish," "peaceful and orderly," etc. In its ancient forms, 台 looks like a fetus with its head facing down toward the birth canal. It originally meant "pregnant." Later, 台 became the simplified version of 臺 (tái) to mean "platform," "stage," "terrace," and a shorter term for "Taiwan."

治　形聲。從氵，台聲。本義為治水，引申義有治理、管理、醫治、研究、懲辦、太平安定等。台，會意。甲骨文像頭朝下的胎兒，是胎的本字。台也作為臺的簡化字，屬於同音替代，在金、元已見。

篆

治理 zhìlǐ to govern; to manage
自治 zìzhì autonomy

政治 zhèngzhì politics
治安 zhì'ān public security; public safety

中

zhōng
center; middle

ASSOCIATIVE COMPOUND   In the Oracle-Bone Inscriptions, the character 中 represents streamers fluttering in the wind, perhaps at the center of a square. The original meaning of 中 was "flag" and it now means "center" or "middle."

中　會意。甲骨文、金文像樹立在場地中央迎風飛舞的旗幟。本義為旗幟，引申為中央。

甲 𝄐 金 𝄐 篆 中

中間 zhōngjiān between; among; middle
中國 zhōngguó China

中心 zhōngxīn center; core
中學 zhōngxué middle school

鐘/钟

zhōng
clock

PICTOPHONETIC CHARACTER   鐘 consists of the radical 金 (jīn, metal) and the phonetic component 童 (tóng), originally referring to "bronze bell," an ancient instrument. Later it came to mean "bell," "clock," "o'clock," or "time." In the Bronze Inscriptions, 童 depicted a male slave, and later extended to mean "young servant" or "children." In Regular Script, 童 is made up of 立 (lì, stand), 田 (tián, field), and 土 (tǔ, earth). In the simplified 钟, the metal radical 金 is simplified to 钅 and the right part 童 is replaced by 中, for the pronunciation of 中 is the same as 鐘.

鐘　形聲。從金，童聲。本義為用銅、鉄鑄製成的一種打擊樂器。引申為寺廟裏懸挂的鐘、計時器等。童，會意。金文像身背重物，眼被刑刀刺入的人，本義為男奴隸，引申為童僕、兒童。簡化字钟偏旁用钅取代金，右部聲旁以中取代童，屬同音替代。

篆 鐘 草 鐘 童 金 𝄐 篆 𝄐

點鐘 diǎnzhōng o'clock
秒鐘 miǎozhōng (time) second

分鐘 fēnzhōng minute
鐘頭 zhōngtóu hour

種／种

zhǒng
kinds; types

zhòng
to plant

PICTOPHONETIC CHARACTER The character 種 consists of the growing grain radical 禾 and the phonetic element 重 (zhòng, heavy), meaning " plant" or "grow." The extended meanings of 種 are "seed," "breed," "species," "kind," "type," etc. In the Bronze Inscriptions, 重 is the sketch of a man carrying a heavy sack on his back, meaning "heavy," or "serious." In the simplified character 种, the right part of 種 is replaced by 中 because the pronunciation of 中 (zhōng) is similar to 重 (zhòng).

種 形聲。從禾，重聲。本義指種植，引申為種子、種族、種類等。重，象形。金文像人身負重物。簡體字种把種字的聲旁重用中替代。

篆 種 種

種地 zhòngdì to farm; to work the land
各種 gèzhǒng various kinds

種子 zhǒngzi seed
人種 rénzhǒng race (of people)

重

zhòng
heavy; serious

chóng
again

ASSOCIATIVE COMPOUND In the Bronze Inscriptions, 重 depicts a figure carrying a heavy sack on his or her back. The initial meaning of 重 (pronounced as zhòng) is "heavy" and its derived meanings include "serious," "grave," "severe," "important," "to emphasize," and "to value". When 重 is pronounced as chóng, it means "to repeat," "double," "again," or "once more."

重 會意。像一個背著一簍重物的人。本義為沉重、分量大，引申為重要、重視、程度深等。重念做 chóng 時，意指重復、兩個、再。

金 重 篆 重

超重 chāozhòng overweight (baggage, freight)
保重 bǎozhòng take care of oneself

重要 zhòngyào important
重新 chóngxīn all over again

州

zhōu
administrative
division;
state

PICTOGRAPH In the Oracle-Bone and Bronze Inscriptions, the character 州 resembles an islet in a river. In Seal Script, 州 became three islets. 州 originally meant "islet" or "sandbar." Later it came to mean "administrative district" or "state," and no longer carried its original meaning. A water radical 氵 was added to 州 to form a new character, 洲, meaning "islet in a river" or "continent."

州 象形。甲骨文、金文像河水環繞的小島嶼。本義是水中陸地。"州"是"洲"的本字。引申為劃分的行政區域。

甲 州 金 州 篆 州

州長 zhōuzhǎng the governor of a state
加州 jiāzhōu California

州立 zhōulì state-run
廣州 guǎngzhōu Guangzhou; Canton

週/周

zhōu
week; cycle

ASSOCIATIVE COMPOUND   In the Oracle-Bone Inscriptions, the character 周 consists of 田 (tián, field) and four dots, suggesting crops planted in an orderly fashion in a field. The primary meanings of 周 are "circumference," "surround," and "all around." Extended meanings include "period," "cycle," and "week." The walk radical ⻌ was eventually added to 周 to specifically mean "week." In Regular Script, 土 and 口 are found inside 冂. The simplified character 周 does not include the walk radical ⻌.

週　會意。甲骨文像田地形，中間四點代表田裏種的莊稼。本義為農田，引申為周圍、環繞、一定循環的時段等。簡體周字去掉⻌。

甲 𠙻 金 𤲅 篆 周

週末 zhōumò weekend　　　　週日 zhōurì Sunday

住

zhù
to live (in a certain place)

PICTOPHONETIC CHARACTER   住 consists of the person radical 亻 and the phonetic indicator 主 (zhǔ), meaning "to stay," "to dwell," "to live," "to stop," or "firm." In its ancient forms, 主 looks like an oil lamp, with the dot on the top standing for the flame of the lamp wick. The original meaning of 主 was "lamp wick," and has been extended to mean "main," "primary," "host," "master," "to take charge of," etc.

住　形聲。從亻，主聲。本義為停留，引申為留下、居住、停止、牢固等。主，象形。古文與篆文下像燈座，上似燈碗與燈芯，本義為燈芯，引申為主要的、主人、主張、主持等。

主 篆 𡊨

住址 zhùzhǐ address
住口 zhùkǒu shut up; stop talking

住校 zhùxiào to live on campus
記住 jìzhù remember; learn by heart

助

zhù
to assist; to aid

ASSOCIATIVE AND PICTOPHONETIC COMPOUND   助 combines the radical 力 (lì, strength; power) and the semantic and phonetic symbol 且 (qiě/jū), referring to the assistance one receives from ancestral spirits. In the Oracle-Bone and Bronze Inscriptions, the character 且 resembles a memorial tablet used in ancestral worship, and originally meant "ancestor." You can also see 且 in the characters 姐 (jiě, older sister), 租 (zū, to rent), and 宜 (yí, suitable).

助　形聲兼會意。從力，從且（祭祀祖先之靈所用的牌位）；且亦聲。指靠祖先之靈鼎力相助。

篆 𦔭

幫助 bāngzhù help; aid; assist
助教 zhùjiào teaching assistant

助手 zhùshǒu assistant; helper
資助 zīzhù to provide financial aid; subsidy

祝
zhù
to wish

ASSOCIATIVE COMPOUND In the Oracle-Bone and Bronze Inscriptions, the character 祝 delineates a person on his or her knees praying next to an altar, meaning "pray" and "prayer." 祝 also extends to mean "express good wishes" or "wish." In its ancient forms, 示/礻 (shì, show) is a pictograph of a stone table upon which sacrificial offerings to gods or ancestors are placed. The radical 礻 is often found in characters related to religious rituals.

祝 會意。從示/礻（用石塊搭起的祭臺），從人，從口。甲骨文、金文中像人跪在祭臺邊向神靈或祖先祈禱。

甲 祝 金 祝 篆 祝

祝好 zhùhǎo Wish you all the best!
祝福 zhùfú blessings; to wish happiness to

祝賀 zhùhè to congratulate; congratulations
慶祝 qìngzhù to celebrate

專/专
zhuān
special

ASSOCIATIVE AND PICTOPHONETIC COMPOUND In the Oracle-Bone Inscriptions, 專 consists of a hand (寸 cùn) and a spindle (叀 zhuān), signifying the act of winding thread on a spindle. Early meanings of 專 were "spindle" and "revolve." Later it came to mean "concentrate," "focus," or "special." The simplified character 专 is derived from the cursive style of the traditional character 專.

專 會意兼形聲。從寸，叀聲，甲骨文像用一手轉動紡錘形。本義為紡錘，後為專一，專心等。簡體字专是繁體字專的草書楷化字。

甲 專 篆 專 草 专

專業 zhuānyè major; specialized field of study
專家 zhuānjiā expert; specialist

專門 zhuānmén specially; specialized
專心 zhuānxīn to concentrate

轉/转
zhuǎn/zhuàn
to turn

ASSOCIATIVE AND PICTOPHONETIC COMPOUND The character 轉 combines the signifying element 車 (chē, vehicle) with the semantic and phonetic component 專 (zhuān, revolve), implying that "the cart wheels are revolving." The meanings of 轉 include "to turn," "to move," "to change," "to transport," and "indirect" when pronounced as zhuǎn, and "to rotate," "to revolve," and "to walk around" when pronounced as zhuàn. In Seal Script, the chariot in 車 is simplified to one wheel on its axle. The simplified character 车 developed from the cursive style of 車. In the character 转, both 車 and 專 are simplified.

轉 會意兼形聲。從車，從專（以手轉動紡錘），專亦聲。表示車輪轉動。本義為運轉、轉動，引申義有變換、間接傳送、改變方向等。以上意思讀作 zhuǎn。讀作 zhuàn 時意為旋轉。車的簡化字是车，專是专。簡化字转將兩字的簡化字合為一體。

金 轉 篆 轉 專 甲 專 草 专

轉學 zhuǎnxué to transfer to another school
轉眼 zhuǎnyǎn in the twinkling of an eye

轉機 zhuǎnjī transfer flight
轉椅 zhuànyǐ swivel chair

準/准

zhǔn
to allow;
standard

PICTOPHONETIC CHARACTER The character 準 consists of the water radical 氵 and the phonetic indicator 隼 (sǔn), originally referring to "level surface of water." Its extended meanings are "level," "even," "standard," "criterion," "accurate," "definitely," "target," and "to aim." In the Bronze Inscriptions, 隼 portrays a hand holding a bird and means "falcon." Although 准 is the variant form of 準, its usage is different: in Traditional Characters, only 准 can be used to mean "to allow," "to permit," or "to approve." Nowadays 准 is also used as the simplified form of 準, and in this case it carries the meanings of both characters.

準 形聲。從氵，隼 (sǔn) 聲。本義為水平面，引申為水準、標準、準確、目標、一定等。准本是準的俗字，但在用法上有所區別。如果意思是同意、准許，只能用准，而不能用準。現在准用作準的簡化字。

篆 𣆟 隼 甲 𠃌 金 𠦝 篆 𠦝

準時 zhǔnshí on time; punctual
準備 zhǔnbèi to prepare

對準 duìzhǔn to aim at
准許 zhǔnxǔ to approve; to allow

桌

zhuō
table; desk

PICTOPHONETIC CHARACTER The character 桌 is built with the wood radical 木 and the phonetic component 卓 (zhuó), signifying that a table is made from wood. 桌 can also be used as a measure word, as in 一桌菜 (a tableful of dishes). In the Oracle-Bone Inscriptions, 卓 portrays a bird caught in a long-handled net. Since one has to raise the net high enough to catch a bird, 卓 means "lofty" or "outstanding."

桌 形聲。從木，卓聲。本義為几案、桌子，引申作為量詞，如：一桌酒席。卓，會意。甲骨文字形的下面是帶把的網，上面是鳥，指用網罩鳥。因人要高舉網罩鳥，引申為高超、卓越。

卓 甲 𠦝 金 𠦝 篆 帛

桌子 zhuōzi table; desk
書桌 shūzhuō desk

飯桌 fànzhuō dining table
桌布 zhuōbù tablecloth

字

zì
character

ASSOCIATIVE AND PICTOPHONETIC COMPOUND The character 字 has the roof radical 宀 on the top and 子 (zǐ, child) underneath, indicating a child in a house. The original meaning of 字 was "give birth to" or "bring up," but later evolved to mean "characters." Children were supposed to remain at home, practicing their characters every day. You could probably memorize all the characters you have learned if you did the same!

字 會意兼形聲。從寶蓋頭，從子；子亦聲。用房屋中有子意指生養孩子。現可想象為孩子在屋中寫字。

金 𡦹 篆 𡧳

漢字 hànzì Chinese character
字典 zìdiǎn character dictionary

生字 shēngzì new character
字母 zìmǔ letter (of the alphabet)

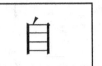

自
zì
self

PICTOGRAPH In the Oracle-Bone Inscriptions, 自 represents the shape of a nose. 自 originally meant "nose," and came to mean "self," "one's own," "from," "since," etc. 自 no longer carries its original meaning, as the character 鼻 now indicates "nose."

自 象形。甲骨文像鼻形。本義為鼻子，後引申為自己，而鼻子則寫作"鼻"。

甲  金  篆 自

自己 zìjǐ oneself
自由 zìyóu freedom; free; liberty

親自 qīnzì personally; in person
自然 zìrán nature; natural; naturally

租
zū
to rent

PICTOPHONETIC CHARACTER The character 租 consists of the radical 禾 (hé, standing grain), and the phonetic element 且 (qiě/jū), meaning "land tax," "rent," "hire," "lease," etc. 禾 is also used in 和 (hé, and) and 秋 (qiū, autumn). 且 also appears in 姐 (jiě, elder sister), 助 (zhù, to assist), and 宜 (yí, suitable).

租 形聲。從禾，且(jū)聲。有田賦、出租、租用之意。

篆 租

租金 zūjīn rent
出租 chūzū to rent out; to rent

房租 fángzū rent (for a room or house)
出租車 chūzūchē taxi

嘴
zuǐ
mouth

ASSOCIATIVE AND PICTOPHONETIC COMPOUND The character 嘴 consists of the mouth radical 口 and the semantic and phonetic component 觜 (zuǐ; zī), meaning "mouth," "beak," "snout," "sprout," or "talk." 觜 combines 角 (jiǎo, horn) with the phonetic 此 (cǐ, this), originally referring to the horn-like hair on an owl's head and extended to mean "beak" or "mouth." Later a new character, 嘴, was created by adding a mouth radical 口 to the left of 觜. In the Oracle-Bone and Bronze Inscriptions, 角 is the pictograph of the horn of an animal. See the entry for 些 (xiē) for more about the origins of 此.

嘴 會意兼形聲。楷書從口，從觜(zuǐ; zī)，觜亦聲。本義為鳥嘴，引申為人或動物的嘴、物體形狀像嘴的部分、説話等。觜，形聲。從角，此聲。本義為貓頭鷹之類頭上的毛角，引申為鳥嘴、人或動物的進食器官。

此 此 甲 此 角 甲 角 金 角 篆 角

多嘴 duōzuǐ to talk too much
嘴甜 zuǐtián honey-tongued

嘴快 zuǐkuài to have a loose tongue
回嘴 huízuǐ to retort; to talk back

The Way of Chinese Characters

223

Z - X

最

zuì
most

ASSOCIATIVE COMPOUND In Seal Script, 最 is made up of 冃 (mào, headgear) and 取 (qǔ, get; take). In the Oracle-Bone Inscriptions, 取 depicts a right hand holding an ear. In ancient times, soldiers cut off the ears of enemies as proof of victory. 取 therefore means to "capture," "get," "take," or "fetch." 最 consists of the headgear, ear, and hand parts. It originally meant "gather," "total," and "the highest military merit," from which is derived its usage as a superlative degree marker. In Regular Script, 曰 replaces the 冃 in 最, but the bottom still combines ear 耳 and right hand 又.

最　會意。篆文從冃（帽子、頭盔），從取（以手割下戰俘耳朵為立軍功的證據）。本義指以士兵殲敵的數目來判斷誰立下頭等戰功，引申為總計、極度等。

篆 〔seal script forms〕

最好 zuìhǎo best; had better
最後 zuìhòu last; finally
最近 zuìjìn recently
最多 zuìduō at most; maximum

昨

zuó
yesterday

PICTOPHONETIC CHARACTER The character 昨 consists of the sun radical 日 and the phonetic component 乍 (zhà/zuò). In the Oracle-Bone and Bronze Inscriptions, 乍 indicates the stitching of a collar. The original meaning of 乍 was "to make" or "to do." Later the character came to mean "for the first time," "spread," or "abruptly." Please compare 昨 with 怎 (zěn, how).

昨　形聲。從日，乍聲。

篆 〔seal script form〕

昨天 zuótiān yesterday
昨晚 zuówǎn yesterday evening; last night
昨日 zuórì yesterday
昨夜 zuóyè last night

左

zuǒ
left

ASSOCIATIVE COMPOUND In the Bronze Inscriptions, the character 左 depicts a hand stretching toward the left with 工 (gōng, tool; work) underneath, suggesting that a tool is a great extension of one's hands. Its original meanings were "to assist" and "subordinate," but now it is used to mean "the left side," "the east side," "left-wing," "the Left," "unorthodox," and "opposite."

左　會意。從左手，從工。表示以左手助右手操持工具勞作。本義為輔佐，此意後被佐取代，左則指左邊，東邊，也指左翼、政治上激進、非正統、相反等。

金 〔bronze script forms〕 篆 〔seal script form〕

左上 zuǒshàng upper left
左派 zuǒpài the left wing
左腿 zuǒtuǐ the left leg
極左 jízuǒ the ultra-left

zuò
to sit

篆 坐

ASSOCIATIVE COMPOUND The character 坐 consists of two 人 (rén, person) on top and 土 (tǔ, earth) at the bottom, representing two people sitting on the ground. In addition to "sit," 坐 also means "to travel by" some kind of vehicle (which one sits in), such as a bus, train, or airplane.

坐 會意。古文中像兩人在土地上面對面而坐。

坐下 zuòxia sit down
坐車 zuòchē to take a bus, a car, etc.
坐位 zuòwèi seat
坐牢 zuòláo to be imprisoned

zuò
to work; to do

甲 止 金 止 篆 作

ASSOCIATIVE AND PICTOPHONETIC COMPOUND In the Oracle-Bone and Bronze Inscriptions, the character 作 is written as 乍, which represents stitching a collar, therefore meaning "to do" or "to make" something. In Seal Script, the person radical 亻 was added to the left of 乍 to form 作. 乍 also appears in the characters 怎 (zěn, how) and 昨 (zuó, yesterday). When 作 is used as a verb, sometimes it can be replaced by 做, a character which was developed later. However, in certain combinations, such as 工作, 做 cannot be substituted for 作.

作 會意兼形聲。從人，從乍，乍亦聲。甲骨文、金文寫為"乍"，意指縫製衣領。篆文加人字旁為"作"

工作 gōngzuò job; work; to work
作家 zuòjiā writer
作業 zuòyè school assignment; homework
合作 hézuò cooperate; to work together; cooperation

zuò
to do

甲 止 金 止 篆 作

ASSOCIATIVE COMPOUND In the Oracle-Bone and Bronze Inscriptions, the character 作 is written as 乍 (zhà). 乍 looks like the stitching of a collar, and its original meaning was therefore "to do" or "to make." In Seal Script, the person radical 亻 is added to 乍 to form 作. 做 developed later than 作, and is the combination of 亻 and 故 (gù, former). When 作 is used as a verb, sometimes it is interchangeable with 做. However, if an action involves body movement, 做 is preferable to 作, such as in 做飯 (zuòfàn, to cook) and 做衣服 (zuò yīfu, to make clothes).

做 會意。"做"是"作"的後起字，在一些意思上二字相通。但在口語中具體東西的製造一般寫為"做"，如做飯，做衣服；較為抽象、書面語色彩較重的詞語及成語，一般寫為"作"，如寫作，作文，自作自受。但區別的標準不是絕對的。

做事 zuòshì to work; to handle matters
做客 zuòkè to be a guest
做飯 zuòfàn to cook
做法 zuòfǎ way of handling something

CHARACTER INDEX
By *Integrated Chinese* Lesson

This index contains all the characters found in *Integrated Chinese Level 1, Part 1* and *Level 1, Part 2* arranged as they appear in each lesson.

*	=	**Bound Form**	
MW	=	**Measure Word**	
P	=	**Particle**	
QP	=	**Question Particle**	
( )	=	**Variant/Radical Form**	

RADICALS

人(亻)	rén	person; people	1
刀(刂)	dāo	knife	1
力	lì	power; strength	2
又	yòu	right hand; again	2
口	kǒu	mouth; entrance	2
囗	wéi	enclose	3
土	tǔ	earth	3
夕	xī	sunset; evening	3
大	dà	big; great	4
女	nǚ	female; woman	4
子	zǐ	baby; child	4
寸	cùn	inch	5
小	xiǎo	little; small	5
工	gōng	tool; work; labor	5
幺	yāo	tiny; small	6
弓	gōng	bow	6
心(忄)	xīn	heart	6
戈	gē	dagger-axe	7
手(扌)	shǒu	hand	7
日	rì	sun; day	8
月	yuè	moon; month	8
木	mù	wood	8
水(氵)	shuǐ	water	9
火(灬)	huǒ	fire	9
田	tián	field; (surname)	10
目	mù	eye	10

示(礻)	shì	to show	11
糸/纟	mì	silk	11
耳	ěr	ear	11
衣(衤)	yī	clothing	12
言(讠)	yán	word; speech	13
貝/贝	bèi	cowry shell	13
走	zǒu	to walk	14
足	zú	foot; enough	14
金	jīn	metal; gold; (surname)	14
門/门	mén	door; gate	15
隹	zhuī	short-tailed bird	15
雨	yǔ	rain	15
食	shí	to eat	16
馬/马	mǎ	horse	16

NUMERALS

一	yī	one	17
二	èr	two	17
三	sān	three	17
四	sì	four	17
五	wǔ	five	18
六	liù	six	18
七	qī	seven	18
八	bā	eight	19
九	jiǔ	nine	19
十	shí	ten	19

LESSON 1

你	nǐ	you	129
好	hǎo/hào	good; fine/ to like; to be fond of	77
請/请	qǐng	please; to invite	139
問/问	wèn	to ask (a question)	177
貴/贵	guì	honorable; expensive	74
姓	xìng	surname	189
我	wǒ	I; me	178
呢	ne	QP	128
姐	jiě	elder sister	94
叫	jiào	to be called; to call	93
什(甚)	shén	*what	148
麼/么	me	QP	120
名	míng	name	124
字	zì	character	222
先	xiān	first	183
生	shēng	to be born; to grow	148
李	lǐ	(surname); plum	110
友	yǒu	friend	204
王	wáng	king; (surname)	10
朋	péng	friend	133
是	shì	to be	152
老	lǎo	old	108
師/师	shī	teacher	149
嗎/吗	ma	QP	118
不	bù	not; no	33
學/学	xué	to study	190
也	yě	also; too	196
人	rén	people; person	1
中	zhōng	center; middle	218
國/国	guó	country; nation	74
北	běi	north	28
京	jīng	capital city	96
美	měi	beautiful	121

紐/纽	niǔ	knob; button	130
約/约	yuē	agreement; appointment	208

LESSON 2

那	nà/nèi	that	126
的	de	possessive P	49
照	zhào	photograph; to shine	213
片	piàn	MW (for tablets, films); slice	134
這/这	zhè(i)	this	214
爸	bà	father; dad	23
媽/妈	mā	mother; mom	117
個/个	gè	MW (general)	68
孩	hái	child	75
誰/谁	shéi	who	147
她	tā	she	163
男	nán	male	127
弟	dì	younger brother	50
他	tā	he	163
哥	gē	elder brother	67
兒/儿	ér	son; child	57
有	yǒu	to have; to exist	204
沒(没)	méi/ mò	(have) not/ to sink	121
高	gāo	tall; high	66
文	wén	(written) language; script	177
家	jiā	family; home	89
幾/几	jǐ	how many; a few	87
兩/两	liǎng	two; a couple of	113
妹	mèi	younger sister	122
和	hé/*huo	and; harmonious/ *warm	78
做	zuò	to do	225
作	zuò	to work; to do	225
律	lù	law; rule	116
都	dōu/dū	all; both/ capital	54
醫/医	yī	doctor; medicine	197

白	bái	white; (surname)	24
英	yīng	flower; hero; *England	201
愛/爱	ài	love; to love	22

LESSON 3

號/号	hào	number	77
星	xīng	star	188
期	qī	period (of time)	136
天	tiān	sky; day	168
今	jīn	today; now	95
年	nián	year	129
多	duō	many; much	56
歲/岁	suì	age	162
吃	chī	to eat	39
飯/饭	fàn	meal; (cooked) rice	59
怎	zěn	how	211
樣/样	yàng	kind; appearance	194
太	tài	too; extremely	164
了	le	P	108
謝/谢	xiè	to thank	187
喜	xǐ	to like; happy	181
歡/欢	huān	happy; joyous	83
菜/菜	cài	dish; cuisine; vegetable	34
還/还	hái/huán	still; yet/ to exchange; to return	75
可	kě	but; to permit	102
們/们	men	*(plural suffix)	122
點/点	diǎn	dot; o'clock	51
半	bàn	half	25
晚	wǎn	evening; late	173
上	shàng	above; top	145
見/见	jiàn	to see	13
再	zài	again	210
現/现	xiàn	now; present	183
在	zài	at; in; on	210

刻	kè	quarter (hour); to carve	103
事	shì	affair; matter	151
很	hěn	very	79
忙	máng	busy	119
明	míng	bright	124
為/为	wèi/wéi	for	176
因	yīn	because	200
同	tóng	same	170
認/认	rèn	to recognize; to know	142
識/识	shí	to recognize	150

LESSON 4

週/周	zhōu	week; cycle	220
末	mò	end	124
打	dǎ	to hit	45
球	qiú	ball	140
看	kàn	to watch; to read	101
電/电	diàn	electricity	52
視/视	shì	to view; to look at	152
唱	chàng	to sing	37
歌	gē	song	68
跳	tiào	to jump	169
舞	wǔ	to dance; dance	179
聽/听	tīng	to listen	169
音	yīn	sound; music	200
樂/乐	yuè/ lè	music/ happy	209
書/书	shū	book	155
對/对	duì	correct; toward	56
時/时	shí	time	149
候	hòu	time; season; await	80
影	yǐng	shadow	202
常	cháng	often; ordinary	36
去	qù	to go	140
外	wài	outside; foreign	172
客	kè	guest	103

昨	zuó	yesterday	224
所	suǒ	*so; place	162
以	yǐ	with	198
久	jiǔ	long time	98
錯/错	cuò	wrong; error	45
想	xiǎng	to want to; to think	185
覺/觉	jiào/jué	to sleep/ to feel; to think	99
得	dé/děi	to obtain; to get; P/ must; have to	48
意	yì	meaning	199
思	sī	to think	159
只	zhǐ	only	217
睡	shuì	to sleep	158
算	suàn	to calculate	161
找	zhǎo	to look for; to seek	212
別/别	bié	other; do not	32

LESSON 5

呀	ya	P	192
進/进	jìn	to enter	96
快	kuài	fast; quick	105
來/来	lái	to come	106
介	jiè	to be between	94
紹/绍	shào	to introduce; to continue	146
下	xià	below; under	182
興/兴	xìng	mood; interest	189
漂	piào/piāo	*pretty/ to float	135
亮	liàng	bright	113
坐	zuò	to sit	225
哪	nǎ/něi	which	126
校	xiào	school	186
喝	hē	to drink	78
茶	chá	tea	35
咖	kā	*coffee	100
啡	fēi	*coffee	60

吧	ba	P (a sentence-ending particle)	23
要	yào	to want	195
瓶	píng	bottle	135
起	qǐ	to rise	136
給/给	gěi	to give	68
杯	bēi	cup; glass	28
玩	wán	to play; to have fun	173
圖/图	tú	picture; drawing	171
館/馆	guǎn	place; building	73
聊	liáo	to chat	113
才	cái	not until; only then	34
回	huí	to return	84

LESSON 6

話/话	huà	speech	82
喂	wéi/wèi	Hello!; Hey!	176
就	jiù	just	99
您	nín	you (polite)	130
位	wèi	MW (for people [polite])	175
午	wǔ	noon	178
間/间	jiān	MW (for rooms); between	90
題/题	tí	topic; question	167
開/开	kāi	to open; to operate	100
會/会	huì	meeting	84
節/节	jié	MW (for classes); holiday	94
課/课	kè	class; lesson	104
級/级	jí	grade; level	86
考	kǎo	test; to test	101
試/试	shì	test; to try	153
後/后	hòu	after; behind	80
空	kòng/kōng	free time/ empty; sky	104
方	fāng	square; side; method	9
便	biàn/pián	convenient; handy/ *inexpensive	31
到	dào	to arrive	48

辦/办	bàn	to manage	25
公	gōng	public	69
室	shì	room	152
行	xíng/ háng	to walk; okay/ firm; bank	189
等	děng	to wait; rank	50
氣/气	qì	air	137
幫/帮	bāng	to help	26
準/准	zhǔn	standard; criterion	222
備/备	bèi	to prepare	29
練/练	liàn	to practice; to drill	112
習/习	xí	to practice	181
說/说	shuō	to speak	158
啊	a	P	21
但	dàn	but; however	46
跟	gēn	with; and	69
面	miàn	face	123

LESSON 7

復/复	fù	to duplicate	64
寫/写	xiě	to write	187
慢	màn	slow	119
枝	zhī	branch; MW (for long, thin objects)	216
筆/笔	bǐ	pen; writing brush	30
張/张	zhāng	MW (for flat objects); (surname)	212
紙/纸	zhǐ	paper	217
教(教)	jiāo/jiào	to teach/ education	92
懂/懂	dǒng	to understand	54
真(眞)	zhēn	true; real; really	214
裏/裡/里	lǐ	inside	110
預/预	yù	in advance; beforehand	206
第	dì	(ordinal prefix)	51
語/语	yǔ	language	205

法	fǎ	method; way; law	58
容	róng	to hold; to contain	142
易	yì	easy	199
詞/词	cí	word	43
漢/汉	hàn	Chinese ethnicity	76
難/难	nán	difficult; hard	127
平	píng	level; even	135
早	zǎo	early	211
功	gōng	skill	70
始	shǐ	begin	150
唸/念	niàn	to read aloud	129
錄/录	lù	to record	115
帥/帅	shuài	handsome; smart	157
酷	kù	cool; cruel	105

LESSON 8

篇	piān	MW (for articles)	134
記/记	jì	to remember; to record	88
累	lèi	tired	108
床(牀)	chuáng	bed	42
洗	xǐ	to wash	181
澡	zǎo	bath	211
邊/边	biān	side	31
發/发	fā	to emit; to issue	57
新	xīn	new	188
腦/脑	nǎo	brain	128
餐	cān	meal	34
廳/厅	tīng	hall	170
網/网	wǎng	net	174
宿	sù	to stay; to lodge	160
舍	shè	house; residence	147
正	zhèng	just; upright	215
前	qián	front; before	138
告	gào	to tell; to inform	67

訴/诉	sù	to tell; to relate	161
已	yǐ	already	198
經/经	jīng	to pass through	97
知	zhī	to know	216
道	dào	road; way	48
封	fēng	MW (for letters)	62
信	xìn	letter; to believe	188
最	zuì	most	224
近	jìn	close; near	95
除	chú	except	41
專/专	zhuān	special	221
業/业	yè	profession	197
希	xī	to hope	180
望	wàng	to hope; to gaze	175
能	néng	can; to be able to	128
用	yòng	to use	203
笑	xiào	to laugh; to smile	186
祝	zhù	to wish (well)	221

LESSON 9

商	shāng	commerce; business	145
店	diàn	store; shop	51
買/买	mǎi	to buy	118
東/东	dōng	east	53
西	xī	west	180
售	shòu	sale; to sell	154
貨/货	huò	merchandise	85
員/员	yuán	personnel	206
服	fú	clothing; to serve	62
件	jiàn	MW (for items)	91
襯/衬	chèn	lining	38
衫	shān	shirt	145
顏/颜	yán	face; countenance	192
色	sè	color	144
黃/黄	huáng	yellow	84

紅/红	hóng	red	79
穿	chuān	to wear; to pass through	42
條/条	tiáo	MW (for long, thin objects)	168
褲/裤	kù	pants	105
宜	yí	suitable	197
如	rú	as; if	143
果	guǒ	fruit; result	74
長/长	cháng/ zhǎng	long/ to grow; leader	36
短	duǎn	short	55
合	hé	to suit; to fit	78
適/适	shì	to suit; appropriate	153
共	gòng	altogether	70
少	shǎo/ shào	few; little; less/ young	146
錢/钱	qián	money	138
塊/块	kuài	piece; dollar	106
毛	máo	hair; dime	120
分	fēn	penny; minute	61
百	bǎi	hundred	20
雙/双	shuāng	pair	157
鞋	xié	shoes	187
換/换	huàn	to exchange; to change	83
黑	hēi	black	79
雖/虽	suī	although	162
然	rán	like that; so	141
種/种	zhǒng/ zhòng	kinds; types/ to plant	219
挺	tǐng	very; rather	170
它	tā	it	163
刷	shuā	to brush; to swipe	157
卡	kǎ	card	100
收	shōu	to receive; to accept	153
過/过	guò	to pass	75
付	fù	to pay	63

LESSON 10

寒	hán	cold	76
假	jià	vacation	90
飛/飞	fēi	to fly	60
機/机	jī	machine	86
票	piào	ticket	134
場/场	chǎng	field	37
汽	qì	steam; gas	137
車/车	chē	vehicle; car	12
或	huò	or	85
者	zhě	(aux. verb)	213
地	dì/de	earth/ P	50
鐵/铁	tiě	iron	169
站	zhàn	stand; station	212
綠/绿	lù	green	117
線/线	xiàn	line; route	184
藍/蓝	lán	blue	107
麻	má	hemp; numb	117
煩/烦	fán	to bother; to trouble	58
出	chū	to go out	40
租	zū	to rent	223
送	sòng	to see off; to deliver	159
郵/邮	yóu	post; mail	204
讓/让	ràng	to allow; to cause; to let	141
花	huā	to spend; flower	81
每	měi	every; each	121
城	chéng	city; town	39
市	shì	city; market	151
特	tè	special	166
速	sù	speed	160
路	lù	road; way	115
緊/紧	jǐn	tense; tight	95
自	zì	self	223
己	jǐ	oneself	87
灣/湾	wān	strait; bay	172

LESSON 11

比	bǐ	to compare	30
雪	xuě	snow	190
園/园	yuán	garden	207
滑	huá	slippery; to slide	81
冰	bīng	ice	32
剛/刚	gāng	just now	66
報/报	bào	to report; newspaper	27
更	gèng/gēng	even more/ to alternate	69
而	ér	(conj.)	57
且	qiě	(conj.)	138
暖	nuǎn	warm	130
冷	lěng	cold	109
碟	dié	disc; saucer	52
非	fēi	not; non-	60
糟	zāo	messy; rotten	210
糕	gāo	cake	67
冬	dōng	winter	53
夏	xià	summer	182
熱/热	rè	hot	142
春	chūn	spring	43
秋	qiū	autumn; fall	140
舒	shū	to stretch; to smooth out	156
加	jiā	to add	89
州	zhōu	administrative division; state	219
悶/闷	mēn/mèn	stuffy/ depressed	122

LESSON 12

像	xiàng	likeness; portrait	185
務/务	wù	affair; task	179
桌	zhuō	table; desk	222
盤/盘	pán	plate; dish	132
餃/饺	jiǎo	dumpling	93

素	sù	vegetarian; made from vegetables	160
豆	dòu	bean	55
腐	fǔ	rotten; to turn bad	62
放	fàng	to put; to place	59
肉	ròu	meat; flesh	143
碗	wǎn	bowl	173
酸	suān	sour	161
辣	là	spicy	106
湯/汤	tāng	soup	164
味	wèi	flavor; taste	176
精	jīng	essence; refined	97
鹽/盐	yán	salt	193
賣/卖	mài	to sell	119
完	wán	finished	172
青	qīng	green; blue	139
渴	kě	thirsty	103
些	xiē	MW (for indefinite amount); some	186
够	gòu	enough	71
餓/饿	è	hungry	56
傅	fù	tutor; instructor	64
糖	táng	sugar; candy	165
醋	cù	vinegar	44
魚/鱼	yú	fish	16
甜	tián	sweet	168
極/极	jí	extremely; pole	86
燒/烧	shāo	to burn	146
牛	niú	cow; ox	7
涼/凉	liáng	cool	112
拌	bàn	to mix	25
瓜	guā	melon; gourd	72
米	mǐ	uncooked rice	12
忘	wàng	to forget	174
帶/带	dài	to bring; to take; to carry	45
清	qīng	clear; clean; pure	139

楚	chǔ	clear; neat	41
關/关	guān	to involve; to close	72
係/系	xì	to relate to	182
海	hǎi	sea	76

LESSON 13

運/运	yùn	to move	209
動/动	dòng	to move	54
旁	páng	side; edge	132
遠/远	yuǎn	far	207
離/离	lí	away from	109
活	huó	to live; living	85
拿	ná	to take; to get	125
次	cì	MW (for occurrences)	43
從/从	cóng	from	44
直	zhí	straight	217
往	wǎng	toward; past	174
南	nán	south	127
拐	guǎi	to turn	72
哎	āi	(exclamatory particle to express surprise or dissatisfaction)	22
燈/灯	dēng	light; lamp	49
右	yòu	right	205
左	zuǒ	left	224

LESSON 14

表	biǎo	surface; matrilineal relatives	32
禮/礼	lǐ	gift; ceremony	111
物	wù	thing; matter	179
本	běn	MW (for books); foundation	29
飲/饮	yǐn	to drink	200
料	liào	material	114
把	bǎ	MW (for objects with handles)	23
蘋/苹	píng	component in apple 蘋果/苹果	136

梨	lí	pear	109
住	zhù	to live (in a certain place)	220
重	zhòng/chóng	heavy; serious/ again	219
接	jiē	to receive; to welcome	93
樓/楼	lóu	multi-storied building; floor (of building)	114
鐘/钟	zhōng	clock	218
頭/头	tóu	head; top	171
聰/聪	cōng	able to hear well; smart	44
暑	shǔ	heat; summer	156
班	bān	class	24
屬/属	shǔ	to belong to	156
狗	gǒu	dog	70
臉/脸	liǎn	face	112
圓/圆	yuán	round	207
眼	yǎn	eye	193
睛	jīng	eyeball	96
鼻	bí	nose	29
嘴	zuǐ	mouth	223
定	dìng	settled; decided	52
蛋	dàn	egg	47
倫/伦	lún	ethics; moral principles	116
姆	mǔ	housemaid	125

LESSON 15

病	bìng	illness; to become ill	33
院	yuàn	yard	208
肚	dù	belly; abdomen	55
疼	téng	to be painful	166
死	sǐ	to die; (a complement indicating an extreme degree)	159
夜	yè	night	196
厕	cè	toilet	35
箱	xiāng	box; case	184
躺	tǎng	to lie (down)	165

檢/检	jiǎn	to inspect	91
查	chá	to check; to look up	35
壞/坏	huài	bad	83
針/针	zhēn	needle	214
藥/药	yào	medicine	195
片	piàn	MW (for tablet; slice); slice	134
遍	biàn	MW (for complete courses of an action or instances of an action)	31
感	gǎn	to feel; to sense	65
冒	mào	to belch; to emit	120
身	shēn	body	148
體/体	tǐ	body	167
癢/痒	yǎng	itchy	194
敏	mǐn	nimble; agile	123
健	jiàn	healthy	92
康	kāng	healthy; affluent	101
保	bǎo	to protect; insurance	27
險/险	xiǎn	risk; danger	183
趕/赶	gǎn	to rush for	65
越	yuè	to exceed	209
休	xiū	to cease; to rest	190
息	xī	to cease; to rest	180
懶/懒	lǎn	lazy	107
亂/乱	luàn	randomly; messily	115

LESSON 16

印	yìn	to print	201
象	xiàng	elephant; appearance; shape	185
成	chéng	to become; to succeed	38
演	yǎn	to act; to perform	193
費/费	fèi	to spend; to take (effort)	61
倆/俩	liǎ	(coll.) two	111
碼/码	mǎ	(symbol indicating a number)	118
搬	bān	to move	24
掃/扫	sǎo	to sweep	144

整	zhěng	to put in order	215
理	lǐ	reason; in good order	110
房	fáng	house	59
旅	lǚ	to travel	116

LESSON 17

吵	chǎo	to quarrel; noisy	38
連/连	lián	even; to link	111
廣/广	guǎng	wide; vast	73
附	fù	to attach; near	63
套	tào	MW (for suite or set)	165
寓	yù	residence	205
臥/卧	wò	to lie (down)	178
廚/厨	chú	kitchen	41
衛/卫	wèi	to guard; to protect	177
傢/家	jiā	furniture	89
具	jù	tool; utensil	99
乾/干	gān	dry	65
淨/净	jìng	clean; pure	97
沙	shā	sand	144
椅	yǐ	chair	199
架	jià	shelf	90
安	ān	calm; safe	22
靜/静	jìng	quiet	98
元	yuán	MW (for unit of Chinese currency); yuan	206
民	mín	the people; folk	123
幣/币	bì	currency; coin	30
差	chà	to fall short of	36
押	yā	to give as security	191
當/当	dāng	to serve as; to be	47
另	lìng	other; another	114
准	zhǔn	to allow	222
養/养	yǎng	to raise	194
趣	qù	interest; interesting	141
寵/宠	chǒng	to dote on	40

LESSON 18

胖	pàng	fat	132
怕	pà	to fear; to be afraid of	131
簡/简	jiǎn	simple	91
單/单	dān	single	46
跑	pǎo	to run	133
步	bù	step; pace	33
受	shòu	to bear	154
拍	pāi	to clap; racket	131
籃/篮	lán	basket	107
游	yóu	to swim	203
泳	yǒng	swimming	202
危	wēi	danger	175
淹	yān	to submerge; to drown	192
願/愿	yuàn	wish; hope	208
提	tí	to lift	167
賽/赛	sài	game; competition	143
際/际	jì	border; boundary	88
式	shì	type; style	151
應/应	yīng/ yìng	should/ to respond	201
該/ 该	gāi	should; ought to	64
腳/脚	jiǎo	foot	92
踢	tī	to kick	166
抱	bào	to hold or carry in one's arms	27
壓/压	yā	to press; to weigh down	191
被	bèi	by; quilt	28
擔/担	dān	to be burdened with	46
棒	bàng	fantastic	26

LESSON 19

司	sī	to take charge of	158
實/实	shí	solid; reality	150
計/计	jì	to count	87
劃/划	huà	to plan; to divide	82
父	fù	father	63

母	mǔ	mother	125
首	shǒu	head	154
政	zhèng	politics	215
治	zhì	to govern; to manage	218
化	huà	to transform; to influence	82
勝/胜	shèng	victory; wonderful	149
古	gǔ	ancient	71
蹟/迹	jì	remains; ruins	88
導/导	dǎo	to lead; to guide	47
遊/游	yóu	to roam; to travel	203
護/护	hù	to protect	81
訂/订	dìng	to reserve; to book (a ticket, a hotel room, etc.)	53
簽/签	qiān	to sign	137
證/证	zhèng	proof; certificate	216
社	shè	organized body	147
香	xiāng	fragrant	184
港	gǎng	harbor	66
臺/台	tái	platform; deck	164
初	chū	beginning; elementary	40
程	chéng	journey; schedule	39
返	fǎn	to return	58
航	háng	to navigate	77
千	qiān	thousand	20
折	zhé	to fold	213
轉/转	zhuǎn/zhuàn	to turn	221
靠	kào	to lean on; to rely on	102
窗	chuāng	window	42
戶/户	hù	door; household	80
份	fèn	MW (for meal orders, jobs)	61

LESSON 20

托	tuō	to entrust	171
包	bāo	bag; sack; bundle; package	26
超	chāo	to exceed; to surpass	37
登	dēng	to climb; to ascend	49
牌	pái	plate; card; brand	131
哭	kū	to cry; to weep	104
顧/顾	gù	to look after; to attend to	71
叔	shū	uncle	155
阿	ā	(a prefix)	21
姨	yí	aunt	198
迎	yíng	to welcome	202
瘦	shòu	thin; slim (of a person or animal)	155
爺/爷	yé	grandpa; (respectful form of address for elderly men)	195
奶	nǎi	milk; (paternal) grandmother	126
烤	kǎo	to bake; to roast; to grill	102
鴨/鸭	yā	duck	191

LEVEL 2

慣/惯	guàn	to be used to	73
啤	pí	*beer	133
酒	jiǔ	wine	98
助	zhù	to assist; to aid	220
葉/叶	yè	leaf	196

CHARACTER INDEX
Alphabetical by *Pinyin*

*	=	**Bound Form**	
MW	=	**Measure Word**	
P	=	**Particle**	
QP	=	**Question Particle**	
( )	=	**Variant/Radical Form**	

A

阿	ā	(a prefix)	21
啊	a	P	21
哎	āi	(exclamatory particle to express surprise or dissatisfaction)	22
愛/爱	ài	love; to love	22
安	ān	calm; safe	22

B

八	bā	eight	19
把	bǎ	MW (for objects with handles)	23
爸	bà	father; dad	23
吧	ba	P (a sentence–ending particle)	23
白	bái	white; (surname)	24
百	bǎi	hundred	20
班	bān	class	24
搬	bān	to move	24
半	bàn	half	25
拌	bàn	to mix	25
辦/办	bàn	to manage	25
幫/帮	bāng	to help	26
棒	bàng	fantastic	26
包	bāo	bag; sack; bundle; package	26
保	bǎo	to protect; insurance	27
抱	bào	to hold or carry in one's arms	27
報/报	bào	to report; newspaper	27

杯	bēi	cup; glass	28
北	běi	north	28
貝/贝	bèi	cowry shell	13
被	bèi	by; quilt	28
備/备	bèi	to prepare	29
本	běn	MW (for books); foundation	29
鼻	bí	nose	29
比	bǐ	to compare	30
筆/笔	bǐ	pen; writing brush	30
幣/币	bì	currency; coin	30
邊/边	biān	side	31
便	biàn	convenient; handy	31
遍	biàn	MW (for complete courses of an action or instances of an action)	31
表	biǎo	surface; matrilineal relatives	32
別/别	bié	other; do not	32
冰	bīng	ice	32
病	bìng	illness; to become ill	33
不	bù	not; no	33
步	bù	step; pace	33

C

才	cái	not until; only then	34
菜	cài	dish; cuisine; vegetable	34
餐	cān	meal	34
厠	cè	toilet	35

INDEXES

查	chá	to check; to look up	35
茶	chá	tea	35
差	chà	to fall short of	36
長/长	cháng	long	36
常	cháng	often; ordinary	36
場/场	chǎng	field	37
唱	chàng	to sing	37
超	chāo	to exceed; to surpass	37
吵	chǎo	to quarrel; noisy	38
車/车	chē	vehicle; car	12
襯/衬	chèn	lining	38
成	chéng	to become; to succeed	38
城	chéng	city; town	39
程	chéng	journey; schedule	39
吃	chī	to eat	39
重	chóng	again	219
寵/宠	chǒng	to dote on	40
出	chū	to go out	40
初	chū	beginning; elementary	40
除	chú	except	41
廚/厨	chú	kitchen	41
楚	chǔ	clear; neat	41
穿	chuān	to wear; to pass through	42
窗	chuāng	window	42
床(牀)	chuáng	bed	42
春	chūn	spring	43
詞/词	cí	word	43
次	cì	MW (for occurrences)	43
聰/聪	cōng	able to hear well; smart	44
從/从	cóng	from	44
醋	cù	vinegar	44
寸	cùn	inch	5
錯/错	cuò	wrong; error	45

D

打	dǎ	to hit	45
大	dà	big; great	4
帶/带	dài	to bring; to take; to carry	45
單/单	dān	single	46
擔/担	dān	to be burdened with	46
但	dàn	but; however	46
蛋	dàn	egg	47
當/当	dāng	to serve as; to be	47
刀(刂)	dāo	knife	1
導/导	dǎo	to lead; to guide	47
到	dào	to arrive	48
道	dào	road; way	48
得	dé	to obtain; to get; P	48
得	děi	must; have to	48
的	de	possessive P	49
地	de	P	50
登	dēng	to climb; to ascend	49
燈/灯	dēng	light; lamp	49
等	děng	to wait; rank	50
地	dì	earth	50
弟	dì	younger brother	50
第	dì	(ordinal prefix)	51
點/点	diǎn	dot; o'clock	51
店	diàn	store; shop	51
電/电	diàn	electricity	52
碟	dié	disc; saucer	52
定	dìng	settled; decided	52
訂/订	dìng	to reserve; to book (a ticket, a hotel room, etc.)	53
冬	dōng	winter	53
東/东	dōng	east	53
懂	dǒng	to understand	54
動/动	dòng	to move	54
都	dōu	all; both	54

廣/广	guǎng	wide; vast	73
貴/贵	guì	honorable; expensive	74
國/国	guó	country; nation	74
果	guǒ	fruit; result	74
過/过	guò	to pass	75

H

孩	hái	child	75
還/还	hái	still; yet	75
海	hǎi	sea	76
寒	hán	cold	76
漢/汉	hàn	Chinese ethnicity	76
行	háng	bank; firm	189
航	háng	to navigate	77
好	hǎo	good; fine	77
好	hào	to like; to be fond of	77
號/号	hào	number	77
喝	hē	to drink	78
合	hé	to suit; to fit	78
和	hé	and; harmonious	78
黑	hēi	black	79
很	hěn	very	79
紅/红	hóng	red	79
後/后	hòu	after; behind	80
候	hòu	time; season; await	80
戶/户	hù	door; household	80
護/护	hù	to protect	81
花	huā	to spend; flower	81
滑	huá	slippery; to slide	81
化	huà	to transform; to influence	82
話/话	huà	speech	82
劃/划	huà	to plan; to divide	82
壞/坏	huài	bad	83
歡/欢	huān	happy; joyous	83
還/还	huán	to exchange; to return	75

換/换	huàn	to exchange; to change	83
黃(黄)	huáng	yellow	84
回	huí	to return	84
會/会	huì	meeting	84
活	huó	to live; living	85
火(灬)	huǒ	fire	9
或	huò	or	85
貨/货	huò	merchandise	85
和	huo	*warm	78

J

機/机	jī	machine	86
級/级	jí	grade; level	86
極/极	jí	extremely; pole	86
己	jǐ	oneself	87
幾/几	jǐ	how many; a few	87
計/计	jì	to count	87
記/记	jì	to remember; to record	88
際/际	jì	border; boundary	88
蹟/迹	jì	remains; ruins	88
加	jiā	to add	89
家	jiā	family; home	89
傢	jiā	furniture	89
架	jià	shelf	90
假	jià	vacation	90
間/间	jiān	MW (for rooms); between	90
檢/检	jiǎn	to inspect	91
簡/简	jiǎn	simple	91
件	jiàn	MW (for items)	91
見/见	jiàn	to see	13
健	jiàn	healthy	92
教(教)	jiāo	to teach	92
腳/脚	jiǎo	foot	92
餃/饺	jiǎo	dumpling	93
叫	jiào	to be called; to call	93

覺/觉	jiào	to sleep	99
教(教)	jiào	education	92
接	jiē	to receive; to welcome	93
節/节	jié	MW (for classes); holiday	94
姐	jiě	elder sister	94
介	jiè	to be between	94
金	jīn	metal; gold; (surname)	14
今	jīn	today; now	95
緊/紧	jǐn	tense; tight	95
近	jìn	close; near	95
進/进	jìn	to enter	96
京	jīng	capital city	96
睛	jīng	eyeball	96
精	jīng	essence; refined	97
經/经	jīng	to pass through	97
淨/净	jìng	clean; pure	97
靜/静	jìng	quiet	98
九	jiǔ	nine	19
久	jiǔ	long time	98
酒	jiǔ	wine	98
就	jiù	just	99
具	jù	tool; utensil	99
覺/觉	jué	to feel; to think	99

K

咖	kā	*coffee	100
卡	kǎ	card	100
開/开	kāi	to open; to operate	100
看	kàn	to watch; to read	101
康	kāng	healthy; affluent	101
考	kǎo	test; to test	101
烤	kǎo	to bake; to roast; to grill	102
靠	kào	to lean on; to rely on	102
可	kě	but; to permit	102
渴	kě	thirsty	103

刻	kè	quarter (hour); to carve	103
客	kè	guest	103
課/课	kè	class; lesson	104
空	kōng	empty; sky	104
空	kòng	free time	104
口	kǒu	mouth; entrance	2
哭	kū	to cry; to weep	104
酷	kù	cool; cruel	105
褲/裤	kù	pants	105
快	kuài	fast; quick	105
塊/块	kuài	piece; dollar	106

L

辣	là	spicy	106
來/来	lái	to come	106
藍/蓝	lán	blue	107
籃/篮	lán	basket	107
懶/懒	lǎn	lazy	107
老	lǎo	old	108
樂/乐	lè	happy	209
了	le	P	108
累	lèi	tired	108
冷	lěng	cold	109
梨	lí	pear	109
離/离	lí	away from	109
李	lǐ	plum; (surname)	110
理	lǐ	reason; in good order	110
裏/裡 里	lǐ	inside	110
禮/礼	lǐ	gift; ceremony	111
力	lì	power; strength	2
倆/俩	liǎ	(coll.) two	111
連/连	lián	even; to link	111
臉/脸	liǎn	face	112
練/练	liàn	to practice; to drill	112

INDEXES

涼/凉	liáng	cool	112
兩/两	liǎng	two; a couple of	113
亮/亮	liàng	bright	113
聊	liáo	to chat	113
料	liào	material	114
另	lìng	other; another	114
六	liù	six	18
樓/楼	lóu	multi-storied building; floor (of building)	114
路	lù	road; way	115
錄/录	lù	to record	115
亂/乱	luàn	randomly; messily	115
倫/伦	lún	ethics; moral principles	116
旅	lǚ	to travel	116
律	lù	law; rule	116
綠/绿	lù	green	117

M

媽/妈	mā	mother; mom	117
麻	má	hemp; numb	117
馬/马	mǎ	horse	16
碼/码	mǎ	(symbol indicating a number)	118
嗎/吗	ma	QP	118
買/买	mǎi	to buy	118
賣/卖	mài	to sell	119
慢	màn	slow	119
忙	máng	busy	119
毛	máo	hair; dime	120
冒	mào	to belch; to emit	120
麼/么	me	*QP	120
沒(没)	méi	(have) not	121
美	měi	beautiful	121
每	měi	every; each	121
妹	mèi	younger sister	122
悶/闷	mēn	stuffy	122
門/门	mén	door; gate	15

悶/闷	mèn	depressed	122
們/们	men	*(plural suffix)	122
米	mǐ	uncooked rice	12
糸	mì	silk	11
面	miàn	face	123
民	mín	the people; folk	123
敏	mǐn	nimble; agile	123
名	míng	name	124
明	míng	bright	124
末	mò	end	124
沒(没)	mò	to sink	121
母	mǔ	mother	125
姆	mǔ	housemaid	125
木	mù	wood	8
目	mù	eye	10

N

拿	ná	to take; to get	125
哪	nǎ/něi	which	126
那	nà/nèi	that	126
奶	nǎi	milk; (paternal) grandmother	126
男	nán	male	127
南	nán	south	127
難/难	nán	difficult; hard	127
腦/脑	nǎo	brain	128
呢	ne	QP	128
能	néng	can; to be able to	128
你	nǐ	you	129
年	nián	year	129
唸/念	niàn	to read aloud	129
您	nín	you (polite)	130
牛	niú	cow; ox	7
紐/纽	niǔ	knob; button	130
暖	nuǎn	warm	130
女	nǚ	female; woman	4

勝/胜	shèng	victory; wonderful	149
師/师	shī	teacher	149
十	shí	ten	19
時/时	shí	time	149
食	shí	to eat	16
實/实	shí	solid; reality	150
識/识	shí	to recognize	150
始	shǐ	to begin	150
示(礻)	shì	to show	11
市	shì	city; market	151
式	shì	type; style	151
事	shì	affair; matter	151
是	shì	to be	152
室	shì	room	152
視/视	shì	to view; to look at	152
試/试	shì	test; to try	153
適/适	shì	to suit; appropriate	153
收	shōu	to receive; to accept	153
手(扌)	shǒu	hand	7
首	shǒu	head	154
受	shòu	to bear	154
售	shòu	sale; to sell	154
瘦	shòu	thin; slim (of a person or animal)	155
叔	shū	uncle	155
書/书	shū	book	155
舒	shū	to stretch; to smooth out	156
暑	shǔ	heat; summer	156
屬/属	shǔ	to belong to	156
刷	shuā	to brush; to swipe	157
帥/帅	shuài	handsome; smart	157
雙/双	shuāng	pair	157
水(氵)	shuǐ	water	9
睡	shuì	to sleep	158
說/说	shuō	to speak	158

司	sī	to take charge of	158
思	sī	to think	159
死	sǐ	to die; (a complement indicating an extreme degree)	159
四	sì	four	17
送	sòng	to see off; to deliver	159
素	sù	vegetarian; made from vegetables	160
速/速	sù	speed	160
宿	sù	to stay; to lodge	160
訴/诉	sù	to tell; to relate	161
酸	suān	sour	161
算	suàn	to calculate	161
雖/虽	suī	although	162
歲/岁	suì	age	162
所(所)	suǒ	*so; place	162

T

它	tā	it	163
他	tā	he	163
她	tā	she	163
臺/台	tái	platform; deck	164
太	tài	too; extremely	164
湯/汤	tāng	soup	164
糖	táng	sugar; candy	165
躺	tǎng	to lie (down)	165
套	tào	MW (for suite or set)	165
特	tè	special	166
疼	téng	to be painful	166
踢	tī	to kick	166
提	tí	to lift	167
題/题	tí	topic; question	167
體/体	tǐ	body	167
天	tiān	sky; day	168
田	tián	field; (surname)	10
甜	tián	sweet	168

條/条	tiáo	MW (for long, thin objects)	168
跳	tiào	to jump	169
鐵/铁	tiě	iron	169
聽/听	tīng	to listen	169
廳/厅	tīng	hall	170
挺	tǐng	very; rather	170
同	tóng	same	170
頭/头	tóu	head; top	171
圖/图	tú	picture; drawing	171
土	tǔ	earth	3
托	tuō	to entrust	171

W

外	wài	outside; foreign	172
灣/湾	wān	strait; bay	172
完	wán	finished	172
玩	wán	to play; to have fun	173
晚	wǎn	evening; late	173
碗	wǎn	bowl	173
王	wáng	king; (surname)	10
往	wǎng	toward; past	174
網/网	wǎng	net	174
忘	wàng	to forget	174
望	wàng	to hope; to gaze	175
危	wēi	danger	175
囗	wéi	enclose	3
位	wèi	MW (for people [polite])	175
味	wèi	flavor; taste	176
為/为	wèi/wéi	for	176
喂	wéi/wèi	Hello!; Hey!	176
衛/卫	wèi	to guard; to protect	177
文	wén	(written) language; script	177
問/问	wèn	to ask (a question)	177
我	wǒ	I; me	178
臥/卧	wò	to lie (down)	178

五	wǔ	five	18
午	wǔ	noon	178
舞	wǔ	to dance; dance	179
物	wù	thing; matter	179
務/务	wù	affair; task	179

X

夕	xī	sunset; evening	3
西	xī	west	180
希	xī	to hope	180
息	xī	to cease; to rest	180
習/习	xí	to practice	181
喜	xǐ	to like; happy	181
洗	xǐ	to wash	181
係/系	xì	to relate to	182
下	xià	below; under	182
夏	xià	summer	182
先	xiān	first	183
險/险	xiǎn	risk; danger	183
現/现	xiàn	now; present	183
線/线	xiàn	line; route	184
香	xiāng	fragrant	184
箱	xiāng	box; case	184
想	xiǎng	to want; to think	185
象	xiàng	elephant; appearance; shape	185
像	xiàng	likeness; portrait	185
小	xiǎo	little; small	5
校	xiào	school	186
笑	xiào	to laugh; to smile	186
些	xiē	MW (for indefinite amount); some	186
鞋	xié	shoes	187
寫/写	xiě	to write	187
謝/谢	xiè	to thank	187
心 (忄)	xīn	heart	6

新	xīn	new	188
信	xìn	letter; to believe	188
星	xīng	star	188
行	xíng	to walk; okay	189
姓	xìng	surname	189
興	xìng	mood; interest	189
休	xiū	to cease; to rest	190
學/学	xué	to study	190
雪	xuě	snow	190

Y

押	yā	to give as security	191
鴨/鸭	yā	duck	191
壓/压	yā	to press; to weigh down	191
呀	ya	P	192
淹	yān	to submerge; to drown	192
言/讠	yán	word; speech	13
顏/颜	yán	face; countenance	192
鹽/盐	yán	salt	193
眼	yǎn	eye	193
演	yǎn	to act; to perform	193
養/养	yǎng	to raise	194
癢/痒	yǎng	itchy	194
樣/样	yàng	kind; appearance	194
幺	yāo	tiny; small	6
要	yào	to want	195
藥/药	yào	medicine	195
爺/爷	yé	grandpa; (respectful form of address for elderly men)	195
也	yě	also; too	196
夜	yè	night	196
葉/叶	yè	leaf	196
業/业	yè	profession	197
一	yī	one	17
衣(衤)	yī	clothing	12

醫/医	yī	doctor; medicine	197
宜	yí	suitable	197
姨	yí	aunt	198
已	yǐ	already	198
以	yǐ	with	198
椅	yǐ	chair	199
易	yì	easy	199
意	yì	meaning	199
因	yīn	because	200
音	yīn	sound; music	200
飲/饮	yǐn	to drink	200
印	yìn	to print	201
英	yīng	flower; hero; *England	201
應/应	yīng	should	201
迎	yíng	to welcome	202
影	yǐng	shadow	202
應/应	yìng	to respond	201
泳	yǒng	swimming	202
用	yòng	to use	203
游	yóu	to swim	203
遊/游	yóu	to roam; to travel	203
郵/邮	yóu	post; mail	204
友	yǒu	friend	204
有	yǒu	to have; to exist	204
又	yòu	right hand; again	2
右	yòu	right	205
魚/鱼	yú	fish	16
雨	yǔ	rain	15
語/语	yǔ	language	205
寓	yù	residence	205
預/预	yù	in advance; beforehand	206
元	yuán	MW (for unit of Chinese currency): yuan	206
員/员	yuán	personnel	206
園/园	yuán	garden	207

圓/圆	yuán	round	207
遠/远	yuǎn	far	207
院	yuàn	yard	208
願/愿	yuàn	wish; hope	208
約/约	yuē	agreement; appointment	208
月	yuè	moon; month	8
越	yuè	to exceed	209
樂/乐	yuè	music	209
運/运	yùn	to move	209

Z

在	zài	at; in; on	210
再	zài	again	210
糟	zāo	messy; rotten	210
早	zǎo	early	211
澡	zǎo	bath	211
怎	zěn	*how	211
站	zhàn	stand; station	212
張/张	zhāng	MW (for flat objects); (surname)	212
長/长	zhǎng	to grow; leader	36
找	zhǎo	to look for; to seek	212
照	zhào	photograph; to shine	213
折	zhé	to fold	213
者	zhě	(aux. verb)	213
這/这	zhè(i)	this	214
針/针	zhēn	needle	214
真(眞)	zhēn	true; real; really	214
整	zhěng	to put in order	215
正	zhèng	just; upright	215
政	zhèng	politics	215
證/证	zhèng	proof; certificate	216
知	zhī	to know	216
枝	zhī	branch; MW (for long, thin objects)	216

直	zhí	straight	217
只	zhǐ	only	217
紙/纸	zhǐ	paper	217
治	zhì	to govern; to manage	218
中	zhōng	center; middle	218
鐘/钟	zhōng	clock	218
種/种	zhǒng	kinds; types	219
重	zhòng	heavy; serious	219
種/种	zhòng	to plant	219
州	zhōu	administrative division; state	219
週/周	zhōu	week; cycle	220
住	zhù	to live (in a certain place)	220
助	zhù	to assist; to aid	220
祝	zhù	to wish (well)	221
專/专	zhuān	special	221
轉/转	zhuǎn/zhuàn	to turn	221
隹	zhuī	short-tailed bird	15
准	zhǔn	to allow	222
準/准	zhǔn	standard; criterion	222
桌	zhuō	table; desk	222
子	zǐ	baby; child	4
字	zì	character	222
自	zì	self	223
走	zǒu	to walk	14
租	zū	to rent	223
足	zú	foot; enough	14
嘴	zuǐ	mouth	223
最	zuì	most	224
昨	zuó	yesterday	224
左	zuǒ	left	224
坐	zuò	to sit	225
作	zuò	to work; to do	225
做	zuò	to do	225

Traditional CHARACTER INDEX
By Stroke Count

*	=	**Bound Form**	
MW	=	**Measure Word**	
P	=	**Particle**	
QP	=	**Question Particle**	
( )	=	**Variant/Radical Form**	

1

一	yī	one	17

2

八	bā	eight	19
刀 (刂)	dāo	knife	1
二	èr	two	17
九	jiǔ	nine	19
了	le	P	108
力	lì	power; strength	2
七	qī	seven	18
人 (亻)	rén	person; people	1
十	shí	ten	19
又	yòu	right hand; again	2

3

才	cái	not until; only then	34
寸	cùn	inch	5
大	dà	big; great	4
工	gōng	tool; work; labor	5
弓	gōng	bow	6
己	jǐ	oneself	87
久	jiǔ	long time	98
口	kǒu	mouth; entrance	2
女	nǔ	woman; female	4
千	qiān	thousand	20

三	sān	three	17
上	shàng	above; top	145
土	tǔ	earth	3
囗	wéi	enclose	3
夕	xī	sunset; evening	3
下	xià	below; under	182
小	xiǎo	little; small	5
幺	yāo	tiny; small	6
也	yě	also; too	196
已	yǐ	already	198
子	zǐ	baby; child	4

4

比	bǐ	to compare	30
不	bù	not; no	33
方	fāng	square; side	9
分	fēn	penny; minute	61
父	fù	father	63
戈	gē	dagger-axe	7
公	gōng	public	69
火 (灬)	huǒ	fire	9
戶/户	hù	door; household	80
化	huà	to transform; to influence	82
介	jiè	to be between	94
今	jīn	today; now	95
六	liù	six	18

毛	máo	hair; dime	120
木	mù	wood	8
牛	niú	cow; ox	7
片	piàn	MW (for tablets, films); slice	134
日	rì	sun; day	8
少	shǎo/shào	few; little; less/ young	146
什(甚)	shén	*what	148
手	shǒu	hand	7
水(氵)	shuǐ	water	9
太	tài	too; extremely	164
天	tiān	sky; day	168
王	wáng	king; (surname)	10
文	wén	(written) language; script	177
五	wǔ	five	18
午	wǔ	noon	178
心(忄)	xīn	heart	6
以	yǐ	with	198
友	yǒu	friend	204
元	yuán	MW (for unit of Chinese currency): yuan	206
月	yuè	moon; mouth	8
中	zhōng	center; middle	218

5

白	bái	white	24
半	bàn	half	25
包	bāo	bag; sack; bundle; package	26
北	běi	north	28
本	běn	MW (for books); foundation	29
出	chū	to go out	40
打	dǎ	to hit	45
冬	dōng	winter	53
付	fù	to pay	63
功	gōng	skill	70
古	gǔ	ancient	71

瓜	guā	melon; guord	72
加	jiā	to add	89
叫	jiào	to be called; to call	93
卡	kǎ	card	100
可	kě	but; to permit	102
另	lìng	other; another	114
民	mín	the people; folk	123
末	mò	end	124
母	mǔ	mother	125
目	mù	eye	10
奶	nǎi	milk; (paternal) grandmother	126
平	píng	level; even	135
且	qiě	(conj.)	138
去	qù	to go	140
生	shēng	to be born; to grow	148
示(礻)	shì	to show	11
市	shì	city; market	151
司	sī	to take charge of	158
四	sì	four	17
他	tā	he	163
它	tā	it	163
台/臺	tái	platform; deck	164
田	tián	field; (surname)	10
外	wài	outside; foreign	172
印	yìn	to print	201
用	yòng	to use	203
右	yòu	right	205
正	zhèng	just; upright	215
只	zhǐ	only	217
左	zuǒ	left	224

6

安	ān	calm; safe	22
百	bǎi	hundred	20
冰	bīng	ice	32

成	chéng	to become; to succeed	38
吃	chī	to eat	39
次	cì	MW (for occurrences)	43
地	dì/de	earth	50
多	duō	many; much	56
而	ér	(conj.)	57
耳	ěr	ear	11
份	fèn	MW (for meal orders, jobs)	61
共	gòng	altogether	70
好	hǎo/hào	good; fine/ to like; to be fond of	77
合	hé	to suit; to fit	78
回	huí	to return	84
件	jiàn	MW (for items)	91
考	kǎo	test; to test	101
老	lǎo	old	108
忙	máng	busy	119
米	mǐ	uncooked rice	12
糸(纟)	mì	silk	11
名	míng	name	124
那	nà/nèi	that	126
年	nián	year	129
肉	ròu	meat; flesh	143
如	rú	as; if	143
色	sè	color	144
式	shì	type; style	151
收	shōu	to receive; to accept	153
死	sǐ	to die; (a complement indicating an extreme degree)	159
她	tā	she	163
同	tóng	same	170
托	tuō	to entrust	171
危	wēi	danger	175
西	xī	west	180
先	xiān	first	183

行	xíng/ háng	to walk; okay/ bank; firm	189
休	xiū	to cease; to rest	190
衣(衤)	yī	clothing	12
因	yīn	because	200
有	yǒu	to have; to exist	204
再	zài	again	210
在	zài	at; in; on	210
早	zǎo	early	211
州	zhōu	administrative division; state	219
字	zì	character	222
自	zì	self	223

7

阿	ā	(a prefix)	21
把	bǎ	MW (for objects with handles)	23
吧	ba	P (a sentence-ending particle)	23
貝/贝	bèi	cowry shell	13
別/别	bié	other; do not	32
步	bù	step; pace	33
吵	chǎo	to quarrel; noisy	38
車/车	chē	vehicle; car	12
初	chū	beginning; elementary	40
床(牀)	chuáng	bed	42
但	dàn	but; however	46
弟	dì	younger brother	50
豆	dòu	bean	55
肚	dù	belly; abdomen	55
返	fǎn	to return	58
附	fù	to attach; near	63
告	gào	to tell; to inform	67
更	gèng/ gēng	even more/ to alternate	69
花	huā	to spend; flower	82
見/见	jiàn	to see	13
近	jìn	close; near	95

快	kuài	fast; quick	105
來/来	lái	to come	106
冷	lěng	cold	109
李	lǐ	plum; (surname)	110
没(沒)	méi/ mò	(have) not/ to sink	121
每	měi	every; each	121
男	nán	male	127
你	nǐ	you	129
汽	qì	steam; gas	137
沙	shā	sand	144
社	shè	organized body	147
身	shēn	body	148
完	wán	finished	172
忘	wàng	to forget	174
位	wèi	MW (for people [polite])	175
我	wǒ	I; me	178
希	xī	to hope	180
呀	ya	P	192
言(讠)	yán	word; speech	13
迎	yíng	to welcome	202
找	zhǎo	to look for; to seek	212
折	zhé	to fold	213
住	zhù	to live (in a certain place)	220
助	zhù	to assist; to aid	220
走	zǒu	to walk	14
足	zú	foot; enough	14
坐	zuò	to sit	225
作	zuò	to work; to do	225

8

哎	āi	(exclamatory particle to express surprise or dissatisfaction)	22
爸	bà	dad	23
拌	bàn	to mix	25

抱	bào	to hold or carry in one's arms	27
杯	bēi	cup; glass	28
表	biǎo	surface; matrilineal relatives	32
長/长	cháng/ zhǎng	long/ leader; to grow	36
到	dào	to arrive	48
的	de	P	49
店	diàn	store; shop	51
定	dìng	settled; decided	52
東/东	dōng	east	53
兒/儿	ér	son; child	57
法	fǎ	method; way; law	58
房	fáng	house	59
放	fàng	to put; to place	59
非	fēi	not; non-	60
服	fú	clothing; to serve	62
狗	gǒu	dog	70
拐	guǎi	to turn	72
果	guǒ	fruit; result	74
和	hé/huo	and; harmonious/*warm	78
或	huò	or	85
姐	jiě	elder sister	94
金(钅)	jīn	metal; gold; (surname)	14
京	jīng	capital city	96
具	jù	tool; utensil	99
咖	kā	*coffee	100
刻	kè	quarter (hour); to carve	103
空	kòng/ kōng	free time/ empty; sky	104
兩/两	liǎng	two; a couple of	113
妹	mèi	younger sister	122
門/门	mén	door; gate	15
明	míng	bright	124
姆	mǔ	housemaid	125
呢	ne	QP	128

夏	xià	summer	182
校	xiào	school	186
笑	xiào	to laugh; to smile	186
員/员	yuán	personnel	206
站	zhàn	stand; station	212
針/针	zhēn	needle	214
真(眞)	zhēn	true; real; really	214
紙/纸	zhǐ	paper	217
准	zhǔn	to allow	222
桌	zhuō	table; desk	222
租	zū	to rent	223

11

菜	cài	dish; cuisine; vegetable	34
厠/厕	cè	toilet	35
常	cháng	often; ordinary	36
唱	chàng	to sing	37
從/从	cóng	from	44
帶/带	dài	to bring; to take; to carry	45
蛋	dàn	egg	47
得	dé/de/ děi	to obtain; to get/ P/ must; have to	48
第	dì	(ordinal prefix)	51
動/动	dòng	to move	54
啡	fēi	*coffee	60
乾/干	gān	dry	65
夠	gòu	enough	71
國/国	guó	country; nation	74
黃(黄)	huáng	yellow	84
貨/货	huò	merchandise	85
假	jià	vacation	90
教(敎)	jiāo/jiào	to teach; education	92
接	jiē	to receive; to welcome	93
淨/净	jìng	clean; pure	97
康	kāng	healthy; affluent	101

累	lèi	tired	108
梨	lí	pear	109
理	lǐ	reason; in good order	110
涼/凉	liáng	cool	112
聊	liáo	to chat	113
麻	má	hemp; numb	117
敏	mǐn	nimble; agile	123
唸/念	niàn	to read aloud	129
您	nín	you (polite)	130
啤	pí	*beer	133
票	piào	ticket	134
清	qīng	clear; clean; pure	139
球	qiú	ball	140
商	shāng	commerce; business	145
紹/绍	shào	to introduce; to continue	146
視/视	shì	to view; to look at	152
售	shòu	sale; to sell	154
宿	sù	to stay; to lodge	160
速	sù	speed	160
掃/扫	sǎo	to sweep	144
甜	tián	sweet	168
條/条	tiáo	MW (for long, thin objects)	168
望	wàng	to hope; to gaze	175
問/问	wèn	to ask	177
習/习	xí	to practice	181
現/现	xiàn	present; now	183
象	xiàng	elephant; appearance; shape	185
雪	xuě	snow	190
淹	yān	to submerge; to drown	192
眼	yǎn	eye	193
郵/邮	yóu	post; mail	204
魚/鱼	yú	fish	16
張/张	zhāng	MW (for flat objects); (surname)	212
這/这	zhè(i)	this	214

專/专	zhuān	special	221
做	zuò	to do	225

12

棒	bàng	fantastic	26
報/报	bào	to report; newspaper	27
備/备	bèi	to prepare	29
筆/笔	bǐ	pen; writing brush	30
遍	biàn	MW (for complete courses of an action or instances of an action)	31
場/场	chǎng	field	37
超	chāo	to exceed; to surpass	37
程	chéng	journey; schedule	39
窗	chuāng	window	42
詞/词	cí	word	43
單/单	dān	single	46
登	dēng	to climb; to ascend	49
等	děng	to wait; rank	50
短	duǎn	short	55
發/发	fā	to emit; to issue	57
飯/饭	fàn	meal; (cooked) rice	59
費/费	fèi	to spend; to take (effort)	61
復/复	fù	to duplicate	64
傅	fù	tutor; instructor	64
港	gǎng	harbor	66
給/给	gěi	to give	68
貴/贵	guì	honorable; expensive	74
寒	hán	cold	76
喝	hē	to drink	78
黑	hēi	black	79
滑	huá	slippery; to slide	81
換/换	huàn	to exchange; to change	83
極/极	jí	extremely; pole	86
幾/几	jǐ	how many; a few	87
傢	jiā	furniture	89

間/间	jiān	MW (for rooms)	90
進/进	jìn	to enter	96
就	jiù	just	99
開/开	kāi	to open; to operate	100
渴	kě	thirsty	103
裡/裏/里	lǐ	inside	110
買/买	mǎi	to buy	118
悶/闷	mēn/mèn	stuffy/ depressed	122
牌	pái	plate; card; brand	131
跑	pǎo	to run	133
期	qī	period (of time)	136
然	rán	like that; so	141
勝/胜	shèng	victory; wonderful	149
試/试	shì	test; to try	153
舒	shū	to stretch; to smooth out	156
暑	shǔ	heat; summer	156
訴/诉	sù	to tell; to relate	161
湯/汤	tāng	soup	164
提	tí	to lift	167
晚	wǎn	evening; late	173
喂	wéi/wèi	Hello!; Hey!	176
喜	xǐ	to like; happy	181
爺/爷	yé	grandpa; (respectful form of address for elderly men)	195
葉/叶	yè	leaf	196
椅	yǐ	chair	199
飲/饮	yǐn	to drink	200
游	yóu	to swim	203
遊/游	yóu	to roam; to travel	203
寓	yù	residence	205
越	yuè	to exceed	209
運/运	yùn	to move	209
週/周	zhōu	week; cycle	220
準/准	zhǔn	standard; criterion	222
最	zuì	most	224

13

愛/爱	ài	love; to love	22
搬	bān	to move	24
楚	chǔ	clear; neat	41
當/当	dāng	to serve as; to be	47
道	dào	road; way	48
電/电	diàn	electricity	52
煩/烦	fán	to bother; to trouble	58
該/该	gāi	should; ought to	64
感	gǎn	to feel; to sense	65
跟	gēn	with; and	69
過/过	guò	to pass	75
號/号	hào	number	77
話/话	huà	speech	82
會/会	huì	meeting	84
塊/块	kuài	piece; dollar	106
際/际	jì	border; boundary	88
腳/脚	jiǎo	foot	92
節/节	jié	MW (for classes); holiday	94
睛	jīng	eyeball	96
經/经	jīng	to pass through	97
裏/裡/里	lǐ	inside	110
路	lù	road; way	115
亂/乱	luàn	randomly; messily	115
媽/妈	mā	mother; mom	117
嗎/吗	ma	QP	118
腦/脑	nǎo	brain	128
暖	nuǎn	warm	130
睡	shuì	to sleep	158
歲/岁	suì	age	162
跳	tiào	to jump	169
碗	wǎn	bowl	173
想	xiǎng	to want; to think	185
像	xiàng	likeness; portrait	185

新	xīn	new	188
業/业	yè	profession	197
意	yì	meaning	199
預/预	yù	in advance; beforehand	206
園/园	yuán	garden	207
圓/圆	yuán	round	207
遠/远	yuǎn	far	207
照	zhào	photograph; to shine	213

14

鼻	bí	nose	29
幣/币	bì	currency; coin	30
碟	dié	disc; saucer	52
對/对	duì	correct; toward	56
腐	fǔ	rotten; to turn bad	62
趕/赶	gǎn	to rush for	65
歌	gē	song	68
慣/惯	guàn	to be used to	73
廣/广	guǎng	wide; vast	73
漢/汉	hàn	Chinese ethnicity	76
劃/划	huà	to plan; to divide	82
餃/饺	jiǎo	dumpling	93
緊/紧	jǐn	tense; tight	95
精	jīng	essence; refined	97
酷	kù	cool; cruel	105
辣	là	spicy	106
綠/绿	lǜ	green	117
慢	màn	slow	119
麼/么	me	*QP	120
漂	piào/piāo	*pretty/ to float	135
認/认	rèn	to recognize; to know	142
實/实	shí	solid; reality	150
瘦	shòu	thin; slim (of a person or animal)	155
說/说	shuō	to speak	158

INDEXES

酸	suān	sour	161
算	suàn	to calculate	161
臺/台	tái	platform; deck	164
圖/图	tú	picture; drawing	171
網/网	wǎng	net	174
舞	wǔ	to dance; dance	179
寫/写	xiě	to write	187
演	yǎn	to act; to perform	193
語/语	yǔ	language	205
種/种	zhǒng/zhòng	kinds; types/ to plant	219

15

廚/厨	chú	kitchen	41
醋	cù	vinegar	44
導/导	dǎo	to lead; to guide	47
懂	dǒng	to understand	54
餓/饿	è	hungry	56
課/课	kè	class; lesson	104
褲/裤	kù	pants	105
樂/乐	lè /yuè	happy/ music	209
練/练	liàn	to practice; to drill	112
靠	kào	to lean on; to rely on	102
樓/楼	lóu	multi-storied building; floor (of building)	114
碼/码	mǎ	(symbol indicating a number)	118
賣/卖	mài	to sell	119
盤/盘	pán	plate; dish	132
篇	piān	MW (for articles)	134
請/请	qǐng	please; to invite	139
趣	qù	interest; interesting	141
熱/热	rè	hot	142
誰/谁	shéi	who	147
適/适	shì	to suit; appropriate	153
躺	tǎng	to lie (down)	165
踢	tī	to kick	166

衛/卫	wèi	to guard; to protect	177
險/险	xiǎn	risk; danger	183
線/线	xiàn	line; route	184
箱	xiāng	box; case	184
鞋	xié	shoes	187
養/养	yǎng	to raise	194
樣/样	yàng	kind; appearance	194
影	yǐng	shadow	202

16

辦/办	bàn	to manage	25
餐	cān	meal	34
錯/错	cuò	wrong; error	45
擔/担	dān	to be burdened with	46
燈/灯	dēng	light; lamp	49
糕	gāo	cake	67
館/馆	guǎn	place; building	73
還/还	hái	still; yet	75
機/机	jī	machine	86
靜/静	jìng	quiet	98
懶/懒	lǎn	lazy	107
錄/录	lù	to record	115
錢/钱	qián	money	138
燒/烧	shāo	to burn	146
糖	táng	sugar; candy	165
頭/头	tóu	head; top	171
興/兴	xìng	mood; interest	189
學/学	xué	to study	190
鴨/鸭	yā	duck	191
澡	zǎo	bath	211
整	zhěng	to put in order	215
嘴	zuǐ	mouth	223

17

幫/帮	bāng	to help	26
聰/聪	cōng	able to hear well; smart	44
點/点	diǎn	dot; o'clock	51
檢/检	jiǎn	to inspect	91
禮/礼	lǐ	gift; ceremony	111
臉/脸	liǎn	face	112
賽/赛	sài	game; competition	143
雖/虽	suī	although	162
謝/谢	xiè	to thank	187
壓/压	yā	to press; to weigh down	191
應/应	yīng/ yìng	should/ to respond	201
糟	zāo	messy; rotten	210

18

蹟/迹	jì	remains; ruins	88
簡/简	jiǎn	simple	91
藍/蓝	lán	blue	107
離/离	lí	away from	109
雙/双	shuāng	pair	157
題/题	tí	topic; question	167
顏/颜	yán	face; countenance	192
藥/药	yào	medicine	195
醫/医	yī	doctor; medicine	197
轉/转	zhuǎn/ zhuàn	to turn	221

19

邊/边	biān	side	31
關/关	guān	to involve; to close	72
壞/坏	huài	bad	83
蘋/苹	píng	component in apple 蘋果/苹果	136
難/难	nán	difficult; hard	127
簽/签	qiān	to sign	137

識/识	shí	to recognize	150
癢/痒	yǎng	itchy	194
願/愿	yuàn	wish; hope	208
證/证	zhèng	proof; certificate	216

20

寵/宠	chǒng	to dote on	40
護/护	hù	to protect	81
覺/觉	jiào/jué	to sleep/ to feel; to think	99
籃/篮	lán	basket	107
鐘/钟	zhōng	clock	218

21

襯/衬	chèn	lining	38
顧/顾	gù	to look after; to attend to	71
屬/属	shǔ	to belong to	156
鐵/铁	tiě	iron	169

22

歡/欢	huān	happy; joyous	83
體/体	tǐ	body	167
聽/听	tīng	to listen	169

23

讓/让	ràng	to allow; to cause; to let	141

24

廳/厅	tīng	hall	170
灣/湾	wān	strait; bay	172
鹽/盐	yán	salt	193

INDEXES

Simplified CHARACTER INDEX
By Stroke Count

*	=	**Bound Form**	
MW	=	**Measure Word**	
P	=	**Particle**	
QP	=	**Question Particle**	
( )	=	**Variant/Radical Form**	

1

一	yī	one	17

2

八	bā	eight	19
刀（刂）	dāo	knife	1
儿/兒	ér	son; child	57
二	èr	two	17
几/幾	jǐ	how many; a few	87
九	jiǔ	nine	19
了	le	P	108
力	lì	power; strength	2
七	qī	seven	18
人（亻）	rén	person; people	1
十	shí	ten	19
又	yòu	right hand; again	2

3

才	cái	not until; only then	34
寸	cùn	inch	5
大	dà	big; great	4
飞/飛	fēi	to fly	60
干/乾	gān	dry	65
个/個	gè	MW (general)	68
工	gōng	tool; work; labor	5
弓	gōng	bow	6

广/廣	guǎng	wide; vast	73
己	jǐ	oneself	87
久	jiǔ	long time	98
口	kǒu	mouth; entrance	2
马/馬	mǎ	horse	16
么/麼	me	*QP	120
门/門	mén	door; gate	15
女	nǚ	woman; female	4
千	qiān	thousand	20
三	sān	three	17
上	shàng	above; top	145
土	tǔ	earth	3
囗	wéi	enclose	3
卫/衛	wèi	to guard; to protect	177
夕	xī	sunset; evening	3
习/習	xí	to practice	181
下	xià	below; under	182
小	xiǎo	little; small	5
幺	yāo	tiny; small	6
也	yě	also; too	196
已	yǐ	already	198
子	zǐ	baby; child	4

4

办/辦	bàn	to manage	25
贝/貝	bèi	cowry shell	13

比	bǐ	to compare	30
币/幣	bì	currency; coin	30
不	bù	not; no	33
长/長	cháng/ zhǎng	long/ to grow; leader	36
车/車	chē	vehicle; car	12
从/從	cóng	from	44
订/訂	dìng	to reserve; to book (a ticket, a hotel room, etc.)	53
方	fāng	square; side; method	9
分	fēn	penny; minute	61
父	fù	father	63
戈	gē	dagger-axe	7
公	gōng	public	69
火(灬)	huǒ	fire	9
户/戶	hù	door; household	80
化	huà	to transform; to influence	82
计/計	jì	to count	87
见/見	jiàn	to see	13
介	jiè	to be between	94
今	jīn	today; now	95
开/開	kāi	to open; to operate	100
六	liù	six	18
毛	máo	hair; dime	120
木	mù	wood	8
牛	niú	cow; ox	7
片	piàn	MW (for tablets, films); slice	134
气/氣	qì	air	137
认/認	rèn	to recognize; to know	142
日	rì	sun; day	8
少	shǎo/ shào	few; little; less / young	146
什(甚)	shén	*what	148
手	shǒu	hand	7
书/書	shū	book	155
双/雙	shuāng	pair	157

水(氵)	shuǐ	water	9
太	tài	too; extremely	164
天	tiān	sky; day	168
厅/廳	tīng	hall	170
王	wáng	king; (surname)	10
为/為	wèi/wéi	for	176
文	wén	(written) language; script	177
五	wǔ	five	18
午	wǔ	noon	178
心(忄)	xīn	heart	6
以	yǐ	with	198
友	yǒu	friend	204
元	yuán	MW (for unit of Chinese currency): yuan	206
月	yuè	moon; mouth	8
中	zhōng	center; middle	218
专/專	zhuān	special	221

5

白	bái	white; (surname)	24
半	bàn	half	25
包	bāo	bag; sack; bundle; package	26
北	běi	north	28
本	běn	MW (for books); foundation	29
边/邊	biān	side	31
出	chū	to go out	40
打	dǎ	to hit	45
电/電	diàn	electricity	52
东/東	dōng	east	53
冬	dōng	winter	53
对/對	duì	correct; toward	56
发/發	fā	to emit; to issue	57
付	fù	to pay	63
功	gōng	skill	70
古	gǔ	ancient	71

瓜	guā	melon; gourd	72
汉/漢	hàn	Chinese ethnicity	76
号/號	hào	number	77
记/記	jì	to remember; to record	88
加	jiā	to add	89
叫	jiào	to be called; to call	93
节/節	jié	MW (for classes); holiday	94
卡	kǎ	card	100
可	kě	but; to permit	102
乐/樂	lè/yuè	happy/ music	209
礼/禮	lǐ	gift; ceremony	111
另	lìng	other; another	114
们/們	men	*(plural suffix)	122
民	mín	the people; folk	123
末	mò	end	124
母	mǔ	mother	125
目	mù	eye	10
奶	nǎi	milk; (paternal) grandmother	126
平	píng	level; even	135
且	qiě	(conj.)	138
去	qù	to go	140
让/讓	ràng	to allow; to cause; to let	141
生	shēng	to be born; to grow	148
示(礻)	shì	to show	11
市	shì	city; market	151
帅/帥	shuài	handsome; smart	157
司	sī	to take charge of	158
四	sì	four	17
他	tā	he	163
它	tā	it	163
台/臺	tái	platform; deck	164
田	tián	field; (surname)	10
头/頭	tóu	head; top	171
外	wài	outside; foreign	172
务/務	wù	affair; task	179

写/寫	xiě	to write	187
业/業	yè	profession	197
叶/葉	yè	leaf	196
印	yìn	to print	201
用	yòng	to use	203
右	yòu	right	205
正	zhèng	just; upright	215
只	zhǐ	only	217
左	zuǒ	left	224

6

安	ān	calm; safe	22
百	bǎi	hundred	20
冰	bīng	ice	32
场/場	chǎng	field	37
成	chéng	to become; to succeed	38
吃	chī	eat	39
次	cì	MW (for occurrences)	43
当/當	dāng	to serve as; to be	47
导/導	dǎo	to lead; to guide	47
灯/燈	dēng	light; lamp	49
地	dì/de	earth	50
动/動	dòng	to move	54
多	duō	many; much	56
而	ér	(conj.)	57
耳	ěr	ear	11
份	fèn	MW (for meal orders, jobs)	61
刚/剛	gāng	just now	66
共	gòng	altogether	70
关/關	guān	to involve; to close	72
过/過	guò	to pass	75
好	hǎo/hào	good; fine / to like; to be fond of	77
合	hé	to suit; to fit	78
红/紅	hóng	red	79

后/後	hòu	after; behind	80
划/劃	huà	to plan; to divide	82
欢/歡	huān	happy; joyous	83
回	huí	to return	84
会/會	huì	meeting	84
机/機	jī	machine	86
级/級	jí	grade; level	86
件	jiàn	MW (for items)	91
考	kǎo	test; to test	101
老	lǎo	old	108
伦/倫	lún	ethics; moral principles	116
妈/媽	mā	mother; mom	117
吗/嗎	ma	QP	118
买/買	mǎi	to buy	118
忙	máng	busy	119
米	mǐ	uncooked rice	12
糸(纟)	mì	silk	11
名	míng	name	124
那	nà/nèi	that	126
年	nián	year	129
肉	ròu	meat; flesh	143
如	rú	as; if	143
扫/掃	sǎo	to sweep	144
色	sè	color	144
师/師	shī	teacher	149
式	shì	type; style	151
收	shōu	to receive; to accept	153
死	sǐ	to die; (a complement indicating an extreme degree)	159
岁/歲	suì	age	162
她	tā	she	163
汤/湯	tāng	soup	164
同	tóng	same	170
托	tuō	to entrust	171
网/網	wǎng	net	174

危	wēi	danger	175
问/問	wèn	to ask	177
西	xī	west	180
先	xiān	first	183
行	xíng/háng	to walk; okay/ bank; firm	189
兴/興	xìng	mood; interest	189
休	xiū	to cease; to rest	190
压/壓	yā	to press; to weigh down	191
爷/爺	yé	grandpa; (respectful form of address for elderly men)	195
衣(衤)	yī	clothing	12
因	yīn	because	200
有	yǒu	to have; to exist	204
约/約	yuē	agreement; appointment	208
再	zài	again	210
在	zài	at; in; on	210
早	zǎo	early	211
州	zhōu	administrative division; state	219
字	zì	character	222
自	zì	self	223

7

阿	ā	(a prefix)	21
把	bǎ	MW (for objects with handles)	23
吧	ba	P (a sentence-ending particle)	23
报/報	bào	to report; newspaper	27
别/別	bié	other; do not	32
步	bù	step; pace	33
吵	chǎo	to quarrel; noisy	38
初	chū	beginning; elementary	40
床(牀)	chuáng	bed	42
词/詞	cí	word	43
但	dàn	but; however	46
弟	dì	younger brother	50
豆	dòu	bean	55

足	zú	foot; enough	14
坐	zuò	to sit	225
作	zuò	to work; to do	225

8

哎	āi	(exclamatory particle to express surprise or dissatisfaction)	22
爸	bà	dad	23
拌	bàn	to mix	25
抱	bào	to hold or carry in one's arms	27
杯	bēi	cup; glass	28
备/備	bèi	to prepare	29
表	biǎo	surface; matrilineal relatives	32
厕/廁	cè	toilet	35
衬/襯	chèn	lining	38
宠/寵	chǒng	to dote on	40
单/單	dān	single	46
担/擔	dān	to be burdened with	46
到	dào	to arrive	48
的	de	P	49
店	diàn	store; shop	51
定	dìng	settled; decided	52
法	fǎ	method; way; law	58
房	fáng	house	59
放	fàng	to put; to place	59
非	fēi	not; non-	60
服	fú	clothing; to serve	62
该/該	gāi	should; ought to	64
狗	gǒu	dog	70
拐	guǎi	to turn	72
国/國	guó	country; nation	74
果	guǒ	fruit; result	74
和	hé/huo	and; harmonious/*warm	78
话/話	huà	speech	82
货/貨	huò	merchandise	85

或	huò	or	85
姐	jiě	elder sister	94
金(钅)	jīn	metal; gold; (surname)	14
京	jīng	capital city	96
经/經	jīng	to pass through	97
净/淨	jìng	clean; pure	97
具	jù	tool; utensil	99
咖	kā	*coffee	100
刻	kè	quarter (hour); to carve	103
空	kòng/kōng	free time/ empty; sky	104
练/練	liàn	to practice; to drill	112
录/錄	lù	to record	115
码/碼	mǎ	(symbol indicating a number)	118
卖/賣	mài	to sell	119
妹	mèi	younger sister	122
明	míng	bright	124
姆	mǔ	housemaid	125
呢	ne	QP	128
念/唸	niàn	to read aloud	129
怕	pà	to fear; to be afraid of	131
拍	pāi	to clap; racket	131
朋	péng	friend	133
苹/蘋	píng	component in apple 蘋果/苹果	136
青	qīng	green; blue	139
绍/紹	shào	to introduce; to continue	146
衫	shān	shirt	145
舍	shè	house; residence	147
实/實	shí	solid; reality	150
始	shǐ	to begin	150
事	shì	matter; affair	151
视/視	shì	to view; to look at	152
试/試	shì	test; to try	153
受	shòu	to bear	154
叔	shū	uncle	155

The Way of Chinese Characters

前	qián	front; before	138
秋	qiū	autumn; fall	140
胜/勝	shèng	victory; wonderful	149
食（饣）	shí	to eat	16
是	shì	to be	152
室	shì	room	152
适/適	shì	to suit; appropriate	153
首	shǒu	head	154
说/說	shuō	to speak	158
思	sī	to think	159
送	sòng	to see off; to deliver	159
虽/雖	suī	although	162
挺	tǐng	very; rather	170
洗	xǐ	to wash	181
险/險	xiǎn	risk; danger	183
香	xiāng	fragrant	184
信	xìn	letter; to believe	188
星	xīng	star	188
养/養	yǎng	to raise	194
要	yào	to want	195
药/藥	yào	medicine	195
姨	yí	aunt	198
音	yīn	sound; music	200
语/語	yǔ	language	205
院	yuàn	yard	208
怎	zěn	*how	211
政	zhèng	politics	215
钟/鐘	zhōng	clock	218
种/種	zhǒng/zhòng	kinds; types/ to plant	219
重	zhòng/chóng	heavy; serious/ again	219
祝	zhù	to wish (well)	221
昨	zuó	yesterday	224

10

啊	ā	(a prefix)	21
爱/愛	ài	love; to love	22
班	bān	class	24
被	bèi	by; quilt	28
笔/筆	bǐ	pen; writing brush	30
病	bìng	illness; to become ill	33
都	dōu/dū	all; both/ capital	54
饿/餓	è	hungry	56
烦/煩	fán	to bother; to trouble	58
赶/趕	gǎn	to rush for	65
高	gāo	tall; high	66
哥	gē	elder brother	67
顾/顧	gù	to look after; to attend to	71
海	hǎi	sea	76
航	háng	to navigate	77
换/換	huàn	to exchange; to change	83
家/(傢)	jiā	family; home/ furniture	89
健	jiàn	healthy	92
紧/緊	jǐn	tense; tight	95
酒	jiǔ	wine	98
烤	kǎo	to bake; to roast; to grill	102
课/課	kè	class; lesson	104
哭	kū	to cry; to weep	104
离/離	lí	away from	109
凉/涼	liáng	cool	112
料	liào	material	114
旅	lǚ	to travel	116
拿	ná	to take; to get	125
难/難	nán	difficult; hard	127
脑/腦	nǎo	brain	128
能	néng	can; to be able to	128
旁	páng	side; edge	132
瓶	píng	bottle	135
起	qǐ	to rise	136

12

棒	bàng	fantastic	26
遍	biàn	MW (for complete courses of an action or instances of an action)	31
超	chāo	to exceed; to surpass	37
程	chéng	journey; schedule	39
厨/廚	chú	kitchen	41
窗	chuāng	window	42
道	dào	road; way	48
登	dēng	to climb; to ascend	49
等	děng	to wait; rank	50
短	duǎn	short	55
傅	fù	tutor; instructor	64
港	gǎng	harbor	66
寒	hán	cold	76
喝	hē	to drink	78
黑	hēi	black	79
滑	huá	slippery; to slide	81
就	jiù	just	99
渴	kě	thirsty	103
裤/褲	kù	pants	105
牌	pái	plate; card; brand	131
跑	pǎo	to run	133
期	qī	period (of time)	136
然	rán	like that; so	141
舒	shū	to stretch; to smooth out	156
属/屬	shǔ	to belong to	156
暑	shǔ	heat; summer	156
提	tí	to lift	167
湾/灣	wān	strait; bay	172
晚	wǎn	evening; late	173
喂	wéi/wèi	Hello!; Hey!	176
喜	xǐ	to like; happy	181
谢/謝	xiè	to thank	187
椅	yǐ	chair	199
游/（遊）	yóu	to swim/ to roam; to travel	203
寓	yù	residence	205
越	yuè	to exceed	209
最	zuì	most	224

13

搬	bān	to move	24
楚	chǔ	clear; neat	41
错/錯	cuò	wrong; error	45
感	gǎn	to feel; to sense	65
跟	gēn	with; and	69
简/簡	jiǎn	simple	91
睛	jīng	eyeball	96
蓝/藍	lán	blue	107
楼/樓	lóu	multi-storied building; floor (of building)	114
路	lù	road; way	115
暖	nuǎn	warm	130
签/簽	qiān	to sign	137
睡	shuì	to sleep	158
跳	tiào	to jump	169
碗	wǎn	bowl	173
想	xiǎng	to want; to think	185
像	xiàng	likeness; portrait	185
新	xīn	new	188
意	yì	meaning	199
照	zhào	photograph; to shine	213

14

鼻	bí	nose	29
碟	dié	disc; saucer	52
腐	fǔ	rotten; to turn bad	62
歌	gē	song	68
精	jīng	essence; refined	97
静/靜	jìng	quiet	98

酷	kù	cool; cruel	105
辣	là	spicy	106
慢	màn	slow	119
漂	piào/ piāo	*pretty/ to float	135
赛/賽	sài	game; competition	143
瘦	shòu	thin; slim (of a person or animal)	155
酸	suān	sour	161
算	suàn	to calculate	161
舞	wǔ	to dance; dance	179
演	yǎn	to act; to perform	193
愿/願	yuàn	wish; hope	208

澡	zǎo	bath	211
整	zhěng	to put in order	215
嘴	zuǐ	mouth	223

17

糟	zāo	messy; rotten	210

15

聪/聰	cōng	able to hear well; smart	44
醋	cù	vinegar	44
懂	dǒng	to understand	54
靠	kào	to lean on; to rely on	102
篇	piān	MW (for articles)	134
趣	qù	interest; interesting	141
躺	tǎng	to lie (down)	165
踢	tī	to kick	166
题/題	tí	topic; question	167
箱	xiāng	box; case	184
鞋	xié	shoes	187
颜/顏	yán	face; countenance	192
影	yǐng	shadow	202

16

餐	cān	meal	34
糕	gāo	cake	67
篮/籃	lán	basket	107
懒	lǎn	lazy	107
糖	táng	sugar; candy	165

Notes

Notes

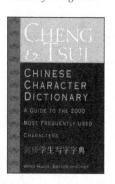